D1207096

SHAFTESBURY

GEORGINA BATTISCOMBE

SHAFTESBURY

THE GREAT REFORMER
1801–1885

With an Introduction by
Elizabeth Longford

Illustrated
with Photographs

HOUGHTON MIFFLIN COMPANY BOSTON

1975

Also by Georgina Battiscombe

Charlotte Mary Yonge
Mrs. Gladstone
John Keble
Queen Alexandra

First American Edition 1975

Library of Congress Cataloging in Publication Data

Battiscombe, Georgina
  Shaftesbury: The Great Reformer, 1801–1885.

  London ed. has title: Shaftesbury: A Biography of the
Seventh Earl, 1801–1885.
  Bibliography: p.
  Includes index.
  1. Shaftesbury, Anthony Ashley Cooper, 7th Earl of,
1801–1885. 2. Reformers—biography. I. Title
HV28.S46B38 1975 362′.92′4 B 74-32370
ISBN 0-395-19953-0

M 10 9 8 7 6 5 4 3 2 1

Printed in the United States of America

To my brother, George Harwood

CONTENTS

ILLUSTRATIONS

following page 174

FOREWORD

The most important printed source of information about Lord Shaftesbury is the three-volume biography by Edwin Hodder, published in 1887. Somewhat to the annoyance of his family, who would have preferred a better-known and more distinguished author, Shaftesbury himself chose Hodder for his biographer. In some respects the choice was a fortunate one. Hodder had access to Shaftesbury's diary as well as to a large collection of public and private correspondence and, wisely, he allowed this material to speak for itself. For this reason his book is invaluable to the student since it contains many long, accurate and almost entirely unexpurgated passages from the diary and letters.

Two other books are particularly helpful to any study of Shaftesbury. In 1923 J. L. and Barbara Hammond published a book whose aim was to describe 'Shaftesbury's life and character and the significant contribution which he made to the politics and history of his age.' The authors specifically state that 'with this object before us we have omitted many incidents which, though interesting in themselves, do not illuminate his place in the life of the nineteenth century.' Inevitably the book has dated a little, particularly in its treatment of Shaftesbury's religious views, but it remains a brilliant, informative, and supremely readable piece of work. Equally brilliant is a small book published in 1964 by Geoffrey Best. Like the Hammonds, Professor Best has adopted the plan of an opening biographical chapter followed by chapters on Shaftesbury and the Factory Acts, Shaftesbury and Lunacy Law reform, and similar topics. He has written what is probably the best introduction to Shaftesbury available to the modern reader but, again like the Hammonds, he has not attempted a full-scale, chronological biography.

Turning to books on general subjects, Professor Owen Chadwick's *The Victorian Church* is essential and very enjoyable reading where religious matters are concerned. Other books which I have found specially useful are *The History of the Factory Movement* by J. T. Ward, and *Edwin Chadwick and the Public Health Movement* by R. A. Lewis. I was fortunate enough to have my attention called to two unpublished theses in the Cambridge University Library. 'English Evangelical Eschatology' by S. C. Orchard was of great help to me in the writing of chapter seven, whilst 'The Evangelical Party in the Church of England' by B. E. Hardman contained much useful information about 'the Shaftesbury bishops.'

Of unpublished material by far the most important are the eleven volumes of Shaftesbury's diary, now in the possession of the Trustees of the Broadlands Archives and at present deposited with the National Register of Archives together with part of Shaftesbury's correspondence. The remaining letters belonging to the Trustees are to be found in the Hampshire County Archives at Winchester. The papers belonging to the present Earl of Shaftesbury appear to be those which the seventh Earl himself selected as material for Hodder to use in writing the *Life*. The Castle Howard papers are of interest for the picture they give of Shaftesbury as a young man. Among them I had the luck to find some uncatalogued letters dating from 1823 to 1825, a period hitherto empty and undocumented, thus filling in a two-year gap in our knowledge of Shaftesbury's life. At Castle Howard there are also a few later letters concerned with the affairs of the Board of Health; the bulk of material on this subject is to be found in the Chadwick papers in the library of University College, London.

Reference for quotations from Shaftesbury's diary presented a difficult problem. I have quoted so frequently from the diary as to make regular references impracticable; in any case such references would be of little use since the diary is uncatalogued and not easily accessible. I have tried to give the date whenever I have quoted at length and I must ask the reader to remember that, unless a reference is given, all short quotations from Shaftesbury are taken from the diary. In general, when giving references, I have referred the reader to an easily accessible printed source rather than to the original document; thus, when possible, references are to Hodder rather than to the Shaftesbury papers, which are not open to students, and to the published letters of Queen Victoria rather than to the Royal Archives.

I am most grateful to all those who have given me access to letters and other unpublished material. By gracious permission of Her Majesty the Queen I have been allowed to use papers in the Royal Archives. I wish also to thank the Trustees of the Broadlands Archives, Lord Shaftesbury, Mr. George Howard, Miss Margaret Holmes,

Dorset County Archivist, Mr. E. G. W. Bill, Librarian at Lambeth Palace, Mr. J. W. Scott, Librarian of University College, Mr. J. E. Fagg, Archivist to the Department of Paleography and Diplomatic, Durham University, Dr. K. W. Noakes, Librarian of Pusey House, Oxford, Sir Fergus Graham and the authorities of the Bodleian Library, Oxford (Graham papers), Miss Monica de Bunsen, the Shaftesbury Society, the Commonwealth and Continental Church Society, the London City Mission, and the British and Foreign Bible Society.

Among the many people who have been kind enough to help me in various ways I would like particularly to thank Miss Jane Langton of the Royal Archives, the staff of the Hampshire County Archives, Dame Annis Gillie, Mr. Harold Ludman, Dr. Kenneth Bourne, Professor Owen Chadwick, Dr. Rhodes Boyson, Mr. Jasper Ridley, Mr. Stewart Perowne, Mrs. Sophie Johnson, the Revd. J. C. Pollock, Mr. Patrick Davis, Mr. H. Babington-Smith, Mrs. Kathryn Gibson, Dr. Mary Woodall, and my sister, Ruth Harris.

I owe very much to Miss Felicity Ranger of the National Register of Archives for her unfailing help and patience with my many demands and queries. Mr. Handasyde Buchanan read the book in typescript and gave me invaluable advice and criticism. Finally, my thanks are specially due to Lady Lettice Ashley-Cooper; without her constant help and co-operation this book about her great-grandfather could not have been written.

INTRODUCTION

by Elizabeth Longford

A hundred years ago people on both sides of the Atlantic would speak reverentially of 'the great Lord Shaftesbury.' They saw him as a powerful aristocrat endowed with outstanding brains and good looks, inhabiting a vast country mansion and splendid town house, wielding enormous social influence and doing incalculable good for the cause of — the weakest, the poorest, the outcast.

Today Shaftesbury is still remembered as a great philanthropist. But the personal flavour of the man who led the most spectacular social crusades of the nineteenth century has become strangely diluted. Compared with the names of Gladstone and Disraeli, for instance, Shaftesbury's name rings a faint bell. Yet he did more to lessen the misery and increase the happiness of actual, living human beings than both the other two put together. What Shaftesbury accomplished with travail during the last century has become the birthright of our own, not only in Britain but throughout the civilised world.

For this reason alone the time has come for a new, major study of his life. There is a second equally valid reason, however, why Shaftesbury the man should not be forgotten but should exert a powerful fascination over the modern mind. He was a genius with a flawed character.

His character suffered acutely from 'instability,' writes Georgina Battiscombe: 'The swing of the pendulum, apparent in every one of us, was in him particularly marked . . .' In his own words, he was subject at the university to 'desponding fits.' Some ten years later he was writing: 'How curious is my character, sometimes for a while in the wildest and most various of spirits, in others, and for a much longer period, in cruel and overwhelming despondency!' Georgina Battiscombe is too good a scholar to make a dogmatic, retrospective diagnosis of Shaftesbury's psychological troubles. While refusing to dub him crudely a 'manic depressive,' she does consider this possibility; and she insists on the importance to his career of this psycho-

somatic condition, whatever it was and however it would be labelled
today. Both his life-long dyspepsia and tinnitus (noises in the ears)
were exacerbated by periods of anxiety.

What was responsible for Shaftesbury's 'desponding fits' and
physical ills? Georgina Battiscombe sees at least an immediate
cause in a syndrome familiar to every modern student of the mind,
amateur or professional: a desperately unhappy childhood. In
reading about Shaftesbury's bullying parents and loathsome first
school, we are inevitably reminded of other great men who as
children were deprived of a steady stream of love. The poet Byron
comes to mind, dying at thirty-six when Shaftesbury was twenty-
three. Byron's mother kept him on a violent emotional see-saw by
her alternate scoldings and spoilings; this, together with congenital
lameness, partly accounted for his later, self-styled 'moping fits.'
Sir Winston Churchill's childhood also resembled Shaftesbury's, in
so far as both suffered from neglectful parents and a sadistic school-
master. Shaftesbury said of his school: 'The place was bad, wicked,
filthy; and the treatment was starvation and cruelty.' Like Shaftesbury, Churchill was visited by fits of depression which he referred
to as the coming of 'Black Dog' — though they were far less traumatic or frequent than Shaftesbury's. The likeness did not end here:
for both were rescued by a devoted servant, in Churchill's case his
beloved nurse Mrs. Everest, in Shaftesbury's case the housekeeper
Maria Millis. Shaftesbury's childish misery went really deep, if only
because his guardian angel Maria died when he was still a small boy.

The distinguished American critic, Edmund Wilson, has demon-
strated in his seminal book, *The Wound and the Bow*, the intimate
connection between suffering and achievement. Of course not every
great man or woman carries a hidden 'wound,' like the legendary
hero Achilles, as the price of drawing the 'bow' or genius and letting
loose its arrows. But Shaftesbury undoubtedly did so. His 'wound'
was a highly nervous, introverted temperament, separated by a
hair's breadth from derangement. His 'bow' was religion — an irresistible weapon in the hands of one so pious and even fanatical in
his beliefs. The flights of winged arrows which he despatched year
after year were destined to penetrate the Victorian carapace of
cruelty and cant.

Shaftesbury's religion, as first taught to him by Maria Millis, was
a religion of love. How could it be otherwise, when he had received
it from one who stood for all he knew of love as a child? Where
others might find their psychological difficulties further entangled
rather than sorted out by religion, Shaftesbury was the opposite.

'For him religion was a stabilising and upholding force,' writes
Georgina Battiscombe, 'soothing, strong, inalterable . . . the Rock
of Ages.' It was only occasionally towards the end of his life, when
his special brand of Victorian belief had ossified into bigotry, that
his religion lost something of its gentle strength and became, like
everything else he touched, tense and strained. In Georgina Battiscombe's words: 'He had the misfortune to be born with, as it were,
a mental skin too few; all his feelings were abnormally intense.'

But if Shaftesbury's temperament was a 'misfortune' for him personally, for the rest of the world it was and is a marvellous blessing.
To his oppressed contemporaries, Shaftesbury's very weaknesses
helped to bring salvation. Religious bigotry was no doubt one face
of the coin; the other was a sense of direct inspiration from on high
which enabled him to defy all humanity, be it the Queen, or the
whole despicable realm of bumbledom. To posterity, it gives his
life-story a compelling readability which a tale of more balanced
progress would lack.

Thus equipped, Shaftesbury was to shoot far and fast. His first
targets were the unspeakable lunacy laws, under which poor crazy
creatures (and often sane people also) were subjected to the horrors
of the 'circular swing' and 'bath of surprise.' Short of Edgar Allan
Poe's 'pit and pendulum,' there was scarcely any torture which
alleged madness did not give the authorities the excuse to inflict.
Next came the pathetic 'factory children,' followed by the children
down the coalmines, and the little illiterates for whom Ragged
Schools were started, and the campaign against scabrous lodging-
houses, and for public health and a hundred other good causes.
When we recollect that many otherwise progressive forces, such as
the radical Chartists and liberal anti-Corn Law League, opposed
Shaftesbury's campaigns to mitigate industrial oppression, we realize
what he was up against. For an economic theory can be as merciless
as a mill-owner. Shaftesbury no doubt erred on the side of paternalism, but at least the waifs and strays of those days were profoundly thankful to find one father-figure who would look after them
in a world that was inconceivably compassionless and cold.

Through all Shaftesbury's struggles against his enemies, internal
and external, runs one gold thread of pure felicity. This was his
romantic courtship and marriage. It is hard to believe that a young
man of such moral earnestness, however handsome, clever and well-
born, could have won the step-daughter (or more likely natural
daughter) of that incorrigible 'Cupid' Lord Palmerston. But so it
was. One rejoices to know that Shaftesbury held his beautiful 'Min'

against all comers. Highly sexed, as one would expect, he developed an over-powering need to get married ('It is better to marry than to burn') which led to some comically desperate entries in his private diary: 'I am dying to be married, but where, Oh, God help me, where is the woman? . . . Oh, my prayer, my prayer, how I repeat it! A wife, a wife!'

Mention of this diary leads me directly to Georgina Battiscombe's *tour de force* as his biographer. She has handled this long life of eighty-four years, and these eleven volumes of diary, with consummate economy and skill. It was in the recesses of his diary that Lord Shaftesbury revealed the full strangeness of his character. A bad judge of people, he saw political and religious adversaries, such as Gladstone, as sheer vipers — but vipers whom he castigated strictly within his own bosom. His diary was a safety-valve for remarkably un-Christian animosities. Only a biographer of Georgina Battiscombe's calibre and experience could be trusted to present this explosive material with complete honesty and openness but without distortion. The overall picture which results is of a man who was much more human and rather more saintly than one ever suspected.

Georgina Battiscombe's preparation, so to speak, for her task has been extraordinarily complete. Through her earlier biographies of famous Victorians she has gained the *entrée* into the worlds of politics, religion and society. Her own descent from the manufacturing Harwoods of the English North Country gives her an understanding of the mill-owners' problems but much deeper sympathy with their victims. 'Descendants of the early mill-owners,' she writes, 'can only admit with shame that their families were to blame for the sufferings of thousands of hapless children.' Her *Queen Alexandra* is already a classic. She reaches her zenith in this book, where a great subject evokes the highest expression of historical art.

PART ONE

Search the records, examine the opening years of those who have been distinguished for ability and virtue, and you will ascribe, with but few exceptions, the early culture of their minds, and, above all, the first discipline of the heart, to the intelligence and affection of the mother, or at least of some pious woman, who, with the self-denial and tenderness of her sex, has entered as a substitute on the sacred office.

Speeches of the Earl of Shaftesbury, p. 114.

It would often be better if children had no parents at all.

Speeches of the Earl of Shaftesbury, p. 240.

Chapter 1

EARLY YEARS

The heir to a great name and a large estate is often a spoilt child; not so Anthony Ashley-Cooper. On both sides he came of distinguished lineage. His mother, Anne Spencer-Churchill, was daughter to the fourth Duke of Marlborough and great-great-granddaughter to the famous first Duke; his father, Cropley Ashley-Cooper, later to succeed as sixth Earl of Shaftesbury, was in direct line from the seventeenth-century politician Ashley, the second 'A' of the Cabal*, who was satirised by Dryden in *Absalom and Achitophel*. This same Anthony Ashley, or Ashley-Cooper, inherited rich and extensive estates from his mother, heiress of the Hampshire family of Cooper. These estates, together with the Ashley property in Dorsetshire, he passed on to his descendants.

Such was Anthony Ashley-Cooper's ancestry and inheritance. Normal parents might have been expected to give a specially warm welcome to the son and heir born on April 28th 1801, following a disappointing string of daughters. Anthony's parents, however, were anything but normal. Lord Ashley, as Cropley Ashley-Cooper then was, in spite of uncouth manners and indistinct speech later made some reputation for himself as Chairman of Committees in the House of Lords. His son, who disliked him intensely and with good reason, admitted that 'he does his duty to the public and is, I really believe, an honest man.' In private life he was a selfish and cold-hearted bully, married to a woman of similar character. We know almost nothing about Anthony's mother, and what little we do know is unpleasant. Her son habitually referred to her as 'a fiend.' She is usually described as an attractive, worldly woman, totally preoccupied with the social round and neglectful of her children; her son's remarks, however, suggest a more active malevolence.

* Clifford, Arlington, Buckingham, Ashley, Lauderdale, members of the Committee of Foreign Affairs, 1672, whose close combination in shifty intrigues has given the word 'cabal' to the English language.

If Anthony himself is to be believed few children have had to endure a more hard and desolate childhood than he did. It is, however, only fair to point out that his parents may not have been quite the monsters that he depicts, though they were certainly bad enough. Lady Holland said of Lord Ashley, 'Father in the kind sense he has never been'; and Lord Melbourne told the young Queen Victoria that both husband and wife had heartily disliked their children. These remarks show that Lord and Lady Ashley were notoriously bad parents; they are not, however, evidence of actual ill-treatment or neglect. The only source of information about Anthony's childhood is a fragmentary autobiographical note which he wrote in old age and gave to his authorised biographer, Edwin Hodder. Even this fragment is suspect. The original has disappeared; and although Hodder appears to have reproduced it intact he may have had occasion to do a little editing. It must also be borne in mind that old people's recollections of childhood, though frequently extremely vivid, are as frequently very misleading. The past is viewed again through the eyes of a child; unusual and perhaps unimportant episodes, which struck the imagination just because they were something out of the ordinary, and which middle-aged recollection rightly discounts, in old age assume again an enormous and horrific importance. Writing on the authority of the eighty-year-old Lord Shaftesbury, as Anthony had then become, Hodder thus describes the boy's neglected childhood:

> He was left, with his sisters, to the tender mercies of the servants, and he knew, times without number, what it was to be kept for days without sufficient food until he was pinched with starvation; and could recall many weary nights in winter when he lay awake all through the long hours, suffering from cold.[1]

The only questionable expression in that passage is the phrase 'times without number.' An occasional painful occurrence could impress itself so deeply on a child's mind as to blot out other memories and to be remembered in old age as an habitual state of affairs.

It must be remembered, too, that Anthony was always to be a poor judge of character, and that his descriptions of people he disliked were as often as not exaggerations. He could, for instance, describe John Bright as 'swinish,' and ascribe to Peel, of all people, 'a singular and marked malignity,' and, although the in-law relationship is a notoriously difficult one, he was surely going a little far in referring to his son's wife as 'an incarnation of Satan.' His words should therefore be taken with a small grain of salt when he describes his mother as a 'dreadful woman' with a 'fiend-warmed heart' or writes of his father as 'venting malignity and horror' against his unfortunate daughters.

When, however, all possible allowances have been made for them the fact remains that Anthony was afflicted with an unnatural and unpleasant pair of parents. 'Most solemnly do I pray,' he wrote in his diary on November 13th 1828, 'that no family hereafter may endure from its parents what we endured.' Though the younger boys – there were to be nine children in all, three daughters and six sons – may possibly have been better treated, Anthony and his three elder sisters suffered under a system of the utmost severity. No sign of affection was ever shown these children or encouraged on their part. In later life, however, what was to trouble Anthony most in his recollections of childhood was the lack of any real religious instruction or training. His own standards on this respect were abnormally high, even for a Victorian parent. In an earlier and less pious age Lord Ashley was really doing all that might be expected of a father in the way of religious education when he occasionally shot a question from the Catechism at his little son, demanding that the answer be word-perfect but never troubling to discover whether the child understood anything of the meaning. As for Lady Ashley, she concerned herself not at all with such matters.

In spite of this total lack of interest on the part of both his parents, Anthony's religious perception awoke early. One person and one only troubled to win the love and devotion of the neglected child. Very little is known about this woman. Even her surname is doubtful; although usually spelt 'Millis' it may well have been plain 'Mills.' She was a Woodstock girl who had 'gone into service' at Blenheim Palace as personal maid to Lady Anne. When her mistress married Lord Ashley she went with her to London, becoming housekeeper. She grew to be particularly fond of little Anthony, giving him the love which he had never had from any other living soul; more important still, she put into his hand the thread which was to guide him through the puzzling labyrinth of his life. She taught him religion.

Brought up in Woodstock, a parish with an Evangelical tradition, Maria Millis was naturally a staunch Evangelical. Her Evangelicalism was not the Evangelicalism of caricature with its emphasis upon hell-fire and a jealous God; it was more akin to the Evangelicalism of the popular Victorian hymn, 'There's a friend for little children, Above the bright blue sky.' Anthony, who needed love so badly, saw

God as someone as kind and loving and generous as Maria Millis herself. Though reputed to be a slow child, he found no difficulty in grasping the meaning of the Bible stories which she repeated to him or in learning a simple prayer which he was to use every day until the end of his long life. Maybe he was a naturally religious character; maybe his deplorable childhood made him especially sensitive to spiritual values; whatever the reason, the religion which he first learnt from Maria Millis was to remain the central driving force of all his thoughts and actions.

Anthony's earliest years had been dreary enough; now even worse was to come. In the early nineteenth century boys were often sent to boarding school at a very early age. John Newman, for instance, was seven; Lord Salisbury, the future Prime Minister, and Gladstone's brother-in-law, Henry Glynne, were both as young as six. None of these children was the son of neglectful or unloving parents so that Lord and Lady Ashley were only following established practice when they sent seven-year-old Anthony to board at the Manor House School, Chiswick. They may even have thought to congratulate themselves on their choice of school, since the Manor House was an expensive establishment kept by a well-known scholar and catering almost exclusively for the sons of the nobility. It was nevertheless a hell upon earth. In later life Anthony was to write of his time there:

> The memory of that place makes me shudder; it is repulsive to me even now. I think there was never such a wicked school before or since. The place was bad, wicked, filthy; and the treatment was starvation and cruelty.[2]

Significantly enough he lays stress on wickedness rather than on physical hardships, severe though these undoubtedly were. Anthony knew what it was to go short of the ordinary necessities of life; his previous experience of cold and hunger had, however, been due to neglect and not to intentional ill-treatment. Now the boy was to come face to face with deliberate cruelty and evil, a traumatic experience for so young a child. Lord Salisbury described life at his first school as 'an existence among devils'; Anthony might have said the same of his time at Chiswick. When he described the school as 'filthy' he was referring to moral as well as physical dirt. Hodder, who had heard the old man describe this shocking school, wrote that 'evil of every kind was rampant.' Anthony suffered more from what Hodder calls 'the general blackguardism of the place' than ever he did from cold, hunger, or the total absence of physical comfort.

Bad though the Manor House was, home was not so very much better. Anthony cried at the end of the holidays when he was forced to return to the horrors of school; he cried at the end of term when he must face the bleak misery of life in the great house in Grosvenor Square or at his parents' country home at Richmond. Only the presence of Maria Millis gave him any reassurance and comfort. No portrait of this good woman exists or any memento of her, except, perhaps, a single sheet of paper. The handwriting on it is clear and firm, though uneducated. At the top right-hand corner are the initials, 'A.P.'; impossible not to wonder how and why a ladies' maid became acquainted with the poems of Alexander Pope. The paper is headed 'To my dear Anthony Ashley Cooper on his Birthday, April 28th, 1809.' Underneath are the lines:

> Oh be thou blessed with all that Heaven can send
> Long health, long youth, long Pleasure, and a Friend
> Let joy and ease, let affluence and content
> And the gay conscience of a life well spent,
> Calm every thought, inspirit every grace,
> Grow in the Heart, and smile upon thy face.
> Let day improve on day and year on year,
> Without a Pain, a Trouble, or a Fear;
> Till Death unfelt that tender frame destroy,
> In some soft dream, or Exstasy of joy,
> Peaceful sleep out the Sabbath of the Tomb,
> And wake to Raptures in a Life to come.
>
> The never-ceasing wishes of an old Friend
> But *most* truly your affectionate Friend
>
> A.M.M.[3]

Though there is no proof that A.M.M. was in fact Maria Millis, young Anthony surely had no other friend whose birthday greeting he would cherish carefully until the day of his death. Her name may well have been the very common combination, Anna Maria, Maria being the one in general use, perhaps to avoid confusion with the other Anne, her mistress.

Whether this particular birthday was spent at home or at school the day must have been brightened for the unhappy child by the arrival of this token of affection. But now the worst possible blow fell on him; Maria Millis died. We do not know either the cause or the date of her death, which took place, according to Hodder, before Anthony

had been long at Chiswick. It must therefore have occurred shortly
after the eighth birthday for which she had written him this greeting.
By her will she left him a gold watch, which he was always to wear
in preference to any other, taking pride in showing his friends this
token 'given me by the best friend I ever had in this world.'

Faced with utter desolation, bereft of the only person whose
presence had made life tolerable to him, any small boy, and more
particularly Anthony, might have been expected to suffer a total
collapse. The Shaftesbury inheritance had both a bright and a dark
side. A spark of brilliance amounting almost to genius had shone in
the first Earl, time-server though he was. It had appeared again,
though less clearly, in his descendant 'the Philosopher.'* The reverse
of this brilliance was a deep melancholy, a lack of balance, and a
failure to come to terms with life, characteristics which showed
themselves in Anthony's brother Lionel and in Anthony's son, the
unhappy eighth Earl. Through Anthony's own character there ran
a strong streak of instability; he himself was several times on the verge
of nervous collapse. Yet with this instability there also went an unexpected toughness; the Ashley-Coopers were not a race who easily
acknowledged defeat. Now, faced at the age of eight with a supreme
crisis of grief, Anthony did not give way. Somehow or other he clung
to the faith which Maria herself had taught him; somehow or other
he continued to say his prayers and read his Bible regularly. After
the death of Maria Millis the child had little or no experience of human
affection. He did not, however, lose his trust in the divine love.
On his belief in that love he was to build his whole philosophy of life.
When Maria Millis died the friendless little boy had nothing to turn to
except the religion she had taught him; and in that black moment
religion did not fail him.

The test was a long and severe one, since Anthony had to endure
four more years at Chiswick before his fortunes took a turn for the
better. In 1811 Anthony's father succeeded his brother as Earl of
Shaftesbury, Anthony himself becoming Lord Ashley, the name by
which he is henceforth to be known. This access of dignity at
first made little or no difference to the family's way of life; far more
important to young Ashley was his own transference in 1813 from
Chiswick to Harrow. The unreformed public schools were barbarous
places; to Ashley, however, after the horrors of Chiswick, Harrow
appeared as a demi-paradise. Under its famous Headmaster, George
Butler, a man who set high standards of conduct and character,

---

* Anthony Ashley Cooper, third Earl, author of *Characteristics of Men* (1711).

Harrow was passing through a happy phase in its history. Bullying
was frowned upon; and most of the boys seem to have found the
school a pleasant enough place. At school with Ashley, though in
a lower form, was a Welsh boy called Isaac Williams, who in later life
was to find Ashley crossing his path in no very amicable manner. In
his autobiography Williams admitted to enjoying himself greatly at
Harrow, as well he might, since he achieved the enviable position of
Captain of cricket. Ashley won no particular distinction, either
intellectual or athletic, though he succeeded in carrying off a few
prizes. He was, however, happier than he had ever been before. As a
boarder in the Headmaster's house he found himself in company
with boys whom Hodder describes as 'a gentlemanly set of fellows,'
in great contrast to the blackguards of Chiswick, his chief friend
among them being Harry Verney of Claydon, who was later to fall
in love with Florence Nightingale and to marry her sister Parthenope.

Pleasant though Harrow might be, the education provided was
not of a very high quality, though Ashley was to blame his own
idleness for the fact that he learnt very little during his time there.
The attitude towards religion was equally uninspiring. In the school
itself there was practically no religious teaching. Of a Sunday the
boys would be taken to the parish church to sit in a gallery where it
was impossible to see or hear anything of the service. Even the
Headmaster was seen to while away the boredom of sermon-time
by reading in his pocket German Bible. Since the vicar of Harrow
was a keen Evangelical the services he conducted may not have seemed
so dreary to Ashley as they did to Isaac Williams, who had been
brought up in a High Church tradition, but to no one can they have
been a source of much interest or inspiration.

Compared with the barbarism of Chiswick Harrow might appear
remarkably civilised, but judged by modern standards it was a
rough and tough place. Though the ill-treatment of small boys
was mercifully infrequent, cruelty to animals was a commonplace
of school life; birds, cats, and even dogs were systematically hunted
down and killed. The boys lived in comparatively comfortable
surroundings; their physical well-being was, however, at the mercy
of their masters' whims. Members of the Shell, for instance, seldom or
never enjoyed a full night's sleep because the master in charge of
that unfortunate form suffered from insomnia and was in the habit
of calling the boys to 'early school' at four o'clock in the morning.
Near the school buildings was a filthy, stinking pond known as
'Duck Puddle,' alive with mosquitoes and other insects. This menace
to health might have remained indefinitely had not Ashley chosen to

make it the subject of a set of Latin verses, thereby shaming the authorities into cleaning up the nuisance.

It would be far-fetched indeed to see in this schoolboy squib the first glimmerings of Ashley's concern with public health problems. With more reason, yet not altogether correctly, another episode of his Harrow schooldays has always been taken to mark the beginning of his lifelong interest in the lot of the poor. When about fourteen years old, walking one day down Harrow Hill he heard from a side street the sound of what Hodder splendidly describes as 'a low bacchanalian song.' He watched in fascinated horror as a party of drunken men came staggering round the corner carrying a rough coffin. Suddenly they let the coffin fall to the ground and broke into a flood of oaths and curses. Not unnaturally, the boy was deeply moved by this shocking sight. 'Before the sound of the drunken songs had died away,' writes Hodder, 'he had faced the future of his life and had determined that, with the help of God, he would from that time forth devote his life to pleading the cause of the poor and friendless.'[4]

The story is famous, the evidence apparently unimpeachable. A tablet now marks the spot where the great philanthropist, another Saul on the road to Damascus, received this sudden and dramatic call to his life's work. According to the usually accepted version, Henry Butler, son to Ashley's Headmaster and himself Headmaster in his turn, was one day walking up Harrow Hill with Lord Shaftesbury, as Ashley had then become. He chanced to ask the old man whether he could point to any particular event which had induced him to devote his life to the betterment of the poor. 'It is a most extraordinary coincidence that you should ask me this question here,' Shaftesbury replied, 'for it was within ten yards of the spot where we are now standing that I first resolved to make the cause of the poor my own.' He than related the incident of the pauper's funeral.

Very few people can repeat conversation verbatim; Butler himself gave another, much less definite version in a commemorative sermon preached after Shaftesbury's death. The truth seems to be that the sight of the pauper's funeral, though an important episode in Ashley's life, was not the supreme turning-point that legend has made of it. In all his voluminous and self-revealing diaries there is only one reference, and that an oblique one, to this apparently decisive moment. Still more significant is the fact that as a young man in his twenties, reflecting on his future prospects, Ashley never gave hint or sign that he considered himself pledged to the service of the poor, nor did he show any interest in what would now be called social problems until he was appointed, at the age of twenty-seven, a member of a Select Committee on Lunacy. His eyes seemed to be fixed on the prospect of a political career, with an occasional glance in the direction of science; and whatever may be true in the twentieth century, in Ashley's day an interest in social questions was certainly not a passport to political office. If it is indeed true that, shocked by the sight of the pauper's funeral, he then and there dedicated himself to the service of the poor it is also true that for at least thirteen years he conveniently forgot all about that dedication, an act of oblivion so out of keeping with his character as to be wholly incredible. Nevertheless, this episode may well have been the first thing that roused the boy to an awareness of the miseries of the world outside his own privileged circle. If so, it was ironic that the realisation should dawn on him at Harrow, a school where, according to Isaac Williams, 'the poor were never spoken of but by some contemptuous term, or looked upon as hateful boors to be fought with,'[5] whilst an historian of Harrow[6] remarks especially upon the boys' insolence and cruelty to those whom they regarded as their social inferiors.

A change in his home circumstances which occurred about this time may have helped to interest Ashley in the lives of the working people. Two or three years after succeeding to the title, his father decided to open up the great house at Wimborne St. Giles in Dorset-shire, which from now onwards Ashley was to regard as his home. The boy took to country life, delighting in dogs and horses, spending much of his time riding over the estate, making friends with the far-mers and labourers, and watching them at work. Here for the first time he felt himself at home amongst his own people. He could never spend enough time in the place; for him Dorset was always to remain the most delightful spot on earth.

The neighbourhood of Wimborne St. Giles is not so obviously beautiful as other parts of Dorset; this wide and rather melancholy landscape has neither the comfortable prettiness of the western valleys nor the sweeping grandeur of the downs about Dorchester and Cerne Abbas. In this rolling chalk country strips of woodland alternate with bare upland pastures sprinkled with long barrows. When Ashley came into his inheritance he would never allow anyone to disturb these burial places of a forgotten race. Beside a shallow trout stream stands the village of Wimborne St. Giles, a pleasantly cosy cluster of well-built, well-cared-for cottages. In the days of the sixth Earl the place must have looked very different. He seems to

have found the estate in poor condition and, being himself totally
unconcerned with the welfare of his tenants, he allowed matters to
go from bad to worse until all was desolation and decay.

The only part of the village which still remains much as it was in
Ashley's boyhood is the charming group of parish church and red
brick alms-houses. In 1732 the fourth Earl pulled down the mediaeval
church and built one in classical style whose exterior forms the shell
of the present building. The fifth Earl altered and embellished the
church built by his predecessor; the sixth Earl, as might have been
expected, left the church severely alone. Ashley, on inheriting as
seventh Earl, immediately set about the business of remodelling
the existing structure. After his death his daughter-in-law, of a school
of Churchmanship very different to his own, lost no time in commissioning Bodley to alter the church yet again in accordance with
her own Anglo-Catholic views and practices. In 1910 a catastrophic
fire destroyed the building, leaving only the outside walls standing.
Today the exterior of the church, which is predominantly eighteenth-
century in style, looks very much as it did when young Ashley first
set eyes upon it; the interior, a fine example of the work of Ninian
Comper, is not so much a reconstruction as an entirely new design.
Beyond the church is the curiously unimpressive entrance to the
grounds of the great house. In Ashley's boyhood the outside of the
mansion remained very much as it had been commissioned by the
first Earl in the manner of Inigo Jones. Inside, the magnificent
decorations in mid-eighteenth-century taste were the work of the
fourth Earl, who also laid out the grounds, embellishing them with
pavilions and temples and a charming shell grotto.

Since London remained the family headquarters, a stay at St.
Giles was for Ashley only an occasional treat. He had done well
enough at Harrow to reach the Sixth Form at the respectable age of
fifteen when his father, for no ascertainable reason, removed him
from the school where he had been so happy and sent him to board
with a clergyman at Eckington in Derbyshire. The next two years
were spent by Ashley in almost complete idleness; he was to write
that perhaps 'no two years were ever so misspent.' They were not,
however, unhappy years; he had horses and dogs for his amusement,
and pleasant neighbours to show him 'abundant hospitality.' With
no work to do and few books to read, much of his time was spent
day-dreaming. Vague aspirations and schemes of all sorts floated
through his head, none of them even remotely connected with the
military career for which he was destined. The thought of Army life
was totally distasteful to him. Fortunately Lord Bathurst, who was

always to be a good friend to Ashley, persuaded Lord Shaftesbury to change his mind and to allow the young man to go to Oxford.

Going up to Christ Church in January 1819 Ashley found himself one of the select company of 'tufts,' titled undergraduates privileged to wear a gold-tasselled cap as a sign of social superiority. Tufts were tacitly expected to spend their University years in pleasurable idleness; Ashley, however, decided to work hard and to 'challenge honours.' Among the freshmen of his year was a fair, curly-headed Etonian called Edward Bouverie Pusey. Ashley and Pusey were related, Ashley's grandmother, wife of the fourth Earl, being Pusey's aunt. As cousins and contemporaries the two young men naturally saw much of each other, and they might well have become intimate friends had it not been for a trivial incident. Since they were attending the same lectures Ashley suggested that they should do their reading together; Pusey, however, declined, preferring to work by himself. His rather ungracious attitude checked the growth of a friendship which might have been of real importance not only to the young men themselves but also to the future of the Church of England.

As matters fell out George Howard, later Lord Morpeth, later still seventh Earl of Carlisle, became Ashley's closest companion at Oxford. A grandson of the famous Georgiana, Duchess of Devonshire, and thus closely related to the 'Devonshire House' group of Whigs, George Morpeth was a shy and scholarly young man who disliked society and concentrated upon his academic work, winning prizes for both Latin and Greek verse. Though in later life best known as a politician, he was also to win some slight fame as a very minor poet.

Unlike George Howard, Ashley enjoyed the social round. By nature extremely serious, not to say solemn, at this period of his life he seems to have developed a surprising and quite uncharacteristic gaiety. From an unhappy, downtrodden boy he had grown into a very handsome, conversable young man, attractive to girls and smiled on by their designing mothers. True, he was very badly off, and his manner was at times a little odd; much, however, might be overlooked in a person of such transparently virtuous character, who was, moreover, the heir to an earldom.

For the summer vacation of 1820 Ashley and George Howard planned a Scottish tour, beginning with a few days spent with George's family at Castle Howard near York. As he afterwards ingenuously confessed, Ashley approached Castle Howard anticipating 'every form of dullness'; in fact, his visit there was to prove one of the happiest times of his life.[7] Though lacking the brilliance and charm of her mother, Georgiana Morpeth was a gentle, kindly

person, possessed of exactly those qualities which were best calculated to win the heart of a young man starved of a mother's love
and care. Between her and Ashley there sprang up a quasi-maternal
relationship spiced by the innocent but intense admiration of a boy
of nineteen for a pleasant, attractive woman in her late thirties. In
a letter to his mother George Howard described Ashley as 'very
tender about you.'

At Castle Howard were the three Howard girls, Caroline, Georgiana
and Harriet, and their little sister Blanche with whom Ashley struck
up a fast friendship. He rolled with her down the grassy garden slopes,
he played with her at a form of billiard fives known as 'Rocket,' and
when he left he wrote her a charming little letter, 'in size equal to a
walnut.' In all his letters to her mother he sends her comic, affectionate messages. It is impossible not to suspect that he used his attachment to Blanche as a stalking-horse for his liking for her elder sisters.
With one or other of the three he was reputed to be a little in love,
though no one could say for certain which. His letters to Lady
Morpeth, however, make clear that it was the lively, argumentative
Harriet who came nearest to touching his heart.

In these letters Ashley gave a long and interesting account of the
Scottish holiday. From Castle Howard he and George went first
to Chatsworth, 'the most admirable spot in all England,' and thence
to Bolton Abbey. 'From there,' he writes, 'we went to sleep at an odd
eccentric hamlet called Shap after passing through a country more
suited to monsters and deformities of imagination than any human
being.' After enduring these horrors of the Pennines, Ashley delighted
in the gentler landscape of the Scottish Border and its many anti-
quities. Best of all was a visit to Sir Walter Scott, whom he had
desired to see 'more than all the wonders of nature and art put
together.' After a long stay at Edinburgh, where a young woman
rather improbably described Ashley as 'the handsomest young man
I ever saw, full of fun and frolic, and his countenance radiant with
youthful hope,'[8] the two friends travelled on to Fort William, staying
in a poverty-stricken inn where their room had 'an enormous hole in
the floor which gave me an exquisite view of the suite of rooms
beneath.' They went on from there to visit Glencoe, Inverary, and
finally Loch Lomond, ending their tour with a second stay with Scott
at Abbotsford – 'the allurement of his society is irresistible.' Scott,
on his side, wrote down Ashley as 'an original.'

For the next two or three years Ashley continued to write frequently to Lady Morpeth. The oddest thing about these revealing
letters is the absence of any mention of religion. Lady Morpeth was

a serious-minded woman to whom Ashley wrote intimately and without reserve; all the more strange, therefore, that he should never refer to what was to him the most important of all topics. He seems to be trying to adopt the tone of the 'Devonshire House set,' gossiping, humorous, with undertones of strong emotion. He cannot, however, achieve the urbanity so characteristic of that society; his letters are almost endearingly naïve and tactless. He was still young enough to find it very difficult to think before making a statement—'the world will name it precipitancy, I call it enthusiasm.' So, in an obvious fit of jealousy, he writes thus of a visit which his own cousin, George Agar-Ellis, had been paying to Castle Howard:

> To my great surprise I heard of the sojourning of George Ellis in your land? What could Agar do? Was he captivated by the repartee of Miss Harriet? But I am certain he did not play at Rocket or roll down the grassplot – that would wear out his clothes.

In other letters he wrote so disparagingly of Agar-Ellis that when that gentleman finally became engaged not to Harriet but to her sister Georgiana he was obliged to eat his words, which, it must be admitted, he did with a very good grace.

Much more inexcusable was his blunt-speaking about Lady Morpeth's beloved sister, Harriet, wife to Lord Granville. For some reason Ashley took a dislike to this fascinating woman, whom he barely knew, and proclaimed aloud his opinion of her. Later, when Lady Granville had shown him much undeserved kindness, he wrote in some embarrassment to express his penitence:

> How I do love Lady Granville! She is the most agreeable, the most captivating, the most kind personage that my good fortune has presented to me. She is so good to my family and so interesting to myself that I can scarcely believe that she is the same person against whom I once poured forth such a violent philippic in your back drawing-room.

Later he wrote criticising his own impetuosity and making a prophecy which was to be exactly fulfilled:

> I cannot exactly decide but I rather think that I have not been so violent and impetuous as formerly. Howard perhaps will say different; there is little doubt, however, that in time I should grow cold; you will remark, like the lava, cold at the surface but heated at the bottom.

In the autumn of 1820 Ashley's letters are full of the affairs of Queen Caroline whom George IV was trying to divorce under a Bill of Pains and Penalties. Ashley was hotly against the Queen, the Howards, and Harriet in particular, as hot in her favour. 'Town and Gown' antagonism was still strong in Oxford, most of the townsmen being for the Queen:

The Radicals assemble in small groups and watch any unfortunate gownsman who may be without the flock; having pursued him to a spot convenient they maltreat him at leisure.

One letter gives an amusing account of the hazards and inconveniences of even the shortest journey. Ashley has been invited to a party at Heythrop, some twenty miles from Oxford:

Road infamous, and latter part really dangerous at night, at which season we return, moonless, lampless, servantless, for we are going in a postchaise, and the gates are innumerable and in the dark too, not allowed a room to dress in, so arrive destroyed and vilified as to the exterior neatness of our dresses, so as to lose all chance of captivating. Weather dreadfully bad, and to sum up, when we arrive, what is the meed of so great trouble? It is like martyrdom, not in this world.

Other people beside Ashley were reluctant to face the discomforts of travel in those days before railways and motor-cars. In vain he tries to persuade Lady Morpeth to pay him a visit at St. Giles:

It is very evident that ye of the North have a certain contempt for the people of the West . . . You anticipate broken roads, dirty inns, a barbarous race, and a cannibal gentry, but I assure you on my honour that in these parts no Lords eat human flesh.

In these Oxford letters Ashley frequently mentions Henry Fox, son of the third Lord Holland. 'Ashley's character seems to me quite unintelligible, and can only be accounted for by a dash of madness,' Henry Fox wrote in his journal. 'From having a dislike that amounted almost to hatred I have grown insensibly to admire and like him.'[9] The friendship between Fox and Ashley was always to be something of a love-hate relationship. Two years later, after they had travelled to Oxford together, Fox wrote, 'We had a very pleasant journey and I got from his conversation a much better opinion of his heart than I ever had before.' Fox must needs, however, add the remark, 'his understanding is so warped by the most violent prejudices that he appears quite ridiculous whenever he finds an opportunity to vent them.'[10]

Fox could recognise and appreciate the warmth of Ashley's heart but he expected that generous heart to be controlled by Ashley's brilliant brain, and he was shocked to find that in fact Ashley's heart ruled his head. It was the confrontation of reason with emotion, of classic with romantic. Delicate, precocious, disillusioned, brought up in an atmosphere almost entirely cerebral, Henry Fox could make nothing of a personality which he could not explain in terms of logic and good sense. As a Tory and an Evangelical, Ashley was something of a fish out of water at Holland House, that temple of Whiggery and rationalism. Its famous hostess, Lady Holland, was one of the first American heiresses to marry into the English aristocracy. Born Elizabeth Vassall, at the age of fifteen she married Sir Godfrey Webster. A few years later she eloped with Lord Holland, whom she married two days after her divorce was completed, but even so too late to legitimise their first child. Ashley was not likely to approve of such a lady nor to be approved of by her. Lady Holland, however, judged her guests less by their opinions than by their entertainment value; if they could 'sing for their supper' all was well. The clever and handsome young Ashley was a very acceptable neighbour at the dinner-table and as such he soon won a place among the regular guests at Holland House parties.

At Oxford Ashley was working very hard for an honours degree in classics, perhaps even over-working, since in later life he would sometimes dream that he was once again up for his Finals, a nightmare all too familiar to those who have worked too hard, or not worked hard enough, for that examination. One of his examiners was a young Oriel don, John Keble by name, whose 'amiable and gentle-manlike demeanour' Ashley long remembered. At this period *viva voce* examinations were attended by the candidate's friends and relatives; George Howard wrote to his mother describing Ashley's examination:

I am sure you will be anxious to hear about Ashley, whose examination I have just been attending. The result has been as favourable as possible; he did all extremely well, and is, I think, quite certain of his first class. He was very nervous before it and I am really particularly happy at his success, as I think he had made a great object of it. If I was to distinguish what he did best, it was those parts which showed knowledge of the subject and memory, and not those which are showy and have more effect, such I mean as the poetry. It was very pretty to see his brother William in the greatest state of anxiety during it all.

When the lists were published, not only Ashley's name but George Howard's appeared in the First Class. 'I can only hope (speaking now in rather a moral style) that as we began our career and ended it, so may we continue through life,' Ashley wrote to Lady Morpeth. 'We commenced the friendship at Oxford, have passed through the University with honour, and I ardently desire that with equal credit and unanimity we may endure to the end.'

Chapter 2

THE YOUNG ARISTOCRAT

When Ashley left Oxford in 1822 he found himself without a settled home. For no apparent reason, his father forbade him to live permanently either at St. Giles or in the family house in Grosvenor Square. In 1826 he gave his address as Norfolk Street, Strand, but he spent much of his time staying with friends. For a year after taking his degree he lived the conventional social life of a young aristocrat, going to parties of all sorts and paying country house visits. In 1823 he dined four times at Holland House and in April of that year attended a Ball at Devonshire House where he danced with Lady Holland's young daughter Mary Fox. Though 'very pretty and much admired,' Mary was a bad dancer who might not have enjoyed herself very much had not Ashley taken her under his wing, 'very anxious and kind in assisting her to keep right.'

After this courtesy towards her daughter it was ungrateful of Lady Holland to write as she did in a letter to Henry Fox dated May 26th 1823:

> Your friend Lord Ashley is going abroad for two years. His absence will be a blessing to young ladies. He is a male coquet, the cruellest of characters and the most cold-hearted. But he is very handsome and captivating; and young ladies are willing to be deceived, and from their own vanity often exaggerate attentions. But if they fall in love it is hard, poor things, let the fault be where it may.[1]

Perhaps Ashley's well-meant kindness to Mary had deceived that seventeen-year-old innocent. It is easy to see how he had acquired this undeserved reputation as a flirt. Nobody is so dangerous to a young woman's peace of mind as a really serious, well-behaved young man. Kisses and the small change of love ensnare only the inexperienced; long and earnest conversations, especially on the subject of religion, are sufficient to persuade any girl that a man's attentions are as serious as his interests. Ashley liked women, and he

liked talking to them about the deep subjects which most interested
him. He could be at times curiously unrestrained; the middle-aged
Lady Lyttelton was amazed when he seized her by both hands and
exclaimed, 'Heaven bless you ten thousand times!' Women might
have been expected to fall in love with him because he was handsome,
charming and aristocratic; in fact, they fell in love with him because
he was earnest.

On August 27th 1823 Ashley set out on the Grand Tour of Europe
which was still an accepted part of the education of an English
aristocrat. With John Denison, afterwards Speaker of the House of
Commons, he spent three weeks in Switzerland before travelling
on to Italy, where he was joined by George Howard. After visiting
Naples, he and Howard settled in Rome for a stay of several months.
Rome was then as now a hotbed of gossip and scandal – 'never
credit any story retailed from Rome,' he warned Lady Morpeth.[2]
Ashley himself seems to have been temporarily affected by this
gossiping humour. He told Lady Morpeth of a Prince Esterhazy
who had sixty-four acknowledged children – 'most probably his
modesty will not allow him to claim the honour, however justly,
of a larger family' — and he repeated the malapropism of a Mrs.
Grant, who announced that she was about to give a classical ball,
'something in the manner of the Rape of the Sabines.' Nevertheless
Ashley found Rome 'a place where cold hearts become warm and
feelings naturally friendly become kinder and more general.' Certainly the relationship between him and his parents temporarily
improved during his stay there; he even referred to his father as
being 'excessively kind' and putting no restriction either on his
movements or his expenditure. Ashley found some of his own in-
hibitions melting away in the Roman atmosphere. Private theatri-
cals were still looked on slightly askance (only a few years earlier
Jane Austen had roundly expressed her disapproval of them in
Mansfield Park). Now, however, Ashley seemed delighted that
George Howard should take the part of the hero in a play got up by
the British visitors, whilst he himself appeared in a tableau in the
feminine role of a sibyl – 'I shall do my best for an inspired countenance.'

Ashley travelled in Italy until August 1824, when he met his brother
William in Milan, and with him journeyed through Germany to Vienna
where he stayed several months, in spite of his disapproval of 'the
sleek, sleepy, sensual Viennese.' The Austrian men he disliked intensely, finding them uneducated, untruthful and mischief-making.
He particularly despised 'the old men who dote yet play the gallants,'

but the women he found 'beautiful, gay, well-educated, open mannered.' With one of these women he now fell head over heels in love.

In his biography of Metternich, Algernon Cecil describes Antoinette von Leykam as 'the daughter of a diplomatist of no great importance and of a lady of no great reputation.' Baron von Leykam was reasonably well-born, though not a member of the high aristocracy; he had, however, made a *mésalliance* with an Italian singer who filled their home with actors and musicians, persons regarded as immoral riff-raff by the members of Viennese society. Ashley himself wrote of his love that 'the object was, and is, an angel, but she was surrounded by and would have brought with her a halo of Hell.'

Even thus haloed Antoinette was sufficiently beautiful and charming to plunge him 'furiously and imprudently in love.' Her looks belied the background from which she sprang; slender, blonde, wide-eyed, she wore an air of untarnishable innocence. She was, moreover, both tactful and intelligent, a girl altogether out of the ordinary. But she was not the girl for Ashley. At first he supposed marriage to be a possibility. Writing in his diary a year later, he declared that at the time he had 'thought the Deity hard in the obstacles to our union,' but in his heart of hearts he had always known that the future Lady Shaftesbury must not be the daughter of a disreputable Italian singer, nor must she be, as Antoinette of course was, a Roman Catholic. We do not know whether prudence prevailed over passion or whether he proposed and was rejected. Whatever may actually have occurred, by the end of the summer of 1825 all was over; Ashley was back again in England, and Antoinette was walking in the woods around Vienna with another even more aristocratic and unlikely lover, the famous statesman, Prince Metternich.

With Ashley the affair had gone very deep; he himself believed that it had started him on 'a course of self-knowledge.' Perhaps with a view to increasing that knowledge he now began to keep a diary, packed full of introspection and self-analysis. In their brilliant but sometimes misleading book, *Lord Shaftesbury*, J. L. and Barbara Hammond have this to say of these diaries: 'They tell of the brooding misery of the man to whose soul, divinely clouded by the sorrows of the world, the religion he had learnt at his nurse's knee offered for light and peace the torment of an incessant and distracting analysis of self.'[3] It is all too easy to attribute Ashley's morbid preoccupation with self-analysis to the workings of a sensitive conscience over-stimulated by Evangelical religion. The truth is not nearly so simple and obvious. In fact, Ashley's conscience was not particu-

larly sensitive. He is curiously free from any sense of guilt; his
diary shows him as not so much preoccupied with his own sins as
with the sins of other people. At times he can even display an unpleasantly smug assurance of his own righteousness. So, on November
13th 1828, he writes of his father:

> I feel that had I broken out years ago into resistance and com-
> plaint I should have done no more than almost every other son
> living would have done . . . Although I cannot feel any esteem
> for Lord Shaftesbury I shall never think in repentance on myself.
> Not a year has passed in which I have not conveyed some favour
> on him.

All this is true; yet surely there is no situation in which a Christian
could not and should not think in repentance on himself. Ashley,
as he reveals himself in his diaries, is tormented not by a sense of
sin but by a sense of failure. He is convinced, or, more accurately,
he tries to convince himself, that he is a person of no ability, yet
on the same page he maintains the complete contradiction, that his
abilities have gone unrecognised and that he has been denied the
high position to which they certainly entitle him.

This complicated, involuted personality was not one to be easily
understood either by his contemporaries or by posterity. People
as a whole admired and liked Ashley, but they also found him a little
disconcerting. Henry Fox was not alone in his half-jesting reference to
'a dash of madness.' Lady Lyttelton admired Ashley for his sincerity,
'mad though he be'; Lord Cowper thought him 'odd'; Georgiana
Howard complained that his opinions were 'more lively than durable,'
whilst her sister, Caroline Lascelles, admitted that 'I have not perfect
confidence in his judgement.' All these opinions of Ashley stress
a certain instability in his character. Yet this was the man who was to
display an unequalled steadfastness in his championship of unpopular
and unpromising causes, the man who doggedly faced disappointment
after disappointment, the man who was not to be turned from his
purpose by opposition or ridicule or the dead weight of sheer inertia.
The truth is that religion, far from being the cause of Ashley's
psychological troubles, was in fact their antidote, even partially
their cure. He was so distressed and obsessed by the machinations
of those whom he believed to be his enemies, whether or not they were
so in fact, that he could not have continued the struggle had he not
been convinced that an omnipotent God was on his side. For him
religion was a stabilising and upholding force, soothing, strong,

unalterable, in his own Evangelical terminology, the Rock of Ages. 'I will spread it out before the Lord,' was one of his favourite texts; time and again, when distressed and disturbed almost beyond bearing, he found comfort and support in prayer. In the contemplation of nature, and later in his relationship with his wife, but most frequently and most profoundly in the practice of religion, he was to discover that serenity which was so conspicuously lacking in his own character.

Evangelicalism as Ashley conceived of it was not what is popularly described as 'Old Testament religion.' Though he believed in the wrath of God, all his preoccupation was with God's love. In his childhood he had equated irreligion with his harsh, unloving parents, religion with the loving, warm-hearted Maria Millis. He had been happy with Maria, unhappy with his parents; for him, therefore, religion spelt happiness. Even his conception of the Last Judgement was of a happy rather than a terrible day; the fear of Hell had little or no place in his thought. A pessimist about the affairs of this world, where the next world was concerned Ashley was a confirmed optimist. Taught by his unhappy experiences in childhood, he saw this world as a dangerous place which he had no difficulty whatsoever in renouncing, except – and it was a large exception – where his political career was concerned. Religion, on the contrary, he found a positive pleasure. 'Church,' said someone apropos of Lady Frederick Cavendish, 'is dear Lucy's public-house'; so could religion be called Ashley's most enjoyable stimulant.

As well as writing page after page of self-analysis Ashley devoted much of his diary to descriptions and criticism of other people. He was not in fact a very good judge of character, but even so his pen portraits are interesting, if only because they are often and obviously wrong. On April 28th 1826 he wrote an account of his brothers and sisters, to whom he felt himself linked by an especially intimate tie – 'we, whom from unhappy circumstances which you well know, are more closely connected by all the sentiments of affection than in general,' he wrote to Lady Morpeth. Because of these 'unhappy circumstances' all three of his sisters, though renowned for their good looks, were looked on rather askance by society. As early as 1820 Ashley had written explaining the situation to Lady Morpeth:

I was anxious that you should become more intimate with my sisters. I am aware that you would have discovered faults, as I do many, but their merits are still great, and your good opinion delivered to the world would have been a great shield for their reputations, for I know full well they are traduced. Here are the consequences of a mother's dereliction of her children; how dreadful they are you will neither learn by experience nor imagine; your own feelings are so vivid and so maternal and so ardent towards your offspring that you almost doubt my assertions that such *unnatural*, such deeply horrid examples are found in a human and a Christian soul.

Charlotte, Harriet and Caroline suffered as much at their father's hands as at their mother's. Lord Shaftesbury kept them in such awe of him that none of them dared speak in his presence. The eldest sister, Charlotte, escaped from the tyranny of this bullying parent, whom Henry Fox describes as 'disgusting, and meaner than any wretch in the world,' by marrying Henry Lyster, a young man 'well spoken of,' according to Lady Holland, 'rich, but not rich enough to have a lovely wife out of a great house, and a hunting establishment beside.'[4] Sydney Smith's nephew described the newly-married couple as 'an insipid pair,' but since he had been rejected by Charlotte in favour of Lyster he was not an altogether impartial judge. Harriet. who was to marry a Member of Parliament called James Lowry Corry, and to become the mother of Disraeli's secretary, Montague Corry, seems at this time to have been Ashley's favourite sister; he writes that 'she conducts herself with all the amiableness that human nature is capable of.' Caroline, on the contrary, 'is neither so amiable nor so generous as her sister, though she has some good qualities.' In later life, when married to Joseph Neeld, a rich and influential Wiltshire landowner, Caroline was to show herself exceptionally amiable and generous towards her brother. In a letter dated January 1827, commenting on Lord Shaftesbury's unnatural behaviour to his children, Lady Holland wrote, 'Lady Caroline Ashley has been living for months with Lady Warwick at the Castle,' the inference being that Caroline's father had behaved to her as he behaved to his eldest son and turned her out of house and home.

William, the brother next in age to Ashley, is described by him as being 'more applied to useful pursuits.' Ashley was particularly fond of William, though he nevertheless found him somewhat irritating, apparently because of a certain lack of determination. A year or so later, in an attempt 'to get William settled in life,' Ashley resolved to ask the great Duke of Wellington to find a post for his brother, adding the sad comment, 'if William, having gained the object of his wishes, do not conduct himself with industry and energetic principle, my heart will be snapped asunder.' The outside world found William a good-hearted and affectionate character, whose abilities some people were inclined to rate higher than those of his elder brother. The next two brothers Ashley deals with in very summary fashion. Henry, now abroad, 'bears a good character in Malta,' whilst John, a plain but sensible young man who was to become a reasonably successful Queen's Counsel, is dismissed as giving 'no cause for disquietude.' Lionel, the youngest child, though only twelve, was already serving with the Navy. Perhaps an instinctive sympathy with anyone who was difficult or different from his kind made Ashley particularly attached to this problem-child. He writes of Lionel more affectionately than of any of the other brothers – 'the dear boy, with his many faults, promises well.' The promise was not to be fulfilled; a few years later Princess Lieven wrote that Lionel 'was certainly a little mad,' whilst Lord Melbourne described him to Queen Victoria as 'a most sad fellow.'

During Ashley's absence abroad, Francis, the brother between John and Lionel in age, had been killed in a fight at Eton. The fourteen-year-old-boy, 'a kind, jolly, curly-headed youngster,' had certainly not lacked courage; he had battled for more than two hours against a boy bigger than himself until he was knocked senseless. Between the sixty rounds of this bloody, bare-fisted fight Francis' seconds had misguidedly plied him with brandy; even so, he need not have died had he not been allowed to lie unconscious for four hours before anyone thought to send for a doctor. 'This event, so novel, so unprecedented, so terrible that it can never be forgotten,' induced in Ashley, who was himself a good boxer, an undying horror of what he described as 'the English bestiality of prize-fights.'

On April 28th 1826, Ashley's twenty-fifth birthday, and the day on which he wrote his description of his brothers and sisters, he chided himself for his idleness during the past three years – 'not a study commenced, not an object pursued, not a good deed done, not a good thought generated, for my thoughts are too unsteady for the honour of that title.' If this were indeed so he was now making up for lost time, studying hard at physics, astronomy, and mathematics. He made some very obscure notes on the connection of physics and astronomy with politics and morals:

Monarchy is the great principle in physics; close relation of physics to morality. Solar system typical of government on earth. Argue that the circle or elliptical form is the most complete (being the most celestial) figure. Form of bodies, course of bodies etc all round infer that morals will follow physics. Mankind begins with monarchy and simplicity. It will return to the point from whence it started by a different route, which in morals is equivalent to a circle. Monarchy is the perfect form, and will prevail again when man, as the planets, can perform his functions as simply and as truly.

Mathematics, as Ashley understood them, 'bespeak the harmonious wisdom of a God.' He describes them as 'the business of pure spirits,' and adds, 'they have substance for their subject and matter, and are part of the science of man here below.'

Ashley intended his studies to fit him for taking his place in Parliament, the obvious destination for the eldest son of a peer with a successful career at the University behind him. 'Politics seem my destination,' he wrote; 'at present I am preparing for the senate, preparing in the hopeless, unsettled way that cannot be called a plan.' His mother's relations, the Marlboroughs, seem to have played a very small part in his life; they did, however, provide him with his first seat in the House of Commons. In June 1826 he and his cousin, Lord Blandford, were elected as Tory members for the Duke of Marlborough's pocket borough of Woodstock.

Ashley was to take his seat for the first time when Parliament reassembled in November. In the interval he and Denison visited Paris and stayed with Lord and Lady Granville at the British Embassy. Ashley wrote to Lady Carlisle, as Lady Morpeth had now become, to tell her how much he was enjoying this visit to her sister:

> Lady Granville is the Queen of Hearts, and I love her much. She has put herself to trouble with the view of doing us kindnesses, and if it but depended on her alone I should be the most charming and sought-after man in all Paris. She not only introduces me to the fashionables, but beautifies and gives system to my manners, making me bow and call upon them, going in when they are at home, and leaving cards when they are not.[5]

For her part Harriet Granville wrote to her sister, 'Lord Ashley and Mr. Denison are behaving beautifully and go out every morning to sit with foreigners of distinction.'[6] Sir Walter Scott was paying a brief visit to Paris and Ashley was distressed to hear him criticised on every hand for attempting to write a life of Napoleon so soon after the Emperor's death. 'He wants money,' Ashley commented sadly and truly; 'and money will make his pen go faster than his judgement.'[7]

Other visitors to Paris were two future premiers, George Canning and the young Lord John Russell, and two well-known figures in London society, Lady Jersey and Lady Cowper. Ashley found Lady Cowper 'a quiet, sensible (outwardly so) and tractable woman'; Lady Jersey was so noisy that he declared 'I see no way of keeping her still except by gagging or starving her.'[8] The other English women in Paris he found 'no great shakes,' but he made himself very popular with the French women he met at the Embassy. 'I introduced him to the *élègantes,* who think him *superbe, magnifique,*' Harriet Granville wrote, 'and he is much pleased, "dear, delicious women".'[9]

It is typical of Ashley that at the very time when he appeared to the perceptive Harriet Granville to be thoroughly enjoying himself with these dear delicious French women he should be writing to Lady Morpeth that he would have nothing to regret in leaving Paris except the loss of Harriet's own company. On his return to England he summed up his views in his diary: 'I hate France. It is a wicked country. It is the Devil's *pied-à-terre.*' There was always to be this discrepancy between his outward behaviour and the opinions expressed in his diary, a discrepancy due in part to his innate good manners but more particularly to his very curious pyschological make-up. His moods fluctuated so violently that he might in a moment of euphoria genuinely delight in France and the French people, and, a day or two later, dislike them both intensely.

To diagnose the physical ills of a person who lived a century ago is difficult enough; to diagnose the mental ones is almost impossible. Perhaps, were Ashley alive today, he might be labelled a manic-depressive and advised to have psychiatric treatment for that condition. The swing of the pendulum, apparent in every one of us, was in him particularly marked; he touched unusual heights of happiness, or, more frequently, lay submerged in the lowest depths of gloom. Whether or not he was technically a manic-depressive, he certainly suffered from unusually severe fits of depression. In his Oxford days he had written to Lady Morpeth of his 'desponding fits,' and time and again in his diary he records periods of almost intolerable depression and despondency.

On November 16th 1826 Ashley noted in his diary, 'took the oaths of Parliament with great good will; a slight prayer for assistance in my thoughts and deeds.' He had, of course, entered Parliament as a Tory, but the Toryism of Lord Liverpool's Government, with Canning its most powerful member as Foreign Secretary, was not the thing that Toryism had been under Castlereagh. It was natural that an enthusiastic young man should be carried away by Canning's brilliance. 'Canning's speech, the finest historical recollection of my life,' Ashley noted on December 10th; 'except the loftier flights of the Bible I never heard nor read such rousing eloquence, such sentiments, such language, such a moment; they almost maddened me with delight and enthusiasm – could not sleep for agitation – feverishly and indistinctly recollecting what I had heard.' Next morning he snatched up his pen to dash off to Mrs. Canning, whom he had known in Paris, a letter which she later described as 'the most eloquent and beautiful effusion of feeling I have ever met with.' Ashley was always to be a person whose easily aroused emotions could on occasion temporarily overrule his naturally sound judgement. So now his enthusiasm for Canning, however well justified, was in fact merely a temporary aberration, his real allegiance being given to Wellington, whom he affectionately if slightly disrespectfully referred to as 'Dukey.' 'The Duke of Wellington is here,' he had written to Lady Carlisle from Woodford, the home of Wellington's friends, Mr. and Mrs. Arbuthnot; 'his conversation is as useful as his battles. I have never heard of such a man.' Ashley was nevertheless sitting rather loose to any definite party affiliation beyond that of a vague and comprehensive Toryism, his attachment to Wellington being a matter of hero-worship and personal friendship rather than one of political conviction.

In February 1827 Lord Liverpool suffered a severe stroke – 'poor man, beloved, trusted, and looked up to by every mind in England!' was Ashley's rather surprising comment – and two months later resigned the Premiership. Canning succeeded to the office, and, through the medium of Mrs. Canning, offered Ashley, who had only been in the House of Commons for five months, a place in the Government. This offer Ashley declined in polite, non-committal terms. 'You know,' he wrote to Mrs. Canning, 'how sincerely I admire his policy in the late affairs on the Continent' – Ashley was always to fancy himself as an authority on European politics – 'and I should have great satisfaction in supporting with my best endeavours so enlarged and so national a system. But there is a concurrence of circumstances which will not allow me to accept his friendly proposal.'[10] In his diary Ashley analysed that concurrence of circumstances. His difficulties really reduced themselves to the fact that to serve under Canning would be a betrayal of his loyalty to 'Dukey,' who, with Peel and five other leading Tories, had resigned from the Cabinet on Canning's appointment as Prime Minister. 'With me,' Ashley wrote, 'the Duke is the first consideration.'

He had also written, 'I feel so unqualified that I almost rejoice in the difficulty.' In writing thus Ashley was not indulging in false modesty but expressing an opinion about himself which at the moment he felt to be exactly and painfully true. At times he was all too keenly aware of gifts and abilities which were not being appreciated at anything like their true value, at others, he honestly believed that 'wherever I go, I am the last in knowledge, in reasoning, in information, in eloquence.' He had the natural self-assurance of the born aristocrat; but the lack of any appreciation or encouragement in the impressionable period of childhood had undermined his self-confidence and left him self-questioning and insecure. He knew too that a good Christian should be humble, and on the many occasions when he wrote himself down as stupid, feeble, incapable, he was making an effort to achieve that difficult virtue of humility. Yet in his heart of hearts he could not but know himself superior, or at the very least not inferior, to his fellows – 'It seems to me that I must be a man of uncommon dullness, and yet I have not the feel, nor, as I have been told, the air of stupidity.'

This spring of 1827 he was engulfed in one of his worst fits of black depression. A year earlier he had written in self-deprecatory mood, 'As advancement is impossible I must be careful not to retrograde, confiding in the Almighty Greatness which will lead me to eminence or suppress me in obscurity as seemeth best to His divine all-knowledge.' Now, however, he felt that God himself had forsaken him. 'The curse of God is upon me,' he wrote, and again, 'I never felt greater depression or more thorough belief that God is opposed to all my advancement in learning and wisdom than I did last evening.' He believed that he had proved himself a complete dunce in the mathematical studies to which he had devoted so much time and attention. 'Even now in mathematics, in common arithmetic, I am beaten by a man who has not perhaps looked at this science for a long period, not at any time seriously!' He despaired of making any sort of success of his apparently promising political career:

Would to heaven I could quit public life and sink down into an ambition proportionate to my ability! But I am cursed by honorable desires (they are so). . . . I care not so much about the wretchedness of my understanding as I am maddened through the ardour of my love for science and true wisdom, and humbled by the poverty of my mind.

Mental stress reacted on Ashley's physical condition; or perhaps some physical weakness helped to produce mental overstrain. By

April 1827 he was ill enough to think it necessary to go to Leamington to consult the fashionable physician, Dr. Jephson, although the nine pounds travelling expenses were a heavy burden on his very limited financial resources. Dr. Jephson declared 'he had never seen a person with a more deranged stomach.' In quoting the doctor's statement Hodder bowdlerised 'stomach' to 'system,' thereby obscuring the fact that this illness is the first recorded instance of the digestive trouble which was to attack Ashley at intervals during the rest of his long life. Because these attacks coincided with periods of exceptional strain or anxiety the trouble was almost certainly either a gastric ulcer or nervous dyspepsia. Ashley was a copybook example of the type of person most liable to develop these complaints; although he intended the expression figuratively he was exactly describing his habitual physical condition when he wrote, 'I am too bilious for public life.'

In spite of his depression and ill-health, all the signs pointed to Ashley as a coming young man in politics. The leaders of the two sections of the Tory party manoeuvred against each other to secure this promising recruit; Canning had already offered him office, Wellington took him very much into his confidence. Among the Shaftesbury papers there is an interesting letter from Wellington, undated, but presumably written sometime in the winter of 1827, before Wellington himself took office in January 1828:

I have observed that since I quitted the Government in April last I have been the *bête noire* of Mr. Canning and his friends. At times I am deemed a *stupid fool* and moreover, everything that is bad; at others when the gentlemen find themselves in a scrape they discover that they have acted exactly as I advised they should act, and therefore they must be right!!! This is the case at present. My objection is that neither Parliament nor the public will be satisfied respecting that *unfortunate* affair, the battle of Navarino* (as all now agree that it was) till they have examined all that preceded it and could have occasioned it . . . Till then I will not say a word. But if any gentleman tells you that any private letter from me to Mr. Canning will be produced you may say that I have

* Fought October 20th 1827. A fleet under Admiral Codrington had been sent to Greek waters to enforce the terms of the Treaty of London, July 6th 1827, between Russia, France and Great Britain, arranging a settlement between Turkey and Greece. When the Turkish–Egyptian fleet refused to withdraw Codrington attacked and annihilated them. Turkey and Britain were not technically at war.

copies as well as Mr. Canning's friends and that not one alone but all must be produced if one is.

Even on the Whig side of the House Ashley's abilities were noted and admired. 'Lady Carlisle wrote me word the other day that Brougham* had been loud in my praises.' It was not only to Lady Carlisle, who was known to take a motherly interest in Ashley, that Brougham praised this up-and-coming young man. 'I wish to God Ashley would come forward well,' he wrote to Lady Jersey. 'I have a high opinion of him as an uncommon young man, and in spite of his father I hope great and good things of him.'

At this period of his life Ashley seems to have given himself wholly to politics as his business, with mathematics and science for his recreation; of any particular interest in the lot of the poor he gives no sign whatsoever. True, he was generous with his money; on the rare occasions when he received an unexpected gift or legacy he was scrupulous in giving a due proportion to charity. Occasionally in his diary he made some such entry as 'I am relieved of an old pensioner, must find out someone else.' This, however, shows no more than a careful habit of alms-giving common to many charitable people. Clearly he does not consider himself a dedicated champion of the poor; equally clearly, though he never says so in as many words, he does consider himself a possible future Prime Minister. Yet, little though he planned or intended any such thing, in this summer of 1827 he was to take his first step in the direction of his true vocation in life. Before he had been a year in the House of Commons he had sat on three Parliamentary committees. In June 1827 he was appointed to a fourth, a Select Committee 'On Pauper Lunatics in the County of Middlesex and on Lunatic Asylums.' For the first time he was to be concerned with the fortunes of the outcast and the destitute.

---

* Henry Brougham, first Lord Brougham and Vaux, Lord Chancellor, 1880, a Whig famous for 'extreme' opinions.

Chapter 3

REFORM OF LUNACY LAW AND PRACTICE

Ashley's appointment to this Select Committee marks a turning-point in his life, definite although unrecognised. It would be interesting to know to whom he owed his nomination. The suggestion may well have come from the Chairman, Robert Gordon, a well-known Dorset character living at Leweston House near Sherborne. Ashley and Gordon probably knew each other, since they were both named in the Dorset Commission of the Peace for 1823. Gordon was recognised as leader of the struggle for the reform of lunacy law and treatment, a position which Ashley was shortly to inherit.

The Committee included such well-known figures as Lord Althorp, William Sturges-Bourne, the Home Secretary, Thomas Spring-Rice, the future Chancellor of the Exchequer and John Cam Hobhouse, friend of such different characters as Byron and the Radical tailor, Francis Place. In her book, *Lunacy, Law and Conscience*, Doctor Kathleen Jones writes of this Committee that 'it was supported by prominent politicians from both sides of the House, but most of the active work was done by back-benchers who were prepared to make a special study of the questions involved.'[1] Among these back-benchers Ashley quickly became pre-eminent.

'Poor mad people and naturals, how treated? The diversion of seeing Bedlam – what a better laugh? See the malignity of this.' So had Ashley's ancestor, the philosopher Earl, written in the previous century. By 1827 matters had improved a little, but they were still bad enough. The horrors inflicted upon lunatics appal the imagination. Pauper lunatics were confined in workhouses, in 'bridewells' or Houses of Correction, sometimes even in jails. They would be kept fastened by the leg to a table, chained in a cellar, garret or outhouse, perhaps shut up in an uninhabited ruin. Conditions in Liskeard workhouse were typical. Here an investigator found two women in a very damp low building without light or air, 'chained down to the damp stone floor, and one of them had only a little dirty straw which appeared to have been there for many weeks . . . We asked if she was allowed water to wash herself and found she was not . . . the whole place was very filthy, filled with excrement, and very offensive.' Other pauper lunatics were boarded out, at the expense of the Poor Law authorities, in private madhouses where conditions were perhaps even more horrible. One such madhouse boasted a structure known as 'Bella's Hole,' an enclosed box built on a base three or four feet square, with a few holes at the top to allow for the passage of air. It was said that a lunatic had been confined in this contraption for several months, naked and in the dark. Since there was no adequate system of registration or certification, unwanted or burdensome people, sometimes merely eccentric, occasionally completely normal, could be committed to these terrible places simply on the authority of a mercenary heir or an impatient relative. Once incarcerated in a madhouse escape was all but impossible since the unfortunate inmates had no means of communication with the outside world.

Perhaps the worst of all madhouses was the famous Bedlam or Bethlehem Hospital. As the philosopher Earl had remarked, a visit to Bedlam to watch the antics of the lunatics had been one of the favourite diversions of eighteenth-century Londoners. At Bedlam the most notorious case of ill-treatment was that of an unfortunate man called William Norris who was confined in a narrow stone trough against a wall:

An iron collar several inches wide encircled his neck, and was fastened to the wall behind his head; his feet were manacled, and a harness fitted over his shoulders, pinioning his arms to his side. It was just possible for him to stand or to lie on his back but he was unable to shift his position when lying down or to move more than one step away from the wall. He had remained thus for many years, never enjoying a moment's freedom from his chains; yet, strange to relate, when spoken to he appeared quiet and rational, able to hold an intelligent conversation and to read and understand anything put before him.[2]

Although Norris's plight was perhaps the most spectacular many other patients in Bedlam were kept in conditions almost as horrible. As a 'hospital' Bedlam was intended to be an institution where lunatics could not merely be safely confined but also, when possible, cured of their lunacy. The treatment consisted of bleeding the patients, placing them on a 'lowering,' semi-starvation diet, and dosing them with strong purges and emetics. Other and even more drastic methods employed were the 'circular swing' in which the patient was rotated faster and ever faster until he lost consciousness, or the 'bath of surprise,' a trap-door which opened beneath the feet of the unsuspecting patient who fell through it into a tub of icy water.

Such tortures were not peculiar to Bedlam. The treatment administered to one particular patient who was confined in his own home is described thus:

> The unhappy patient was no longer treated as a human being. His body was immediately encased in a machine which left it no liberty of action. He was sometimes chained to a staple. He was frequently beaten and starved, and at best he was kept in subjection by foul and menacing language.[3]

The individual so maltreated was no pauper lunatic but His Majesty King George the Third. Beatings, starving, chains, purges and so forth were not cruelties inflicted by brutal and ignorant men; they were the accepted treatment for lunacy, and as such they were applied by the best available doctors to the most notable patient in the land. Willis, the specialist in charge of the King, was under great pressure from Queen Charlotte and the Tory politicians to bring about the speediest possible cure in order to avoid the necessity for a regency; he therefore employed the methods which he considered most likely to effect this. (The curious fact is that these methods were to some extent successful; in February 1789 George III made a sudden recovery, though he was to relapse again in 1801.)

This illness of George III was responsible for the first real change in the public attitude towards lunacy. The brutal methods of treatment which had been employed in his case were survivals of the time when lunatics were believed to be possessed by a devil. This attitude of mind, if not the actual belief, survived well into the eighteenth century, the so-called age of enlightenment. The existence of a lunatic in the family was a terrifying and shameful fact to be mentioned as little as possible and hidden from public knowledge. Lunacy was the forbidden topic, under the same taboo which banned sex as a subject of conversation among polite Victorians. Now, however, lunacy suddenly became an absorbing topic, spoken about freely and discussed in the newspapers. Moreover, as Doctor Jones points out, it was scarcely possible, at least in Tory circles, to assume that the King of England was being punished for his sins. The result of this awakening of public interest was a real effort in the direction of reform. Between 1800 and 1808 three Select Committees reported to the House of Commons, and four Acts were passed dealing with the subject of lunacy. The Lunacy Laws were consolidated and amended, although the Lords threw out the proposal to appoint a Board of Inspection which alone could have made those laws effective. Two specific reforms were achieved: Justices of the Peace at Quarter Sessions were empowered to order the building of county asylums, and conditions at Bethlehem Hospital were so improved that 'New Bedlam' could compare favourably with most private madhouses.

Meanwhile, a Quaker called William Tuke had achieved what would now be called a breakthrough in the treatment of lunacy. He founded at York a private asylum known as the Retreat, a comfortable, pleasant place where the patients were treated with kindness and, above all, with respect. Tuke banished chains and all forms of mechanical restraint, treating the patients as one family with the staff. His humane, enlightened methods proved very successful, and the number of cures was remarkably high.*

The Retreat had been opened in 1796. By 1827, when Ashley took his seat on the Select Committee, Tuke's ideals and ideas had begun to spread, and a change, faint but perceptible, had come over the general attitude towards lunatics and their treatment. In this, as in so many of the other reforms with which Ashley was later to be concerned, a beginning had already been made. Other men had sown the seed; it was for him to reap. The fact that he entered into another man's labour did not make his part in the work any the less strenuous. His shining vision of the end never blinded him to the prosaic details of the means. He was not one of those reformers who shirk dull, routine business; if there was hard, unspectacular work to be done he did it himself. So it was to be with his work on behalf of lunatics.

The Select Committee's terms of reference in fact confined it to an examination of the conditions existing in the madhouses kept by a certain Doctor Warburton, to whose care the vast majority of the London pauper lunatics were committed. The Committee concerned itself almost exclusively with the White House, Bethnal Green, the largest of Warburton's houses. The members of the Committee examined many witnesses, but they did not visit the White House.

* Oddly enough, Ashley, who was to be one of the greatest opponents of 'mechanical restraint' and a keen advocate of the more humane methods Tuke adopted, never seems to have visited the Retreat or to have corresponded with the various members of the Tuke family who carried on this pioneer work after the founder's death.

Ashley, however, went there personally on their behalf to enquire
into the facts of a disputed case.

The treatment of the 'crib cases' at the White House was to become
notorious as an instance of cruelty and neglect. 'A crib-room,' said
Richard Roberts, assistant to the Overseers of the Poor in the parish
of St. George's, Hanover Square, 'is a place where there is nothing
but wooden cribs or bedsteads, cases in fact, filled with straw and
covered with a blanket, in which these unfortunate beings are placed
at night, and they sleep most of them naked on the straw, and of
course do all their occasions in their cribs.' In these cribs, as another
witness described, 'they were chained by their hands and feet and if
they were to get up on a great state of fury they might dislocate
their wrists and ankles.' Thus chained, the patients were left in their
cribs from Saturday afternoon till Monday morning when they were
cleaned of their accumulated filth. A kind-hearted if ungrammatical
witness described the way in which this was done:

> They were washed in such a manner as would make tears come out
> of any Christian's eyes; they were taken to a tub where there was
> ice in cold, frosty weather, and there they stand by the side of the
> tub and are mopped down just the same as if they were mopping
> an animal.

The White House infirmary was rightly described as 'a mere place
for dying,' since no adequate treatment was given there to the sick.
The whole establishment was appallingly overcrowded; food, particularly meat, was scanty and disgusting, 'that nasty thick hard
muscle a dog could not eat'; cleanliness was totally disregarded,
no soap being provided and only one towel, changed weekly, allotted
to one hundred and sixty persons. Patients suffering from every type
of mental disease were herded together without any attempt at
classification. One Doctor MacMichael, when asked whether he
considered that 'in the lunatic asylums in the neighbourhood of
London any curative process is going on with regard to pauper
patients,' replied succinctly, 'None at all.'

Many a person had been confined in these madhouses who was, in
the words of one witness 'a great deal sounder of mind than those that
sent him.' A Mrs. Pettingale, reported cured in 1825, was still shut
up in a madhouse two years later; even then, in order to procure
her discharge, 'it was necessary to expostulate somewhat warmly
with her husband.' Sir James Williams, a Director of the Poor in
St. Pancras' parish, found in the White House 'a little boy, about

thirteen or fourteen years of age, a fine lad, with the dress of a fisherman upon him, perfectly sane.' It is good to know that Sir James saw to it that this fisherboy was set at liberty.

With such evidence before them, it is not surprising that in their Report the Select Committee declared that 'if the White House be taken as a fair specimen of similar establishments your committee cannot too anxiously or too thoroughly express their conviction that the greatest possible benefit will accrue to pauper patients by the creation of a County Lunatic Asylum.' Eighteen counties had failed to send in any returns, and as yet asylums had been built in only nine counties. The Committee proposed that 'legislative measures of a remedial character should be introduced at the earliest period at the next session,' and they made a number of recommendations, including the establishment of a Board of Commissioners appointed by the Home Secretary and possessed of real and extensive powers of licensing, inspection and control.

On February 18th 1828 Robert Gordon moved for leave to bring in a Bill to put these recommendations into effect. At Gordon's special request Ashley seconded this motion in a maiden speech. 'So, by God's blessing,' he wrote in his diary, 'my first effort has been for the advance of human happiness. May I improve hourly! Fright almost deprived me of recollection but again thank Heaven, I did not sit down quite a presumptuous idiot.'

Ashley might well pray for improvement in the art of public speaking, for the short report in Hansard was enough to daunt any beginner:

> His Lordship spoke in so low a voice that he was nearly inaudible in the gallery. He alluded to evidence given before the committee to prove that it was highly necessary that something should be done relative to the treatment of pauper lunatics, and he cited several instances that had come within his own knowledge which clearly proved that the present system was greatly defective.

Knowing Ashley to be 'mighty sensitive,' kind Lord Bathurst wrote immediately to assure him that this maiden speech had not been quite the failure that might be supposed – 'Peel said that if your speech had been uttered with as loud a voice as that of Lord Morpeth everyone would have said it was an excellent speech' – and to point out that it was no bad thing to begin his parliamentary career with a speech that was not over-successful – 'you will feel when next you speak that you are risking nothing, and the very feeling will encourage you to speak with more confidence.'[4] The Bathursts had always been Ashley's very good friends. At this period Lady Bathurst had become the 'mother figure' in his life, taking the place once filled by Lady Morpeth. 'They seem very familiar,' wrote Lady Morpeth's daughter, Georgiana Agar-Ellis; 'it reminds me a little of what he used to be with Mamma and makes me feel half angry with him.'

Ashley had a hand in framing two bills, the County Asylum Bill and the Madhouse Bill, which passed easily through both Houses of Parliament, an agreeable change from earlier days when the House of Lords had invariably rejected any such measures of reform. By these Acts fifteen commissioners were appointed for the metropolitan area and given extensive powers of licensing and inspection. Among these commissioners was Ashley, who thus began fifty-seven years of unrewarded, disagreeable, and very fatiguing work on behalf of those whom he once described as 'the most helpless, if not the most afflicted portion, of the human race.'[5]

It was not work likely to appeal to a politically ambitious young man like Ashley. Familiarity with the working of lunatic asylums or with the intricacies of lunacy law could lead to no office or to any sort of political employment. He admitted to feeling 'unusual sympathy' with the mentally afflicted, but otherwise he had no reason to interest himself particularly in their plight. Why then did he undertake so thankless a task and, what is still more surprising, pursue it for so long and with such unwavering tenacity? The answer lies in one short and simple word, 'duty.' He had not sought out the work himself; the work had, as it were, sought him. It was a duty to which he believed himself called by God. On one Sunday, when for once he broke the Sabbath rule to which he usually adhered so strictly, finding himself 'from eleven o'clock till half-past six engaged in the good but wearisome cause of lunatic asylums,' he commented, 'did not wish for such an employment but duty made it imperative.' So he might have written about all his work on behalf of lunatics. But what was begun as a duty ended as a matter of the heart. Once he had seen for himself the neglect and brutality endured by these helpless people he found himself personally involved in their misery: a sensitive and compassionate man, he could not see such suffering and pass by on the other side. Where the welfare of lunatics was concerned Ashley acted simply in the spirit of the Good Samaritan and continued so to act until almost the last day of his long life.

The years 1827 and 1828 which saw the beginning of this work on behalf of lunatics were a period of great confusion in the political world and of almost equal confusion in Ashley's political thinking.

When Canning took office as Prime Minister in April 1827 he was already a sick man. His death four months later greatly shocked and distressed Ashley. 'Canning died yesterday; I am really quite agitated and can be alive to nothing but pity and horror,' he wrote in his diary on August 9th, and, forgetting that good Evangelicals should not pray for the dead, added the sentence, 'I do feel true compassion and pray sincerely God rest his soul.'

In the month following Canning's death Ashley paid a visit to his sister Charlotte Lyster at her home at Rowton Castle near the Welsh border. From there he made an expedition into Wales where a chance encounter led to one of the oddest episodes of his whole career. At Aberystwyth he fell in with a pleasant Welsh parson, an enthusiast for the Welsh language, who fired him with a desire to learn Welsh. He settled down at Aberystwyth for a few weeks and studied to such effect that a year or so later, when a scheme was on foot to launch a magazine to be called *The Cambrian Quarterly*, he was asked to write the prospectus. Hodder does not say whether this was in Welsh or in English; the quotation which he gives would probably read best in the more poetic of the two languages:

> Inhabiting a land which came a virgin to the arms of our ancestors, unmixed in our race, uncorrupted in our language, civilised though not adulterated by foreign intercourse . . . we can vie with every nation in examples of honour, courage, and dignified obedience.[6]

Though he had no drop of Welsh blood in his veins, Ashley is here taking upon himself to speak as a Welshman. Whilst he was at Aberystwyth the local Welsh people, astonished that an Englishman should trouble to learn their neglected language, 'regarded me,' said Ashley, 'with great reverence and held a great meeting at which I was created both a Bard and a Druid.' Whatever his racial origin a Druidic Bard might surely consider himself a fitting spokesman for the Welsh people. Englishmen of the eighteen-twenties regarded Wales very much as their sons and grandsons regarded Africa in the days of imperialism; Ashley even goes so far as to write of 'my residence among the natives.'

On his return to London Ashley found Goderich installed as Prime Minister in Canning's place. 'Goody' Goderich, 'as firm as a bulrush,' was the very last man to preside successfully over an amorphous coalition Cabinet. In January 1828 he resigned, to be succeeded by the Duke of Wellington. Not a year previously Ashley had claimed

Canning as a personal friend, and, although refusing to serve under him, had declared, 'I agree with Canning in nine-tenths of his system.' (Very rarely indeed was Ashley to be as much as nine-tenths in agreement with any political leader.) Now, however, he worked himself into a frenzy because 'Dukey' planned to include a few Canningites in his Cabinet. In particular he objected to the appointment of Lord Dudley as Foreign Secretary – 'Can the Great Duke sit in Cabinet with the man who signed that prodigy of injustice, the treaty?* What shall I myself do if they offer me a place? Can I submit, all insignificant as I am, to such a compromise?'

To just such a compromise did Ashley submit exactly one week later when, as he had foreseen, Wellington offered him a place as a Commissioner on the India Board of Control. By this time he had cooled down a little and was able to admit that Wellington was acting with wisdom and good sense in his effort to reunite the two sections of the Tory party – 'I regret deeply our reunion with the Canningite party, but the Duke has according to his usual style done that which is best.'

To suppose that the prospect of office had in itself sufficed to calm Ashley's excitement and alter his views would be to make a totally unfair simplification of his very complicated reactions. No man was ever less of a place-seeker than he; time and again he was to refuse office for much less substantial reasons than those scruples which he now abandoned so easily. He had been honest in his objection to the appointment of Canningites to Cabinet office; he was equally honest in withdrawing that objection. Sober reflection, not the glittering prospect of office, had convinced him that Wellington was right after all. In the heat of the moment he was always apt to make hasty, ill-founded judgements, which, on more careful and cool consideration, he recognised as wrong; sometimes but not always, he was wise and humble enough to admit his mistake. So it was now, when he had the grace to be ashamed of his childish outburst of temper, and to admit that he had altered his opinion, even though such an admission laid him open to the charge of placing preferment above principle.

Painfully enough, Ashley was learning that essential lesson for any politician, 'Always think twice before you speak.' The memory of his ill-considered remarks caused him some embarrassment:

Can one be too guarded in the expression of one's thoughts? At the first moment of surprise, while yet in doubt as to the conditions granted to Mr Canning's party, I vented some indignation against the admitting of Lord Dudley. A few hours convinced

* Treaty of London, July 6th 1827: see ante Chapter II, p. 30.

me of my error, but it was too late. I had vented it before Agar-Ellis who yesterday threw it in my teeth. This silly childish ebullition of sentiment may give someone the power of calling me a dishonest man. How unpleasant, but I must steel my heart against such trifles, and learn caution in studying philosophy, not that of the schools but the philosophy of man, and of a life of passion.

This philosophy he was never wholly to comprehend; for him life was always to be 'a life of passion,' not of philosophic calm. Now he prayed with desperate earnestness for 'discretion and calmness to reflect,' adding the petition, 'now office can no longer be avoided I pray the Heavenly Father to give me the will to discharge my duty, and the strength to perform it.'

Ashley was not a hypocrite in thus speaking of office as something he might have wished to avoid. A remarkably single-minded and determined man where other peoples' interests were concerned. in matters affecting himself he was hesitant, contradictory, unsure. swinging first one way then the other. In part this strange inconsistency sprang from the mistrust and self-consciousness induced in him by his unhappy upbringing, in part from the inner conflict between his religious aspirations and his unregenerate self. By nature Ashley was a proud and very ambitious man; with the help of what he would have described as God's grace he was doing his best to become a humble and selfless one. Of course he did not wholly succeed in this effort, though he came nearer to success than most of us can ever hope to do. The battle had its ups and downs; there were times when he honestly wished to flee from the trials and temptations of a political career – 'would to God I could quit public life!' – and there were other, more frequent occasions when the pull of ambition was paramount. Try as he might to convince himself that he was a person of small ability and that worldly success was a snare and a delusion, an inner voice kept whispering that he had gifts far above the average and that his ambitions were not ignoble ones – 'I am cursed by honorable desires (and they are so).' One day he would be certain that he disliked the very idea of office and would record this conviction in his diary; on the next he would see office as no more than his just due, and declare himself bitterly aggrieved if it were not offered to him.

The appointment to the India Board did not merely gratify Ashley's ambition, it also eased his financial position. All his life he was doomed to go short of money. Though not gifted with much financial sense, judged by the standards of his own day he was cer-

tainly not extravagant, and he might have managed well enough
had he ever had the good fortune to possess an income in any way
equal to the demands of his position. In 1828 the eldest sons of peers
not merely would not but could not earn their own living except
by obtaining a political post. Ashley was dependent upon a ludi-
crously inadequate allowance from his father, and, moreover, he was
always to be dogged by financial misfortune. Thus in 1827, on the
death of a Mr. Parkes, who had 'given hints to myself and positive
declarations to others of making me a monied man,' it was found that
the perfidious old gentleman had left Ashley exactly one hundred
pounds. He was therefore the more relieved when, five months later,
he was appointed to the India Board and for the first time received
a regular salary.

Though the sum involved was nothing remarkable, to Ashley it
seemed as if 'riches have of late poured in upon me.' With obvious
relief he adds the remark 'I have discharged two-thirds of my debts.'
Thus early had he begun to suffer under the burden of debt from
which he was never to free himself. His next thought was to send a
large donation to the parson at St. Giles to be used for the relief
of the poor of the parish. The neglected state of the people in his
home village weighed constantly upon Ashley's mind but, so long
as his father lived, he could do next to nothing to improve their
state. Other charitable donations disposed of much of the money
which might have gone to clear the remainder of those outstanding
debts. King's College in the Strand had recently been established as
a counterblast to the 'godless' University College, and to it Ashley
gave a surprisingly generous gift – 'I did well in giving a hundred
pounds to King's College; the sum, though large for me, is rightly
laid out in erecting an embankment against the overflow of irreligion.'
With equal satisfaction – the unkind might perhaps say self-satis-
faction – he records a donation of twenty pounds to a memorial to
Bishop Heber, author of the hymn 'From Greenland's icy mountains,'
a prelate whom Ashley described as being 'like Orpheus, who led
even stones and trees by the enchantment of his music.' A further
five pounds went to rescue a girl from prostitution and to help pay
for her education.

Control of Indian affairs was at this period divided between the
governmental India Board and the independent East India Company.
Some of the Board's Commissioners were inclined to treat 'John
Company's' directors 'with vulgar insolence'; not so Ashley, who was
glad to dine with them, welcoming any occasion to cultivate friendship and good feeling. He does not seem to have been so popular

with his own colleagues. Lord Ellenborough complained frequently
that 'Ashley came and bored me,' whilst an interesting letter from
Lady Harriet Granville to Wellington's friend and assistant,
Charles Arbuthnot, seems to show that 'Dukey' and his friends were
disappointed in their protégé. It is dated September 14th 1829:

> You really are very provoking about Ashley. It is but a year and
> a half that you were so much *coiffé* with him and that you told
> me the Duke wished especially to bring him forward. I told you
> *then* to be cautious how you went to work, and that you might
> perhaps be disappointed in him. You formed too great expecta-
> tions from him and they *have* been disappointed. The reaction
> is now much stronger than it ought to be, and in your mortifica-
> tion at having been mistaken in the political character of the man
> you have lost sight of many redeeming qualities, and are too ready
> to find fault with *all* that he does, rather dwelling upon his failures
> than trying to forget them. I dare say he is quite wrong about his
> India affairs ... You seem to value his services in the public line
> so little that I do not imagine you would care much if he did no
> longer adhere to the Duke, and took to Madame de Lieven.[7]

Perhaps Ashley had fallen from favour because he was clearly
prepared to ride full tilt against practices which his colleagues preferred to leave unchecked out of deference to religious prejudice.
Speaking at Wimborne nearly thirty years later he recalled his fight
against one such practice:

> I recollect perfectly well, when I was at the India Board in 1828,
> on the question of Sutteeism (that is, the burning of widows on
> the death of their husbands) coming before us, thinking it a matter
> of most outrageous cruelty and wrong. On saying so I was put
> down at once as if I were a madman; I was wondered at for even
> daring to mention such a thing. Well, my Lord William Bentinck
> was appointed to the command in India. My Lord William Ben-
> tinck thereupon, with a stroke of his pen, put the unnatural
> practice down, and the whole of India was satisfied that it was
> right, because his Lordship appealed to those great principles of
> the human heart, which are implanted by the hand of God, and
> which may be overcome by abominable incrustations; but con-
> science is still there, the mistress of truth, and does its work;
> and if you appeal to the conscience, depend upon it the millions
> will go along with you.[8]

With the 'abominable incrustations' of Hinduism Ashley would have
no truck whatsoever – 'I hate the folly of persons who, conceited in
Deism and the ostentation of abstruse learning, find a hidden beauty
in all the beastly nonsense of the Hindu religion.' He summed up
his views on India's needs and England's obligations in a rhetorical
question and answer:

> India, what can I do for your countless myriads? There are two
> things, good government and Christianity.

Ashley's condemnation of the Hindu religion did not, however,
imply any condemnation of Hindus themselves. He was years ahead
of his time in disapproving of what he described as 'the rigid characteristics of English behaviour' towards Indians, and in looking forward
to the day when India would be granted her full independence. He
never wavered in this opinion; as late as 1876 he declared that 'a
time may come when, after a long period of happy rule, we may
surrender India to the natives, grown into a capability for self-
government.' The free India to which he looked forward was, however,
an India that would be British, not Indian, in outlook and ideals:
before these 'natives' could become fit for self-government 'we must
train them in British sentiments, infuse into them British principles,
imbue them with British feeling.'[9] This was always to be Ashley's
view of Empire; and it was not an ignoble one. Educated in the classical tradition of Greece and Rome, an alien culture long ago imposed
upon Britain by an Imperial power, the men of the nineteenth century saw no harm but rather great good in imposing their own culture
upon other nations and races. They did not believe that they were
forcing an uncongenial civilisation upon an unwilling people; they
thought to offer those people the very best they had to give. So
Ashley writes in his diary for November 25th 1845, 'I should like to
make each colony, so far as possible, a transcript of the Mother
Country; I would protect it and train it unto its riper years, and then
give it, like a full-grown son, free action and absolute independence.'
With this end in view he welcomed the arrival of Indian students in
England to enjoy the advantages of English education, and he urged
his fellow-countrymen to adopt a more hospitable and appreciative
attitude towards them:

> India's sons come hither from every presidency and every pro-
> vince; they enter our colleges, inns of court, and schools of science,
> in preparation for professional careers in their own country. They

dash boldly into competitive examinations with the European
and not infrequently carry the day. In sense, justice, policy, in
the spirit of Christianity, are these men to be overlooked? Attentions shewn to them in England strike a chord that thrills through
the whole of Hindustan. Their manners and conversation are
graceful, their thoughts high, and their views of the blessings of
the British rule sagacious and solid.[10]

Where more practical matters were concerned Ashley was especially concerned with efforts to improve Indian agriculture and food
supplies. He became positively lyrical in praise of the potato as an
alternative to rice as a staple crop and item of diet, and he enthusiastically urged the foundation of a 'Scientific Corporation of the
institution and Improvement of Horticulture and Husbandry throughout the Provinces of India.' All this was interesting and important
work, but it was not work likely to win the attention either of Ashley's
political leaders or of the general public. From 1827 to 1829 the
question of Catholic Emancipation overshadowed all other issues,
whether at home or abroad. The admission of Roman Catholics to
Parliament and to high office under the Crown was of course a
burning question in Ireland, where a successful agitation led by
Daniel O'Connell forced the matter once again upon the attention
of the British government. In 1828 O'Connell was returned at a
by-election in County Clare, although as a Catholic he could not take
his seat in Parliament. The Tory leaders, Wellington and Peel,
realised that at the next General Election similar tactics would be
adopted all over Ireland, and they decided that the time had come
to give way. Naturally enough, this decision was very unwelcome
to many members of the Tory party, but not to Ashley. Although
at times he could behave like a fanatic, at others he could show an
admirable detachment and impartiality of judgement. So now, though
the most Protestant of Protestants, he was nevertheless convinced
that Emancipation was not merely inevitable but right and desirable.
In this he differed absolutely from his father, who was hot against
Emancipation. Though this was by no means the first time that father
and son had disagreed on a political issue the two had never before
clashed openly upon a matter of first-class importance. Ashley's
brother William was also a member of Parliament, and Lord Shaftesbury expected both his sons to vote according to his own views.
Of the two, William was the more amenable to parental pressure.
'William still at Brighton,' Ashley recorded on January 9th 1829;
'to a certainty the Earl has won him and we shall have him excul-

pating and justifying all these sad proceedings. To justify Lord Shaftesbury is to condemn me.' On March 9th, writing to her son Henry about the progress of the Emancipation Bill, Lady Holland remarked, 'Lord Shaftesbury is behaving abominably and would not let his son William, who had promised, vote the other night.'[11]

Ashley was made of sterner stuff than his brother, and he refused to bow to such dictation, but he dreaded the prospect of an open quarrel with his father so greatly that he could describe the opening of the parliamentary session as 'the beginning of sorrow.' However, though he had himself given an anti-emancipation pledge to his constituents, he was sincerely pleased that Wellington and Peel should have admitted to a change of heart and declared themselves in favour of giving full civil rights to Roman Catholics. 'I have long and deeply desired this policy,' he wrote on February 5th 1829, and in defiance of his father's anger, he both spoke and voted in favour of the Catholic Emancipation Bill, which became law in April.

Chapter 4

LOVE AND MARRIAGE

As relaxation from politics, the India Board, and the work of a Commissioner in Lunacy, Ashley would frequently turn to his favourite scientific pursuits. 'In early life I was passionately devoted to science,' he recollected in his old age, 'so much so that I was almost disposed to pursue science to the exclusion of everything else.' Astronomy was his especial love – 'what a study is that of the heavens!' He made friends with the astronomer James South, spending many hours in the observatory on Campden Hill where South was building a great telescope, and in May 1830 he invited Peel, who was then Home Secretary, to call upon South 'to view this noble specimen of art and make acquaintance with a man whose zeal and skill in the cause of science have never been surpassed.'[1] South had been given promises of financial help by the French government should he decide to move his telescope to Paris; Ashley hoped that Peel might arrange for funds to be made available to enable South to remain in England. 'I feel an irresistible desire to maintain as long as God will permit, the superiority of England in the discovery of the perfections of scientific truth.'[2] He concerned himself too with the appointment of an astronomer in Bombay, urging that at least one of the observatory assistants should be an Indian – 'This man, by contemplating the purity of Almightiness will soon learn to despise Brahma and Vishnu.' The interweaving of science and religion, still possible in that pre-Darwinian age, is typical of Ashley's thought. 'I held forth last night upon Astronomy a little,' he writes on July 20th 1829. 'It was to persons who had not considered its glories; I hope that the few remarks I made will lead them to reflect more deeply on the immensity of power and goodness in the Creator.'

Yet, busy though he was about his work and his scientific hobbies, the diary shows that in the years from 1827 to 1830 one subject filled Ashley's mind to the exclusion of almost everything else – 'I am dying to be married, but where, Oh, God help me, where is the

woman?' In the autumn of 1827, solitary at Aberystwyth, he had
begun to play the child's game of Imaginary People, inventing for
himself an ideal woman and worshipping this 'imaginary darling.'
Back again in England he had no lack of opportunity to meet and
make friends with flesh and blood females. Women found Ashley
very attractive, though they laughed at him a little; he and his
brother William were nicknamed 'the Sublime and Beautiful.' About
this time he was reputed to be engaged to Lady Augusta Brudenell, a
rumour he hotly denied. Perhaps he was in danger of becoming a
little spoilt. After conducting a mild flirtation with two young women
known to us only as Henrietta and Olivia he made a solemn entry in
his diary:

> I find that Love is not likely to have a mastery of my heart. Man
> loves fiercely but once; the next time is reason or convenience or
> plain matter-of-fact. I shall marry no doubt, but not yet. I feel
> great kindness towards a select few, nay, towards some it is even
> warm and tender affection, but it is the warmth of a brother's
> love, and probably they would not thank me for such a gift.

Though he might try to believe that he would marry for 'reason
or convenience or plain matter-of-fact,' like many extremely virtuous people he was really an incurable romantic. He must marry
for love, and the girl of his heart must be a goddess. The truth was
that he had never been able to free himself from the memory of
Antoinette, or 'Liebe' as he privately called her.* He grieved fiercely
over a report sent him by Lord Clanwilliam of her supposedly unseemly behaviour with Prince Thurn und Taxis – Antoinette's
lovers were a remarkably aristocratic collection – and tormented
himself with the notion that when he had believed her entirely

---

* On August 13th 1827 there is a puzzling entry in the diary, following an erased
sentence: 'You are now married and happy as one so thwarted and represesd
can be with the aid of talents and religion. Two years have gone by; she had been
oftentimes out of my memory, not this the presence of another but lost in my
business and active life. Solitude, however, brings her back and then I remember
all with sorrow. There is now much to soothe, even to delight me. [word erased]
you are the most surprising female I ever heard of, your virtues are heroic,
your whole character made up of the greatest qualilties, but I am convinced
(and Providence, I feel, points it out) I could not have been happy with you as a
wife, and yet you border upon perfection. It is very odd.' The pronouns 'you'
and 'she' must refer to two different women. Antoinette is clearly the 'she'
whom he had loved two years previously but she cannot be the 'you' who is
now married and happy, because at this date she was still unmarried. Presumably the clue lies in the erased sentence and word.

devoted to himself she had been laughing up her sleeve at him and flirting with someone else – 'surely the mother and daughter must consider me the very silliest puppy they ever associated with.'

In December 1827 news reached him of Antoinette's marriage to Prince Metternich, which had taken place on November 3rd. This *mésalliance* was a nine days' wonder in all the courts of Europe; Metternich's mistress, Princess Lieven, was not alone in expressing surprise at the sight of the great man 'taking notice of a little girl' and choosing that little girl for his second wife. Ashley's reaction was a generous one:

> So Liebe is married; I cannot but feel some return of love; the affection I entertained once was so painfully strong that its influence must endure for a time. I rejoice in her bettered condition, and pray for her happiness, for nothing, I am told, could have surpassed her open conduct, her frank avowal in answer to Metternich's offer. She has command of the most heroic virtues; I never doubted these.

Typically enough, after writing this high praise Ashley must needs have second thoughts – 'But is she worthy of such reflections? I do not like to doubt it, and I will not. Heaven protect her!'

Ashley solaced himself for his regret that Liebe was now for ever out of his reach with the affection shown him by 'my dear sweet friend,' Lady Francis Egerton. This friendship with a married woman gave rise to a little unkind gossip:

> It is well to contemplate a female mind rich in pureness and anxious for truth. I know that some people fancy such a friendship the cloak for passion but God knows better and to Him I appeal.

Meanwhile, he was constantly dreaming of his ideal woman – 'Methinks that if I could find the creature I have invented I could love her with a tenderness and truth unprecedented in wedlock. I pray for her abundantly; God give me this purest of blessings.'

The following year, 1828, Ashley spent Christmas at St. Giles, alone but happy in 'the ancient seat of my forefathers.' In his daydreams he saw himself living there with the wife of his imagination, both of them blissfully occupied in 'patriarchal duties.' Then, a month later, came news which grieved him greatly yet in a strange way set his heart at rest – 'This day what do I hear? Liebe, Liebe

herself is dead.' After ten months of ideally happy married life with
Metternich, Antoinette had died in childbed.

It seems that this news reached him when he was staying with the
Egertons:

> Immediately afterwards I saw a bandbox which I had given to my
> dear Lady Francis, on it was a view which I last saw in company
> with Antoinette; at that moment Francis demanded of me where
> I got the little shawl I wore round my neck; the whole together
> almost overpowered me for an instant.

His grief for Antoinette was long-lasting; references to her constantly
recur in the diary. He could not easily forget 'the many walks, the
many sentiments, the many tears we have known together.' Nevertheless, her death seems to have freed him from an inhibition, turning
him from his preoccupation with an imaginary ideal to the serious
search for a flesh and blood wife. On March 22nd 1829, during a visit
to the opera, he was smitten with 'a feeling the most sudden on record,
it can hardly be called love,' at the sight of the sixteen-year-old
Lady Selina Jenkinson, daughter of Lord Liverpool. The idea of
marriage seems to have crossed his mind immediately, since the
entry in his diary ends with the reflection, 'Providence ordained
marriage with all its grievances as the comfort of the human race.'

At first it seemed that Lady Selina must be as good as she was
attractive, 'most excellently educated and accomplished, perfect in
virtue and female delectability.' The excellent education of the
Jenkinson girls was a matter of general comment; 'I think Lord
Liverpool has taken great pains in educating his daughters,' Lady
Charlotte Neville wrote to her niece, Catherine Glynne. Their behaviour, however, was not always as excellent as their education.
One of them, Charlotte, stole away Catherine Glynne's betrothed,
Francis Harcourt, a piece of meanness which in the end turned
greatly to Catherine's advantage, since it left her free to marry that
rising young politician William Gladstone. So now Charlotte's
sister Selina seems to have played slightly fast and loose with Ashley's
affection. There were, however, at least as many faults on his side
as on hers. Most of the pages dealing with this abortive love affair
have been cut out of the diary, but what remains shows him as a
painfully intense and critical suitor. Even Lady Selina's sister is
made the subject of severe analysis – 'I am become very nice and
fastidious; I found fault with her as over-taught and instructed to
discriminate by rule and not by nature, feeling and judgement.'

Lady Selina herself is described as 'most captivating.' He yearns for a chance to meet her quietly and alone, not in the rush and bustle of Society; after dancing with her at a ball he comments, 'Oh, what a place for nurturing a love such as I desire to feel!'

The marriage was confidently predicted by society gossips and pressed upon Ashley by his brother William and his sister Harriet; in his heart of hearts, however, he knew that this girl was not, and could never become, the ideal wife of his dreams, attracted though he was to her. He was not so much distressed as piqued when, at the beginning of June 1829, Selina's father put an end to the affair. Ashley believed Lord Liverpool to be flying at higher game – 'he had one of two purposes, either to make me propose,' which Ashley never did, 'and then to raise his daughter's value by a refusal of me, or else to retain me secretly as a *pis aller*.'

Back Ashley went to his urgent quest – 'Oh, my prayer, my prayer, how I repeat it! A wife, a wife!' His sexual desires were strong; he prayed for someone 'with whom I might be safe from the snares of temptation.' He admired beauty in women as intensely as he admired it in art and nature – 'I love all beautiful things.' His wife must be lovely to look at and sexually attractive; she must also be 'the companion of my life and of my mind,' and, he might well have added, of his soul also, since it was essential that she should be able to share his religious faith. Engaged as he was in this search for what seemed an unattainable ideal, it is not surprising to find Ashley frequently falling from the heights of bliss to the depths of depression. 'How curious is my character,' he wrote on July 3rd 1829, 'sometimes for a while in the wildest and most various of spirits, in others, and for a much longer period, in cruel and overwhelming despondency!' He knew well enough that such a character as this was not able to stand alone; he needed a wife to give him steadying balance. Because he had never known a normal family life he yearned all the more for the companionship of someone loving and stable with whom he could share all the ups and downs of life, the trivialities of every day as well as the aspirations and struggles towards some great achievement as yet unspecified to which, obscurely but certainly, he felt himself destined.

On August 2nd Ashley recorded his hopes and feelings in his diary:

It is time, high time, that I should marry. Temporal comfort a little but eternal welfare specially demand a sacred and lawful connection. I am now twenty-eight and it suits neither my dignity nor my principles to continue the life of a headstrong youngster just emancipated from college . . . Marriage is a state appointed by God to which we must all submit. 'It is better to marry than to burn.' I have looked around, I have found many amiable girls, two or three *especially* so, but none entirely satisfactory as companions.

Thus far his musings read as if his attitude towards love was a deliberately cold and calculating one; he seems to be as distant as ever from the attainment of his goal of matrimony, 'that state to which we must all submit.' But suddenly comes a hint of delighted discovery and deeper involvement – 'There is one that I know not well; she is lovely, accomplished, clever, with an almost virgin indifference towards her admirers.'

All would seem perfection; there is, however, a major drawback attaching to this paragon: 'By the mother's side she is sprung of a family which, gifted with talent and good humour, seems to confound the distinction between right and wrong. The mother herself has laboured under heavy suspicions of faithlessness to her marriage vows.'

The girl in question was the most admired beauty of the year, nineteen-year-old Lady Emily Cowper, known as Minny to distinguish her from her mother Lady Cowper, who had been born Emily Lamb. Nobody in their senses would have thought to suggest that Ashley should look for his ideal wife in the ranks of 'the Grand Whiggery,' least of all among the members of the Lamb family. Fire and ice were not more different than the Tory, Evangelical Ashley, and the Whig, free-thinking Lambs, described by Lord David Cecil as 'vital, sensual, clever, positive, and unidealistic.' People did not always take to the Lambs – 'they complained that they were hard and mocking, unappreciative of delicacy and romance; they were scandalised by the freedom alike of their morals and their conversation; and they disliked their manners.'[3]

It might have been argued that Minny Cowper was a Lamb only on her mother's side. In her case, however, the maternal line of descent counted for much more than the paternal. That shadowy character, Lord Cowper, was in all probability not her father. Who that gentleman might have been no one could say for certain, possibly not even Lady Cowper herself. Though no real evidence was forthcoming, the most likely guess was Lord Palmerston. Whether this assumption was or was not correct Minny was always to be Palmerston's especial darling. A charming letter from him, written in January of this same year, 1829, is addressed to 'My dear Minny, if indeed it is still allowable to address by so familiar a diminutive a Lady so formed and so distinguished.' He begs her to accept 'this little Box, and the small Fan, and the Smelling Bottle,' which he had brought her from Paris, 'more as tokens of Recollection and Regard than for their own particular merits.' These New Year's gifts, he continues, come with the wish 'that the return of this season may for many, many years bring with it as much Happiness to you as it now does through you to all those who belong to you.'[4]

How closely Minny did in fact belong to Palmerston can never now be known. Ashley was being extremely charitable when he referred merely to suspicions attaching to Lady Cowper. He might have added that Lady Cowper's own mother, the first Viscountess Melbourne, laboured under similar suspicions, or rather, near-certainties, of unfaithfulness to her husband. Lord David Cecil describes the first Emily's parentage as 'shrouded in mystery.' If Minny's legal father, Lord Cowper, was not in fact her father, neither, it seems, was her legal grandfather, Lord Melbourne, her real grandfather. Viewing her as a possible wife for a particularly strait-laced young man, it must be admitted that her heredity was anything but ideal.

Ashley, however, had good reason to know that daughters did not of necessity take after their mothers – 'Have I not seen daughters the very reverse of their mothers, domestic, loving, faithful?' Lady Shaftesbury was certainly neither domestic nor loving; is this sentence a hint that she was also unfaithful? 'If the world were to judge of my sisters by the infernal wickedness of the parent who bore us what would the conclusion be?' He decided that the mother's reputation was no adequate reason to 'abstain from enquiry into the character of a person whose outward appearance presents such qualities.' Such enquiries were to be pursued in the spirit in which Christians are urged to enter upon the holy estate of matrimony, discreetly, advisedly soberly, and in the fear of God – 'I will enquire, and I will implore Almighty Providence to aid my judgement and direct my choice.'

On August 2nd, the same day on which he wrote that entry in his diary, Ashley found occasion to see Minny again. The meeting was apparently a satisfactory one. 'Why now, what a paradise of ecstasy it would be to share with this lovely girl all the sublimities of religion if she has a good and affectionate heart,' he commented, then added in a more spontaneous outburst of feeling, 'there is something in her too fascinating.' Later in the month he went down to Tunbridge Wells, where the Cowpers were staying. There he was able to see

Minny constantly. On a warm summer's evening they stood side by side on the balcony, and Minny, who was not inexperienced in dealing with young men, tactfully questioned him about astronomy. They strolled together in the town – 'what could she mean by withdrawing her hand from mine in the Pantiles?' – they drove together to the High Rocks. Passionately in love though he was, Ashley could not or would not silence all his misgivings; his eagle eye fastened on the slightest fault, the smallest deviation from his standard of perfection. He felt 'dispirited' when, by way of a joke, she peeped into a stranger's room in the lodging-house, believing her action to show 'a curious and prying disposition, with something of indelicacy.' Just because he loved her so deeply he was determined to note her every failing, as if to prove to himself that he was not the victim of a blind infatuation, but that he could still criticise her dispassionately and withdraw his heart if his head should tell him that it would be prudent so to do.

He was, of course, far beyond the stage of emotion that would admit of any withdrawal. 'I do believe she is the woman whom God will give me as His choicest gift,' he wrote on August 11th; 'I feel as though I could love her beyond the love of mortals. Oh, great God, what a treasure to possess such a darling!' Significantly, he still used the conditional 'could,' as if even now hesitant to admit himself fully committed. On August 10th he resolved on no account to be precipitate; on August 13th he decided to propose. His chance came that very day when walking with Minny to call on Princess Lieven – 'I seized her hand repeatedly, I gave every possible sign; she did not *correspond* but she did not *discourage* me.' Thus not discouraged he made his proposal – 'I was, I know not what, but certainly not accepted.' Minny put him off with the time-honoured plea, 'I have not known you very long'; her manner, however, was 'soft and tender.' A wiser or a more cold-blooded man than Ashley would have rested content for the present with much gained; Ashley, however, lost his temper and made a foolish little scene:

I became very angry and irritated and refused to enter Madame Lieven's house, she seemed alarmed and entreated me. I went. We walked home. I could not but admire her decision. It was so honest and unworldly.

In Ashley's heart hope alternated with despair. 'I will endeavour to pique her by indifference,' he decided haughtily, then, recollecting himself, 'I will have recourse to prayer.' Neither expedient succeeded.

On August 17th 'she positively rejected me.' Nevertheless, she begged
for time for further consideration, promising him a definite answer
at Panshanger, the Cowpers' home in Hertfordshire, where they
were to meet again in September. Ashley agreed to this delay, though
at times he trembled lest after all Minny should prove a heartless
flirt, regarding him merely as yet another conquest – 'it may be a
feather in her cap but it is a dagger in my heart.'

Ashley took some comfort from an interview with Lady Cowper.
Minny's mother told him to his face that she found him 'exceedingly
handsome' and his conversation 'most agreeable.' He was troubled
to think what the reaction of his own parent would be to the idea of
the proposed marriage. 'Now will Lord Shaftesbury make objections?'
he asked himself, knowing the answer only too well – 'Yes, he will,
money, money, money.' He tried to persuade himself that this hard-
hearted father must at least relent and show a little kindness towards
his son and heir – 'he has so embittered my happiness in earlier days
that he will scarcely presume to close it forever by a ferocious edict;
not that I should obey.'

Meanwhile Minny hesitated, unable to make up her mind. Describing Cup Day at Ascot, Lady Granville had remarked that 'all
the men are more or less in love with Emily Cowper.' The diarist
Creevey called Minny 'the leading favourite of the town,' a phrase
which it is tempting to paraphrase as 'the deb of the year.' Ashley was
by no means her first or only suitor. In 1827, before she was 'regularly
come out,' Lady Holland had reported that 'already two swains are
poorly, a young Wortley and a young Talbot.' Since then at least
three eligible suitors had made offers for her hand, only to be rejected.
She had also won the heart of a diminutive and rather delicate young
man who was one day to be Prime Minister. In 1829 Lord John
Russell certainly wanted to marry her though we do not know
whether he actually proposed. Ashley, however, was quite unlike
Minny's many other suitors. He both attracted and scared her;
she was drawn to his goodness but frightened by his intensity. She
felt him to be unstable, 'everything today and nothing tomorrow,'
and she knew that many people, including various members of her
own family, considered him to be a little mad. Bewildered by the
puzzle of Ashley's character, beset and harassed by her over-anxious
mother, the poor girl took refuge in tears. 'Indeed, indeed, it is not
a rejection,' she declared, but when pressed by Ashley for a more
definite promise she could only repeat, 'What a difficult situation!
What a difficult situation!'

After several unsatisfactory meetings in London, Ashley followed

Minny to Panshanger. Here she was all kindness, wearing the dresses
which she knew pleased him most, and taking off all her bangles and
bracelets because he liked to see her lovely arms bare of ornament.
She even went so far as to confide to him her doubts and difficulties
about her mother – 'she has touched upon the character of Lady
Cowper's society and conversation and principles, her caprice and
changeableness.' Still, however, Ashley remained uncertain of his
fate – 'yet she will not say the words "I love you!" '

All through the winter of 1829–30 Ashley was kept dangling as
the acknowledged suitor of a lady who would not make up her mind.
In this unenviable and embarrassing situation he bore himself with
gentle dignity. Everyone's love affairs were common knowledge
among the small, enclosed circle of aristocratic London society.
During their stay at Tunbridge Wells Lady Granville was already
referring to Ashley and Minny as the *amanti* and telling her sister,
Ashley's old friend Lady Morpeth, now become Lady Carlisle, about
his admirable behaviour – 'his manner of making up to her is so
exactly what we all like and admire that everyone was in astonishment at her *insouciance*, so *passioné*, so devoted, yet so manly, *si
noble*, nothing of the commonplace *rôle* in it.'[5] She also described
Lady Cowper as being 'very much in love with Lord Ashley, much
more than the girl'; yet one of Ashley's greatest difficulties was the
equivocal attitude of his would-be mother-in-law. A charming but
infuriating woman, Lady Cowper suffered from a chronic inability
to make up her mind. One day she would warn Minny against him.
'He is so enthusiastic he must be capricious,' she told her daughter,
then added, using the slang term for an Evangelical, 'take care, he
has a high sense of religion, he is almost a Saint.' ('I rejected the last
charge,' Ashley commented.) On another occasion she would declare
that of all the men she knew he was the one whom she considered
as most likely to make her daughter happy.

Meanwhile, other members of Minny's family were taking alarm
at the prospect of a marriage between this apparently ill-assorted
pair. Lord Cowper does not appear to have expressed any opinion
beyond commenting on Ashley's oddity. Minny's uncle, Frederick
Lamb, was not so reticent. His letter to his sister Lady Cowper is
worth quoting at some length as showing the opinion currently held
of Ashley and his family, especially in Whig circles. Much as Frederick
Lamb disapproved of Ashley's character, political views, and family
background, he disapproved still more of his financial prospects:

Three thousand a year, whereof the third comes from a place

which he will probably lose very shortly and which you and I both devoutly hope that he may. An odious father and four beggarly brothers. What has poor Min done to deserve to be linked to such a fate, and in a family generally disliked, reputed mad, and of feelings, opinions, connections directly the reverse of all of ours? Do you know what £3000 a year, or *probably two,* can furnish to a couple and a family? You people who have had profusion all your lives imagine that it can be done very well upon, but I can tell you it is a privation of everything. If it were for a man she doated upon and who would live well with all of us it might be endured and softened, but in this case Cowper thinks him odd, William* laments it as a bad look-out and an undesirable connection. The girl herself has no fancy for him and what the devil there is in its favour I am at a loss to perceive, except his being what you call in love with her and a person as you think to be fallen in love with.

Frederick goes on to scold his sister for what he describes as her 'shillyshallying,' and to bestow some very discerning praise on Minny herself:

This mode of dealing with these things is in my opinion neither safe nor fair nor creditable, and if she cares as little for him as you say, I recommend the getting rid of him at once and for ever. As for his love I suppose it's about as violent as it was for Lord Liverpool's daughter, and as it will be for some other six weeks after Minny shall have turned him off.

As to her, I can't say how much I admire her. She shows in everything a good sense and a resolution which will bring her through all things – but in God's name when this is got rid of (as I have no doubt it will be when you come to look fairly at it) do try to know beforehand what is suitable and what is not, and do not be balancing about after a thing is proposed and when a negative if it is to be pronounced ought to be so at once. Of all the matches that have offered I have not a hesitation in saying that this is the least desirable, Ossulston was forty times better, Bob Grosvenor was better, F. Robinson is infinitely better, but if anything can cloud her happy and brilliant prospects, it will be this way of dallying with undesirable offers.[6]

* Minny's uncle William Lamb, 2nd Viscount Melbourne, Prime Minister 1834 and 1835–41.

By this time Minny was rather more in love than her Uncle Frederick supposed her to be. When Ashley, in the usual manner of rejected suitors, threatened to resign his appointments and depart for America, she besought him to do no such thing. This highly-strung, slightly priggish young man was someone altogether outside the range of her previous experience; she had quite genuinely needed time in which to get to know him and to learn to understand and appreciate his complexities. At first she had shrunk from the force of his emotions – 'I fear the vehemence of your character' – but now she was learning to respond. She felt too that she had already all but committed herself, and she rounded on her uncle with the exclamation, 'If I am not to marry him, I ought not to have had anything to do with him!' Other people thought as she did in this respect. 'I think Minny's marriage to Lord Ashley is thought to be more likely, as he is a great deal there and one cannot conceive what they are at if it is not to end so,'[7] Georgiana Agar-Ellis wrote rather tartly to her sister Caroline Lascelles.

Yet still Minny hesitated, too uncertain both of herself and of him to be able to come to a definite decision. Ashley believed that more than his earthly happiness was hanging in the balance – 'if I fail to win her all is lost and I shall tremble for my eternal salvation.' It is tantalising to find that during this fateful winter he made no entries in his diary. The last one is dated October 24th:

> The day is at hand to decide my fate. I opened the Book to read the psalms for the day; the first was the 116th* – it encouraged comfort – it seems to me as if God had prepared a happiness in store for me – I shall soon see.

Minny, however, refused him yet again. On October 25th he was reported by Lord Dover to be 'very low and disconsolate about his rejected love,' and two days later he was found 'drinking tea with Georgiana and recounting his grief respecting Lady Emily Cowper.' The Lamb family persisted in their doubts and misgivings, accusing him of 'tyranny, violence, moroseness.' As late as February 1830 Minny had still not made up her mind, to judge from what Lady Granville told Lady Carlisle:

> Lord Ashley behaved most beautifully last night. How that girl can help liking him, seeing his devotion to her, with something so

---

* The 116th psalm begins, 'I am well pleased that the Lord has heard the voice of my prayer.'

noble, so manly in his whole manner and conduct! He danced all night with the girls, did not follow her at all, and his spirits appeared good without being forced, though I, who know, could have cried over him.[8]

In mid-April, however, Princess Lieven was writing to Lady Cowper, 'your marriage is so well-known that everyone takes me for a fool when I deny the rumours,'[9] and advising her not to keep the matter secret any longer. The engagement must have been announced by April 20th, because on that day Minny's one-time suitor, Lord John Russell, wrote to Lady Holland expressing magnanimous good wishes for the couple's happiness:

Lord Ashley and Lady Emily were much loving as might have been expected – he is the most of the two, but she seems very well pleased with his devotion. I believe him to be an excellent and amiable man, and I hope it may all turn out right.[10]

On June 10th 1830 the wedding took place at St. George's, Hanover Square, the bridegroom's father refusing to attend the ceremony.

The marriage thus begun in doubt and disapproval was to be an enduring success. On April 28th 1831 Ashley again took up his neglected diary to make a brief entry, the last for three years – 'no man, I am sure, ever enjoyed more happiness in his married life, God be praised.' As for Minny, once she had made up her mind to marry Ashley she fell deeply and passionately in love with him. In the early years of their marriage she would write him charmingly artless love-letters. 'I really am quite miserable without you; I would not have believed I would have minded so much your going away for two days,' reads one dated July 26th 1830. 'There certainly never was such a darling as you are, dearest Ashley.'[11] A year-and-a-half later her expressions of affection are still as warm and unrestrained:

I do think you are such a kind Hub to write me such long letters. I always find I have got tears in my eyes when I read them. It does make me so happy to think that you love me.[12]

They were of course to have their difficulties and differences, but up to the very end Ashley remained devoted to Minny and she presumably to him, though except for these early letters nothing remains to give any direct indication of her feelings. People of opposite temperaments need not of necessity disagree; if they love one another well enough they can be complementary, each supplying what is lacking to the other. Minny's sunny, even nature provided the right antidote to Ashley's depressive temperament. Improbable though it seemed at the time, he had in fact done very well for himself by taking a bride from the Lamb family. 'What stuff people are made of,' wrote a member of that family, 'who find life and society tiresome when they are in good health and have neither liver nor spleen affected; and have spirits enough to enjoy, instead of being vexed by, the ordinary little *tracasseries* of life.'[13] A typical Lamb in everything but morals, Minny had plenty of spirit to enjoy those little *tracasseries* which her husband found so exasperating, and when larger difficulties threatened she showed, as her Uncle Frederick had foretold she would, 'a good sense and a resolution which will bring her through all things.' As her husband was later to write 'her dear-smiling face made everything shine.' Her beauty and charm were Ashley's perennial delight; she was his lover, companion and friend. Together they were able to make for their children the happy home for which he, as a child, had longed in vain. All his life he had been starved of affection; now his whole being could expand in the warmth of her steadfast, loving heart.

If Minny gave much to Ashley, he in his turn had much to give to her. In 1829 Harriet Granville, whilst admitting that Minny was natural, gay and good-humoured, wrote that she had been 'so perseveringly spoilt' that her only chance of salvation was 'to marry a good sort of man whom she likes very much.'[14] Minny made just such a marriage, with the result that in 1838 Sarah Lady Lyttelton could write of her that 'from being a flirting, unpromising girl, she has grown into a nice, happy wife and mother.' Lady Lyttelton attributed this desirable change entirely to Ashley, 'a very sensible, most highly principled man, full of useful good qualities, having married his beautiful wife and taught her all the good she could not learn from her mother.'[15] Very patiently, and with a touching tenderness, Ashley taught Minny to value and practise the religion that meant all-in-all to him. He found her anything but an unwilling pupil. Though she was never to become so single-minded, or, to put it more bluntly, so bigoted, as her husband, though she was sometimes to be bored and proclaim aloud her boredom with the minutiae of Evangelical faith and practice, she was more in tune with Ashley than she could ever have been with a worldly man. In spite of her gaiety, her frivolity even – 'don't be angry with your *facetious* little wife!' – something fundamental in her responded to her husband's religious teaching. More serious-minded than either her mother or her grandmother, she could never have been really content to lead the type of life or acquiesce in the view of marriage which both Lady Melbourne and Lady Cowper found perfectly satisfactory. If Ashley made his Minny into a good woman he also made her into a happy one.

Chapter 5

AFFAIRS POLITICAL AND FINANCIAL

The beginning of the Ashleys' married life was bedevilled by political upheavals and financial cares. On June 26th 1830, little more than a fortnight after their wedding day, King George IV died. At that period the death of the sovereign entailed a general election. This time Ashley chose to stand not for Woodstock but for the Borough of Dorchester in Dorset, where he was returned with very little expense of time, money or trouble, except for a short but unwelcome absence from his Minny. Elsewhere, however, the Tories suffered a significant loss of seats, with the result that in November Wellington resigned, to be succeeded by Lord Grey at the head of a Whig administration.

As a result of this change of government Ashley lost his place on the India Board. The new Foreign Secretary, Lord Palmerston, offered him an Under-Secretaryship, which he refused, not wishing to take office under the Whigs. The loss of an official salary was a serious matter to the newly-married couple, since as a married man Ashley had from his father an allowance only one hundred pounds larger than the one he had enjoyed as an undergraduate. Fortunately Minny's mother was more open-handed. Lady Cowper was a warmhearted, generous woman who delighted in showering gifts of money and kindnesses of all sorts upon her daughter and son-in-law. The Cowper house at Panshanger was always open to them. No one thought to reproach Ashley for his inability to keep Minny in the comfort and luxury which a richer husband could have provided for her, whilst Minny in her turn learnt to manage well enough as the wife of a comparatively poor man. Nevertheless, for Ashley himself the situation was not a pleasant one; and the year 1831 was to see his financial difficulties swollen to alarming proportions.

In March the Whig government brought in their first Reform Bill, which was defeated in Committee. At the election which followed this defeat Ashley was again returned for Dorchester without undue effort. A few months later, however, he found himself engaged in the

expense and turmoil of a hard-fought by-election. Calcraft, one of
the members for the county seat of Dorsetshire, committed suicide
almost immediately after the general election. Although he was
already a sitting member of the House of Commons, Ashley accepted
an invitation to stand for this vacant seat. In a letter to the Duke of
Wellington Ashley wrote, 'I embarked on the Dorsetshire contest
from no motives of private ambition whatsoever but was solely
induced to it by political feelings and the persuasions of those who
felt strongly upon the Reform question.'[1] After their defeat in the
general election a win in Dorsetshire could give the Tory party some
badly-needed encouragement, since it might be taken as a sign
that the tide which had flowed so strongly for Reform was beginning
to turn in their favour. Ashley was the ideal candidate for this
important by-election. Not merely was he a Dorset man of high social
standing, the member of a family with much local influence, but, as
Lord Granville once remarked of him, 'he had those manly good
looks and that striking presence which help a man more than we
sometimes think' – and nowhere more than on an election platform.
'Dorsetshire offered the first ground on which a stand could be made,'
the poet Southey was to write to Ashley, 'and when you took your
stand there everyone knew it was not for your own sake but for the
common cause.'[2]

Since the Tories were so anxious to secure Ashley as candidate it is
not surprising that proposals of some sort should have been put
forward as to the payment of election expenses. Clearly, a man as
badly-off as he was could not afford the immense sums which a
contested election for a county seat then entailed. Ashley himself
later declared, 'I honestly protested my inability to pay my expenses
before I stood and I received assurance that such an event would
be as improper as it was unlooked for.'[3] However, he was himself
to admit the wide difference between a positive promise and reasonable expectations, and he seems to have had no more than a 'reasonable expectation'[4] that the necessary money would be forthcoming
either from the pockets of the local Tory gentry or from the rather
exiguous fund at the disposal of the party managers. All his life he
was to be singularly trustful – it would be more truthful to say
foolish – in entering into financial arrangements without receiving
any adequate or binding guarantee. So now he embarked on a
ruinously expensive election campaign relying merely on what
Hodder describes as 'a distinct understanding'; and how distinct
that understanding may have been it is impossible now to say.

Ashley's opponent was William Ponsonby, afterwards Lord de

Mauley. The two men were doubly connected by marriage, Ponsonby being the husband of Ashley's first cousin, Lady Barbara Ashley-Cooper, and brother to Lady Caroline Lamb, who had married Minny's uncle, Lord Melbourne. These family links, however, did not serve to make the struggle any less bitter.

Ashley was the last in the field, but he made up for his late start by assiduous canvassing. He was so anxious to have his wife by his side during the struggle that although their first child, Anthony, was only three months old, Minny decided to leave the baby behind and to travel to Dorchester, where she stayed in the house of a family called Frampton. Her hostess described her as 'pretty, very young in ideas, and unknowing of common things, but very good-tempered, amiable and interesting, and perfectly unassuming, most desirous not to give any trouble, and civil to everyone.'[5] Minny's charm was something of an electioneering asset; Lady Cowper wrote to tell her that 'our William heard today that you had made a *great effect* among the gentry.'

'To represent my native country would be one of the highest honours I could attain, but I am nevertheless, impelled by no personal ambition,' Ashley declared in his election address; 'I wish to identify my cause with the cause of the constitution.' He stood squarely as an anti-Reform candidate, objecting to Reform as bringing about 'the destruction of equipoise and the consequent collision of interests' and, more specifically, 'the aggrandisement of the towns at the expense of the agriculturalists.' Polling continued for fifteen days, opening on September 30th and closing on October 17th. On October 18th the result was to be declared at Poundbury, a prehistoric fortification outside Dorchester. Here fighting broke out between the supporters of the rival candidates, who had to be dispersed by a body of mounted yeomanry. When quiet had been temporarily restored Ashley was declared the victor by a majority of thirty-six. His brother John leading his horse, he rode bareheaded in triumph into Dorchester, followed by three or four hundred gentlemen and farmers on horseback and a vast crowd of ordinary citizens on foot, 'a very respectable cortège.' The evening passed quietly with only 'as few drunken riots as could be expected at the conclusion of so severe a contest.'[6] Dorsetshire, however, was in a state of turmoil; after the election the High Sheriff remained in Dorchester, fearing to be attacked on the road to his home, and when Minny and Ashley left the town they travelled with a pair of loaded pistols in their carriage. A week later the disappointed Whigs burnt effigies of Ashley instead of Guy Fawkes on their Fifth of November bonfires.

Ashley had enjoyed his hour of triumph; now the day of reckoning was at hand. His election expenses topped the enormous figure of £15,000. Of that sum more than £12,000 had been spent in public houses. Since Ponsonby had presumably spent a comparable sum in similar manner the three or four thousand Dorset electors must have enjoyed a splendidly drunken election. To meet these expenses Ashley had £1900 from a party fund controlled by Wellington's friend, Charles Arbuthnot, and £500 from local subscription; the rest had to be found out of his own pocket. The situation was a very serious one since he could never hope to pay off a debt of such magnitude. To add to his troubles Ponsonby was planning to unseat him by bringing a petition alleging bribery and other malpractices. Although Ashley was right in describing the case against him as 'an uncommonly bad one' his financial position was such that he could not possibly afford to contest this petition. In his extremity he turned to his old friend and idol, the Duke of Wellington. Tactfully but firmly he pointed out that unless money were forthcoming the Dorset seat must inevitably be lost to the Tories. A long correspondence ensued between Ashley on the one hand and Wellington and Charles Arbuthnot on the other. Finally Wellington declared none too politely, 'I cannot interfere in these matters any more.'[7] 'Dukey' was irritated by what he regarded as Ashley's tiresome and unjustifiable importunity; Ashley himself was deeply wounded by this brusque, unhelpful attitude on the part of the man who had been his friend and hero. The happy relationship between them was at an end; 'you will never come here again, I am sure, you are missed,'[8] Arbuthnot wrote sadly from the Duke's home at Stratfield Saye.

That most hidebound and determined of Tories, the Duke of Cumberland, to whom Ashley had also applied, wrote a sympathetic and flattering letter but produced no cash. Some support came from an unexpected quarter. Although Lady Cowper belonged to the innermost circle of the Whig oligarchy she rushed to the support of her Tory son-in-law, though with no very conspicuous results. 'Mamma is indefatigable,' Minny wrote on December 17th, 'and goes on writing the most *violent language* left and right. She wrote to Lady Jersey to tell her to see what she could do. Upon my word, I think Sir Robert Peel's conduct in not even offering to subscribe and giving you such a cool answer is quite atrocious and scarcely credible. I can't but think that they will all feel desperately ashamed of themselves when they find that they have lost your seat in the House; but that will do us no good.'[9]

Minny herself was not in favour of any attempt to contest the petition. She considered the expense unjustifiable and in her heart of hearts she would have been glad to have her husband at home for a while, free of the ties of parliamentary business – 'my dearest love, I hope you love me and are not angry with me for thinking that I could be very happy if you were out of Parliament for a little while.' Minny's family, however, thought otherwise, both Lady Cowper and Frederick Lamb believing that Ashley should fight the petition if only because he was more likely to have his election expenses paid out of party funds if he did not abandon the seat. In the end the petition was successfully opposed, the Tory party finding the necessary money, an action which roused Minny to scorn – 'What a shabby thing for the Tories that they can fork out for the petition but not to help your expenses!' On January 18th 1832 Sir Henry Hardinge wrote to Charles Arbuthnot's wife, Harriet, 'Lord Ashley is very sulky and cross but will keep his seat.' Sulky and cross Ashley might well be; he had his seat in Parliament, but he had on his back a huge burden of debt from which he was never to free himself:

> We must submit to the evils which await an insolvent debtor. God be praised that I have done nothing to disgrace my character, though much to diminish our happiness, yet it was in the hope of maintaining a great cause and fighting a battle for the institutions of the country.

So Ashley wrote to Minny on March 10th 1832. In all these trials and difficulties she was his support, consolation, and dear delight. He was entirely devoted to his pretty young wife and she to him. Minny's charm was such that it could melt even her stony-hearted father-in-law. Only eight months after the wedding at which Lord Shaftesbury had been conspicuous by his absence she was writing, 'The Earl was very gracious to me last night and *kissed* me when he went away.' A year or so later the Earl had become positively jocose, sending little notes to say that he would have his revenge for some imagined piece of neglect by making her dine with him the very next day. Very tactfully, Minny sometimes hinted to her husband that he did not go the right way about conciliating his difficult relatives – 'I cannot judge so well not being on the spot, but I cannot help thinking that it would have been better had you called at St. Giles. However, I dare say you did it for the best.' She herself took pains to keep on good terms with his sisters and to see much of them when they were in London.

If circumstances forced them apart, even for a short while, husband

and wife wrote to each other almost daily. 'My dearest darling,' Minny writes, 'I cannot let the post go without just sending you one line to say goodnight. I don't know how it is, I not only love you but when you are away I *hate* everybody else.' Sometimes she reproaches herself for excessive devotion – 'It really is almost wrong to doat on anybody as I do on you. It makes me miserable to be separated from you (even for a day) and I can't bear my room without you sitting in the arm-chair.' Ashley was equally devoted and disconsolate in absence. 'The house is a dungeon without you,' he writes, and again, 'It is wonderful, sweet wife, how all my hopes and affections are centred on you; without you everything is dull and my feelings never seem to be in any way satisfied.' He addresses her as 'my own dearest pet,' 'my blessed and perfect darling'; she in her turn calls him 'my dearest darling' or 'my dearest Hub.' He was the older by nearly ten years, and he could at times be almost paternal towards his 'sweetest child.' When he was away he would gently urge her not to neglect those religious practices which he had been at such pains to teach her; 'my own dear wife, say your darling little prayers,' and again, 'Minny, my pet, the Sacrament will of course be administered on Christmas day; you will not forget that.'

Minny was quick to respond to his concern. When staying at Brighton with Lady Cowper she wrote to tell him that she had liked the place much better when she had stayed there alone with him – 'It is so difficult to keep good hours and to get out early with Mamma' – and she speaks severely of 'the way in which Mamma goes on thinking of *nothing* but going out, gadding right and left.' She makes a valiant effort to read family prayers on Sunday and becomes quite incoherent in an attempt to describe an occasion when Lady Cowper chose to join in these devotions:

Only think what a fancy to seize Mamma, she would come and read passages with Fanny, little T. and me. I did not go to church on account of my cold and so both last Sunday and this one I have read prayers with them and it was so unlucky the two chapters there were for today, one of them in the Acts,* particularly because it is like what the Irvingites pretend is happening now, and therefore Mamma thinks that if the one is *stuff* the other must be too.

'My child,' Ashley writes back in his most solemn mood, 'your

* Presumably this refers to the description of the Day of Pentecost, Acts, Chapter Two.

mother's reading prayers is, I fear, a superstition, but God be praised for that even.'

Minny was doing her very best to accommodate herself to her husband's severe standards in manners, morals, and religion. Occasionally, however, the unregenerate Minny Cowper peeps over the shoulder of the sober Lady Ashley. Her account of a conversation between King William the Fourth and Princess Lieven would have delighted her Lamb relatives but it may not have been so pleasing to Ashley:

What an odd man the King is! He said to her the other night by way of conversation *'Quelle drôle de societé nous avons, Madame, quelle quantité de bâtards!'* and he then proceeded to make out that everybody nearly in the room who were not bastards themselves were descended from some. I think this was pretty well considering that five or six of them were his own.

The birth of a son and heir on June 27th 1831 had given great joy to this devoted couple. The child was christened Anthony, the name given to all Ashley-Cooper sons, although by tradition the common use of it was restricted to the first-born. His nickname in babyhood was 'Sir Babkins,' and as such he figures prominently in his parents' correspondence. On December 18th 1831 he sends his father 'a *slobbering* kiss.' Three months later, when his mother is staying at Brighton with Lady Cowper, he breakfasts every day with his father and looks in again on his way out for a walk – 'Babs has just been in here on his way out, he looks *too* heavenly.' Both parents were openly besotted with their son's beauty, brains and goodness, although Minny, whilst describing him as 'the admiration of the town,' could nevertheless complain 'he grows so wilful there is hardly any managing him, so *violent*,' adding the impudent comment, 'It is *astonishing, how like his father* he is!'

Unfortunately, from 1831 to 1834 Ashley kept no diary. The years 1831 and 1832 seem to have been one of the very few periods in his life when he was comparatively idle. Free of the cares of office and occupied with nothing very much except his parliamentary duties he could enjoy himself at leisure with his wife and child. His work on the Lunacy Commission was not at this time very onerous, although in 1829 he had become Chairman of that body. In 1828, for instance, he inspected and reported upon seven madhouses, in 1829 only three. As yet he was concerned with no other social reform nor with any active, practical work for the benefit of the poor. A new friendship, however, was soon to turn his thoughts towards social problems.

Ashley was a great admirer of the writings of the Poet Laureate, Robert Southey. In September 1830, whilst still a member of the India Board, he had written to offer Southey, who was personally unknown to him, a Writership in the East India Company 'for any son or nephew whom you may wish to advance in an honourable and advantageous career.' This offer was the beginning of a correspondence which ended only with Southey's last illness. Southey described Ashley, whom he was never to meet face-to-face, as 'a right-minded young man, deeply imbued with religious principles and feelings – without which the principles are nothing.'[10] As for the poet himself, 'for a man who led such a rigidly *bourgeois* life,' says his biographer, Jack Simmons, 'Southey showed, in occasional flashes, an extraordinarily vivid perception of the miseries of poverty.'[11] He was especially perturbed by the appalling housing conditions in big cities, by the cruelties inflicted on the 'climbing boys' who swept chimneys, and by the scandal of child labour in mines and factories, three causes which Ashley was later on to make particularly his own. Already Southey had protested strongly against 'a new sort of slave trade,' the system by which the London workhouses supplied waggon-loads of children to those mills and factories which would take them off the hands of the parish. By the time that Ashley and Southey began to correspond this pauper apprentice system was practically at an end. The substitution of steam for water power had caused industry to move from the banks of streams in remote country valleys to the neighbourhood of towns where a plentiful supply of child labour was available. Because these 'free' children lived at home with their parents their lot was not quite so pitiable as that of the pauper apprentices, herded together in bleak, insanitary factory 'barracks,' but it was nevertheless unhappy enough. Children of five years old and upwards worked in the factories, usually for twelve hours a day, often for fourteen or sixteen hours. Not infrequently they continued working all through the night. Some were caught in the unfenced machinery and terribly injured; many more were crippled by the actual nature of the work they had to perform; others fell victims to the various forms of tuberculosis caused by the unhealthy, dirt-laden atmosphere of the mills. They snatched their food as they worked, because during the official meal-breaks it fell to them to clean the machinery. Hungry and exhausted, towards the end of the day they fell asleep at their work and could only be roused by blows from the overseer's whip. They had no time free for schooling, and at work they learnt no skills which could be of use to them in later life. Thousands upon thousands of children were growing up with damaged, stunted bodies, and minds quite untouched by education.

These conditions were more or less universal, and not confined to any one industry or neighbourhood. They were, however, most conspicuous in the textile towns of Lancashire and Yorkshire, because of the large number of children employed in the cotton and woollen industries. Here the first people to make any efforts towards reform were themselves mill-owners. The better type of employer was only too anxious to shorten hours and improve conditions of work, but he dared not do so on his own account, fearing a rise in prices or a fall in production that would give an advantage to his competitors. It was therefore in his interest to press for uniform regulations to be imposed on the trade as a whole. Sir Robert Peel, father of the statesman and himself a master cotton-spinner, brought in the first Act regulating child labour in the cotton industry. In Yorkshire the pioneer of reform was John Wood, a rich worsted-spinner from Bradford. Having failed to persuade his fellow mill-owners to limit the hours of children's work by voluntary agreement, Wood turned to Richard Oastler and succeeded in interesting him in the matter. Oastler was a combative Yorkshireman, a keen Evangelical who had already made a name for himself locally as the leader of a successful fight against the payment of Church tithes, and as a supporter of the Anti-Slavery movement. He opened his campaign on behalf of the factory children with a forceful letter in the *Leeds Mercury* headed 'Yorkshire Slavery.' From now onwards the factory children were to be known as 'the white slaves.' A movement was soon on foot to demand a limitation of children's working hours to ten a day, and Short-Time committees sprang up spontaneously all over Lancashire and Yorkshire. Oastler was their leader in the North of England and Michael Sadler their spokesman in Parliament. Like Oastler, Sadler was a Yorkshireman, a Tory, and an Evangelical; unlike Oastler, he was a gentle, reflective man, who had for a long time been concerned with the plight of the factory children. His hobby was the writing of poetry; a few verses from a long poem entitled *The Factory Girl's Last Day* give a fair example of his style:

> Alas! what hours of horror
>   Made up her latest day;
> In toil, and pain, and sorrow
>   They slowly passed away;

It seemed as she grew weaker
  The threads the oftener broke,
The rapid wheels ran quicker,
  And heavier fell the stroke.

At last, the engine ceasing,
  The captives homeward rushed;
She thought her strength increasing –
  'Twas hope her spirits flushed:
She left, but oft she tarried;
  She fell, and rose no more,
Till, by her comrades carried,
  She reached her father's door.

All night, with tortured feeling,
  He watched his speechless child;
While, close beside her kneeling,
  She knew him not, nor smiled.
Again the factory's ringing
  Her last perceptions tried:
When from her straw-bed springing,
  ' 'Tis time!' she shrieked, and died![12]

In December 1831 Sadler introduced a Ten Hours Bill into the
House of Commons. The Bill passed its second reading, the subject
being then referred to a Select Committee of the House, with Sadler
acting as Chairman. At the end of June this Committee produced a
report on the working conditions of the factory children which has
become a classic document in the social history of England. Almost
simultaneously the great Reform Bill of 1832 passed the House of
Lords and became law. A general election followed in December,
when Sadler was defeated at Leeds by the famous Whig historian,
Thomas Babington Macaulay. The Ten Hours campaign had lost
its parliamentary leader.

On January 13th 1833 Southey wrote Ashley a letter discussing
the results of the general election. 'I am more sorry to perceive what
good men are thrown out of Parliament than what scamps and
miscreants have got in,' he commented. The Leeds result filled him
with particular regret:

Sadler too is a loss; he might not be popular in the House or in
London society, but his speeches did much good in the country,
and he is a singularly able, right-minded, religious man. Who is

there that will take up the question of our white slave trade with equal feeling?[13]

When Southey wrote thus to Ashley he could have had no idea as to what the answer to his question was to be. Three weeks later Ashley himself reluctantly stepped into Sadler's place and stood up in the House of Commons as the declared champion of the 'white slaves.'

The Ten Hours men feared that the loss of Sadler might mean the defeat or abandonment of his Bill. Time pressed; Ashley's old friend, George Howard, now Lord Morpeth, was about to bring in an Eleven Hours Bill which would take the wind out of their sails. Someone must immediately be found to steer the Ten Hours Bill through Parliament and to join Oastler in the leadership of the campaign in the country at large. On January 11th 1833 delegates from the various Short Time committees met in conference at Bradford. The secretary and moving spirit of this conference was George Bull, 'the Ten Hours Parson,' curate-in-charge of the industrial district of Byerly. The conference decided to send one of their number up to London to find a successor to Sadler, and chose Bull as the most suitable person for this task.

Bull took with him a list of Members of Parliament, including Ashley, recommended to him by Sadler. He had tried every other name on this list before he approached Ashley, who was introduced to him by Sir Andrew Agnew, a Scottish Evangelical. When Bull put forward his proposition Ashley was taken completely by surprise. He knew nothing whatsoever about the subject; he had never visited the industrial North nor as much as set eyes on a textile mill or a factory child. So little interest had he taken in the matter that he had not even known of the existence of Sadler's Select Committee until he chanced to read in a newspaper some extracts from its report. These made such an impression upon him that he wrote to Sadler offering to help in any way he could, but, receiving no answer, he forgot the whole business.

The proposal that he should take Sadler's place therefore came to Ashley as a profound and rather unpleasant shock. Hodder prints a memorandum written in 1838 in which Ashley says that he can 'perfectly recollect my astonishment and doubt and terror at the proposition,' and adds that he had by now forgotten 'the arguments for and against my inter-meddling with the affair.' Hodder, who may have discussed the matter many years after the event with the aged Lord Shaftesbury, proceeds to set out those arguments:

On the one hand lay ease, promotion, and troups of friends; on the other, an unpopular cause, unceasing labour amongst every kind of opposition; perpetual worry and anxiety; estrangement of friends; annihilation of leisure; and a life among the poor. It was between these that he had to choose. Had he been ambitious of political distinction there can be no doubt that, with his abilities, his popularity, and his great oratorical powers,* he would have commanded a prominent position in his party . . . The alternative before him was to voluntarily cut himself off from these prospects, to associate himself with the most unpopular question of the day, to become a victim of a virulent opposition from all parties.[14]

The alternatives were in fact not nearly so clear-cut as Hodder makes out. Not for many years after 1833 did Ashley cease to hope for and to expect high political office. Several times he was to be pressed to take office and refuse, in later years certainly because he felt himself too deeply committed to the cause of factory legislation but on earlier occasions simply because he believed himself deserving of a higher position than any offered. Only as late as 1841 did it become clear to him that the championship of the factory children necessarily meant the abandonment of all his hopes for a political career. Nor were his efforts on behalf of the factory children to involve him in 'a life among the poor'; that was to come later with his work for public health and for the betterment of the outcasts of London. Nevertheless the arguments against accepting Bull's proposition were powerful enough to make any man pause. The championship of the Ten Hours cause meant much hard work, a great loss of leisure, and the enmity of many important people both inside and outside Parliament. Against this catalogue of certain losses no possible gains, either political, personal, or financial, could be set to the credit side of the account. Ashley had no personal responsibility for the plight of the factory children; neither he nor his family was even remotely to blame for the conditions existing in the mills of Lancashire and Yorkshire. If he chose to accept Bull's proposal it would not be because he felt any sudden or special sympathy with 'little piecers' and other child workers; it would be because Bull's words sounded in his ears as the voice of God. Before he made up his mind he must pray and meditate and seek for guidance in the pages of the Bible – 'divination' was his own word for this process. He must also take

* Up to this date Ashley had in fact displayed no 'great oratorical powers' but rather the reverse.

counsel with his beloved Minny, who was within a few weeks of the birth of their second child.

Husband and wife had very little time in which to reach a decision. Ashley asked for a short while for consideration; Bull replied that he must have an answer within twenty-four hours.* Minny did not hesitate; she too believed that she could recognise the voice of God in this demand. Her husband had received a call he dare not disobey; his answer must be 'yes.' Thus almost fortuitously and at a moment's notice did Ashley come to take up the work which was to make him world-famous and to lessen so vastly the sum of human misery.

---

* Shaftesbury's letter of acceptance to Bull (Shaftesbury papers) is dated February 5th. A letter to Morpeth dated February 6th (Castle Howard papers) seems to imply that he was approached before and not after the other members and that he had rather more time for reflection than is here supposed: 'It would be difficult to describe to you with what reluctance I undertook to bring forward Mr Sadler's Bill – until almost all his friends had been tried and had given their refusal, I withheld my consent.' This rather vague sentence is hardly adequate evidence on which to reject Ashley's own account as given in the memorandum quoted by Hodder (Vol I, pp. 148–9).

PART TWO

Where is the faith that should remove mountains? I have a whole
range before me.

Shaftesbury's Diary, March 29th 1842

Chapter 6

CHAMPION OF THE FACTORY CHILDREN

No sane person would, or indeed could, gloss over the evils of the factory system, least of all the evil of child labour. The facts are horrible and beyond dispute. Descendants of the early mill-owners can only admit with shame that their families were to blame for the sufferings of thousands of hapless children. If ever there was an issue where right was upon one side and wrong upon the other this would seem to be it.

Yet black is not completely black nor white entirely spotless, even where the question of the factory children is concerned. Not all mill-owners were as heartless as one Marshall, Member of Parliament for Leeds, who spoke of the many deaths from tuberculosis caused by unhealthy working conditions in his mill 'with as little compunction as a general would calculate the probable consumption of lives in a campaign.' Among them were also men such as the Ashworths, owners of the famous mills at Turton, near Bolton, a model industrial enterprise and a favourite sight with visitors making a tour of the North of England. Here wages were invariably paid in money, never in 'truck' payment in goods; thrift was encouraged by savings clubs; and an exceptionally generous amount of time was allowed off for holidays. The mills were clean, spacious and well-ventilated. Anyone found beating or otherwise maltreating a child worker was at once dismissed. The Ashworths provided excellent cottages and gardens for their work-people, built four schools for the children, and paid a resident doctor to provide free medical care. Although their Rochdale mills were not such a show-piece as those at Turton, the Bright brothers had also built a school for the children and a reading-room for adults. When a political opponent libelled John Bright – 'he has been hooted away from his own premises; his own people distrust him' – the mill-hands came forward with an address in which they declared 'your conduct as our employer has been such as to meet with our entire approval; you have always endeavoured to improve our moral, social, and intellectual well-being.'

Both the Ashworths and the Brights were members of the Society of Friends, a body justly famous for its concern with social problems. It is not to be supposed that these highly responsible, serious-minded Quakers were so greedy for gain that they allowed themselves to acquiesce callously in a system which obliged young children to work from twelve to sixteen hours a day in conditions which frequently crippled their limbs and injured their health. Of course, profits were a major consideration; a partnership agreement between Henry Ashworth and his sons stated a fact which must be true of any business concern, 'the object of the partnership is money-making.' Yet Dr. Rhodes Boyson, historian of the Ashworth enterprise, can write of this same Henry Ashworth:

Mill-owning was to him not merely a means to personal wealth, but also an aid to national and international progress. It was part of the good life; not something from which to escape when wealth was acquired. He signed himself always not as gentleman, but proudly as cotton-spinner or manufacturer.[1]

Ashley also had his vision of the good life and the right ordering of society, an ideal which he set down very clearly in his diary for June 29th 1841 after a visit to his family home at St. Giles:

What a picture contrasted with a factory district, a people known and cared for, a people born and trained on the estate, exhibiting towards its hereditary possessors both deference and sympathy, affectionate respect and a species of allegiance demanding protection and repaying it in duty!

Such was not at all Henry Ashworth's view of the ideal relationship between master and man. Ashley lays no stress on initiative or independence, two qualities which Ashworth valued very highly. 'I would rather be esteemed even parsimonious than see them deprived of their independence,' he wrote of his work-people, and he defined his motive in providing schools and other educational facilities as 'a desire to enlarge their views and to teach them not to be satisfied with the condition in which they were born, but to induce them to be uneasy under it, and to make them feel uncomfortable if they do not improve upon the example their parents have set before them.'[2]

Here is a very different conception from Ashley's notion of a people born and trained upon the estate of hereditary possessors. The one is essentially dynamic; the other static. The Industrial Revolution was not the social disaster that many historians would have it appear; this upward thrust is something new and vastly important in the history of the British labouring classes. A few individual Dick Whittingtons had always succeeded in making their way to wealth and gentility; now, however, for the first time the door was flung wide open. For the clever, the ambitious, the determined, or the merely lucky, work in a cotton mill could very well prove *'la carrière ouverte aux talents.'* Not every soldier in Napoleon's army carried a Marshal's baton in his rucksack, nor did every little piecer become a master cotton-spinner; the possibility, however, was there, and with the possibility a hope and an incentive that were, and still are, lacking to the agricultural labourer.

Few or none of the early mill-owners came from the ranks of the gentry. Though the majority of them were of farming or artisan stock, many were poor working people who had worked their way up from the very bottom of the ladder. In the Ashworth mills alone some dozen or so operatives rose to become mill-owners. Joseph Brotherton, mill-owner, Member of Parliament, and supporter of the Ten Hours Campaign, started life as an operative; Robert Knowles, head of a famous Bolton firm, had worked as a mechanic in a spinning mill; and the list is one which could be prolonged indefinitely. Not merely did these working-class mill-owners make money; they also rose in the social scale, an achievement almost impossible for the farmer or the farm labourer. The barrier between gentry and non-gentry, not altogether negligible even today, was in the nineteenth century an all-important line of division, and nowhere was it crossed so easily as in Lancashire and the West Riding of Yorkshire. The first generation of successful mill-owners might remain people a little apart; but their sons and grandsons, who were usually given the conventional education of public school and university, would be accepted without much question as gentlefolk.

There remained, however, a subtle difference in social tone between the agricultural South and the industrial North. Where master and man were so nearly akin in origin there was likely to be very little of the deference which Ashley thought so desirable, nor would there be much demand for 'protection.' Paternalism has always been a dirty word in Lancashire. In her novel, *North and South*, a book written from personal experience, Mrs. Gaskell draws a vivid picture of life and manners in a Northern industrial town. She makes Higgins, an unemployed mill-hand, thus address John Thornton, the mill-owner from whom he is seeking work:

> I've been thinking, ever since I saw yo', what a marcy it were yo' did na take me on for that I ne'er saw a man whom I could less abide. But that's maybe a hasty judgement; and work's work for such as me. So measter, I'll come; and what's more, I thank yo', and that's a deal from me.[3]

No worker on the St. Giles' estate would have spoken to Lord Shaftesbury in such a manner. Factory children were as disrespectful as their elders. The members of Sadler's Committee were scandalised to learn in reply to a question about the children's moral state, that 'you cannot go into a mill where even the most wealthy master clothier is called Sir or Master – they all call them Old Tom or Young Tom.' (Incidentally, this use of Christian names for mill-owners was current in Lancashire as late as 1912.) To illustrate the difference in manners between North and South it is amusing to turn to a period-piece description of Hampshire village children of about the same date:

> It so happened that the little girls were at play, some singing, others dancing in a ring; all paused and curtsied to us as we passed. At once that description in the *Lyra Innocentium* flashed across my mind of village maidens making
>
>> 'Their obeisance low,
>>   As forest bluebells in a row
>> Stoop to the first May wind, sweeping o'er each in turn,'[4]

It has been finely said that one of the great achievements of Evangelicalism was to make clear the essential connection between privilege and responsibility. This, of course, was the more noticeable because so many famous Evangelicals belonged to the privileged classes. An article on *Infant Labour* which Ashley wrote for the *Quarterly Review* of December 1840 expresses this Evangelical point of view very clearly:

> We cover the land with spectacles of misery; wealth is felt only by

its oppressions; few, very few, remain in those trading districts to spend liberally the riches they have acquired;* the successful leave the field to be ploughed afresh by new aspirants after gain, who, in turn, count their periodical profits, and exact the maximum of toil for the minimum of wages. No wonder that thousands of hearts should be against such a system, which establishes the relations, without calling forth the mutual sympathies, of master and servant, landlord and tenant, employer and employed.

The aristocratic and Evangelical Ashley, rather unfairly judging them as a class rather than as individuals, condemned the mill-owners for accepting the privileges of wealth whilst neglecting to exercise its responsibilities; the mill-owners in their turn raged against Ashley's calm assumption of privileges which, in the opinion of these egalitarian North Country men, no amount of responsibility could justify.

If the better stamp of mill-owner was neither heartless nor irresponsible, why did such men as John Bright and Henry Ashworth fight so determinedly against Ashley's endeavours to bring in the legislation necessary to shorten hours and improve conditions? Some historians maintain that the influence of the doctrine of *laissez faire* has been considerably exaggerated. The fact remains that in 1833 political economy was the fashionable cult; very few people thought to question its findings. The mill-owners' consciences and also, it is to be supposed, their powers of observation, had been lulled to sleep by the easy speeches of the economists who, for the most part, held to the full, uncompromising gospel of *laissez faire*. There must be no legislative interference between employer and employed; all bargaining must be free between free agents. (Here, of course, the economists tripped up; a small child carried to work on its father's back could hardly be described as a free agent.)

Holding the view that bargaining should be free, the mill-owners

---

* This is an odd accusation to bring against the mill-owners of the 1830s and '40s, though all too true of their sons and grandsons. To take a few Lancashire names at random, Ashtons, Ashworths, Harwoods, Brights, all lived in the town or village where their mills were situated; Mrs. Gaskell's John Thornton (1855) lived on his mill premises. In Yorkshire the cotton-spinning Dewhursts, moving about this time to a house in a large park outside their native Skipton, cut a gap in a screen of trees so that the smoke of their mill chimney could be seen from their drawing-room windows. Nor is Ashley just in blaming the mill-owners for paying 'minimum wages' when in point of fact the average wage of a Northern mill-hand was about double that earned by a Southern agricultural worker.

believed that trade should be free also. They had their own remedy
for the woes of the working classes, and that remedy was the repeal
of the Corn Laws. The removal of import duties, and in particular
the duty on imported corn, would provide the workers with cheap
food and would also benefit industry as a whole by stimulating the
flow of foreign trade. In the North the battle for the factory acts
developed into a straight fight between the Ten Hours men and the
Anti-Corn-Law League. Among the leaders of the Ten Hours campaign Oastler in particular was a strong protectionist, regarding the
Corn Laws as an essential bulwark of the old agricultural England
now threatened by the flood of urban industrialisation. A high Tory
and a convinced Church of England man, he ranted against the
Free Trade mill-owners as 'liberal, dissenting, deaconised blood-
hounds.' Another Yorkshire leader standing four-square for agricultural protection was a John Bull of a country squire called William
Buisfield Ferrand, who became very friendly with the group of
romantically-minded politicians calling themselves 'Young England,'
and entertained the two most prominent Young Englanders, Disraeli
and Lord John Manners, at his home at Bingley. Both Oastler and
Ferrand held views very similar to the Young England philosophy, if
philosophy it deserves to be called; looking back to a golden age of
rural England which had in fact never existed, they saw the new
industrialism as a wholly evil menace. In his book on the Factory
Movement Mr. J. T. Ward thus describes their views:

> Ferrand, Oastler, and many Northern reformers represented an
> ancient Toryism, local, paternal, and long 'out-dated' in 'pro-
> gressive' circles. They adopted traditional dislike of centralisation
> against Benthamite social planning, and old doctrines of social
> cohesion against liberal individualism. They announced no strictly
> 'new' philosophies but sought to leaven squirearchic Toryism's
> defence of Church and State by stressing the social duties of
> both.[5]

Though Ashley, of course, was much in sympathy with such views
the Anti-Corn-Law League leaders were both unfair and mistaken
in classing him with Oastler and Ferrand as a bigoted protectionist.
In fact, he supported the Corn Laws merely because they were part
and parcel of the traditonal Tory creed to which by ancestry and
upbringing he had found himself committed. He took no part in the
campaign against the Anti-Corn-Law League as such; he opposed
its leaders, Cobden and Bright, not because they attacked the Corn

Laws – on that issue his feelings were no more than lukewarm – but because they opposed the Ten Hours Bill.

Both sides, of course, loudly denounced the 'hypocrisy' of their opponents, and both sides were wrong in their denunciations. Though the increase in trade which was expected to follow the repeal of the Corn Laws would be to their own benefit, the mill-owners were nevertheless honest in their belief that cheap bread was the one thing of vital importance to the poor; they, in their turn, were unjust in rating Ashley a hypocrite for interfering with the factory children's hours and conditions of work whilst benefiting, as a member of the land-owning class, from the retention of the laws which kept those same children hungry. They were the more bitter against him because his interference on behalf of the factory children offended their feelings of local patriotism. Who was this South Country lordling, so ignorant that he did not know a spinning-mule from a jenny, that he should tell good North Country men how to go about their own business and accuse them of cruelty and oppression towards their own people?

At first sight Ashley does indeed seem a strange person to emerge as champion of the factory children. George Bull had picked on him simply because no one else was available. Bull was, however, delighted with the new leader he had so providentially discovered, writing to the Short Time Committees that, 'as to Lord Ashley, he is noble, benevolent, and resolute in mind, as he is manly in person.' Sir Reginald Coupland's description of an ideal parliamentary spokesman for an unpopular social reform can hardly be bettered. Coupland, of course, is writing of William Wilberforce and the anti-slavery agitation, but his words apply so exactly to Ashley and the Ten Hours campaign that they are worth quoting at some length:

If the country must first be schooled and roused the second step must be to break through the apathy of Parliament . . . And for this a politician is needed, and a politician endowed with very rare gifts indeed. He must possess, in the first place, the virtues of a fanatic without his vices. He must be palpably single-minded and unself-seeking. He must be strong enough to face opposition and ridicule, staunch enough to endure obstruction and delay. In season and out of season, he must thrust his cause on Parliament's attention. Yet, somehow or other, Parliament must not be bored. He must not be regarded as the tiresome victim of an *idée fixe*, well-meaning possibly, but an intolerable nuisance. Somehow or other he must be persistent, yet not unpopular.

D

Secondly, he must possess the intellectual power to grasp an intricate subject, the clarity of mind to deal with a great mass of detailed evidence, the eloquence to expound it lucidly and effectively. He must be able to speak from the same brief a score of times without surfeiting his audience with a hash of stale meat. And he must have a natural delicacy of feeling. He will have terrible things to say; they will form an important part of his case; but in the choice of them and in the manner in which he says them he must avoid the besetting sin of the professional humanitarian. He must never be morbid. He must not seem to take a pleasure in dwelling on the unsavoury vices of his fellow men. He must not pile up the horrors and revel in atrocious detail. He must shock, but not nauseate, the imagination of his hearers. Finally, he must be a man of recognised position in society and politics. It must be impossible to deride him in London drawing-rooms as an obscure crank, a wild man from beyond the pale. And he must have, or by some means must obtain a footing in Downing Street. For without at least some shadow of support from Government his task might well prove desperate.[6]

Oastler was busy rousing the country; it was Ashley's part to deal with an apathetic Parliament. Without shadow of doubt he was both single-minded and unself-seeking. Like Wilberforce, he was possessed of great strength and tenacity of purpose when and if he believed a religious principle or duty to be involved. (He had told Bull that to him the Ten Hours Bill appeared an affair less of policy than of religion.) Speaking so often from the same brief, he was always fearful of boring Parliament but in fact seldom did so. He was gifted with unusual intellectual power and clarity of mind, and although in 1833 no one would have described him as eloquent, with time and practice he was to develop into one of the most effective and sought-after speakers of the day. And his natural delicacy was remarkable. Although the horrors he had to describe were only less repulsive than the terrible details of the slave trade his speeches were models of good taste and restraint. Finally, as the son and heir of one earl and the son-in-law of another, he could hardly be regarded by the inhabitants of London drawing-rooms as a wild man from beyond the pale – whilst as a one-time junior Minister and a recognised candidate for Cabinet office he had at least one foot very firmly planted in Downing Street.

Having made up his mind to the task, Ashley lost no time. Within a day or two of his first meeting with Bull he gave notice of his intention to re-introduce the Ten Hours Bill brought in by Sadler in the previous Parliament. Almost simultaneously Lord Morpeth gave similar notice of his intention to introduce an Eleven Hours Bill. In a polite but slightly chilly exchange of letters between the two old friends Morpeth stated his conviction that a Ten Hours Bill could have no chance of passing through Parliament whilst Ashley declared that he would stand by 'the most just demands of the Short Time Committees' for a working period for children of no more than ten hours, with an eight-hour day on Saturdays, and total freedom from night-work. The fight was on.

On February 23rd 1833 a great meeting was held in London under the auspices of the Society for the Improvement of the Condition of Factory Children. In a forceful speech Ashley described nineteenth-century Englishmen as more brutal than the Indians who practised infanticide, or than those ancient peoples who sacrificed their children to Moloch – 'those nations sacrificed at once their wretched offspring, and prevented a long career of suffering and crime; but we, having sucked out every energy of body and soul, toss them on the world a mass of skin and bone, incapable of exertion, brutalised in their understandings, and disqualified for immortality.' The real pith of his denunciation lay in the last three words. Ashley was to do almost more than any other Englishman to lessen physical evils and to provide the poorest of the poor with opportunities to improve their minds, but he was always to believe that the damage to men's souls weighed far heavier in the balance than the corresponding damage to their minds and bodies.

At this meeting Ashley found himself on the same platform as Robert Owen, the pioneer Socialist, Daniel O'Connell, the Irish patriot and agitator, and the economist, Robert Torrens. (Not all economists opposed the Ten Hours Bill; John McCulloch wrote to Ashley wishing him success with the measure and adding the sensible comment, 'I would not interfere between adults and masters; but it is absurd to contend that children have the power to judge for themselves in such a matter.')[7] Here also Ashley met Richard Oastler for the first time. Strangely enough, no one seems to have suggested that Ashley should go North, see conditions in the mills for himself, and meet the other leaders of the movement who were as yet unknown to him. Like Ashley himself, nearly all those men were Tories and Anglicans. Too many people persist in believing that the men who fought to reform industrial conditions were of the same Liberal and Nonconformist breed as the men who campaigned for Parliamentary Reform and freedom of trade. John Wood, George Bull, Richard

Oastler and William Ferrand were all Tories and Anglicans; Michael Sadler, a strong Tory, seems to have combined membership of the Church of England with Methodism. Only John Fielden was both a Radical and a Nonconformist. An admirable man, he was also an extremely obstinate one, who earned for himself the nickname of 'the self-acting mule.'

None of the leaders of the Ten Hours campaign came from the working class. Sadler was a merchant, Oastler a land-agent, Ferrand a landowner and Bull, of course, a parson. Though Ashley persisted in believing the opposite to be true – 'the clergy in the trading districts fear the face of man; the frown of a mill owner or a capitalist is beyond their endurance' – the evidence goes to show that many, perhaps the majority, of the clergy were in favour of the Ten Hours Bill. The Archbishop of Canterbury had himself presented to the House of Lords a petition urging the limitation of children's working hours, commenting that 'it was a disgrace to a Christian and civilised country to allow such a system to continue.' The Archbishop of York subscribed twenty pounds 'for the benefit of the poor bairns,' a sum which appears somewhat meagre when set against the forty thousand pounds or more which John Wood expended in the same cause. In some places, Halifax for example, the clergy were apathetic or even hostile; nevertheless, at one rally Bull counted no less than sixty-four parsons present, an attendance which suggests that the movement did not lack supporters among the Yorkshire clergy. As to the Lancashire clergy, there is less evidence. In the early days of the movement for factory reform all its most prominent supporters were Yorkshiremen; and John Fielden, who came from the border town of Todmorden, was the only one of them engaged in the cotton industry. In Lancashire, however, the Short Time committees set up by the operatives were at least as strong as in Yorkshire and more advanced in their views.

In his speech at the London meeting Ashley had declared that 'he had taken up the measure as a matter of conscience, and as such he was determined to carry it through.' The conduct of the campaign must reflect the spirit in which he had embarked upon it. He himself described the agreement he came to with the operatives on this subject: 'they agreed from the first that all should be carried on in the most conciliatory manner; that there should be a careful abstinence from all approach to questions of wages and capital; that the labour of children and young persons should alone be touched; that there should be no strikes, no intimidation, and no strong language against their employers, either within or without the walls of Parliament.'[8]

Ashley was being slightly disingenuous when he said that he had no intention of touching adult labour. In a letter to Morpeth, dated June 24th 1833, now in the Castle Howard papers, he wrote, 'I have always declared, and so has every man who supports this question from his heart, that, if the labour of adults were not *indirectly* limited, one half of the benefits to be looked for from the bill could never ensue.' This statement to Morpeth stands unsupported and alone; on all other occasions Ashley was to maintain that he had no concern with the hours worked by adults. Other supporters of the Ten Hours Bill knew well enough that a limitation of children's working hours, unless the limit were so fixed as to admit of a relay system, must inevitably mean a limitation in adult working hours. A spinner could not work without his little piecer or a weaver without his draw-boy. Here lies the original reason for the almost fanatical insistence on the exact figure of ten hours. A limitation of children's hours to eleven or twelve would be of no appreciable benefit to adults because these were already the most usual, though by no means the universal, working periods; a reduction below the ten-hour limit would allow children to be worked in relays, thus increasing rather than lessening the hours of adult labour. However, by the time Ashley took over the leadership from Sadler the rallying-cry of 'Ten Hours' had become a cherished shibboleth rather than a reckoning of nicely calculated less or more, as he was later to discover to his cost.

Ashley's ban on strong language was bound sooner or later to bring him into collision with Oastler, an honest demagogue all too apt to allow himself to be carried away on the flood-tide of his own eloquence. Already he had caused some embarrassment by publishing a letter on the subject of Morpeth's Eleven Hours Bill, in which he described Ashley's old friend as 'the sleek and oily Judas,' who would 'betray the infants' sacred cause with a kiss.' Tact is a quality usually associated with more smooth and worldly characters than Ashley. Judging by his diaries it was something foreign to his character which he was obliged to cultivate with a conscious effort, a gift, as he himself would have said, not of nature but of grace. Now at the very beginning of his association with the Ten Hours campaign he was faced with a situation demanding all the tact and diplomacy he could muster. Oastler was on the warpath in Lancashire, delivering a series of inflammatory speeches to crowded meetings of cotton operatives. Meanwhile, divisions had arisen among the ranks of the Ten Hours men. Bull, Oastler, and the Yorkshire operatives were strongly of the opinion that the bill should contain a penal clause

providing that on a third conviction for infringing its regulations a
mill-owner could be given a prison sentence. They argued with some
justice that since previous acts had been openly and frequently
defied, the new measure must be enforced with the strongest possible
deterrent. Because he considered it wise to conciliate rather than
to antagonise the mill-owners, Ashley was against any such clause.
Famous for his rigid attitude where private morals were concerned,
in public affairs he was something of a pragmatist. He would never
have set expediency above principle, but in a matter which involved
no real abandonment of principle he was prepared not to insist
on his pound of flesh but to compromise and to exercise a little discretion. So now he saw that although this penal clause might be
right and just in theory, in practice it was not expedient. The measure
as it first appeared before Parliament did indeed contain such a
clause; Ashley, however, succeeded in getting it dropped during the
Bill's progress through the House of Commons. On another controversial issue he sided with the Yorkshiremen against their Lancashire colleagues. In Lancashire the cry was for the enforced stop-
page of machinery; in Yorkshire it was held that the compulsory
keeping of a time-book would provide an adequate sanction. The Bill
as finally drafted contained provision for the keeping of a time-book
but not for the stopping of machinery.

On March 3rd Morpeth withdrew his Eleven Hours Bill, finding no
adequate support for that measure. Ashley's Ten Hours Bill, which
had its first reading a few days later, provided that in the cotton and
woollen industries no child was to be employed before reaching the
age of nine; no child or young person under the age of eighteen was
to work more than ten hours a day or eight hours on Saturdays; and
no one under the age of twenty-one was to be employed on night-
work.

The Government chose not to oppose this measure; instead, they
countered it by proposing a Royal Commission to examine afresh
the whole problem of children's employment in the cotton and
woollen industries on the ground that Sadler's Select Committee
had only heard one side of the question. This argument was fair
enough; reading that Committee's report the evidence does not appear
to be untrue – it is painfully clear that the witnesses spoke the
exact and horrid truth – but it does appear to be slanted. Henry
Ashworth pointed out that of the eighty-nine witnesses not one was
a mill-owner and only twelve came from Lancashire. The majority
of the operatives who gave evidence were known to be supporters
of the Ten Hours movement and some of them were members of

Short Time committees. Although many operatives opposed any limitation of children's working hours, fearing the inevitable drop in family income, not one witness spoke up for this point of view. Many of the questions were phrased in such a way as to put the desired answer into the mouth of the witness, as, for instance, this question put to a Keighley operative, 'You conceive the degree of labour you were subjected to deprived you of your education, interfered with your home duties, and rendered you a cripple for life?' Some of the witnesses had been instructed beforehand as to what to say and how to say it. In *Ten Hours Parson* Mr. Gill describes the care taken to prepare the more unsophisticated for the ordeal of giving evidence:

> It was important that they should be able to give evidence convincingly and stand up to close cross-examination. Witnesses must tell only of what they knew. Hearsay evidence would harm their case and impair the value of their genuine evidence. Every care therefore was taken to test the veracity of every witness; a document . . . was issued by the Central Committee which stressed all this. It posed twenty-two questions covering the ground which the Select Committee was likely to cover.[9]

Although such preparation was legitimate, even perhaps desirable, the fact remained that these witnesses had been briefed previous to their appearance before the Committee. Good reason certainly existed for further enquiry. Ashley and his supporters were, however, right in supposing that the proposal for a Royal Commission had been put forward as a means of delaying and possibly destroying the Ten Hours Bill. On April 3rd the motion to establish a Royal Commission passed the House of Commons by a majority of one, Ashley protesting forcibly. The plan was to send Assistant Commissioners to the factory districts to collect information which they would pass on to three Chief Commissioners sitting in London. Ironically enough, Ashley was later to count two of these three men, Edwin Chadwick and Thomas Southwood Smith, among his most valued friends and fellow-workers. Now, however, he made no protest when his Northern supporters decided to boycott the Commission completely. They refused to give evidence before the Assistant Commissioners and they harassed and beset those unfortunate men in a manner deliberately calculated to make them look foolish. At Leeds and Bradford, for instance, the Commissioners were mobbed by crowds of factory children singing a popular catch:

We will have the Ten Hours Bill,
That we will, that we will,
Else the land shall ne'er be still,
Never still, never still.
Parliament say what they will
We will have the Ten Hours Bill;
We want no commissioning,
We will have the Ten Hours Bill.

It is something to know that after long hours of work in shocking conditions these poor children still had spirits and energy enough for such mischief. Their cheerful resilience was indeed astonishing. One of the few bright moments of relief in the woeful stories told by the witnesses before Sadler's committee came when a pauper apprentice, the class of child whose lot was of all the most miserable, was asked whether the children on night-shift were tempted to play rather than to sleep during their free day-time hours. 'Yes,' came the answer, 'and in such weather as this to go a-blackberrying.'

Ashley's Bill passed its second reading on June 18th. On July 13th the Report of the Royal Commission was laid on the table of the House of Commons. Contrary to all expectation this report confirmed in every particular but one the findings of Sadler's committee. The Commissioners stated categorically that in their opinion the long working hours and bad conditions of labour to which children were subjected damaged their physique, deprived them of education, and in some cases caused incurable disease and deformity. The report cut the ground from under the feet of the economists by declaring that 'at the age when children suffer these injuries from the labour they undergo they are not free agents.' The Commissioners' summing up was definite and decisive: 'We are of the opinion that a case is made out for the interference of the legislature on behalf of the children employed in factories.'

So far, so good. The Commissioners, however, differed from the Ten Hours men in their assessment of the age at which children could be fairly described as free agents no longer requiring the protection of the law. Ashley and his supporters wished to protect all 'young persons' up to the age of eighteen; the Commissioners drew the line at thirteen, believing children of that age to be physically capable of enduring long hours of labour and mentally advanced enough to manage their own affairs, which presumably included the business of striking a bargain with their employers. In coming to this conclusion the Commissioners were disregarding their own statement that long hours of work were 'to the young persons, especially to the young female workers, extremely irksome and harassing,' and also the evidence of such witnesses as the teenage girl who declared that 'many a time she had been so fatigued that she could hardly take off her clothes at night; her mother would be raging at her because when she sat down she could not get up again.'

When confronted with the Commissioners' report, the Whig Government decided that legislation was inevitable, but that rather than introduce a measure of their own they would amend Ashley's bill. On July 18th, on the motion for the Bill to go to Committee, Lord Althorp moved to substitute 'thirteen' for 'eighteen' as the age at which the restriction on working hours ceased to operate. The amendment was carried by a majority of 145. Having seen his measure thus mangled Ashley could only accept defeat, which he did very gracefully – 'He found that the noble lord [Althorp] had completely defeated him; he would therefore surrender the Bill into the hands of the noble lord, but having taken it up with a view to do good to the class intended, he would only say, into whatever hands it passed, God bless it.'

Ashley had no intention of giving up the struggle; for the moment, however, there was nothing more that he could do. Althorp's Bill as finally amended gave the factory children much that was of great value; for those under thirteen it limited working hours to nine, it insisted that they should attend school, and, most important of all, it appointed inspectors equipped with adequate powers to enforce the law. 'The Government,' wrote the Hammonds, 'had wanted to do as little as possible in the way of a Factory Act; they had done a great deal more than they intended.'[10]

Robert Southey wrote to assure Ashley that in spite of the failure of his own bill he could look back with satisfaction on his labours in the cause of the factory children. Neither the Government nor the mill-owners would have taken any action whatsoever had he not shamed them into so doing – 'they have given to the younger children more than you could venture to ask, and they will, ere long, be obliged to give at least as much as you asked to the adolescents.' Southey ended his letter with the wise advice, 'turn away from it now, and you will be the better able to stir in it hereafter when opportunity offers.'[11]

Chapter 7

RELIGIOUS VIEWS AND ACTIVITIES

Southey had proposed a visit to the Lake District; Ashley, however, decided to take a longer and more interesting holiday. Leaving behind baby Francis, who had been born the previous March, Ashley, Minny and 'Sir Babkins' set out on October 10th 1833 for a Continental tour with Lord and Lady Cowper. They drove through France to Geneva, 'a terrible place for shopping,' then travelled on by Lausanne and Brigue across the Simplon to Lake Maggiore and Milan. Here Ashley and his 'little Min' left their child in the care of his grandparents and set off by themselves on a six-weeks' tour of Italy, visiting the better-known Northern Italian cities and, more surprisingly, making a special journey to the little republic of San Marino. They behaved as very ordinary tourists, enjoying a trip in a Venetian gondola in spite of bad weather, scolding their driver for cruelty to his horse, and in the picture galleries going into raptures over Raphael and Guido Reni but finding it difficult to appreciate the works of Carracci. Good Protestant though he was, Ashley cherished a special attachment to the sacred symbol of the Cross. In the Catholic cantons of Switzerland almost the only thing he had found to admire was the frequent appearance of 'the ensign of the Cross, comely in its form and adapted to the scenery.' Now in Padua he bought himself a halfpenny crucifix, thinking it no offence 'to bear about a memorial of what God once did for the world.'

Christmas was spent in Rome, where the Ashleys found themselves caught up in the social round with other English visitors. At a 'lively and pleasant' ball given by a Mrs. Montague, Ashley was delighted that a stranger should beg to be introduced to '*Mademoiselle* Ashley.' Praise of his Minny, 'looking heavenly,' as he described her on this occasion, always won his heart – 'but surely there is nothing so pretty and fascinating as my Min.' Much of their time was of course given to sightseeing. After a visit to the Vatican gallery Ashley expressed a curious and perhaps revealing preference – 'whatever may be the condemnation of my judgement I most boldly declare my preference for the "Madonna di Foligno" to all the pictures of the world.' An extremely sophisticated piece of composition, this Raphael Madonna is by no means an easy or an immediate picture. Something in its intricacies of stress and counter-stress may have found an echo in the complicated pattern of Ashley's psychology.

The travel diary which Ashley kept on this holiday has now disappeared. According to Hodder, 'one of the most interesting entries is that occurring under the date, January 15th, 1834, "Dined with Pusey".' Hodder supposed this entry to refer to Edward Pusey, who was on that day staying with his mother at Holton Park in Oxfordshire. The Pusey with whom Ashley dined was in all probability Edward's elder brother Philip, who had been living in Rome in 1829 and may well have been there also in 1834. At this dinner Ashley sat next to the Prussian diplomat, the Chevalier de Bunsen, 'a most simple, unaffected learned man,' with whom he immediately struck up a friendship that was to mean much to him in later life.

Rome was a place particularly dear to Ashley; when the moment for departure came he recorded 'it was pain and grief to leave it,' though he was cheered by the prospect of seeing 'our darling child,' now in Nice with Lady Cowper. The little boy delighted his parents by recognising them immediately in spite of their long absence and greeting them with obvious joy. Ashley was annoyed that the journey home must be broken by a stay in Paris, a favourite place both with Minny and her mother, and he rejoiced when they left 'that pavilion of Belial' to arrive back in England on April 19th 1834.

On his return Ashley recommenced the keeping of a regular journal which he had neglected for the past three years. The volumes from January 1835 to September 1838 are missing; but entries must have been made during that period, since Hodder gives several quotations from between those dates. Otherwise the diaries run unbroken until the middle of 1885, within a very few months of the death of their writer.

Ashley was a truthful man; yet his diaries must be taken with a large grain of salt. Some diarists keep a record of events; others write a chronicle of gossip; more introspective and repressed characters use their diary as a safety-valve. The eleven volumes of Ashley's diaries are far and away the most important material available to a biographer, but they should be used with discretion and carefully checked against the recollections and impressions of those who knew him personally. Otherwise the shadows will be too dark and the highlights not sufficiently conspicuous. As Coupland wrote of Wilberforce's diary, 'Many men might be misjudged by later generations if they ventured to keep and to leave unburnt behind them so candid a record of their innermost thoughts.'[1]

The publication of Hodder's book, containing as it did large extracts from the diaries, shocked and surprised many people who had hitherto believed themselves to have been on the best of terms with its subject. Among them was Gladstone. 'I could not have believed,' he wrote, 'from the constantly kind relations between us that I could have presented to one sustaining those relations a picture of such unrelieved and universal blackness . . . I am now inclined to regret, what I used to reflect upon with pleasure, that I had broken bread at Lord Shaftesbury's table, for he must have been a reluctant host.'[2] Gladstone would have been still more grieved had he seen some of the references to him which Hodder tactfully suppressed.

The case of Gladstone is a typical one. The diaries record, with unsparing frankness, all occasions of strife, disagreement and bitterness between Ashley and Gladstone; they do not record such occasions as an encounter at the Carlton Club on March 17th 1837 when the two men argued amicably about Gladstone's favourite theory that revelation was to be found in pagan literature as well as in the Bible, and parted with an exchange of blessings. Taking an instance at the other end of his life, in a letter to Gladstone dated July 13th 1880, Shaftesbury describes himself as 'an old personal friend,' yet in that same year he writes in his diary on December 2nd, 'I have long thought Beaconsfield a *bad* man and Gladstone a *mad* man,' a mild enough remark compared to some of his strictures on Gladstone. On November 23rd 1870 he describes Gladstone as 'low, tortuous and timid,' and on May 10th 1871 he pronounces the damning judgement, 'surely the man is not far removed from the Roman Church.' Yet this was the man whom he knew so intimately that he could send him 'a little book which pray accept; it is good to put on your desk, and every now and then in the midst of business, read a thought as a kind of pick-me-up.'[3] When Ashley greeted Gladstone as a friend he was not making a deliberate effort to obey the command to love one's enemies, still less was he playing the hypocrite. We are all of us inconsistent; and Ashley was more inconsistent than most people. There were times when he liked and admired Gladstone; there were others, and more frequent ones, when he came near to hating him.

Ashley was a highly-strung introvert whose precarious balance of mind hung upon a thread. In a moment he could plunge from the heights to the depths. A thought-provoking description of the elder Pitt applies even more aptly to him:

Pitt experienced fits of deep depression, which, when they had passed, were replaced by moods of elation and great excitement. It has been suggested by present-day psychologists that he may have been what is called a 'manic-depressive', or, in other words, that he suffered all his life from a well-recognised mental disease. If this was indeed the case, he was a manic-depressive of outstanding genius and great vision.[4]

Though it would not be right to describe Ashley definitely as a manic-depressive, his tendencies were certainly in that direction. In times of depression he would unburden his soul in his diary, but in his manic moments he would only write the shortest of entries. André Gide, a dissimilar character, who yet in certain respects closely resembled him, wrote thus of his own journals:

Si plus tard on publie mon journal, je crains qu'il ne donne de moi une idée assez fausse. Je ne l'ai point tenu durant les longues périodes d'équilibre, de sante, de bonheur; mais bien durant les périodes de dépression, où j'avais besoin de lui pour me ressaisir, et où je me montre dolant, geignant, pitoyable. Dès que reparnit le soleil, je me perds de vue et suis tout occupé par le travail et par la vie. Mon journal ne reflète rien de cela, mais seulement mes périodes de désespoir.*

So Ashley recorded his times of happiness and success briefly, if at all, but set down at great length his feelings of depression, frustration and defeat. Aware of his own lack of stability and making great efforts to attain to Wesley's ideal, 'to run my course with *even* joy,' he could not have succeeded as well as he did had he not allowed himself this safety-valve.

Where other people were concerned Christian charity and gentlemanly good manners, two qualities which Ashley supremely valued, forbade him to speak angrily or offensively, whilst common sense taught him that such speech would hinder rather than help the causes he had so much at heart. He, who was so fierce in his denunciation of

---

* If later my journal should be published I am afraid that it will give rather a false impression of me. I have not kept it during long periods of equilibrium, health and happiness, but of course during periods of depression, when I needed it to regain self-control, and when I showed myself as plaintive, fretful, wretched. As soon as the sun breaks through again I lose sight of myself, becoming entirely preoccupied with my life and work. My journal shows nothing of this, but only my periods of despair. (February 13th 1924).

abuses, carefully refrained from attacking individuals, excepting perhaps if they chanced to be Tractarians, and even then he seldom descended to personalities. His contemporaries were anything but mealy-mouthed, casually flinging the most abusive epithets at one another, whilst he remained studiously polite. Yet his feelings were frequently at boiling point, and boil over they did, more or less harmlessly, in the pages of his diary. Though all sensible men naturally keep some of their more unflattering judgements to themselves, their public behaviour towards a person will usually approximate to their private opinion of that individual. In Ashley's case, however, the gap between the two was sometimes so abnormally wide as to give rise to considerable misunderstanding.

The difference, at times the complete contradiction, between the Ashley of the diaries and the Ashley whom his contemporaries knew and for the most part loved, can often be extremely baffling. The Christian might maintain that Ashley's public image was in fact his true personality, disciplined, friendly, courteous, a character changed and controlled by divine grace; the psychologist would argue that the real Ashley was the suppressed ego which erupted in the pages of the diaries; the biographer must hope to find something approximating to the truth in a synthesis of these two very different figures.

The diary for the summer of 1834 shows Ashley once again sunk in depression and anxious about many things. The very first entry begins with the sadly prophetic words, 'I am very anxious about my child Anthony.' However, all that at present disturbs him is Anthony's excessive 'sensibility of feeling'; he describes the child as 'a noble fellow' and looks forward to his future development with hope and confidence. The diary also records, 'much anxiety about our house and its purchase money; we must resign our hopes of a fixed home.' Until he inherited St. Giles Ashley was never to enjoy the pleasures of a country home of his own, but as time went on he was to become more and more attached to his London house in Brook Street. An interesting entry on August 4th shows that his affectionate hero-worship of 'Dukey' had now changed into something much more cold and critical. After recording the death of Mrs. Arbuthnot, who had been Wellington's especial friend though not his mistress, he comments 'I feel deeply touched by this event; how will the Duke take it? If he have either sentiment or sense, he will begin to reflect.'

Curiously enough, no entry for this year of 1834 makes even the remotest reference to factory legislation, though many entries are concerned with political affairs. Ashley is constantly lamenting his own inadequacy. 'I hate the House of Commons,' he writes on May 6th; 'I never hear anyone speak without thinking how much more skilfully he does it than myself.' In point of fact he was steadily improving as a speaker, and he was already showing himself a skilled parliamentary hand in his management of the House and his know-ledge of its rules and procedure. Yet still he laments his incapacity: 'In my own mind I find nothing but weakness; I dream much, hope much, endeavour little, and do nothing. Now seriously, have I the power of discharging public duties with any degree of skilfulness and service?'

If Ashley were to be taken at his own expressed valuation the answer to that query would inevitably have been 'no.' As late as November 6th he was maintaining that 'office I regard with dismay, the very thoughts of it are disagreeable to me.' He nevertheless worked himself into a state of frenzied anxiety when, in December, William the Fourth dismissed the Whigs and called upon Peel, who chanced to be on holiday in Italy, to form a Tory Government. Peel's journey back to England took a fortnight; and all this time Ashley was on tenterhooks. Would Peel offer him a post, and if so, what would be his proper course of action? 'Sir Robert Peel may not invite me to take office, and if he overlooks me in the resolution to appoint a better man I shall have no right to complain of neglect,' he wrote on December 6th. 'He must even for the smaller places be attentive only to the efficiency and character of his Government. I then must be content to have *no* office or *any* office, as he may determine.'

Peel started off badly by sending for Ashley on Sunday, December 14th, thus outraging his sabbatarian principles. Ashley's account of the interview is a curious one. Peel opened the conversation by saying he 'invited me into the King's service.' Ashley replied that he had nothing to offer but 'sound principles, and, by God's grace, a good character.' 'There it is,' Peel exclaimed, 'I must have the union of ability and integrity.' When Ashley took his leave, having agreed to accept an as yet unspecified office, he declared himself to be 'like a man heart-broken' at the prospect of exchanging his domestic ease and cherished pursuits for the cares of official life – 'Everything of taste, utility and enjoyment is now lost to me . . . What have I to compensate for this? Justified ambition! I have no ambition.'

A day or two later this unambitious man found himself once again 'heart-broken,' this time because Peel had offered him nothing better than a seat on the Board of Admiralty. Forgetful of his resolve to be content with '*no* office or *any* office,' he wrote Peel a thoroughly peevish letter. Its mock protestations of unfitness leave a peculiarly nasty taste in the mouth: 'When I see that all my contemporaries have been promoted and many who have never served put over my head, I cannot but feel that, having neither merit enough to advance, not even to retain the scale of my old position, I had better give way to other men.'[5] Peel delegated the answering of this sorry epistle to Lord Granville Somerset, who succeeded in smoothing down Ashley's ruffled feelings and in persuading him to take the proffered seat on the Admiralty Board. When writing to tell Peel of Ashley's acceptance Granville Somerset added the mordant postscript, 'perhaps I ought to add my condolences and apologies, having (as you feared) convinced Ashley for *his* benefit.'[6]

This stormy little episode proved to be of no great importance, since Peel's ministry was only to last four months. It marked, however, a worsening of the relationship between Ashley and Peel, which had hitherto been a comparatively friendly one. In 1830 Joseph Planta, the Treasury Secretary, had drawn up a list of Members of Parliament for Peel's information classifying them under such heads as 'doubtful, favourable,' or 'doubtful, unfavourable.' Ashley's name was entered under the most favourable category of 'friends.'[7] He had been in the habit of passing on to Peel small pieces of information which he thought might be of interest, such as the opinions expressed by various City Aldermen or 'some trifles which had passed in evidence before the Northampton Committee.' He had begged Peel's interest on behalf of the Royal Astronomical Society and he had boldly recommended Doctor Barnes for the vacant bishopric of Calcutta. Even so, the two men were not of a kind to like one another or to work together easily. Already Ashley had complained that Peel was 'civil but cold'; before long he was to liken him to 'an iceberg with a slight thaw on the surface.'

Nowhere in these letters and conversations is any mention made of the Ten Hours question. Clearly Peel did not consider Ashley's commitment to that cause as a serious barrier to office nor did Ashley yet regard it as the prime object of his life. The passage of Althorp's Act had been followed by a lull in the Ten Hours campaign. Some of its discouraged and disappointed supporters transferred their energies to such causes as the promotion of the Trades Union movement. Fielden, Robert Owen, and other enthusiasts were planning a strike to enforce the working of a forty-eight-hour week to be paid at the rate of wages current for a sixty-nine-hour one. Neither this hare-brained scheme nor the temper of its promoters was likely to be approved by Ashley, who withdrew, as it were, to the side-lines, contenting himself with seeing that fair play was given to Althorp's

Act, a measure which was to prove of real benefit to the factory
workers.

The years from 1834 to 1839 mark a temporary lull in Ashley's
public career; they are, however, an important period in the development of his inner life. Professor Best believes that the evidence of
the diary goes to show that during the summer of 1834 Ashley under-
went some sort of conversion. A careful reading of the diary for that
year does not seem to confirm this view. No existing record suggests
that at any period of his life did Ashley experience that sudden
and definite assurance of salvation which is the classic Evangelical
conversion. If he in fact ever had such an experience it most probably
would have been during his childhood under the influence of Maria
Millis. Certainly by the mid-thirties he was more of a committed
Evangelical than he had been in 1829, when he had hotly denied
the imputation of being 'a Saint'; but it is interesting to notice that
as late as 1843 he still approved of praying for the dead, a practice
which was, and is, anathema to strict Evangelicals. In that year,
commenting on an account of the murder of Peel's secretary, Edward
Drummond, he lamented that there was 'no prayer, no commendation
of his soul to Christ.' Not till 1844 does he write regretfully, when
recording the death of a friend, 'It is not commanded to pray for the
dead, or I would say, "God rest his soul".'

It seems probable that the deepening – perhaps 'sharpening'
would be the more accurate word – of Ashley's religious views dates
not from 1834 but from 1835. In that year he first met the man who
was to be one of the chief influences in his life, and through that man
he in all probability first came in contact with a mode of belief
which was to be all-important to his view of religion. The man was
Edward Bickersteth, a leading Evangelical; the belief was that
curiously explicit teaching about the end of the world and the Last
Judgement usually known as Millenarianism.

In the course of his biography of his own forebear, Marianne
Thornton, a member of the group of rich Evangelical families nicknamed 'the Clapham sect,' E. M. Forster puts his finger very exactly
on one of the weakest spots in Evangelicalism. After quoting a little
poem sent to the nine-year-old Marianne by her father, Henry
Thornton, he points out that these charming verses are not typical
of Thornton's correspondence as a whole:

> His exhortations were sincere like everything else that he wrote
> or did, and the anxieties he expressed were genuine. But the words
> he used – like many of the words then used – will not travel.[8]

Very much of Evangelical writing is wine that will not travel. The only
full-scale book about Edward Bickersteth is an over-long, quite
unreadable memoir by his son-in-law, T. R. Birks. The letters from
Bickersteth which are there printed are no more than pious plati-
tudes, all personal and possibly unedifying passages having been
presumably cut out. No figure of a living man emerges from this haze
of hagiography. Yet, according to the testimony of the many people
who knew and loved him, Bickersteth was a gentle, clever, attractive
person, lacking in powers of leadership – a brief memorial pamphlet
mentions 'his want of the particular characteristic by which men are
qualified to direct others' – but yet exercising much influence within
the Evangelical party. This same pamphlet describes 'his irrepressible
natural buoyancy,' 'his cheerful gaiety in general society,' and splendidly comments on his activities as a peacemaker, 'the waves of
vehement argument were often calmed down by the oil of Mr Bickersteth's affection.'

Ashley first met Bickersteth some time in the course of the year
1835. The following summer he spent several days at Watton Rectory,
Bickersteth's Hertfordshire home, a visit which Birks describes as
'a season of peculiar privilege to all who were present.' The two men
found themselves immediately attracted to one another in mutual
liking and friendship. 'I am much gratified that I have left a favourable
and lasting impression among you,' Ashley wrote on his return
home; 'few things have given me more pleasure than my visit to
Watton.'[9] From now onwards Bickersteth, whom he once described as
'a jewel, and a jewel of the first water,' was to be his most intimate friend
and counsellor. The two men wrote to each other frequently, Ashley
regarding Bickersteth's letters as 'a balm in Gilead, grapes of Eschol.'

Bickersteth was a Millenialist, that is to say, he believed that
Christ would return in person to establish a glorious kingdom and
reign on this earth for a fixed period before the final Day of Judgement. The Millenialists were otherwise orthodox Evangelicals who had
launched out into a strange scheme of eschatological chronology
based on their own interpretation of the Old Testament prophecies
and the Book of Revelation. Naturally these interpretations varied so
much that the exact details gave rise to bitter quarrels among the
Millenialists themselves. According to the 'pre-Millenial' theory
which Ashley learnt from Bickersteth, the sequence of supposed
happenings ran as follows. First would come the fulfilment of prophecy
by the return of the Jews to Palestine; not till they were re-established
in their ancient home could the Second Coming of Christ take place,
which would coincide with, or perhaps immediately follow, the bodily

resurrection of the righteous. Then would come Christ's glorious earthly reign of a thousand years. At the end of this Millennium the final Day of Judgement would occur; the wicked would rise from their graves to be condemned to Hell; the world would come to an end; and the righteous would return with Christ to heaven.

This neat and tidy reckoning of events about which we are explicitly told that it is not for us to know the times and the seasons is today only found among the more eccentric Christian sects. In the eighteen-thirties, however, it was a fashionable belief in Evangelical circles; intelligent and even intellectual Christians seem to have found in it some very special comfort for their souls. Ashley in particular made the Second Coming and Christ's subsequent earthly reign the point on which all his hopes centred. Then, and only then, did he believe that earth's wrongs could be righted and sorrow turned to joy – except, of course, for the wicked. It is to be doubted whether he was in the exact and literal sense of the word a Millenialist, that is to say, one who believed that Christ's earthly reign would span a period of precisely one thousand years; more probably he would have said with Bickersteth that 'he dreaded attempting to fix the exact time.' He would, however, have agreed with the most literal Millenialist in stressing the essential link between the return of the Jews to Palestine and the Second Coming of Christ, a theory that was to have a vital influence not only on his religious outlook but also upon his political activities.

Most Christian thought centres round the first coming of Christ in the Incarnation; for Ashley the Second Coming was a more frequent and, it would seem, a more important subject of thought and prayer. From the mid-thirties onwards his diaries are full of references to the Second Coming, many entries ending with some such phrase as 'Even so come Lord Jesus.' These words from the Book of Revelations became his favourite prayer; he had them stamped in Greek on the flaps of envelopes where more worldly persons put a crest or an initial;* he gave a signet-ring so engraved to his favourite little grandson (with the gift he also sent detailed instruction for the care of a puppy called Sandy). To some extent he must have passed on his beliefs to Minny, for when their sixteen-year-old son lay desperately ill she comforted the dying boy with talk about the exact date of the Second Coming, which, she reckoned, 'might be nearer than was ordinarily calculated by one hundred and sixty years.'

* Other envelopes, as a reminder of his preoccupation with the return of the Jews, were stamped with the words, 'O pray for the peace of Jerusalem,' this time in Hebrew.

All this seems strange, almost ludicrous today, even to professing Evangelical Christians. It must, however, be taken seriously. To understand Ashley at all it is essential to understand his religion, and to understand his religion it is necessary to understand his ideas about the Second Advent and the immense hold which they had upon his mind. These ideas were very definite and almost to be described as practical; there was no trace of mysticism about his religious attitude.

At first sight Millenarianism would not seem to be a doctrine to appeal to a practically-minded man nor one likely to foster exceptional zeal for good works, least of all that particular school of Millenarianism to which both Ashley and Bickersteth belonged. These premillenialists believed that only after the Second Advent could the world be converted and evil overthrown; no efforts on the part of men could possibly bring about that desirable result beforehand. Why then try? The question is an obvious but superficial one. An intense preoccupation with the next world, or, to speak more accurately of the Millenialists, with the coming dispensation in this one, often goes hand in hand with a deep concern for life as it is lived here and now. A man who knows that he is about to die busies himself putting his affairs to rights and doing what he can to repair any harm he may have caused. The Millenialists were in very much the same position. Believing that the Day of Judgement would occur within time and space, like any other historical event, and that its date might perhaps be calculated from careful study of biblical prophecies, they were convinced beyond shadow of doubt that the end was approaching. Much remained to be put in order before this world and its inhabitants were in a fit state to face the coming judgement. 'Are you zealous to redeem the time?' asked John Wesley. As Mr. Orchard remarks in his essay on *English Evangelical Eschatology*, that question was essentially an eschatological one. An eschatological awareness rather than a compassionate humanitarianism gave strength and urgency to Ashley's efforts on behalf of the poor, the oppressed and the outcast. The force which drove him was a passionate concern for souls. He believed that factory children, chimney-sweeps and lunatics all had souls to be saved and that very little time remained in which to save them. 'It is eternity work,' said a Welsh Evangelical on his death-bed; men like Wilberforce and Ashley and, indeed, the Evangelicals as a whole, saw all social and charitable efforts as 'eternity work.'

There is something almost disreputably odd about Millenarianism, a fact which may explain what Mr. Orchard describes as 'a conspiracy of silence on the part of biographers.' No one has as yet openly and unequivocally called Ashley a Millenialist; yet such he undoubtedly was. The excess of the Irvingites, who preached an extreme form of Millenarianism, helped to bring ridicule upon all Millenialists. They could indeed be very ridiculous. It is impossible to treat with becoming seriousness divines who calculated that the Second Advent must occur on some date between 1790 and 1914, or who preached sermons with such titles as 'Every eye shall see him, or Prince Albert's visit to Liverpool used as an illustration of the Second Coming of Christ.' 'May the sight of the Crystal Palace lead to a desire to enter the New Jerusalem!' exclaimed one enthusiastic believer. Ashley himself referred to the laying of the Atlantic cable as 'one of the preliminaries of the Second Advent, of Christ's personal and human reign on earth.' Yet many Millenialists were highly respectable and respected figures both in the Church and at the universities; it is worth noting that Bishop Baring chose 'the Millennium' as the subject for his Bampton Lectures at Oxford. Millenarianism deeply influenced the whole of Evangelical thought and practice. For that reason this strange system of belief is something of real historical importance, not to be dismissed as mere folly. Literal-minded and humourless they may have been, but men like Ashley and Bickersteth were not fools.

The intensifying of Ashley's religious views which took place about 1835 had its visible counterpart in his increasing connection with official Evangelicalism. By 1840 he had emerged as not merely the leading Evangelical layman but as the only real leader of a party which was at this period sadly lacking in outstanding or distinguished clergy. At the centre of Evangelical life and work were the organisations known as 'the six societies,' the Church Missionary Society, the Religious Tract Society, the Colonial and Continental Church Society, the London Society for Promoting Christianity among the Jews, the British and Foreign Bible Society, and the Church Pastoral Aid Society. With all of these Ashley came to be closely connected; he was, for instance, President of the Bible Society, Chairman of the Jews' Society, Vice-President both of the Church Missionary Society and the Colonial and Continental. He was in ever-growing demand both as a speaker and chairman, especially during the month of May, which was for Evangelicals as well as for Quakers the great period for meetings, reunions, and pious junketings of all sorts.

Closely connected as he was with all six societies, Ashley's particular concern was for his own creation, the Church Pastoral Aid Society. In February he took the chair at a meeting which resulted in the formation of a society with the laudable aim of 'benefiting the population of our own country by increasing the number of working clergymen in the Church of England, and encouraging the appointment of pious and discreet laymen as helpers to the clergy in duties not ministerial.' Curiously enough, those pious and discreet laymen proved a terrible stumbling-block. High Churchmen, always jealous for clerical privilege, jibbed at the idea of official lay-workers, almost certainly Evangelical in tone, paid by an independent society, and therefore not amenable to episcopal control. A group of High Churchmen, headed by young William Gladstone, walked out of the C.P.A.S. to found their own society which was to supply High Church parishes with properly ordained curates only.

The affair was no more than a silly storm in a tea-cup in which the right was surely upon Ashley's side, but it is interesting on two counts. In the first place it illustrates something fundamental and curiously modern in Ashley's approach to religion. He believed passionately in what is now called 'the priesthood of the laity,' objecting, for instance, to the revival of Convocation because that body was purely clerical. Unlike Gladstone, who shared his absorption in religious matters, Ashley was in no sense a 'priest *manqué*.' He dreamt of himself as Prime Minister, whereas Gladstone, who, of course, four times achieved the Premiership, may well have dreamt of himself as Archbishop of Canterbury.

Secondly, the split in the Pastoral Aid Society is important as marking the first clash between Ashley and the new generation of High Churchmen, who had little or nothing to do with the old 'high and dry' party. On July 14th 1833, four days before the crucial debate on Ashley's Ten Hours Bill, John Keble entered the pulpit of the University Church at Oxford to preach an Assize Sermon, his subject being 'National Apostasy.' That apparently trivial event marked the beginning of a movement which was to make a tremendous impact upon the Church of England and to be bitterly opposed by Ashley throughout the rest of his long life. The men of the Oxford Movement were usually called Tractarians after the series of *Tracts for the Times,* which they began to publish in the autumn of 1833; Ashley, however, preferred to use the derogatory epithet of 'Puseyite,' which came into use in 1834 after the publication of a tract signed with Pusey's initials. 'The sound is smooth and comic and disrespectful,' writes Professor Chadwick, adding that Puseyite was a word used by 'those without perfect manners.'[10]

An hysterical dislike of the Tractarians was something common to many, perhaps the majority, of English people. The most extraordinary tales were believed about them; the lady in a tram who declared that Doctor Pusey was in the habit of sacrificing a lamb every Friday – 'Madam,' said one of her fellow-passengers, 'I *am* Doctor Pusey, and I assure you that I have no notion as to how to kill a lamb' – was no worse informed or more extravagant in her views than the generality of good Protestants. Ashley's reactions, however, passed the bounds of sanity and are only to be explained by supposing that on this issue he was slightly but definitely unbalanced. Where the Tractarians were concerned he suffered from what might be called the hidden-hand complex. 'The claw of a Puseyite' was to be found in every attack made upon him personally or upon the causes which he championed. His fixed belief that the Tractarians were deliberately planning his downfall was pure delusion; they were, in fact, curiously oblivious of his declared enmity. Even when Newman was passionately opposing the creation of the Jerusalem bishopric he seems to have been unaware of, or at least quite unperturbed by, Ashley's part in promoting that scheme. Of the Tractarian leaders only Pusey seems to have been fully aware of Ashley's enmity towards the Oxford Movement and its ideals. After the years spent together at Christ Church the two cousins continued to meet occasionally, Ashley, for instance, staying with Pusey for the installation of the Duke of Wellington as Chancellor of Oxford University. Once the Oxford Movement had begun they clashed ever more frequently and seriously; there were, however, times when they found themselves unexpectedly in agreement. One of these occasions was the dispute over Jowett's salary as Professor of Greek, another, the controversy over *Essays and Reviews*. On this second occasion Pusey wrote to Shaftesbury, as Ashley had then become, declaring that for thirty years 'the deep longing of my soul' had been that 'we should understand each other and strive together against the common enemy of souls.'[11] There is no reason to suppose that he was insincere in writing thus, since in all their battles he had never once been the aggressor.

Today the Tractarians are often charged with a lack of concern for the reforms to which Ashley devoted his life. His own quarrel with them was a purely religious one; he appears to have been untroubled by their disregard for social problems but profoundly disturbed by their attitude towards religious ones. Politically, and perhaps philosophically, Ashley and the Tractarians had much in common. In his essay on *The Spirit of the Oxford Movement* Christopher Dawson has some pertinent things to say about the Tractarians' reaction to Liberalism:

The anti-Liberalism of the Oxford Movement is not a proof of its insensitiveness to the need for social reform. On the contrary, its hostility towards Liberalism was due, at least in part, to its dissatisfaction with a social system which seemed dedicated to the service of Mammon. Its Toryism was not that of the defenders of vested interests, the 'Conservatives' who aroused Hurrell Froude's scorn, but that of Southey and Coleridge and the young Disraeli, who were among the first to denounce the injustices of the Industrial Revolution, and the new Poor Law, and the evils of the Factory System.[12]

What Dawson writes of the leaders of the Oxford Movement could equally well be written of Ashley. And if he shared their hatred of political and philosophical Liberalism he also shared their hatred of the theological Liberalism which he was to stigmatise as 'Neology.' Unfortunately, however, Ashley had more than his fair share of that atavistic horror of Popery which is part of the English inheritance. He saw the Tractarians as disguised Papists, and for that reason he both hated and feared these good Christian men with whom he was on many points so nearly in agreement.

Chapter 8

QUEEN VICTORIA AND SIR ROBERT PEEL

It is a pleasant change to turn from Ashley the militant Protestant to Ashley the social reformer. In this sphere of action he displayed all the wisdom, tact and patience that were so conspicuously lacking from his dealings with the Tractarians. By 1835 he had drifted a little out of touch with the Northern leaders of the Ten Hours movement. In Yorkshire Oastler was now all-powerful as 'the factory king.' His fiery personality and his provocative oratory were not such as to commend him to Ashley, who nevertheless loved the man for his zeal and his devotion. 'No man has finer talents or a warmer heart,' Ashley wrote on July 13th 1841; 'his feelings are too powerful for control, and he has often been outrageous because he knew that his principles were just.' Exactly how outrageous Oastler could be is shown by a long letter written to Ashley and dated April 17th 1835. After pages peppered with capital letters, underlining and exclamation marks he exclaims, 'Oh, my Lord, do excuse me; I must write as I feel.' This obviously true remark is followed by some astonishing ranting about the assassin's knife and a cold stone bed in a dungeon. 'Oh! what a field for declamation does the *juggling trickery* of our foes open to us!' he continues. 'I'd give a world, if I had it, just for four hours at them in your Honourable(?) House.'[1]

Meanwhile, across the Pennines the Lancashire men were laying their own plans and choosing a new leader, a move very much disapproved of by Oastler, who, for all his extravagances, was still Ashley's loyal supporter. The reasons for their action are obscure. The Lancashire leaders were much more Radical than their Yorkshire counterparts. Towards the end of 1855 a new figure emerged, a Methodist minister called Joseph Rayner Stephens, who was to be an important figure in Lancashire in connection with both the Ten Hours campaign and the Chartist agitation. His influence was all on the side of the extremists. Unlike Bull and Oastler, the Lancashire men considered that Ashley had made a grave mistake in abandoning the Ten Hours Bill after the passing of Althorp's amendment, not realising that this was the wisest and, indeed, the only practicable course. Maybe, too, the traditional rivalry between the Red Rose and the White had something to do with the matter. Ashley had originally been the choice of the Yorkshire men, and he had backed the Yorkshire plan for the use of a time-book against the Lancashire plan for the restriction of moving power.

Whatever their motives may have been, at a meeting held at Preston in December 1835 the Lancashire men decided to ask Charles Hindley, a mill-owner and Member of Parliament for Ashton-under-Lyne, to bring in a new Ten Hours Bill including a clause restricting moving power. As a local man calling himself a 'Liberal-Radical,' he may have appeared a more suitable leader than a South Country Tory lord. Very soon, however, doubts began to be felt as to Hindley's ability and even his sincerity. The idea of a new bill did not appear to arouse much enthusiasm among the operatives, and the attempt to revive interest in the Ten Hours campaign might have fizzled out like a damp squib had it not been for an unexpected move on the part of the Whig Government which had succeeded Peel's administration in April 1835.

Althorp's Act had given the protection of the law to all children up to age of thirteen. Poulett Thomson, the Whig President of the Board of Trade, now proposed to lower the age-limit to twelve. At once the North was in an uproar. Enthusiasm revived; delegates from the Short Time committees met in London; Hindley's suggested bill was set aside; and Ashley was asked to lead the opposition to Poulett Thomson's measure. This was for him a congenial and an easy task, since the proposed change went clean against the findings of the Royal Commission of 1833. At its second reading in May 1836 Poulett Thomson's bill secured a bare majority of two votes whereupon the Government decided to withdraw the measure. Meanwhile, there was little he could do except encourage individual efforts to arouse sympathy for the cause of the factory children. When, for instance, Frances Trollope, mother of the better-known novelist, Anthony Trollope, wished to visit Manchester in search of material for *Michael Armstrong*, her propaganda novel of factory life, he supplied her with introductions to many people who could be of use to her.

Though the Ten Hours men had won a victory it remained clear that as yet a Ten Hours Bill stood no chance of acceptance by Parliament. Nevertheless, on June 24th Hindley moved for leave to bring in such a bill. Although he considered the moment extremely inopportune, Ashley loyally promised this bill his full support. Parliament, however, proved so unsympathetic that the motion was withdrawn. Hindley faded quietly out of the picture, and Ashley resumed his old position as leader of the campaign in the House of Commons. His influence over the House and his Parliamentary expertise were at last beginning to be recognised at their proper value; so too was his sincere dedication to the cause. 'If there was one man in England more devoted to the interests of the factory people than another, it was Lord Ashley,' declared one Lancashire delegate in July 1836. 'They might always rely on him as a ready, steadfast and willing friend.'[2]

During 1837 Ashley was content to call attention to any flagrant infringements of the existing law, but in 1838 he again renewed the attack in the House of Commons. In June Lord John Russell, now Home Secretary, brought in a bill to amend and enforce the Act of 1833, but he refused to press his measure, which was ultimately abandoned. On July 20th Ashley made what was perhaps the most powerful speech he had yet delivered, charging the Government with turning a blind eye to the many and glaring evasions of their own Act. Protesting hotly against the abandonment of Russell's bill, he declared, 'Thus had a great measure, closely affecting the temporal and eternal welfare of so vast a portion of the population, been set aside and treated like a turnpike bill.' He moved the resolution, 'that this House deeply regrets that the regulation of the labour of children in factories having been found imperfect and ineffective to the purpose for which it was passed, has been suffered to continue for so long without any amendment,' and lost his motion by the small majority of fifteen votes.

In spite of this near-success the truth was that at this particular date very little interest was taken in factory reform, either in Parliament or out of it. 'The agitation for factory legislation,' wrote the Hammonds, 'had become one aspect, and a subordinate aspect, of a general social conflict.'[3] In that conflict Ashley was emphatically not on the side of such men as Stephens, Oastler and Fielden, who were among the most vehement opponents of the new Poor Law, a measure to which he was not opposed. When the famous 'Charter' appeared in May 1838, demanding universal male suffrage, vote by ballot, annual Parliaments, payment of Members, abolition of the property qualification, and equal electoral districts, many of the Lancashire Ten Hours men joined the Chartists. Since Ashley held Chartism in special dread and dislike it is much to his credit that he did not break with these men but continued to work with them in the cause of factory reform.

The absence of any diary for this period is a sad loss. It would have been fascinating, for instance, to have had Ashley's own reaction when temporarily supplanted by the ineffectual Hindley. As some compensation for this loss Hodder gives us an anonymous 'word-portrait' written in 1838:

Lord Ashley possesses perhaps the palest, purest, stateliest exterior of any man you will see in a month's perambulation of Westminster; indeed, it would be difficult to imagine a more complete *beau-ideal* of aristocracy.

His Lordship looks about six-and-twenty, but is some ten years older. He is above the medium height – about five feet eleven, with a slender and extremely graceful figure, which might almost pass for that of some classic statue attired in a fashionable English costume; and the similarity is not at all impaired by the rigidity of his Lordship's muscles.

His forehead has also much of the marble about it; his curling dark hair, in its thick masses, resembles that of a sculptured bust, and his fine brow and features are distinctly yet delicately cut; the nose, perhaps, a trifle too prominent to be handsome. He has light blue eyes, deeply set, and near each other, with projecting white eyelids; his mouth is small, retiring, and compressed.

The whole countenance has the coldness, as well as the grace, of a chiselled one, and expresses precision, prudence, and determination in no common degree. To judge from the set form of the lips, you would say not only that he never acts from impulse, but that he seldom, if ever, acted from an impulse in his life. All that Lord Ashley does seems to be done from conviction and principle, and not even a muscle dares to move without an order from headquarters. Every separate lock of his hair appears to curl because it has a reason for so doing, and knows that to be the right course of conduct. . . .

When he addresses an audience he stands with his hand resting on the platform rail, and as erect as such a position will possibly allow; he looks his hearers coolly in the face, and, with a very slight bowing movement, barely sufficient to save him from the appearance of stiffness, he delivers, without a moment's hesitation, and with great dignity of voice and manner, a short, calm, serious address. The applause with which he is always heard (for he is very popular in the Societies over which he presides) seems rather an interruption than a pleasure to him, as it breaks into the mutual dependence of his sentences.

I have understood that his Lordship is very nervous, and yet the most striking feature of his public deportment is his apparently rigid self-possession, which he never loses for a moment.[4]

This is a picture of a man whose outward appearance is at variance with his inner personality. The writer is correct in supposing that under his 'apparently rigid self-possession' Ashley was in fact extremely nervous. Far from being a man who 'seldom if ever acted on an impulse' he was essentially an impulsive person, but one who had learnt by bitter experience to mistrust his own impulses. Sometimes, of course, his defences broke down, and he showed himself to be 'a fiery soul,' as Dryden had described his famous ancestor, the first Earl. Normally, however, he maintained strict self-control in public, and only in private and in his own family circle did he appear in his original character, emotional, excitable, uncalculating.

Lacking the evidence of the diary, it is difficult to reconstruct Ashley's family life at this period. When the entries begin again at the end of September 1838 the Ashleys have been bidden to stay at Windsor Castle. Writing from there on October 11th Ashley remarks 'I could not restrain an internal chuckle that I and mine were the guests of the Queen of England.' Queen Victoria had invited Ashley and Minny to bring their two eldest children with them; Sarah Lady Lyttelton, who found the Ashleys 'a very interesting ménage to watch,' described a splendid game of romps with Accy, as Anthony was now called, and young Francis:

> Their two eldest boys are two very dear creatures, seven and five years old, most lovely to behold in their green velvet frocks and long perfumed hair. Their beauty is most striking, and not wonderful, considering their parents. And they are all spirits and naturalness, and so tractable and well-trained! the Queen had them to play with her for an hour in the corridor Saturday. She had neither nurse nor Mamma with them and they were most funny and good, throwing great balls at us, and then screaming, '*Queen*, look, I have killed the lady!' having first declined playing at ball – 'I don't think it right *in a palace*; I might hurt something – ' and talking with such spirits of 'lessons with Papa, reading and saying by heart'. I am glad to have made acquaintance with the family; it is pleasant to think about.[5]

At home were three more little boys, Maurice, or 'Mice,' born 1835, Evelyn, or 'Edy,' born 1836, and Lionel, or 'Vava,' born 1838.

A daughter known as 'Vea' had been born in 1837 and christened Victoria after the Queen, who was delighted to stand as godmother to a great-niece of Lord Melbourne. She would often bid Minny bring the children to spend an afternoon at Buckingham Palace, little Maurice being an especial favourite, 'a most lovely, beautiful dear little creature.'

On several occasions in 1837 and 1838 when the Ashleys dined at Buckingham Palace the Queen commented favourably on Minny, 'a very nice and very pretty young person,' whilst maintaining a significant silence on the subject of Minny's husband. Before Ashley's first visit to Windsor, Melbourne had, as usual, coached the Queen a little, telling her of 'his being very anxious to ameliorate the sufferings of the factory children which Lord Melbourne thinks very doubtful,' as she recorded in her journal, adding 'If they don't work they must starve and the greatest philanthropists only wish to reduce the number of hours from fourteen to ten; but then the manufacturers say they will be ruined and that they can't compete with the Continent.'[6]

Almost against his will Ashley had become very fond of Lady Cowper, Melbourne's sister and his own mother-in-law, but he could never really like or approve Melbourne himself. 'My dear Melbourne,' one letter of this period begins, 'You and I differ so widely even on these matters that I fear I shall obtain nothing from you beyond a good-natured acceptance of the copy of the speech I have enclosed.'[7] Melbourne's easy, ironic attitude towards life was something which Ashley could neither understand nor accept, so foreign was it to his own nature. As for Melbourne's opinion of Ashley, Queen Victoria commented years later, 'he disliked *cant* and Lord Shaftesbury's narrowness.'[8] Nevertheless, Melbourne bestowed on Ashley some tempered praise, telling the Queen that 'he is a very good man, and less eager in politics than he was.'[9] On May 15th 1838 the Queen recorded that she and Melbourne had talked of Ashley's courtship and marriage, discussing 'Lord and Lady Ashley's happiness together, his being of a fidgetty temper, but that she managed him very well.'[10]

Like many other people, Ashley was uneasy about the relationship existing between 'Lord M.' and the Queen. In an entry in his diary, written during this visit to Windsor, he sums up the situation with insight and sympathy:

This state of things cannot last, it must be changed in the ordinary course of human affairs; and a sad prospect it is for our little Queen. She has an unlimited confidence in Melbourne and the warmest friendship for him and pleasure in his society, and many hours of every day are passed in his company, and the smallest concerns, even of her private arrangements, are submitted to his opinion. What habits are hereby engendered, and what pain on the rupture of them which nature or political change must necessarily induce! I grieve, deeply grieve, to think of her 'futurity'; it must arrive and she is not by any means prepared for it. Such a transition would be mournful to anyone, but to a Sovereign it is without hope at least of a similar confidence and entire satisfaction. Her next Prime Minister, whatever his public merits, can never be her private and particular friend; their alliance will be formed under different circumstances, and he might not have the leisure or inclination to live away so long from his family and business. This intimacy is natural, very natural, though far from prudent. Her youth and accession to the throne, her inexperience and pressing difficulties and the constraint and reserve under which she had lived, all combined to invest the first man she could trust and speak to openly on every subject with many attractions which few youthful minds could resist. I question the foresight and propriety of judgement in allowing such manifestations of unusual preference though he too has had difficulties. He is a singularly engaging man and sixty years of age sit as pleasantly on him as thirty-five on any other. I believe his real and hearty zeal for her honour and interests; as a public minister he will tarnish her reputation and destroy her kingdom, but as a private counsellor and friend he will know nothing but her comfort and welfare, according to the best of his judgement.

The young Queen's devotion to Melbourne was the underlying cause of the absurd affair known as the Bedchamber Crisis when her determination to retain her Whig ladies of the bedchamber upset all the calculations of the politicians and brought about the fall of the new Tory Government. In May 1839 the Whigs at last gave up office. 'All, ALL my happiness gone,' the tearful Queen wrote in her journal for May 7th, 'that happy life destroyed, that dearest, kind Lord Melbourne no longer my Minister!' Two days later Ashley received an urgent summons from Peel. Once again Peel offered him a post; once again Ashley went through his version of the formula *Nolo episcopari*, but this time with better reason, since the proffered position was one in the Queen's Household. Naturally enough he disliked the very thought of 'the trivialities of a Court life, the loss of time, the total surrender of my political ambitions and of all that honourable ambition had prompted me to hope for; instead of being a Minister to become a mere puppet.' Again it is noticeable that he makes no mention of his leadership of the Ten Hours campaign. When referring to this conversation two years later he described how Peel had 'pooh-poohed' his objection on that score, but writing at the time he does not seem to think it a difficulty worthy of mention.

Peel himself admitted that such an offer was almost an insult to a man of Ashley's capacity and standing – 'I am *ashamed* to ask such a thing of you.' He urged the difficulty of finding suitable attendants and companions for a young woman whose 'moral and religious character' was of such importance. 'Now,' he begged, 'will *you* assist me? Will *you* take a place in the Queen's Household? Your character is such in the country; you are so connected with the religious societies and the religion of the country; you are so well-known and enjoy so high a reputation that you can do more than any man.' Confronted with such arguments Ashley could only reply that although the prospect of Court life was extremely distasteful, 'I would, if he *really* and truly thought I could serve his purpose, accept, if he wished it, the office of Chief Scullion!'

'I thought he would have burst into tears,' was Ashley's comment on Peel's reaction. A very great weight had in fact been lifted from Peel's mind. He had been honest in saying that he offered Ashley a court post, because he wished to have about the Queen someone conspicuous for moral character and religious zeal, but he had another and even more pressing reason for wishing that Ashley might accept such a post. The Queen's entourage consisted almost entirely of Whigs; Peel had now to set about the ticklish business of persuading her to dismiss some of her ladies and to accept Tory ladies in their place. Ashley's appointment to some such office as Treasurer might be thrown in as a sop to make these changes more palatable. It might be supposed that the Queen would be pleased to have about her someone so nearly related to her dear Lord Melbourne; and, in fact, when Peel put forward Ashley's name the Queen readily agreed, although she had no great personal liking for Ashley himself.

The conversation between the two men finished, Peel drove off immediately to his interview with the Queen, Ashley accompanying him as far as the door of Buckingham Palace. In the carriage he improved the occasion by giving Peel some good advice: 'The Queen should be the Queen of the kingdom, not of a party;' Peel must therefore get rid of intriguing Whiggish females such as Lady Normanby, but on the whole he would do well to make as few changes as possible.

A few days later Peel again sent for Ashley to tell him the surprising news that the Whigs were back in office. The nineteen-year-old Queen had defeated the combined forces of Peel and Wellington. She had refused to surrender any of her ladies of the bedchamber; and rather than attempt to carry on the business of government in the face of court intrigues and opposition, Peel had handed in his resignation. Ashley congratulated him on this decision – 'I told him I thought he was a fine fellow and that I rejoiced both in his conduct and in the step he had taken.' This is the son of an earl speaking to the son of a cotton-spinner, not a junior politician addressing his party leader, a man thirteen years his senior who had just been invited to become Prime Minister of England for the second time. Ashley all too frequently used this patronising tone in his dealings with men who, however eminent in their own walk of life, were yet by the convention of the age his social inferiors. As a very young man indeed he had written of a party given by the Lord Mayor of London, 'I was able to compliment the Lord Mayor, a gallant, honest fellow, by opening the ball with his wife; nothing like doing these things now and then.' Ashley was perfectly at home with the poor and outcast; he was not so happy in his dealings with the middle classes.

The Bedchamber Crisis, which had brought Melbourne back into office, set Ashley reflecting again upon the relationship between the Queen and her Prime Minister. This time his conclusions were not nearly so favourable to Melbourne:

He [Melbourne] has, I believe, a sincere and even ardent affection for the Queen but he has either no knowledge or no courage to act and advise her according to her real interests. He will be, if not checked, her political and moral destroyer. His society and con- versation are pernicious to a young mind. I have seen this much of late – his sentiments and manner blunt the moral sense and lower the standard of judgement and feeling. His past life, his present opinions, his reckless language, the intimacy in short subsisting between them, are perpetual sources of poison to her mind. This last affair has been the desperate struggle of a wilful unthinking, untaught girl to recover the society of a man whom she loves. It is love and nothing else, love perhaps less ardent in her because her natural disposition may be cold; but love in her and amusement in him have brought about this fresh crisis of affairs. The vista now open is dreadful, for she is obstinate to manage.

Ashley was less than fair to Melbourne in supposing that his feelings went no farther than mere amusement, nor was he right in supposing the Queen's disposition to be a cold one. Fortunately her marriage to Prince Albert of Saxe-Coburg-Gotha, which took place the following year, radically altered the perspective of that 'dreadful vista.' The comment is none the less interesting as showing what a perceptive and well-informed person thought of a touching and curious relationship.

Throughout the eighteen-thirties financial stringency had slightly marred the happiness of Ashley's home life. As early as 1834, in an endeavour to ease the situation a little, he had raised money on an estate in Yorkshire belonging to his family. Though this money was earmarked for the payment of outstanding debts, he scrupulously set some of it aside for charity, sending a donation to 'the Tuam Diocesan Society founded for the education of benighted papists in the most benighted district of Ireland.'

Perhaps because of the perennial shortage of money, perhaps because of the punctual arrival of the yearly baby, Ashley and Minny had made no major excursion since their holiday abroad in 1833–34. In August 1839 husband and wife, taking young Accy with them, set out on a long tour of Northern England and Scotland, travelling by way of Birmingham to Liverpool. Here Ashley was struck by the wealth of the city, and horrified by the Irish slum-dwellers – 'thousands of the dirtiest, worst-clad children I ever saw throng the streets, presenting a strange inconsistency with the signs of luxury all around.' From Liverpool the Ashleys went on to Bowness-on-Windermere. Ashley delighted in the Lake District scenery but grieved to find it impossible to arrange a meeting with his friend Southey, whom he had never yet seen. 'I may never perhaps have an opportunity of seeing him in this world,' he wrote sadly and truthfully since Southey was already in a state of physical and mental decay from which he was not to recover.

In the Border country Ashley and Minny visited Lord Lothian at Newbattle Abbey, saw Roslyn Chapel and Castle, and on Sunday, no other place of worship being available, betook themselves 'to Kirk! absolutely the Presbyterian Kirk.' The service offended Ashley's standard of worship – 'it appeals neither to the senses, the feelings, nor the reason.' He was particularly hardly tried by the extempore prayers, describing the minister as 'labouring under the weight of his own tautologies.' This form of devotion never appealed to Ashley. 'The gift of extempore prayer is the rarest of all gifts; you may have a dozen good speeches for one good prayer,' he was to write on

September 10th 1874, adding, 'I have it not, even for private devotion.' Though Ashley could not approve the Kirk service he was pleased to notice a welcome improvement in Kirk architecture, 'various parts of the edifice being surmounted by a cross,' a novelty in which he hoped he might see 'a proof of the abatement of the bigoted ignorance and furious spirit of the Covenanters, a *practical* advance towards the reasonable services of the Church of England.' Though he was an Evangelical, at this period of his life Ashley was none the less a typical Anglican in his liking for a decent order of Church worship and in his love of ancient and beautiful buildings. On a visit to Dunkeld Cathedral he moralised over the destruction done by the Reformers: 'Perhaps a certain degree of violence toward these splendid and eye-striking edifices which had so often and so long been abused to superstition, was inevitable in the then state of men's minds; perhaps it was not; but in the present day it would be an act of sacrilege to lay hands on these, or any part whatever of these venerable churches.' Later on this journey, after visiting Fountains Abbey, he asked the sensible question, 'Why could we not retain the buildings when we got rid of the inhabitants?'

Beauty of music and ceremonial moved him as deeply as beauty of architecture. 'People would destroy this service and call it a vain ceremonial, a useless form,' he wrote on October 15th after attending Evensong in York Minster. 'Cloaking their real stinginess under utilitarian argument they calculate pounds, shillings and pence and show that, for an organist and a choir, they might have two curates. So they might, and they might have ten times as many for the keep of a dozen gilded footmen, or a third of their usual port wine, or for any imperceptible abatement of luxury, be their rank high, middling, or low. Why not have both?' In 1833 he had compared High Mass in Milan Cathedral very unfavourably with 'the Cathedral service of an Abbey Church, the liturgy, the chanting of the psalms, the singing of the responses in the Communion, all closed with a pious and learned sermon,' adding that in his opinion 'the chastened splendour of this ceremonial leads us, as near as is possible on earth, to the heavenly pattern of the saints above.'

After visiting Edinburgh the Ashleys toured the Highlands, travelling as far north as Inverness. Ashley was favourably impressed by the appearance of the Highlanders, well-clothed and healthy in spite of the squalor of their dwellings, which he described as 'a corporation of pigsties.' He was not to be deceived by the apparent prosperity of the more frequented parts of the country where landlords had erected 'sweet cottages' to catch the eye of the less dis-

cerning tourist. The beauty of the children both in the Lake District
and in Scotland particularly delighted him – 'I feel a sympathy and a
love for the whole infantine world.' He was less pleased with the
Highland farmers who at harvest-time exacted twelve hours' work for
a wage of a shilling or one and three-pence a day and grudged their
workers the ancient biblical right of gleaning in the fields after the
corn had been carried.

As good tourists should, the Ashleys visited the Trossachs and
Loch Lomond. When husband and wife walked together at the head
of the lake, Minny, moved by the melancholy loveliness of the scene,
'talked of "olden time" and people long since dead, and living ones
growing old.' These walks alone with Minny, when he could enjoy
'much interesting conversation with the darling,' were one of the
dearest delights of Ashley's holidays. From the Trossachs they
went on to Glasgow to stay with Sir Archibald Alison, author of a
once-famous *History of Europe.* As president of the Indigent Blind
Visiting Society, Ashley was particularly interested to see Glasgow
Blind School. He also visited engineering shops and calico printing
works and walked with Alison through the worst of the Glasgow
slums, 'crammed with houses, dung-hills and human beings', to see
for himself 'the black pit of misery' in which so many factory workers
were obliged to live.

On their way home the Ashleys stayed at several of the great houses
of Northern England, Chillingham, Alnwick, Ravensworth, Newby,
and Castle Howard, where Ashley reflected solemnly on the nineteen
years which had passed since he had last visited the place, and
finally Chatsworth, 'far too large for use and infinitely too extended
for comfort.' This happy holiday ended with a pleasant stay at
Rowton, home of Ashley's sister Charlotte Lyster and a place specially beloved. On the last page of the diary written during this tour
is a note added forty years later: 'Believe never to have read this
since it was written.

> *"Nessun maggiore dolore*
> *Che ricordarsi del tempo felice*
> *Nella miseria."* '

On their return home the Ashleys found the Cowper family involved in matrimonial dramas. Minny's sister Fanny was being
courted by Lord Jocelyn, a suitable but not very inspiriting *parti.*
Fanny herself was hesitant. Her uncle, Frederick Lamb, now Lord
Beauvale, put the matter in a nutshell. 'As to Fanny, what could I

say to the girl?' he wrote to Lady Cowper on September 17th. 'Billy tells me she wants a hero, someone to look up to and be afraid of, not a smock-faced youth, a second Ashley, in short. I always foresaw this. If Minny can't succeed in showing her the inconvenience of it nobody can. She must follow her destiny.'[11] Fanny was in fact destined to become Lady Jocelyn, though not until 1841.

The other proposed marriage was a more interesting and important affair. Lord Cowper had died two years previously; now his widow announced her intention of marrying her old lover, Lord Palmerston. At first her family was opposed to this middle-aged marriage (Palmerston was fifty-five and Lady Cowper three years younger). Frederick Lamb, however, was not wholly disapproving, being obviously a fatalist where matrimony was concerned. Once again he summed up the situation very neatly: 'The fact is that with her feelings and disposition she can do no otherwise, so it is not worth canvassing the pros and cons; let her take it as Kismet, her destiny, and I hope it may be happy to her.' After a liaison of nearly thirty years' standing his sister must surely be well-enough acquainted with Palmerston to see for herself where her happiness lay – 'whether he suits her or not must be known to her or the Devil's in it.'[12] The Ashleys had endeavoured to remain strictly neutral in this business – 'for our part Minny and I neither persuaded nor dissuaded' – but later they found themselves forced to approve the marriage, if only for the sake of preserving some semblance of propriety – 'the matter had come to such a pass that one of two courses was inevitable, either she should marry him or she should decline the frequency and familiarity of his visits and this she would not do.' Publicly, therefore, Ashley favoured the marriage; privately, he considered it 'a sad, dangerous, and most worldly step,' believing that at the advanced age of fifty-two Lady Cowper, who could scarcely be described as 'a widow indeed,' should have been thinking of her latter end rather than of a second husband.

Palmerston and Lady Cowper were married on December 16th 1839. Of them it might be said in fairy-tale language that they lived happily ever after. Their marriage was the beginning of an oddly successful friendship between Ashley and Palmerston. Hitherto Ashley had not unnaturally disapproved of Palmerston's behaviour. To Minny he had commented quite openly on her mother's liaison; on one occasion, apropos of Lady Cowper's delay in returning to Panshanger, he remarked, 'London has so many charms with its conveniences and Lord Palmerston.' He frequently referred to Palmerston by his nickname of Cupid, 'Cupid will, I am sure be

beaten,' he wrote during the 1835 elections; 'this will indemnify me
for many disappointments.'[13] The change in his attitude seems to
date from Palmerston's marriage. As early as November 1840 he
was writing, 'It is very curious to see me an ardent supporter of
Palmerston,' and very soon he was to learn to like and trust and
approve Palmerston as he liked and trusted no other politician.

Ashley regarded his mother-in-law with mixed feelings. He could
not possibly approve of her, but neither could he avoid liking, in
fact almost loving, her. For her part Lady Palmerston, as she must
now be called, made spasmodic efforts to fall in with her son-in-law's
awkward fancies and foibles. On one occasion she went so far as to
express a desire for a copy of an illustrated edition of the Bible.
Though Ashley suspected that she was more interested in the pictures than in the letterpress, he decided to give her the benefit of
the doubt and to present her with the book – 'but will she read it?'
On other occasions, irritated beyond bearing by his pieties, she
would break into a storm of anger and vituperation. Since she had
enough good sense not to abuse Ashley to his face, poor Minny was
usually the recipient of these attacks. Minny loved both her strict,
believing husband and her lax, agnostic mother; caught between
their two fires she had indeed much to endure.

These outbursts were mercifully rare. On the whole Ashley got on
well enough with his 'dear Mum,' as he would flippantly call her. He
enjoyed what he described as her 'spirit of affection,' so unlike the
chilliness of his own parents, and he was deeply grateful to her for
her unending generosity – 'my mother-in-law has been abundantly
kind towards us.' Her second marriage meant that Palmerston's
splendid house of Broadlands, near Romsey in Hampshire, was
henceforward to be the Ashleys' second home, taking the place of
Panshanger, the Cowper family house. They paid their first visit to
Broadlands immediately after Christmas, 1839. Ashley described
Lady Palmerston as being 'happy as a bride and thoughtless as an
animal,' looking forward to a blissful succession of 'balls, parties,
foreign ministers and foreign ladies, drawing-rooms and royalty,
all thrown together to form a very *macedoine* of future pleasure.'
He wondered rather sourly whether it might be 'in the order of God's
providence to wean her from the world by giving her a surfeit of it.'

Christmas itself had been spent at Wimborne St. Giles for the first
time since Ashley's own marriage. Some time during the year 1839 –
we do not know when or why – Ashley had been reconciled to his
father, and welcomed back to the home he loved so dearly. He
rejoiced to see 'the kids,' as he rather surprisingly called his children,

playing on the lawns, 'giving life and health and joy to the whole scene'; he rejoiced to be given a free hand in the garden, enjoying himself planting and cutting down bushes, but most of all he rejoiced when on Christmas Day, in a holly-decked church thronged by 'a decent, well-behaved, well-dressed congregation,' he knelt beside his father to receive the Sacrament.

Chapter 9

REFUSAL OF OFFICE

The eighteen-forties were to be for Ashley a time of anxiety and disappointment both in public and private life. As the years went by the clouds gathered more and more thickly round his head. Never a cheerful or a carefree character, he became more harried and hurried, more overworked, more depressed, more convinced that every man's hand was against him. His health began to give way; he suffered from physical ills almost certainly caused by mental strain. Though still a comparatively young man – in 1840 he was only thirty-nine – time and again he complained of failing mental and physical powers.

Yet never did he give way, never did he abandon any cause he had at heart, but rather added to his burden of work. His powers of speaking improved so greatly that he became famous as an orator both in Parliament and out of it. In the conduct of affairs he showed a remarkable grasp of principle combined with a vast and accurate knowledge of detail and great skill in the art of man-management. Far from his powers falling into decline they appeared to be actually on the increase. In July 1844 Richard Sheil, a well-known Member of Parliament, thus eulogised Ashley in the House of Commons:

> It is a saying that it does one's eyes good to see some people, and I may observe that it does one's ears good to hear others; one of them is the noble Lord. There is something of a *sursum corda* in all that the noble Lord says. Whatever opinion we may entertain of some of his views, however we may regard certain of his crochets, there is one point on which we all concur – namely, that his conduct is worthy of the highest praise for the motives by which he is actuated, and for the sentiments by which he is inspired.[1]

To few people is it given to hear themselves so described; yet, of the speech which had called forth Sheil's generous praise Ashley had only disappointed criticism to make:

I was singularly feeble and when I came to my winding up, almost silenced. What is the reason hereof? Surely I perceive a decay of intellectual power.

Sheil had in fact accurately voiced the general opinion held of Ashley. The outside world saw him as a praiseworthy, noble figure; only in the pages of his diary did his depression deepen, his persecution-mania become more acute, and the note of hysteria sound more frequently and more shrilly.

In the new year of 1840 the chief topic of interest was the Queen's marriage to Prince Albert. Ashley went curiously astray in his estimate of the Prince's private character, believing that 'he will soon tire of her [the Queen] and betake himself to other women.' To this inaccurate prophecy he added the strange remark, 'he is a literary character, I hear, with a turn for science; these tastes may lead him into very pernicious society.' Though he strongly disapproved of the motion giving the Prince an annuity of £50,000, fearing that the possession of so large a fortune might be a source of undue political power – 'half the income (which he could not legitimately spend) might bribe a party in the House of Commons, determine elections, and subsidise O'Connell' – he decided not to vote against it lest he might be thought ungrateful for past kindness. This prudent abstention did him no good at all with the Queen, who believed that he should have given positive support to the motion, which was defeated in the House of Commons, the annuity being reduced to £30,000. On February 6th, four days before the Royal Wedding, Lady Wilton wrote a letter to the Duke of Wellington:

> Our Gracious Sovereign is very much out of temper! Lord Ashley had not voted on the annuity for Prince Albert. He was one of those who stayed away. H.M. did not care so much about the money as about the precedence.* Lord Ashley was invited to dine with her yesterday . . . He received through Lord Cowper a message from H.M. yesterday afternoon to desire that he would not come to dine, as H.M. could not receive those who opposed her Ministers!![2]

Though Queen Victoria refused to have Ashley to dinner she did not withdraw his invitation to the Royal Wedding, where he was one of the five Tories present, all the other guests being Whigs. 'The sad thing is that the Queen will not be the Queen of England but the

* The Queen wished Prince Albert to be granted precedence next to herself, but owing to strong Tory opposition this idea had to be abandoned.

Queen of a party,' he not surprisingly commented. He owed his own
invitation to the fact that he was the husband of Melbourne's niece.
In quoting the account of the wedding given in the diary, Hodder
wisely omitted the acid little phrase, 'rather a showy pageant but
wanting in enthusiasm and impressiveness.'

Though he was a most loyal subject of the Queen, Ashley never
really approved of Victoria as a person, lamenting her 'small, girlish
mind, wholly unequal to the business of government or even of common
life.' Within a very few years, however, he was on good enough
terms with Prince Albert to write, 'Your Royal Highness desired me
to speak at all times without reserve,' and even to send the Prince a
jeu d'esprit written by the teenage son of Ashley's extremely Protestant
friend, Alexander McCaul, and entitled *The Pilgrimage of Cardinal
Wiseman Undertaken at the Suggestion of Saint Impudence.* He
nevertheless remained suspicious of the Prince's interference in
foreign affairs and mistrustful of what he described as 'Coburg
ambition and conceit.'

An interesting memorandum[3] by the Prince's Private Secretary,
George Anson, dated Panshanger, July 30th 1841, shows that on
one subject at least the Prince and Ashley were in full agreement.
Anson records how, in the course of a long and confidential conversation, Ashley expressed the alarm which he felt in common with
Peel and the Tory party in general at the continual intrigues of the
Queen's old governess, Baroness Lehzen, a trying character and a
source of perpetual trouble – 'they dreaded her violence and in-
temperance, they felt she used her influence against them by misrepresentations and false reports, and thereby unfairly prejudiced
the Queen's mind.' Lehzen's pernicious influence, they believed,
had been to blame for the Bedchamber Crisis, for the sad affair of
Lady Flora Hastings,* and for the estrangement between the Queen
and her mother, the Duchess of Kent. 'They all felt that if they could
remove the evil influence from about the Queen they could depend
entirely upon the honesty of the Queen but they could not feel any
confidence whilst the ready channel for intrigue existed.' Anson
replied that 'the Prince was quite alive to the danger,' a remark
which was something of an understatement, since no one was more
anxious for Lehzen's removal than was Prince Albert. Lehzen knew
well enough that Ashley was her enemy, and she revenged herself on
him by trying to prevent the Queen from reading his speeches.

* In 1839 great scandal had occurred when the Queen declared her belief that the
Duchess of Kent's lady-in-waiting, Lady Flora Hastings, was pregnant. Lady
Flora, who was unmarried, was in fact suffering from cancer.

After the excitement of the Royal Wedding came a renewal of the serious business connected with the Ten Hours Bill. The beginning of 'the hungry forties' was not a good time in which to press on with such a measure. Trade and industry were faced with a severe depression; prices fell; factories closed or worked short time; wages dropped to their lowest level for twenty-five years; and distress was acute. The mill-owners believed that a reduction in children's working hours would dislocate industry still further, whilst the operatives feared that by lessening children's earnings such a reduction would cause yet another drop in the family income. Men's minds were turning to other remedies for their troubles. The workers were becoming more and more enthusiastic in their support of Chartism, whilst the middle classes looked to the repeal of the Corn Laws to provide cheap bread for the starving masses and to bring back prosperity to British trade.

The manner in which Ashley conducted the Ten Hours campaign during these years of frustration and disappointment shows him at his very best. He had by now taken the measure of the House of Commons, whilst the House in its turn was allowing itself to be impressed by his integrity, patience and determination. In theory, 'dogged does it'; in practice, dogged does not often do it except in combination with a certain finesse. Ashley had learnt how to take advantage of every turn of Parliamentary practice and procedure and how to sum up very accurately the tone and temper of the House. In the prevailing climate of opinion he knew that it would be folly to attempt to introduce a new Ten Hours Bill, but that it would be even worse folly to allow the question of factory reform to lapse altogether. He therefore moved for a Select Committee to consider the working of the 1833 Act, and then for a Royal Commission to enquire into the employment of children in industries outside the scope of the existing law. In March he obtained the Select Committee with himself for Chairman, in August the Royal Commission which was to prove so important. Meanwhile, he had taken up another measure concerned with the employment of children, a bill to prohibit the use of 'climbing boys' to sweep chimneys.

The Water Babies, with climbing-boy Tom for hero, has made the pathetic but picturesque figure of the sooty little chimney-sweep a part of nursery folk-lore. The real facts are too ugly to make pleasant reading for children. Many climbing-boys were illegitimate children; Liverpool and other seaports with a large population of prostitutes were fruitful sources of supply. Some children were actually sold by their parents:

My Father sold me while yet my tongue
Could scarcely cry 'Weep! weep! weep! weep!'
So your chimneys I sweep and in soot I sleep.[4]

Others were paupers from the workhouse. It will be remembered how narrowly the young Oliver Twist escaped apprenticeship to a sweep. Forced screaming and sobbing up dark, narrow chimneys, their skin scorched and lacerated, their eyes and throats filled with soot, these small children – Ashley found a child of four-and-a-half working as a climbing-boy – faced suffocation in the blackness of a chimney or perhaps a slow and painful death from cancer of the scrotum, the climbing-boys' occupational disease. Of all unhappy child-workers these were perhaps the most ill-used and forlorn.

The first person to call attention to this scandal had been Jonas Hanway, inventor of the umbrella. In 1788 an act was passed regulating the terms of apprenticeship for climbing-boys; in 1834 a more stringent act specified the measurements required in building new chimneys and forbade the employment of children under ten years of age. Neither of these acts proved effectual. In 1840 a bill was brought in entirely prohibiting the use of climbing-boys, a measure warmly supported by Ashley both in the House of Commons and out of it. In this matter of the climbing-boys he was perturbed to find himself opposed by Conservatives and Evangelicals but supported by Radicals and men whom he regarded as worldlings. The bill passed the House of Commons, only to run into difficulties with the Lords. 'Anxious, very anxious, about my sweeps,' Ashley wrote on July 4th; 'the Conservative (!) Peers threaten a fierce opposition.' The bill nevertheless passed the House of Lords and became law, only to remain in many places a dead letter. Although in London the use of climbing-boys ceased completely, in other districts magistrates continued to turn a blind eye to the practice. In 1847 a terrible case occurred in Manchester where a little seven-year-old boy was forced up a hot flue, pulled out half-suffocated, and then cruelly beaten. The child later died in convulsions. This and other similar cases led to the foundation of the Climbing-Boys' Society, with Ashley for Chairman, pledged to the total abolition of the scandal. In 1851, 1853 and 1855 he introduced Chimney Sweeps' bills into Parliament, but in spite of the shocking evidence given before a Select Committee all these bills were defeated. In 1864 he succeeded in passing through both Houses yet another act to forbid the use of climbing-boys; but, like all its predecessors, this measure remained almost wholly ineffectual. In 1872 Christopher Drummond, aged seven, died in a flue in Washington Hall, County Durham. 'A death has given me the power once more to appeal to the public,' Shaftesbury wrote in his diary. Three more years had to pass and another child to die in a flue at Fulbourne Asylum near Cambridge before he could finally win deliverance for the climbing-boys. In 1875 he introduced a bill which prescribed the annual licensing of chimney-sweeps, once again prohibited the use of climbing-boys, and gave the enforcement of the law into the hands of the police, a measure which proved powerful enough finally to put an end to the scandal.

It is difficult to explain the protracted and determined opposition to this obviously necessary and humane reform. Climbing-boys did not work far from the eyes of the general public in factories or coal-mines; their appalling misery must have been apparent to everyone whose chimneys needed sweeping. Adequate machines for sweeping chimneys had been available as early as 1856 and their use approved by many insurance companies. To adapt old chimneys to the use of these brushes was not a costly business; 'there is not one house in a thousand,' Ashley declared, 'where ten pounds would be required to make the use of climbing-boys altogether unnecessary.' Women were the most bitter opponents of any attempt to prohibit the use of climbing-boys; the well-known reluctance of the British housewife to adopt new ways and methods must be held accountable for the quite unnecessary terror, torture, and misery of these unhappy little children.

In his work for the climbing-boys Ashley interested himself in individual cases as he was never able to do with the factory children. Personal contacts were very important to him, a fact which perhaps explains a certain air of remoteness about his approach to the Ten Hours question. He could do no personal acts of kindness to factory children who lived and worked in a distant part of the country which he was always to find strange and slightly uncongenial. Climbing-boys, on the contrary, were on his very doorstep; one little chimney-sweep he discovered living just behind his own house in Brook Street. He went to great pains to rescue this child and to send him to 'the Union School at Norwood Hill, where, under God's blessing and special merciful grace, he will be trained in the knowledge and love and faith of our common Saviour.' That phrase may read like a pious commonplace but in it lies the secret of the driving power behind all Ashley's efforts on behalf of the poor and the oppressed. He was shocked that the climbing-boys should be beaten, starved, and exposed to a horrid death, but he was still more shocked that they should grow up without the knowledge of the love of God and the hope of Heaven. His attitude is puzzling, maybe inexplicable, to a generation incredulous of immortality and determinedly humanitarian in outlook, but it is something which cannot be ignored or dismissed as historically irrelevant. In his own mind he knew – or thought he knew – that he was fighting God's battles; and the knowledge gave him a terrible strength.

Ashley's concern for souls shows his religion at its best and highest; his waspish remarks about Melbourne's ecclesiastical appointments – 'when will it please God to relieve the Church from this hateful oppressor and prostitutor of her sacred possessions?' – illustrate its less attractive aspects. When Melbourne very properly appointed to the see of St. David's the Cambridge scholar Connop Thirlwall, according to Professor Chadwick 'the ablest academic mind on the bench of bishops,'[5] Ashley, who had very little use for academically-minded bishops, fulminated against this 'noisy, turbulent, clever man with much learning and no principles.'

This autumn of 1840 Ashley was particularly preoccupied with a question which was to most people a purely political issue but to him a matter of great religious importance. As Professor Chadwick writes, 'Ashley's mind united the practical with the prophetic in a fascinating harmony.'[6] So now, when anxious to promote Jewish colonisation in Palestine, though his own thoughts were running on the fulfilment of prophecy and the hastening of the Second Advent, he was shrewd enough to recognise that Palmerston as Foreign Secretary cared for none of these things and to put before him a case based on solid practical arguments. Two years previously he had sent Palmerston 'a paper drawn up to exhibit the capabilities of the soil of Palestine and the likelihood of a beneficial commerce between that country and our own.'[7] In this paper he had pointed out that the fertility of the soil of Palestine had been attested by many authorities and denied only by Voltaire, 'an author of very little authority except for witticisms either blasphemous or obscene.' In particular, the cultivation of cotton would be a great benefit to the British cotton industry, which might thus become 'free and independent of the Yankees and slave labour.' Distance from England was short and communications comparatively good; only labour was lacking and that could best be supplied by Jewish immigrants. And if the commercial profit would be great the political gain would also be considerable. By sponsoring Jewish settlement in Palestine Britain would be dealing a blow to Russian influence in the Near East. Napoleon himself had seen the importance of the Jewish question and had done his best to win the support of the Jewish people;

'what he attempted for the injury of England and mankind, you may attempt for our benefit and human happiness.'

Now Ashley took up the subject once more. On September 25th 1840 he wrote Palmerston a second letter as practical as the first, making no mention of his real motives in urging support for a scheme of Jewish colonisation.[8] 'These vast regions,' he pointed out, 'are now nearly desolate; every year the produce of them becomes less, because the hands that till them become fewer. As a source of revenue they are nearly worthless, compared at least with the riches that industry might force from them. They require both capital and labour.' His remedy was the establishment of a stable government in Palestine, guaranteed by the great powers, and recognising the equality of Jew and Mahomedan before the law. The result would be an influx of industrious Jews who would quickly develop the land's potential riches – 'Long ages of suffering have trained their people to habits of endurance and self-denial; they would joyfully exhibit these in the service and settlement of their ancient country.'

It would be a mistake to read this letter as a remarkably accurate prophecy of the appearance of modern Israel, tempting though it may be to do so. Ashley was no Zionist; he never proposed the establishment of a Jewish sovereign state in Palestine. What he sought to promote was a settlement of Jews living under British protection but subjects of the Turkish Empire – 'they will submit to the existing form of government, they will acknowledge the present appropriation of the soil in the hands of its actual possessors, being content to obtain an interest in its produce by the legitimate means of rent or purchase.'

For the present nothing came of these schemes. The situation in the Near East was extremely confused and disturbed. The Egyptian Pasha Mehemet Ali and the Sultan of Turkey struggled for supremacy; the great powers were involved in this crisis; France and England found themselves dangerously near to a serious quarrel; and not all his Cabinet colleagues agreed with Palmerston's handling of the situation. On November 9th Ashley sent him yet another letter and with it something to cheer his spirits:

I have sent you a dozen of strong beer, brewed at St. Giles, for your own especial drinking. It is too good for any strangers who may dine at your house.

Taken in moderation, it will give you enormous pluck, and enable you to stand firm against Mehemet Ali, and every Frenchman, whether they be found in Paris or in the Cabinet.[9]

In December came news that Richard Oastler had been arrested
for debt at the instance of his employer, Thomas Thornhill, and
committed to the Fleet prison. This misfortune did not put an end
to his work for the Ten Hours campaign; three weeks after his arrest
he issued the first number of an eight-page paper *The Fleet Papers*,
in which he championed the cause of the factory children, attacked
the new Poor Law, and expounded his naïve philosophy of 'the
Altar, the Throne, and the Cottage.' Ashley, who had broken with
Oastler in 1836 after he had openly incited the workers to sabotage,
visited him in the Fleet and sent him various presents.

The Select Committee on the working of the 1833 Factory Act
reported in February 1841. Both the report itself and the evidence
heard before the Committee went to show that the Act had done
much to improve conditions; it was nevertheless so badly framed as
to be at one and the same time a burden on the mill-owners and an
insufficient protection to the child-workers. Richard Birley, a Manchester mill-owner, declared 'the Act is so imperfect that it is difficult
to tell where we stand.' The redoubtable Henry Ashworth insisted
that with the best will in the world no mill-owner could avoid small
but frequent violations of the law. He took advantage of his position
as a witness to assert his belief that the Committee was altogether
on the wrong track and that the one thing which could really help
the workers was the repeal of the Corn Laws – 'Give the operatives
labour and cheap food and let them look after themselves.' He had
himself been charged with a technical offence against the Act and
had refused to pay the two-pound fine imposed on him. The voice
of all true Lancashiremen, impatient of regulation and fiercely
independent, sounds clearly in the very last sentence of his evidence:
'Legally speaking I consider myself not guilty and morally speaking
I am answerable to myself alone.'

Where the age-limit clause was concerned it had been found that
it was all too easy to falsify or fake a doctor's certificate. The education clause had also proved easy to circumvent; such schooling as
was provided had often been of the poorest quality, and proper
time off had not been given. Tired children would find themselves
doing lessons from half-past seven to half-past nine at night after
working all day in the factory, or rising at five in the morning to
attend school before going to work. Another fault in the Act was the
smallness of the penalties it imposed. In districts where the magistrates favoured the mill-owners fines might even be as low as five
shillings; a joke current in Rochdale told of mill-owners with 'the
sovereign remedy' ready in their pockets.

A bill remedying these defects in the previous measure appeared reasonably sure of a safe passage through Parliament, more especially as it was to be sponsored by the Whig Government, which had always shown itself more sympathetic to factory legislation than had Ashley's own Tory party. He was most anxious to extend the scope of this Amending Bill to include children employed in the silk and lace industries, but he knew that any such clause might encounter opposition strong enough to endanger the bill as a whole. He therefore asked the Government to bring in two bills, the one to amend the existing Act, the other to deal with children employed in these two industries. Both bills were introduced into the House of Commons; but once again Ashley was to be disappointed. In May 1841 the Whigs were defeated on a vote of confidence; a dissolution of Parliament followed; and of necessity both bills were indefinitely suspended.

In the General Election which followed Lord Jocelyn, now married to Minny's sister, Fanny, stood as Tory candidate at Leeds. Ashley was most anxious for his success, less because he thought Jocelyn would be a valuable addition to the House of Commons than because 'it will save him from temptation and mischief to be in Parliament and to have plenty of occupation.' Lady Fanny, his wife, incurred the Queen's wrath by forsaking the Whig principles in which she had been bred and embracing the political views of her Tory husband. Meeting Palmerston at a Drawing-Room the Queen complained that Fanny, as a Lady-in-waiting, ought to have given more thought to the feelings of her Royal mistress – 'had she tried she might certainly have made him into a Whig.' Ashley's comment on the Queen's attitude is harsh, but not undeservedly so:

What a monstrous thing to hear the Queen of three realms speaking and acting in a more party sense than any agent at a contested election! . . . I much fear that, in her total ignorance of the country and the constitution, her natural violence, false courage, her extreme and ungovernable wilfulness, she will betray a disposition and a conduct which, while they do no harm to us [the Tories] will be injurious to herself and to the Crown.

At the beginning of June 1841 Ashley found himself bidden to Windsor to make one of the Royal house-party for Ascot races. The Queen was 'in a high taking' to find that many of her guests were Tories who were about to fight contested elections against her beloved Whigs. Ashley himself was uneasy in his conscience at the prospect of attending a race meeting – 'I am sorry for it but I cannot refuse to go there; I am the Queen's guest and I cannot think it right to put upon my sovereign such a rebuke as would be conveyed by my declining to accompany her.' So to the races he duly went, and found them 'a dull affair and, I hope, harmless.'

Although Jocelyn failed to win the Leeds seat at the election the Tories triumphed in the West Riding, thanks in great part to the power of Ashley's name and fame. This was perhaps surprising because he was almost unknown personally in that district. In August of the same year, 1841, he made what appears to have been his first tour* of the industrial North, visiting Manchester, and addressing successful meetings at Bolton, Ashton, Huddersfield and Leeds. He was delighted by the reception he received from the factory workers:

> What a sin it is to be ignorant of the sterling merit and value of these poor men! A few words of kindness are as effectual with them as 50,000 soldiers on a French population. Never have I met with such respect and affection as on this journey. I see and feel the truth of Oastler's observation, 'they are neither infidel nor Jacobin; they love the monarchy and they love religion'. It is most [illegible] that they have been denied the blessings of the one and excluded from the benefits of the other.

He described the clergy of the industrial towns as 'cowed by capital and power,' an accusation which he himself partially disproved when he recorded offers of help from parsons in Leeds and Huddersfield, and from two further afield, a Mr. Spark Byers and the better-known Archdeacon Robert Wilberforce of the East Riding, a notable Tractarian and brother to Bishop Samuel Wilberforce, who was later to be one of Ashley's most doughty opponents.

In the course of the West Riding elections Ashley had been asked by Mark Crabtree, spokesman for the Yorkshire operatives, whether, if the Tories were successful and he were offered a place in the Government, he would continue with his campaign for a Ten Hours Bill.

---

* Hodder quotes Shaftesbury as saying in 1879 that he was shown a collection of crippled and deformed factory children when he visited Bradford *in 1838.* I can find no other reference to a Northern tour in that year. The Hammonds include one under 1838 in their 'List of Dates' but make no mention of it otherwise. It seems probable that speaking as an old man Shaftesbury made a slip as to the date and substituted 1838 for 1841. He had of course visited Liverpool and he had seen the silk mills at Macclesfield, but neither of these places can properly be called the industrial North. Since no diaries exist for the first nine months of 1838 it is difficult to be certain of his movements during that year.

Ashley's reply was unequivocal: 'I will never place myself in any situation where I shall not be as free as air to do everything that I may believe to be conducive to the happiness, comfort, and welfare of that portion of the working classes who have so long and so confidingly entrusted to me the care of their hopes and interests.'[10] He recognised now, as he had not recognised in 1839, that his first concern must be the leadership of the Ten Hours campaign and that he must not take office if such a step might hinder him in that task. Nevertheless, when the election resulted in the return of the Tories to power with Peel as Prime Minister, Ashley found himself a prey to longings which he believed he had long ago subdued. The old Adam of ambition was not dead in him. On February 13th 1841 he had written, 'As for office, I do not greatly fancy it; I could not submit to be controlled in all my peculiar views and independent actions; their restraint would hardly be compensated by the means of usefulness that high office presents, certainly not by the drudgery and inefficiency of an inferior post.' On August 27th he made another and more explicit entry:

> The master-spinners have held a meeting in Manchester and have resolved to oppose any bill that I can bring in. This determines much of my course. I knew what *I* should do before; now I know what Peel will do; he will succumb to the capitalists and reject my factory bill. No human power therefore shall induce me to take office.

Still, however, he yearned for that very thing; he could not bring himself to abandon all his hopes of a political career. When Peel sent for him on August 30th he supposed that he was about to be asked to take a Cabinet office and went prepared to make the great renunciation; instead, he found himself offered what he had already scorned and accepted only under the most powerful pressure, a post in the Royal Household.

It is a little difficult to see why Peel should have made this obviously unacceptable offer. Ashley himself pointed out that the arguments which influenced him two years previously no longer held good – 'The Court was no longer the same, the Queen was two years older, had a child, and a husband to take care of her.' He described the suggestion of a Court post as 'a plain, cruel and unnecessary insult,' and wrote on September 1st that 'it would have been far more becoming, and indeed, more kind, to have left me unnoticed altogether.' His standing in the House of Commons and with the nation at large fully entitled him to expect high office in any Tory government; nevertheless, Peel had very good reasons for not wishing to include him in the administration. The two men were antipathetic. Peel had a natural distaste for fanaticism, and of necessity he would find such a fanatic as Ashley a difficult and uncongenial colleague. In February Ashley had written that a speech of Peel's betrayed 'a latitudinarian spirit,' adding the comment, 'but such is the man; he is ever seeking the praise of his fellows, not the truth of principles.' For his part, Peel rather aptly described Ashley as 'impracticable.'*

Ashley had done nothing to improve matters by a letter he had written to Peel on July 24th. A statesman about to become Prime Minister for the second time would hardly appreciate a reminder from a junior colleague that 'you are now about to be summoned to the highest and most responsible of all earthly positions.' Ashley lectured Peel as the Victorian father of popular caricature might lecture a schoolboy son:

In these days of speciousness, of peril and perplexity, there is nothing to guide you through the false shoals on every side of your course but a vigorous and dauntless faith which, disregarding the praise of men, and having a single eye to the glory of God, shall seek none but that which comes from Him alone.

Ashley ends by declaring, 'As for myself, let me say that, whether you should be destined, in God's wisdom, to success or defeat, to power or to retirement, I shall ever desire your real honour and your real happiness, both in time and in eternity.'[11]

One of the most curious points about this lamentably pompous letter is the omission of any mention of factory legislation – 'My purpose is simply to point out to you the consequences which must flow from the elevation to high ecclesiastical offices of persons distinguished for the new opinions,' that is to say the Tractarians. Peel had no desire to become entangled in Church quarrels, and he knew very well that a government which had Ashley among its members could not hope to steer clear of such prickly matters.

However, in spite of these temperamental differences between the two men, Peel now urged Ashley to accept the proffered post. Whether, as Ashley himself believed, 'he wanted my name and nothing but my name'; whether, seeing the growing friendship between Ashley and Palmerston, Peel feared that, unless given office, this

* Practicable = that can be used. (*O.E.D.*)

promising Tory might defect to the Whigs; or whether he genuinely appreciated Ashley's gifts of intellect and character and wished to make use of them in the new administration, it is impossible now to say. Professor Gash takes for granted that the offer was honestly intended. Although Ashley described Peel as 'totally disregarding and treating as unworthy of mention, my difficulties on the score of the factory bill,' Peel was in fact well aware of that difficulty, and, according to Gash, suggested a Court post as a means of circumventing it. Acceptance of political office would have tied Ashley to party commitments, but a position in the Household might leave him more free to take his own line in this matter. 'Peel argued that Ashley could reserve his position on a question which in any case could not come up until the spring, and he emphasised the difference between a Court and a political appointment.'[12]

If Peel's offer had not been meant seriously it is difficult to see why he should have pressed it with such persistence, even calling in Goulburn, the new Chancellor of the Exchequer, to help persuade Ashley into acceptance. On the second day of interviews and conversations he went so far as to say, 'If I believed you preferred *civil* office I should of course make arrangements to that end.' But if he had really wished for Ashley's support he had gone the very worst way about obtaining it. Understandably enough, Ashley had been deeply offended by the offer of a Court post, a position wholly unacceptable to any rising politician – 'I cannot but feel indignation when I remember the cool, careless way in which Peel endeavoured to shelve me on the establishment of the Palace, not an apology, not a regret, not a civil word!' In consequence he had made up his mind that in no circumstances could he or would he accept any office whatsoever. He believed that Peel had not been sincere in his belated suggestion of a political post – 'When he saw I was obstinate he purchased a little power of flourish by appearing to propose what, it was evident, I could not accept.'

Ashley's pride had been badly wounded; but the pain had taught him a lesson. The cause of the factory workers must not merely come first with him; it must be an all-important commitment, overriding all other concerns, except, of course, religious ones. Peel's derisory offer marks the real turning-point in Ashley's career; he had made up his mind, or rather, Peel had made it up for him. Finding that high office was denied him he determined to turn his eyes away from the prospect of a career in politics, though at times he could not help casting lingering, backward glances in the direction of that attractive might-have-been. Maybe he would have been strong-minded enough

to make the same sacrifice had Peel offered him, say, the Foreign
Secretaryship; as events turned out, Peel's attitude served to confirm him in his already half-formed resolution to devote himself
entirely and without reserve to the cause of the poor and helpless.
From now onwards he was to regard himself as a dedicated man.
Never again was he seriously to consider taking office, though it was
to be offered to him several times. This renunciation did not mean that
he lost his interest in politics. To the very end his diaries keep their
distinctively political flavour; they reflect the interests of a statesman
and politician rather than those of a philanthropist and social reformer. The measure of his continuing interest is the measure of his
sacrifice.

Chapter 10

CHILDREN IN COAL MINES

Eighteen forty-one had been a year of disappointed hopes. The fall of the Whig Government had meant the abandonment of both factory bills; the Chimney Sweeps' Act, as amended by the House of Lords, was proving an ineffectual measure; Peel had dashed Ashley's hopes of high office to the ground. Private anxieties followed on political disappointments. In October Edward Bickersteth suffered a paralytic stroke – 'I know nothing that would give me greater pain than his incapacity or removal,' Ashley wrote apprehensively. At home he was troubled by vague, indefinite fears for two of his children. For some time he had suspected that all was not entirely as he would have wished with the beloved Accy; on November 26th he wrote half-jestingly but in a tone of alarm, 'my boy Accy dreams sadly of hunting; I fear he will imitate Esau rather than Jacob.' Still more ominous was a small, apparently trivial entry made a few months earlier, 'Darling Maurice not very well.'

Against these troubles and disappointments could be set one achievement which Ashley himself regarded as being of immense importance. Today the affair of the Jerusalem bishopric is remembered if it is remembered at all, because of a single sentence in Newman's *Apologia Pro Vita Sua*, 'This was the third blow which finally shattered my faith in the Anglican Church.'[1] 'All things are now wonderful,' Ashley wrote of the event which proved so fatal to Newman's Anglicanism; he himself believed that the establishment of a Protestant bishopric in Jerusalem was a portent of the Second Coming of Christ.

Other people as well as Newman saw the matter rather differently. The tangled political situation in the Near East had much to do with the King of Prussia's scheme to appoint a bishop in Jerusalem with jurisdiction over all Protestants. France's position as protector of the Roman Catholics and Russia's as protector of the Orthodox gave these powers a certain standing; now the King of Prussia, wishing to obtain a comparable political advantage, planned to pose as protector of the Protestants, few in number though they were.

Ashley was innocently blind to this side of the question. He believed that the scheming King Frederick William IV was 'an unequalled sovereign' who must be honoured as 'an especial instrument of God's surpassing wisdom and mercy.' It was proposed that the bishopric should be an Anglo-Prussian affair, the bishop to be consecrated by the English bishops and nominated alternately by the sovereign of England and the sovereign of Prussia. Though his position seems to have been an entirely unofficial one, Ashley was the person most concerned with the negotiations on the English side whilst his friend the Chevalier de Bunsen acted as special envoy of the King of Prussia. In July the British Government, together with the Archbishop of Canterbury and the Bishop of London as spokesmen for the Anglican Church, agreed to accept Bunsen's proposals. Ashley's excitement and delight knew no bounds. The long-suffering Minny was beginning to be more than a little bored by the Jerusalem bishopric. She realised that her husband was so carried away by his enthusiasm as to be in danger of making a public fool of himself. Her patience snapped. 'You din this perpetually in my ears,' she protested, 'and it sets my back up against it, always talking of "how wonderful, how wonderful!" ' Ashley's exuberance collapsed like a pricked balloon at this unexpected attack. 'Never till now have I recorded words so painful,' he moaned in his diary. Next day, when Minny took back her wounding remarks, all was once more sweetness and light; this, however, was not to be the only occasion when her pagan Lamb blood was to move her to rebellion against her husband's more extreme Evangelical extravagances.

The change of Government after the Election meant that Palmerston's place at the Foreign Office was taken by Lord Aberdeen, of whom Ashley wrote, 'he has no more *religion* than Palmerston and far less wit, experience, generosity, and British feeling.' Aberdeen proved less than lukewarm in his support of the Jerusalem bishopric, and he succeeded in bringing Archbishop Howley round to his point of view. 'Truly so sacred a work could not proceed without the opposition of the Devil,' Ashley wrote on October 5th. All, however, went well; Ashley himself selected for bishop a converted Jew of Prussian nationality called Michael Alexander, Professor of Hebrew at King's College, London. Alexander was consecrated on November 7th and travelled out to Palestine in a British man-of-war rather unsuitably named H.M.S. *Devastation.*

In the midst of all these preoccupations Ashley found time to

record his delight when 'my four blessed boys' brought a contribution from their pocket-money for the new bishopric. Little Maurice
and Edy could only produce three-farthings apiece, 'but it was all
they had.' This same day, November 20th, Ashley heard from Bunsen
that Queen Victoria had invited King Frederick William to be
godfather to the Prince of Wales (born November 9th) and to attend
the christening at Windsor. Immediately Ashley seized up his pen
and wrote Bunsen a letter urging him to see that the King accepted
this 'clearly providential' invitation:

> If the King of Prussia does not come over in person he will commit
> the greatest [illegible] of his life. Never have I known such a
> wonderful Providence; such an event at this moment, the union
> of the Churches, the friendship of the Crowns, the religious sym-
> pathies of the Protestant Powers, and all this effected over a
> combined operation for the temporal and eternal welfare of the
> People of God!
> If His Majesty desire the hearty alliance and real affections of
> *this* country, let him come – he will do more by his presence to
> curb France, to nullify the Pope and to exalt Prussia than by a
> course of diplomacy for fifty years. The effect in Europe will be
> prodigious, *that* you can answer for; the effect in England will be
> greater, *that* I can answer for.
> This act of Prince Albert's will sink deep (God bless the Queen)
> into the hearts of this Kingdom; let the Sovereign of Prussia aid
> our cause and his own, by seizing the occasion that God has given
> him of rooting immovably a political and religious confederacy
> that will defy all the malignity of Sin, Satan, and Sedition through-
> out the whole world. Let him come; in God's name pray him to
> come – he *must not*, he *dare not* throw away such an opportunity.
>
> God bless you,
> Ashley

He must come
Take care that Peel do not step in with his timidity and narrowness.[2]

The King of Prussia duly arrived, to be greeted enthusiastically
by the Eton boys who were given a holiday on his account. His visit,
however, did not have quite the earth-shaking results that Ashley
had predicted. As for the Jerusalem bishopric which he had welcomed
with such enthusiasm – 'a native Hebrew appointed, under God,

to revive the episcopate of St. James and carry back to the Holy
City the truths and blessings that we Gentiles have received from it' –
it was to drag on a precarious existence for forty-eight years, fizzling
out slowly like a damp squib.

Ashley had rejoiced the more in Bishop Alexander's appointment
because it was a slap in the face for the Tractarians – 'This bishopric
strikes at many things, at Popery and Puseyism.' The more extreme
men among the Tractarians, who shared Newman's view of Lutherism
and Calvinism as 'heresies repugnant to scripture,' had deplored
this scheme 'to admit maintainers of heresy to communion, without
formal renunciation of their errors.'³ Others, whilst cordially dis-
liking both Lutherism and Calvinism, yet rejoiced to see the Anglican
Church established in the Holy City. Among these was Gladstone,
whose support of the scheme won him unusual praise from Ashley.
'This is delightful,' he wrote of a dinner given by Bunsen when
Gladstone 'stripped himself of part of his Puseyite garments' and
proposed Bishop Alexander's health; 'for he is a good man, and a
clever man, and an industrious man.'

Pusey himself had been of the same opinion as Gladstone so that
in this matter of the Jerusalem bishopric he had not come into collision with Ashley. Early in 1842 the cousins were to clash head on over
the question of Keble's successor as Professor of Poetry at Oxford.
(Even today elections to this Chair can and do degenerate into acrimonious struggles decided on grounds which have nothing to do with
poetry.) Ashley's fellow Harrovian, Isaac Williams, was put forward
by the President and Fellows of his own College, Trinity. A quiet,
retiring man, and a moderately competent minor poet, Williams
would have been generally acceptable had it not been for his religious
views, which were in fact anything but extreme. Disapproving of
Newman, he belonged to the moderate group known as 'the Bisley
School,' which centred round Keble's brother Thomas, but he was
none the less a Tractarian and author of a tract with the slightly
unfortunate title, *Reserve in Communicating Religious Knowledge*.
Of this Ashley wrote, 'There is no power on earth that shall induce
me to assist in elevating the writer of that paper to the position of a
public teacher.'⁴ Meanwhile, the anti-Tractarians put forward as
rival candidate an obscure individual called James Garbett, justifying their action on purely party grounds – 'The election of Mr.
Williams would undoubtedly be represented as a decision of Convocation in favour of his party; and the resident members of our
college are unanimous in thinking that this would be a serious evil,
as well as highly discreditable to the University.'⁵

The part which he played in the ensuing tussle does Ashley's reputation no good at all. Pusey made the mistake of sending to all members of Convocation,* including, of course, Ashley, a letter which, though moderate enough in tone, yet cast aspersions on the motives of Garbett's supporters. 'I will not conceal from you,' Ashley wrote in reply, 'that if I do nothing against you it is because I have not the power. I have never had much predilection for the peculiar doctrines of the party to which Mr. Williams belongs; but their late opposition to the appointment of the Bishop of Jerusalem has made me abhor their opinions as much in practice as I before feared them in speculation.'[6]

Pusey's answer was notably different in tone. 'You have not probably grey hairs, as I have,' his letter begins, 'nor have you had sorrows like me,† and both ought to soften your mind; yet I could wish that without them your language could be a little softened. I often used to think it stronger than you meant, and you are, doubtless, all the while milder and more loving than one's self.'[7] He goes on to point out that there was more agreement between them than Ashley supposed. The last paragraph reads, 'Try to think more mildly of us; love us more; perhaps you will understand us better; pray for us, as I do daily for you.' Ashley's reply was uncompromising in the fierceness of its attack on the tenets of 'Puseyism,' but at least it contained one kind, cousinly sentence, 'I wish we were one; it is sad that we differ, but let not that difference amount to enmity.'[8]

Ashley followed his letter of protest to Pusey with a letter to Roundell Palmer, afterwards Lord Selborne, a leading Tractarian layman. In it he declared 'I will not consent to give my support, however humble, towards the recognition of exoteric and esoteric doctrines in the Church of England, to obscure the perspicuity of the Gospel by the philosophy of paganism, and to make the places set apart for the ministrations of the preacher, whose duties must mainly be among the poor, the wayfaring, and the simple, as mystic and incomprehensible as the grove of Eleusis.'[9]

Pusey's biographer, Dean Liddon, merely remarks, 'Mr. Palmer's reply was worthy of the occasion.' He might fairly have described it as spirited.[10] Roundell Palmer flatly denied every imputation Ashley had made against Williams' teaching, castigating especially the resounding sentence about the grove of Eleusis; in fact, he went very near to calling Ashley a liar. This was fair enough, since, to all

---

* Convocation at Oxford included all Masters of Arts, whether resident in the University or not.

† Pusey's wife had died in 1839; his only son was an incurable invalid.

intents and purposes, Ashley had called Williams a pagan. Strange
though it may seem today, a hundred and thirty years ago these
asperities were the usual small change of religious controversy;
neither Ashley nor Palmer had overstepped the recognised bounds of
politeness. Where Ashley sinned both against courtesy and good
sense was in his fierce opposition to a compromise solution put
forward by a number of members of Convocation, including several
bishops and such influential laymen as Gladstone and Lord Devon.
These would-be peace-makers proposed that both Williams and Garbett should be asked to withdraw in favour of a candidate acceptable
to all parties. As chairman of Garbett's committee Ashley fought
tooth and nail against this sensible suggestion and succeeded in
securing its rejection. Finding that he stood little chance of success,
Williams withdrew his candidature, leaving the field to Garbett. Not
merely did Ashley rejoice with unseemly glee over a victory which he
described as 'a signal mercy,' but he thanked God especially 'that I
resisted the compromise though not a few were disposed to it.'

Only one small touch of kindliness and good manners relieved the
general ill-temper and rudeness of this foolish squabble. Although
it was a book highly valued by many Evangelicals Ashley had little
use for John Keble's *Christian Year*, describing its contents as
'sundry poems of admitted talent but disputed theology.'[11] In a
letter to the press he now made the mistake of describing Keble as
'author and editor' of a book of religious verse known as *Lyra
Apostolica*. Keble wrote a courteous letter correcting this error. He
very gently rebuked Ashley for dragging the affair into the newspapers, and hinted that the reserve referred to in the title of Williams'
tract might not be an altogether undesirable quality:

> Perhaps your lordship will agree with me in thinking that it would
> be best for all parties and for the truth itself, if we could avoid
> bringing names and private matters before the public especially
> in the newspapers. Should this remark appear too free your lord-
> ship will please to consider that . . . it comes from an elderly man
> and a clergyman, and from one who not only sees but feels every
> day how much unintentional harm is done by want of reserve
> in all sorts of statements.[12]

In his reply Ashley wrote 'I am delighted to have heard from you,'
and reminded Keble of a long-ago encounter:

> Perhaps you have forgotten what I well recollect, that you were

one of the examining masters when I took my degree some eighteen or nineteen years ago. Your amiable and gentlemanlike demeanour then made an impression on my mind which has never been effaced.[13]

Though usually so ready for argument, Ashley now declared, 'I show unwillingness to pass in review the various points on which I might presume to differ from you; we should neither of us gain anything by conviction, we might lose something by irritation.' He ended his letter with the sentence, 'I cannot take leave of you without adding that I shall always think of you with respect not unmingled with affection.'

On January 24th 1842 Ashley wrote in his diary, 'God has blessed us with a victory over the Puseyite party in the retirement of Mr. Williams'; he also noted that he had twice written to Peel to ask for a definite decision on the question of government support for a new factory bill. The gist of Peel's reply to these letters was contained in a single sentence, 'I am not prepared to pledge myself, or other members of the Government to the support of a bill limiting the hours of labour to ten for all persons between the ages of ten and twenty-one.'[14] He nevertheless informed Ashley that the Government had under consideration a bill for regulating hours and promoting the education of factory children. An acrimonious correspondence followed, which Peel forwarded to the Home Secretary, Sir James Graham, with the acid comment, 'there are limits to coaxing a gentleman who is angry with everybody because he has embarrassed himself.'[15]

On February 2nd 1842 Ashley wrote to the Short Time Committees of Cheshire, Lancashire and Yorkshire to inform them of Peel's attitude towards the Ten Hours Bill:

It is with the deepest regret that I am obliged to announce to you that Sir Robert Peel has signified his opposition* to the Ten Hours Bill; and I conclude, therefore, as you will conclude, that his reply must be taken as the reply of the whole Government in this important question.

Though painfully disappointed, I am not disheartened, nor am I at a loss either what course to take, or what advice to give. I

---

* 'This was not strictly true since Peel had merely said that he could not support it. But the distinction was not one which Ashley in his emotional frame of mind was ready to appreciate.' (Gash, op. cit., p. 331.) So fine a distinction was not likely to be better appreciated by the operatives than by Ashley.

shall persevere unto my last hour, and so must you; we must exhaust every legitimate means that the Constitution affords, in petitions to Parliament, in public meetings, and in friendly conferences with your employers; but you must infringe no law, and offend no proprieties; we must all work together as sensible men, who will one day give an account of their motives and actions; if this course is approved, no consideration shall detach me from your cause; if not, you must elect another advocate.

I know that, in resolving on this step, I exclude myself altogether from the tenure of office; I rejoice in the sacrifice, happy to devote the remainder of my days, be they many or be they few, as God in His wisdom shall determine, to an effort, however laborious, to ameliorate your moral and social condition.[16]

In spite of these brave words Ashley was at this time very near to despair. He was passing through one of his phases of emotional instability, at one moment down in the depths, 'particularly dejected' and overcome by 'an unusual conviction of incompetency,' then, a day or so later, waking up in inexplicable high spirits with 'a strong feeling that all will go well.' He was particularly upset by a malicious leading article which appeared in the *Morning Post* for February 4th. Criticising Ashley's letter to the Short Time Committees, the writer complained, 'He anxiously directs attention to his own great virtue in excluding himself from office,' and added, 'We think the noble Lord would have acted more gracefully if he had left to others the task of exhibiting his self-denial to the public.' He took Ashley to task for 'a habit of using a sanctimonious phraseology, resembling that of the conventicle, in his communications with the public,' and referred to 'the whine of Puritanism' which was described as 'inexpressibly odious.' Appearing when it did, and in an admittedly Conservative paper, Ashley believed this effusion, which he described with good justification as 'the most violent and venomous article I ever read directed against any public man,' to be officially inspired either by Peel or the Puseyites:

Is it a statement by authority? I confess it breathes the spirit of a man personally offended; it must be the resentment of the writer. Was Peel the author or furnisher of the matter? Or is it a Puseyite article paying me off for my resistance to Mr. Williams?

When both Peel and Sir James Graham condemned the article Ashley fastened on Roundell Palmer as its most probable author.

This piece of abuse strengthened Ashley's conviction that every man's hand was against him – 'I must be very watchful for I perceive that everybody is on the *qui vive* to catch me at fault.' Loneliness oppressed him – 'I am like a pelican in the wilderness or a sparrow on the house-tops.' Sadly he contrasted what he persisted in regarding as his solitary struggle for the Ten Hours Bill with the nation-wide committees and the host of sympathising friends who had helped Wilberforce with the Anti-Slavery campaign. Ashley had what he himself rather inaccurately described as 'two or three co-adjutators,' but none of these men was really congenial to him. In the House of Commons he was in truth a solitary figure, in spite of the presence of both Ferrand and Fielden. He rightly mistrusted Ferrand as headstrong and ungovernable – 'he had taken no advice, had formed no plan, made no preparations, and been governed altogether by his own wisdom' he wrote of Ferrand's efforts to obtain a Select Committee to enquire into the system of truck payment. As for John Fielden, he was a man 'who ever thinks zeal a higher quality than judgement.'

Ashley was indeed a person of many acquaintances but few friends of his own standing, and none of them on his side of the House of Commons. Only Minny was an ever-present support, and this summer Minny was an invalid, pregnant yet again and threatened with a serious miscarriage or with death in childbed. Minny was very well aware of the situation and steeled herself to face it; Ashley, however, remained strangely unperturbed, full of 'a deep and solemn confidence in God.' His unconcern was certainly not due to lack of affection; the passage of the years had only taught him to love and appreciate his Minny more and more. 'Yesterday the anniversary of our wedding day,' he wrote on June 11th; 'twelve years with the wife of God's gift.' Long ago, before his marriage, he had devised for himself a remarkable pocket Bible. He had a copy of the Bible taken to pieces and re-bound in twenty-five separate volumes of a convenient size to fit into his pocket. Some of the volumes are much annotated, in particular the one which includes the Book of Proverbs. Against the description of the virtuous woman whose price was far above rubies he had written, 'Would to God I had a wife such as this!' In the eighteen-forties he added the comment 'And so I have, God be everlastingly praised!'

To Ashley in one of his fits of depression his opponents always appeared as a collection of cunning knaves determined to thwart his every move. In January 1842 Lord John Manners and George Smythe, who were soon to emerge as leaders of that 'Young England' party which Lord Blake describes as 'the reaction of a defeated class to a sense of its own defeat'[17] had gone down to Lancashire and Yorkshire to see for themselves the conditions existing in the industrial districts. Ashley was convinced that the real object of their journey was to upset his own plans and to undermine his personal influence. The two young men were the more suspect because they both attended that stronghold of Tractarianism, the Margaret Street Chapel, afterwards rebuilt as All Saints Church. Peel was, of course, the archenemy – 'Not a cheer is given to Peel in the House of Commons that does not retard my success, multiply my toil, and add to my anxiety.' Sir James Graham ran Peel very close in villainy. Graham was a much misunderstood character. Outside a small circle of intimate friends his unfortunate manner made him generally unpopular. Ashley excelled everyone else in the bitterness of his criticism: 'there is not a chord in Graham's bosom that can be struck by any key of sympathy, justice, or common humanity,' he wrote on March 3rd. In his diseased imagination he saw Peel and Graham at the head of a host of enemies ranged against him, 'ever on the spot, fearful in their capital, resistless in their energy, unsparing in their falsehoods, and terrible in their prophecies.' Yet at this moment of black depression, when he imagined himself on the verge of total failure, Ashley was in fact within sight of one of his greatest achievements.

In May 1842 the Royal Commission on Children's Employment which had been set up two years earlier issued a report on the employment of women and children in coal mines. Among the Commissioners signing this report was Dr. Thomas Southwood Smith, who had been one of the three Commissioners of the 1833 Royal Commission on the Employment of Children in Factories. Southwood Smith was a physician practising in the City of London, an authority on fevers, and an enthusiast for all kinds of sanitary reform. In 1841 and again in January 1842 he had taken Ashley and his brother William Ashley-Cooper on a 'perambulation' of Whitechapel and Bethnal Green, visiting such misnamed spots as Pleasant Place, 'a perfect quagmire,' and Rose Court, a collection of 'most wretched hovels.' Now Southwood Smith had the wit to realise that many people who would not read an official report might well turn over the pages to glance at the pictures, and he persuaded the Commissioners to illustrate the report on mines with clear, simple linedrawings. Even today, when the horrors they depict have mercifully become matters of ancient history, these pictures arouse feelings of shocked protest. When they first appeared the effect was electric; at once a wave of horrified indignation swept across the country.

Today the drawings which shock us most are those which show little girls carrying huge baskets of coal up long, steep ladders, small five- or six-year-old 'trappers' sitting alone in the darkness opening and shutting ventilation doors, and, most horrifying of all, a woman or child harnessed to a truck by a chain passed between their legs and fastened to a heavy girdle, crawling on all fours to pull loads of coal through passages eighteen inches to two feet high. Ashley's contemporaries were more shocked by a drawing of a half-naked boy and girl sitting face to face astride a bar, she holding the rope and he with his arms round her body, whilst a decrepit old woman turned the hand-windlass which lowered them down the shaft. It was not the obvious danger of this mode of descent but its 'obscenity' which so troubled the Victorian conscience.

Those who turned from the pictures to the letterpress of the Report found more shocks awaiting them. In Halifax a child of three had been taken down the pit by its father – 'It was made to follow him into the workings, there to hold the candle, and when exhausted cradled upon the coals until his return home at night.' In Oldham it was said that some children working in the pits were so young that they were carried down in their nightgowns. Most shocking of all was the excuse put forward in perfect good faith by a Shropshire witness: 'There are very few under six or seven who are employed to draw weights with a girdle round the body, and only when the roof is so low as to prevent the smallest size of horses or asses being employed.'

Working conditions for women were equally horrible. Harnessed with girdle and chain they crawled backwards and forwards dragging the coal-tubs through sloping passages less than two feet high. As the writers of the Report truthfully commented, 'the dangers and difficulties of dragging in roads dipping from 1 in 3 to 1 in 6 may be more easily conceived than explained.' Pregnant women were often employed in this 'sore, sore work,' as one woman witness called it. Another woman witness stated bluntly, 'I had a child born in the pit, and I brought it up the pit-shaft in my skirt; it was born the day after I were married – that makes me to know.' Unlike this witness, most women in the pits discarded skirts and dressed themselves exactly like the pitmen, going naked from the waist up with a pair of ragged trousers their only clothing.

Several witnesses declared that the coal-owners were quite unaware of the state of affairs – 'The coal owners seldom or never descend into the pits; few of them have any personal knowledge or take any superintendence whatever of their work-people.' A particularly bad, wet pit at Mirfield in Yorkshire 'belonged to a gentleman reputed for benevolence but who knew nothing of his own pits.' This ignorance was not altogether to be wondered at, remembering the only available means of descent; Lord Londonderry, for instance, could hardly be expected to allow himself to be lowered in a small, open bucket, or to share a seat on a wooden bar with a half-naked colliery lass. Even in the vastly improved conditions of today only a bare handful of people unconnected with the industry have seen for themselves the bottom of a coal pit. The Miners' Memorial in Durham Cathedral is inscribed with an aptly-chosen text from the Book of Job: 'They break out a shaft away from where men sojourn, they are forgotten of the foot that passeth by.' Pitmen always have been, and perhaps always will be, a race a little apart; their conditions of work are inevitably unseen and therefore too often ignored by their fellow-country-men.

This being so, it is surprising to find that the nation at large, which had been so slow to admit the necessity for the regulation of child-labour in factories, awoke to loud and immediate protest over the scandal of conditions in the pits. Ashley's Ten Hours Bill was to take fourteen years to become law; his Mines Bill passed through both Houses of Parliament in as many weeks, although difficulties inevitably arose in the House of Lords, where the great mine-owners were very powerful. No peer could be found to sponsor the Bill until Lord Devon, generously forgetful of old differences over the Poetry Professorship, at last agreed to undertake the task. Although the passage of the Bill through Parliament was a comparatively smooth one Ashley was on tenterhooks until it finally became law at the beginning of August. 'Anxiety and doubt will make mincemeat of me,' he wrote on May 30th.

Although Ashley complained, and with good reason, that the Lords 'left the Bill far worse than they found it,' the measure never-theless proved effectual in putting a stop to the labour of women and children underground – too effectual, perhaps, since it caused great temporary hardship to the women thus thrown out of work, who could find no other employment. Some Lancashire 'pit-brow lassies,' who had been lucky enough to be taken on as surface workers, went so far as to declare that they 'liked it reet well – would like well to work below again – liked it better than working up here.'[18] Taken as a whole, however, the Mines Act of 1842, described by the Hammonds as 'the most striking of Ashley's personal achievements,'[19] proved to be one of the greatest and most successful of all measures of in-dustrial reform. Southwood Smith, who had played a major part in bringing about this achievement, would often tell his little granddaughter stories about the unhappy children working in the pits. On the day when the Act came into force this child insisted on decorating the Doctor's carriage-horses with festive rosettes of blue ribbon. 'There now,' she exclaimed, 'the little children are all running over the green fields.'

Ashley's work on behalf of the women and children in coal mines won him the respect and approval of two very different characters. After reading his speech in support of the Bill, Prince Albert sent him a warmly congratulatory letter which ended, 'with best wishes for your *total* success.' When Ashley, by special invitation, called at Buckingham Palace to discuss the matter, he found the Prince 'hearty, kind, sensible and zealous,' and summed him up as 'an admirable man.' The other convert was Richard Cobden, leader of the Anti-Corn-Law League, who had been, and was to remain, Ashley's convinced opponent on the issue of the Ten Hours Bill. The two men were opposed to each other both in temperament and in outlook. In an *Open Letter to Lord Ashley* Cobden expressed a point of view very similar to that which had been put forward by Henry Ashworth: 'Mine is that masculine species of charity which would lead me to inculcate in the minds of the labouring classes the love of independence, the privilege of self-respect, the disdain of being patronised or petted, the desire to accumulate and the ambition to rise.'[20] He objected to all factory legislation as tending to destroy the self-reliant spirit of the working-classes. The assertion that a restriction of moving power was the only satisfactory way of enforcing the restrictions on child-labour he regarded as 'an avowal that the parents cannot be trusted to obey a law which forbids them to sacrifice their own children.' Such mistrust was indeed only too well founded; nineteen years later another Commission on Children's Employment was to declare that 'against no persons do the children of both sexes require so much protection as against their own parents.'[21]

Enmity between Cobden and Ashley had been strong and bitter; but Cobden was a generous character quick to recognise and own up to his own mistakes. When Ashley sat down at the end of the same great speech which was to please Prince Albert so much, Cobden walked across the House and shaking him warmly by the hand declared, 'You know how opposed I have been to your views; but I don't think I have ever been put into such a frame of mind in the whole course of my life as I have been by your speech.' From now onwards, although the two men were still to disagree, relations between them were to be much more cordial. Cobden indeed continued his attacks on Ashley in the House of Commons but, unlike his friend and fellow-worker John Bright, he always kept within the limits of courtesy and good taste. The future was to bring much personal tragedy both to Cobden and to Ashley, who were to be drawn closer together by feelings of mutual sympathy.

On July 25th, the day when the Mines Bill went into Committee in the House of Lords, Minny had safely given birth to a daughter. By September she was so far recovered that she yielded to her husband's persuasion and agreed to accompany him on a tour of the industrial North. The hunger and distress that the years of 'the hungry forties' were bringing to these districts had resulted in a series of riots culminating in the disturbance known as 'the Plug Plot,' when the strikers drew the plugs out of boilers, thus putting factories out of action. Chartism too was much on the increase. Ashley attributed all this disaffection to Peel's refusal to support the Ten Hours Bill, believing that the working people regarded a politician's attitude towards that measure as the touchstone of his sympathy towards them and their grievances. Part of his own business on this coming tour would be to urge the Ten Hours men to keep cool heads and to steer clear of these outbreaks of violence so that no act of lawlessness should damage their just cause.

Ashley and Minny extended their journey a little in order to enjoy a holiday together in North Wales, visiting Chirk Castle and the area now known as Snowdonia, where Ashley was particularly impressed by the great slate quarries near Llanberis. From Wales they travelled to Lancashire, where they stayed at Gawthorpe with Dr. James Kay-Shuttleworth, a pioneer of sanitary reform and Secretary to the Manchester Board of Health. Ashley and Kay-Shuttleworth had crossed swords in the past; now, however, he recognised the Doctor as a kindred spirit: 'The grace of God has done much for the man; he always had a kind heart, now he has a religious heart.' Their three days' stay at Gawthorpe was spent visiting colliers and hand-loom-weavers in their cottage homes, in making friends with mill-owners and in non-stop conversation on that absorbing topic, 'the moral and physical condition of the poor.' From Gawthorpe the Ashleys went on to Worsley, home of 'that dear and excellent woman, Lady Francis Egerton, the truest friend I have in this world,' and a friend with whom unkind gossip had once hinted that Ashley was a little in love. At Worsley, Ashley met a Colonel Shaw, who took him on a tour of the slums, gin-palaces, gaming-houses and brothels in the worst parts of Manchester. Ashley was particularly moved by the sight of 'a darling little girl, seven years old, in the very depth of dirt and uproar; never did I witness such beauty of natural, untaught affection towards its rough and unkind mother.' A day or two later he bravely descended a coal pit, believing it 'easier to talk after you have seen.'

On September 26th Ashley was back in Manchester to receive an address from the Lancashire Short Time Committee. The answer which he returned to this address is particularly interesting because he intended it to be in the nature of a manifesto. After thanking the Committee for their address he pointed out that the troubles of the working classes were due to the fact that 'over a large surface of the industrial community man has been regarded as an animal, and that an animal not of the highest order; his loftiest faculties, when not prostrate, are perverted, and his lowest exclusively devoted to the manufacture of wealth.' The inevitable result had been 'a mighty multitude of feeble bodies and untaught minds, the perilous materials of present and future pauperism, of violence and infidelity.' The passing of the Mines Act showed that public opinion was now awakening to these evils; the working men should therefore take encouragement to persevere in their 'just and reasonable demands' for the Ten Hours Bill. They should also fight hard against the growing tendency to replace male by female labour since 'when the women of a country become brutalised that country is left without hope.' Above all, they must remember that their great aim was to see the children of the working classes provided with adequate opportunities to benefit from a good moral and religious education – 'We must keep before our eyes the undeniable but ill-considered fact that every child in these districts is an immortal being; and that another generation, neglected like the present, and left in ignorance and sin, will probably witness the final extinction of the British Empire.' In working towards this goal they must always be careful to keep within the law and to avoid damage to other people's rightful interests. He ended by expressing the hope that he might one day see 'the restoration of content amongst all classes, the revival of good will between master and man, a blessing on every house, and a home for every labourer.'²²

This manifesto is typical of Ashley in the total absence of any appeal to self-interest, in the stress laid on moral rather than physical evils, the concern with the immortal value of each individual, and the insistence that all must be done lawfully and without violence. There is no hint of the operatives' own grievances but a reference to the damage done the whole nation, no talk of the children's physical sufferings but a strong plea for their moral and spiritual betterment. That a point of view at once so disinterested and so impersonal could be made acceptable to a body of working-class people speaks volumes for Ashley's powers of persuasion; it also says something for the good sense and intelligence of the Lancashire working men.

In spite of his success over the Mines Act, on his return from the North Ashley was once again plunged into depression. He saw evil everywhere, at home in the 'arrogance and despotism' of the hated Puseyites, abroad, and more justly, in the behaviour of British troops in China and Afghanistan. In November news of the end of the first Opium War drew from Ashley the truthful comment, 'We have triumphed in one of the most lawless, unnecessary, and unfair struggles in history.' His patriotism was of that rare and noble kind which is not blind to the misdeeds of the beloved country but grieves over them even more passionately than it rejoices over successes. So now he commented sternly apropos of the Afghan War, 'Everything in India is disgraceful; we are reduced to the level of the French; their *razzias* in Africa fall short of ours – is the British name brought to this?'

Trouble had arisen when in 1839 the British had intervened in Afghanistan in order to counteract Russian influence there, and had reinstated an unpopular and incompetent ruler called Shah Shuja. The ensuing occupation of Kabul, the capital, had given rise to so many difficulties that it was decided, too late, to withdraw the garrison. During the retreat the entire British force was cut to pieces by Afghan tribesmen, only one man escaping. The new Governor-General of India, Lord Ellenborough, who had taken office early in 1842, now ordered an expeditionary force to march through the Khyber Pass and relieve the garrisons still holding out at Jullalabad and Kandahar. With horror and bitterness Ashley quoted a passage from the Indian papers describing the behaviour of this force:

'While our troops were advancing, parties were detached to set fire to the houses and villages; and the force afterwards remained on the ground, *employed in cutting down the vineyards and mulberry trees* to which much value and importance is attached by the enemy. The inhabitants were seen watching the ravage and destruction *which continued after resistance had ceased.*' Among the other mercies and righteousnesses of this delightful transaction there is this one prominent, that it is immediately and literally forbidden by Scripture.
(Deuteronomy XX 19–20).

After capturing Ghazni and Kabul, the British troops returned in triumph bringing with them the gates of the Temple of Somnath, spoils of war carried off from India by the victorious Mohammedans as long ago as 1024. In a proclamation to 'the Princes and Chiefs and Peoples of India' Ellenborough declared, 'the insult of eight hundred years ago is at last wiped out; the gates of the temple of Somnath, so long the memorial of your humiliation, are become the proudest record of your national glory, the proof of your superiority in arms over the nations beyond the Indus.'

This piece of bombast irritated Ashley intensely. He was particularly disapproving of this restoration of the treasures of a Hindu temple, 'the house of a beastly image.' So strongly did he feel on the subject that he voted with the Whigs against his own party on a motion censuring Ellenborough's proclamation. (He need not have worried; the gates now brought back proved to be mere replicas of the originals.) In his diary he wrote bitterly and with truth, 'After four years of unparallelled trial and disaster, everything was restored to the condition in which we found it, except that there were so many brave Englishmen sleeping in bloody graves.'

Ashley saw trouble looming too in America. He gloated rather ghoulishly over the financial crisis there – 'so much for the model democracy!' – and expressed alarm at the recrudescence of the dispute between the United States and Great Britain over the Oregon boundary:

The dishonesty of the Americans individually and as a nation is perfectly shocking – not content with private and public repudiation of just debts, the People, in the person of their Secretary of State, have uttered the grossest lies to over-reach Lord Ashburton on the boundary treaty. The moral state of the country is more disgraceful and alarming to the world (for the wretches have power) than that even of France.

On Christmas Day 1842 Ashley expressed his view of the world situation in one tense and typical sentence: 'There is very little seeming, and no real, hope for mankind but in the Second Advent.'

A few days later this gloom had vanished. The Christmas holidays were being spent at St. Giles, where the air of his native place was always the best cure for Ashley's fits of depression. The New Year came in with a spell of exceptionally lovely weather which gave him the opportunity for a solitary walk to a favourite spot on the downs above Brockington. Here he had stood a year previously and commended himself and the coming year to God. Now he came again, his heart full of thankfulness for the past and prayer for the future. As he turned back to St. Giles, the beloved home where, after so many years of banishment, he could now live reconciled to his father, he remembered the words of the patriarch Jacob. 'If God will be with me, and will keep me in this way that I go, and will give me bread to eat and raiment to put on, so that I come again to my father's house in peace, then shall the Lord be my God'.

Chapter 11

POLITICAL AND PERSONAL TROUBLES

The years from 1843 to 1846 were to be overshadowed by two vital issues, the state of Ireland and the repeal of the Corn Laws. The connection between them was not at first apparent. In 1843 it was the political rather than the economic problems of Ireland which loomed so large; O'Connell and his followers were demanding repeal of the Union with England, not repeal of the duties on imported corn. Meanwhile, Ashley's ten years of patient work for the Ten Hours Bill were beginning to bear fruit; little by little opposition to that measure was beginning to break down, both in the House of Commons and out of it. Victory, however, was still to elude him, partly because the issue was to be bedevilled by its connection with education, partly because Peel's opposition was to prove unexpectedly strong.

Ashley opened the year 1843 with an attack on the Government's policy in China. That, for reasons of trade and revenue, the British should force a foreign power to open its ports to the opium traffic seemed to Ashley, as it does to posterity, a grossly immoral act, 'more black, more cruel, more satanic, than all the deeds of private sin in personal history.' In his attack on the opium trade Ashley had the support of the famous Quaker families of Gurney and Fry. With Elizabeth Fry, the prison reformer, he was on terms of personal friendship. His relations with other Quakers were less happy. Many of his most determined opponents among the North Country mill-owners were members of the Society of Friends, one of the best known being John Bright of Rochdale, friend and fellow-worker with Codben in the Anti-Corn-Law League. This summer of 1843 Bright stood for the city of Durham at a by-election, and, failing to win the seat, petitioned against the successful candidate, Lord Dungannon, on grounds of corruption. Ashley was Chairman of the committee which considered this petition and, being 'resolved to run breast-high against all cases of bribery,' he had much to do with its decision to unseat Dungannon and declare Bright elected. Thus inadvertently Ashley was himself the means of admitting to Parliament the man who was to be his own most determined opponent in the House of Commons, 'my enemy, Quaker Bright.'

The total lack of understanding between Ashley and Bright is one of the most lamentable facts of nineteenth-century history; had they been able to agree, together they might have achieved wonders for the betterment of the working people, the cause which they both had so much at heart. At first glance the two men would appear to have had very much in common. Both were deeply religious, intensely serious, and absolutely committed to the tasks they took in hand; both hated oppression and injustice with an almost pathological hatred; in politics they were both lone wolves, impatient of party ties. Yet instead of working together they were perpetually at each other's throats; on no important occasion were they to be found standing side by side as colleagues.

The cynical would explain the constant friction between them in terms of self-interest. As a mill-owner John Bright had good reason to oppose the Factory Acts, and, as an alternative means of improving the condition of the workers, to urge the abolition of the Corn Laws, a policy which was calculated to give Lancashire cotton goods an easier entry into foreign markets. Ashley, on the other hand, had nothing to lose from the Factory Acts and much to lose from repeal of the Corn Laws, coming as he did from a land-owning, agricultural background. Both men were genuinely anxious to better the condition of the working classes but in their choice of methods to bring about this end both were subconsciously influenced by selfish motives.

Self-interest, however, counted for very little either with Ashley or with Bright. These two good men were consumed by a burning desire for the welfare of their fellow men, a desire so fierce that in the face of its light and heat the charge of selfishness shrivels to nothing. Hard facts also discount the accusation. Though Ashley was not affected either personally or financially by the results of factory legislation he lost very much by his championship of the Ten Hours Bill; to it he sacrificed both personal comfort and political ambition. So too, though the firm of Bright Brothers may have gained from the increase of trade following the repeal of the Corn Laws, for John Bright himself the financial balance was an adverse one. When Bright stood for Durham as a declared opponent of the Corn Laws he did so at a great financial risk, since his brother Thomas, who alone could deputise for him in his business, was lying dangerously ill. Though Thomas recovered it remains true that had John Bright decided to give his time and energies to the affairs of Bright Brothers rather than to those of the Anti-Corn-Law League he might have become a very rich man.

The antagonism between Bright and Ashley was certainly not caused by selfish motives; rather, it was due to a personal antipathy between two men of differing social background. A very faint, subtle difference, so subtle that no foreigner could hope to detect it, still exists between a member of a family, however undistinguished, which has been for generations both armigerous and land-owning and a person whose forebears made their fortunes 'in trade,' to use the favourite Victorian expression. In the nineteenth century this difference was plain for all to see. The Gladstones and the Peels were accepted as gentlemen by their fellow Etonians and Harrovians, but they were gentlemen of a slightly different flavour to George Howard or Ashley. Men like Bright, who did not join the Church of England, attend a public school or acquire a landed estate, remained much nearer the border-line. The difference between Bright and Ashley is not the difference between businessman and humanitarian, still less is it the difference between Liberal and Tory; it is the much deeper atavistic antipathy between plain man and aristocrat, between North and South.

It is significant that although he differed from him politically Ashley found it easy to keep on good terms with Bright's friend and ally, Richard Cobden, who came of South Country farming stock and who retired to end his days in his native Sussex. No Southerner is ever heard to say, with a note of pride and challenge in his voice, 'Well, I'm a South Country man.' The Northerner, on the contrary, is touchy and self-conscious, for ever aware of his origin, and proud of it. For him his northern birth is something of very special importance. By tradition the Northerner has certain characteristics: he is tough, friendly, outspoken, hard-working and egalitarian. No matter that vast numbers of Northerners are gentle, reserved, devious, idle and class-conscious; the legend still remains. John Bright was the typical North Country man of this potent myth. Ashley neither liked nor understood the North; it was therefore unlikely in the extreme that he would either like or understand John Bright.

Whether by chance or design, in his classic biography of Bright Sir George Trevelyan played down the antagonism between his hero and Ashley. It is difficult to know whether Bright cherished a personal hatred of Ashley as strong as Ashley's personal hatred of Bright. Certainly Ashley was a good hater. During these years of the early forties his dislike of Graham and Peel assumed fantastic proportions.

Though intimate friends such as Gladstone held Graham in high esteem, Ashley described him as 'so thoroughly odious that I cannot find one human being who will speak a word on his behalf.' On June 30th 1843 he called Graham 'the most dishonest of all public officers,' and later wrote of him as 'mean, false, and hard-hearted beyond himself.'

Ashley's hatred of Graham was only less fierce than his hatred of Graham's friend and leader, Peel. In her biography of Peel, Miss Ramsay writes of Ashley, 'Single-minded, devoted, passionate, he was ready to sacrifice every other consideration to the cause he served, and he expected all its supporters to be equally ready.' Peel, she says, 'was equally capable of sacrifice' – his behaviour over Catholic Emancipation and again over the repeal of the Corn Laws is proud proof of this statement – 'but he liked to be very sure of his facts before he threw his cap over the mill.'[1] Ashley saw only one side to the questions which interested him; Peel saw many sides to every question. Ashley was an idealist; Peel was a pragmatist and a practical man. Having been perhaps the best Home Secretary that Britain ever had, he was by temperament an administrator rather than a politician.

Ashley's dislike of Peel was much exacerbated by what he described as Peel's 'latitudinarian' attitude towards religion. When Peel attended a dinner-party on a Sunday Ashley exploded with indignation – 'This is the example the Prime Minister sets to the people of England; this is the solemn consideration he exhibits for the responsibilities of his office.' Worse still was Peel's reaction to the hated Tractarians, whom he disliked for all the wrong reasons. Ashley justly declared that Peel had 'no doctrinal antipathies,' adding the comment, 'his feelings are governed by far other principles than those of internal and conscientious abhorrence of their tenets and principles.'

For his part, Peel must have found Ashley's high-flown religious views very hard to stomach. Ashley was in the habit of writing him long, pious and slightly impertinent letters similar in tone to the one written on July 24th 1841 when Peel was about to take office as Prime Minister. On January 20th 1843 a madman called Daniel McNaghten shot and killed Peel's private secretary, Edward Drummond. McNaghten's bullet had clearly been intended for Peel himself. Ashley's letter of condolence on Drummond's death is intolerably patronising in tone:

It has pleased God in His wise and merciful, though unsearchable Providence, to permit him to fall by the blow that was, no doubt, intended for another. I cannot believe that it was a disconnected act; it is the beginning of sorrow. *Sursum corda*; these events must prove to us of what avail are all human precautions; that in the everlasting arms is our only safety, and that, as we hope to die, so must we learn to live, in His faith and fear. May God, of His mercy, guide, protect and cherish you! May He reserve you for His gracious purpose towards this country and mankind, for His service in this world, and for His glory in the next![2]

To this effusion Peel replied kindly but briefly in a letter which contained no reference whatsoever to the Almighty. No more than Melbourne did Peel relish that Evangelical turn of expression which Queen Victoria was pleased to describe as 'cant.'

Ashley himself seems to have been in some doubt as to the wisdom of sending Peel such a letter. Strange though it may seem, he feared that it might be construed in too favourable a sense – 'I had written to Peel to say what *I prayed for him*, not what *I thought of him*; my mind misgave me afterwards lest I should be misunderstood.' Such misgivings look odd in the light of Ashley's diary, where almost every page bristles with hatred and contempt for Peel. (Now, as always, it must be remembered that Ashley expressed in his diary emotions and sentiments which he otherwise kept carefully hidden.) Hodder is usually indiscreet rather than otherwise in his selections from the diary, but in dealing with this period he has found it necessary to expunge some of the more violent passages. For instance, he quotes Ashley's account of Peel's speech in defence of British policy in China:

He *sneered* at our care for the health and morals of the Chinese, and altogether assumed the tone of a low, mercantile, financial soul, incapable of urging or conceiving a principle, which finally disgusted me, and placed him in my mind much below the Christian level, and not any higher than the heathen.

This may seem fierce enough; Hodder has, however, seen fit to omit the final and most telling sentence, 'It passed again and again through my mind, "I will never serve under such a fellow as you!" '

Ironically enough, in the all-important matter of the Corn Laws Ashley found himself in precisely the same position as Peel. He could not entirely approve of repeal but he was beginning to realise that repeal was inevitable – 'Matters have come to such a pass that the Corn Laws, I believe are a nominal benefit, but Sir Robert Peel

must not be the man to effect such a change.' He was less alarmed
by Peel's slow and cautious movement towards repeal than by a
more obvious change of front on the part of the up-and-coming young
Tory who was making such a name for himself at the Board of
Trade:

> Gladstone has written a Free Trade article in the *Foreign and
> Colonial Review*. The principles laid down there will not permit
> a delay in the enactment of more liberal measures . . . How Glad-
> stone can arrange his one set of principles for the closet and the
> other for the debate is his own affair. The Government meanwhile
> are seriously compromised by the writing of the Vice-President
> of the Board of Trade.

In January 1843 the Royal Commission on the Employment of
Children issued another report, this time dealing with such industries as calico-printing, pin-making, and hosiery, where conditions and hours of labour were in many cases even worse than in the
textile mills. Everywhere one of the greatest problems was the lack
of opportunity for schooling. On February 28th Ashley rose in the
House of Commons to propose the motion, 'That Her Majesty will be
graciously pleased to take into her serious and immediate consideration the best means of diffusing the benefits and blessings of a moral
and religious education among the working classes of her people.' Of
set purpose he made no attempt to put forward an educational
scheme, but instead, with the help of statistics and reports, he pointed
to the increase of crime and immorality among the uneducated
masses in the industrial towns. (In doing so he made a slight tactical
error which cost him some popularity; the citizens of these towns,
and Leeds in particular, resented being described as abnormally
criminal and immoral, pointing out that Leeds had 'more education,
more religion, and less vice,' than the city of Westminster which
contained the Houses of Parliament.) Ashley reckoned that, taking
the whole population of England and Wales, some 1,014,000 children
and young persons were without any form of daily schooling. Since
the population was rapidly increasing, in ten years' time, if no
effective steps were taken to provide more and better education,
'we shall then have, in addition to our present arrears, a fearful
multitude of untutored savages.' Such schools as had come into being
as a result of the 1833 Factory Act were totally unable to provide
that 'moral and religious education' which Ashley believed to be
essential for the well-being of the nation. The mistress of a Dame's

school – and the vast majority of existing schools could be so described – when asked if she gave any moral instruction to her pupils, replied succinctly, 'I can't afford it at threepence a week.'

In this speech Ashley did not confine himself to his ostensible theme of education but ranged over a variety of subjects connected with the welfare of the working classes. (Incidentally, the speech contains one sentence which, though obviously intended as a hit at Peel's new police force is yet painfully relevant to the world of the twentieth century: 'It is very well to rely on an effective police for short and turbulent periods; it is ruinous to rely on it for the government of a generation.') He described the appalling housing conditions in the great cities, making good use of his memories of the Glasgow slums, he denounced the system of truck payments, and he pointed to the prevalence of drunkenness as the inevitable result of life in such surroundings. His speeches were usually closely-argued and to the point; this one was long and rambling. The House, however, listened attentively and gave it a good reception; 'a triumph for my public career,' he noted next day, 'to God in His mercy be all the honour.'

On March 7th the Government duly brought in a Factory Bill shortening children's working hours to six a day and introducing compulsory education in factory schools. A surprisingly amicable correspondence passed between Graham and Ashley on the subject of this measure. 'Your note has gratified me most sincerely,' Graham wrote on March 4th. 'There is no man whose approbation I value more highly or whose displeasure has given me greater pain. I am willing to hope that the new Factory Bill will in most important particulars satisfy your wishes'. He went on to express the wish that Ashley would reconsider his decision not to take Government office: 'It would delight me if the reasonable settlement proposed should in any degree remove your honourable scruples and smooth the way to future arrangements which I consider so desirable in the public service.'[3]

Graham's Factory Bill soon ran into trouble over its educational clauses. The factory schools were to be managed by the local parsons and churchwardens together with four other persons appointed by the magistrates. This in effect gave the control of these schools into the hands of the established Church. Immediately the Nonconformists rose in their wrath; and Ashley found himself in the ironical position of defending, in the House of Commons and out of it, a measure described in one political squib as 'this Pusey scheme.' Ashley himself was not wholly in favour of the plan, more especially when Graham, in a vain attempt to save the Bill, made concessions which were most unacceptable to a rigidly Anglican and Evangelical conscience:

> I never thought that I could have accepted such a scheme, and yet it was wise both to make it and receive it . . . All was gulpable, but when called on to adopt 'the teaching of the Bible' as proposed by Sir James, the simple text without note or comment or word of interpretation, the grammatical sense and nothing else, the actual leaving, as the case may be, of a Socinian in Socinian ignorance or a Socialist in Socialist impurities, except in so far as the grace of God might bless even the 'letter of His word', I did feel a nausea, even to faintness; nevertheless, for the sake of peace, I agreed to even that.

It would have been odd indeed to find that even one of the thousands of overworked, ignorant factory children had ever heard the word 'Socinian,' or had any notion as to what was meant by it or by the more usual term, 'Unitarian.'

Though he was much disappointed by the Government's decision not to persevere with the non-educational clauses, Ashley was not altogether broken-hearted when this Bill was withdrawn. He had learnt a useful lesson too often ignored by later educationalists. Where religion was concerned a school should be either secular or sectarian; a 'lowest common denominator' form of religious teaching satisfied no one. 'Combined education must never again be attempted,' he wrote on June 16th; 'it is an impossibility and worthless if possible.' In order to save the Bill as a whole he had felt himself obliged to support the compromise put forward by Graham, little as he liked it. Now that it had proved unacceptable he was free to concentrate attention and effect on 'our own schools, our Catechism, our Liturgy, our Articles, our Homilies, our faith, our own teaching of God's word.' An Ashley so rigidly Anglican seems a strange contrast to the later Lord Shaftesbury, the promoter of undenominational services and the enthusiastic believer in Anglican-Nonconformist co-operation in the running of the Ragged Schools.

Although Ashley was not unduly perturbed by the failure of the Factory Bill, wherever else he looked he could see nothing but political and religious trouble. Scotland was in the throes of the dispute which split the Church of Scotland in two and resulted in the formation of the Free Kirk. Ashley regarded this split with disapproval: 'the Scotch Secession is now manifestly in most instances the effect of ambition and vanity operating strongly on a native, inherent, demo-cratic spirit.' (To Ashley 'democratic' was a pejorative term, as 'liberal' was to Newman.) 'Wales almost in insurrection,' he wrote on July 3rd, commenting on the activities of the rioters known as 'Rebecca and her daughters.' In Ireland the situation was far worse. 'Peel will yet find his difficulties in Ireland,' Ashley had written pro-phetically at the beginning of this year. O'Connell's campaign for repeal of the Union was in full swing whilst controversy raged over the position of the Protestant established Church of Ireland, especi-ally in matters of education. Peel summed up the position as 'the problem of peaceably governing seven millions of people and main-taining intact the Protestant Church Establishment for the religious instruction and consolation of one million.'[4] Ashley saw matters in a rather different light when he wrote, 'the evils of that country spring from her social system and her religion.' He was not referring to the invidious position of the Church of Ireland as the Church of a minority supported by the forced contributions of a majority, but to the erroneous teachings of the Church of that majority, the Church of Rome. He saw clearly enough that in ordinary, mundane justice no case whatsoever could be made out for the predominant position of a Protestant Church in a Catholic country, but he supported the Church of Ireland for a reason which seemed to him sufficient and self-evident: 'the Irish Church is in fact assailable on twenty points, defensible only on one, that it testifies and teaches the truth.'

Meanwhile Ireland was threatened by an appalling but as yet unrecognised catastrophe. The summer of 1843 was a most un-seasonable one – 'coughs and colds are as abundant as in the month of November.' Ashley noted that the corn was standing knee-high in water, and that the prospect for the potato-crop was a most un-favourable one. 'This is a sore judgement, but a merited one,' he commented; neither he nor anyone else guessed just how sore that judgement was to be. The bad harvest did, however, add force to the argument against the retention of the duties on foreign corn. Ashley disapproved strongly of the action of seventy county members, who called a meeting and resolved to oppose any move which Peel might make towards repeal, even if by so doing they ran the risk of turning him out of office. Much as Ashley disliked Peel, he was troubled by the atmosphere of doubt and mistrust which was beginning to surround the Prime Minister as a result of the many rumours current about his changed views on the subject of the Corn Laws – 'be it true or not, distrust, when once excited, is not easily allayed.' He likened Peel to 'a ship on the Goodwins between two heavy seas, the League and the landlords,' a metaphor curiously akin to Trevelyan's fine description of Peel and his change of front over the Corn Laws, 'coming round, like a great ship veering with the wind.'[5]

All through this busy spring and summer Ashley seldom had leisure even to open a book. On the evening of May 25th he chanced to find himself for once alone and unoccupied, 'a rare thing to befall me.' Thus free to indulge in a fit of introspection, he set down in his diary the results of his self-analysis:

> I do believe that if one were to pluck from me my knowledge and hope of a future state I should be of all men the most miserable . . . I am by nature foolishly sensitive, passionately fond of applause; disappointment, envy, irritation would madden me if I saw not the end of this life and the dawn of another. In many respects I feel and acknowledge my inferiority to other public men; in one or two, by God's grace, I am superior to them, but any one of their superior points is, for all ambitious purposes, better than both of mine. I perceive it and quail before the conviction. With much thought and deliberation I can effect something; there is perhaps not a man in the House of Commons less able than myself to do the slightest thing unprepared. This is tantamount to incompetency for great public station. Yet I may rejoice in this issue, that I have given a direction to men's thoughts . . . and turned them into a deep and flowing channel which carries them to the great sea of duty to the poor and the whole aggregate of moral and religious obligations.

This passage makes two points very clear: the importance to Ashley of his belief in a future life and his acute awareness of his own shortcomings. It is not necessary to share his religious belief, with its eschatological emphasis, to understand how much reassurance and stability this ultra-sensitive and mentally unstable man drew from such a faith. He could not have borne the disappointments, slights and sorrows which were so much more agonising to him than to a less sensitive person had he not implicitly believed in the coming of a new and perfect dispensation to redress the injustices and imperfections of this one. The thought of the Second Advent of Christ was his lifeline; without this belief he would have sunk finally in despair.

In time most people reconcile themselves to their own limitations; not so Ashley. Both his pride and his acute sensibility kept him perpetually aware of his own weak points and of other people's reaction to them. He was right in describing himself as passionately fond of applause; it was this yearning for approval which made him 'quail

before the conviction' of his own inferiority. Yet in the depths of
his mind a doubt constantly stirred – was he really so inferior?
Trying his hardest to still this doubt and to become genuinely
humble he merely succeeded in destroying his own self-confidence,
or what little remained to him after his unhappy childhood experiences. A basic lack of self-confidence produces an over-assertive
attitude towards life; thus, by an unhappy paradox, Ashley's struggles towards humility tended to make him both obstinate and
aggressive.

As he himself noted, one of Ashley's weak points was an inability
to act or speak without careful preparation. In Parliament this
failing was particularly noticeable; he could not speak well extempore and he was of little use at the cut and thrust of debate. Yet
he was wise and perceptive enough to make an asset out of this
disability. Because he knew that he could not speak well unprepared
he took peculiar care over the preparation of his speeches and worked
so hard over them that in the end he achieved greater power over the
minds of his audience than did many more naturally gifted speakers.

When Ashley wrote that perceptive piece of self-analysis he was
sitting sad and lonely, Minny having been called away to her sick
sister. Minny's brother, William Cowper, had just become engaged
to Harriet Gurney, a girl with a great reputation as a beauty. Ashley,
however, wrote her down as 'a pretty woman but no Venus,' adding
with fond and touching pride, 'she is no more comparable to my
wife, although she enjoys the advantage of twelve years of greater
youth, than I to Hercules.' In July Minny suffered a miscarriage
and though she recovered quickly she seems to have developed
some lurking trouble. 'The seeds of disorder may have been sown,'
Ashley wrote cryptically; 'it is wise to uproot them if possible.'
He himself was 'in very low spirits, hardly able to make any efforts,
so weary yesterday that I could hardly walk.' On the doctor's advice
it was decided to try the cure at Carlsbad. Though the expenses of
such a journey appalled Ashley he decided that Accy and Francis
with their tutor must be of the party. All too soon he would be
deprived of Accy's daily company, since the boy was to go to boarding school in the autumn. His eldest son was particularly dear to
Ashley, who prayed repeatedly that 'like David, I may die and leave
to a Solomon to construct that temple which I may imagine but
may not behold.' Unfortunately the construction of temples was
not to be Accy's hobby.

Before leaving England Ashley set in motion, 'in zeal, in faith
and fear, and full hope,' a memorial to the Vice-Chancellor of Oxford

University protesting against 'Puseyism,' then, saying goodbye
to the younger children, 'a sad and sickening drawback to any pleasure,'
he set out for the Continent with Minny, Accy and Francis. From
Antwerp the party drove on to Carlsbad in their shabby, fourteen-
year-old travelling carriage, going by way of Aachen, Cologne, and
Frankfurt. On arrival at Carlsbad, Ashley for once relaxed and gave
himself up to rest and enjoyment. Very simple his enjoyments were:
he sat with his family by the river, revelling in 'a pretty scene, a
splendid day, delicious air, well-dressed company, green trees, and
coffee and milk enough to satisfy five persons for about a shilling';
he talked to the German working people, finding them kindly and
polite and their children 'quite darlings'; he made friends with Prince
Galitzine and with a Russian Colonel, 'a good-natured chap but the
veriest coxcomb I ever saw'; he climbed to the top of a neighbouring
hill and meditated on the prospect of the Second Advent.

Rested and refreshed after five weeks of this quiet life the party
moved on to Prague, where Ashley visited a hospital and a lunatic
asylum, and from Prague to Vienna, where he inspected two cotton
mills. He spent much time in solitary wanderings about the city,
searching out his old haunts. In his moralisings over the past he
makes no mention of Antoinette, but he must have had her specially
in mind when, at the old statesman's personal request, he called one
day upon Prince Metternich.

Back in England at the beginning of October Ashley first visited
his father at St. Giles, and then took Accy to the school which had
been carefully chosen for him, a small, Evangelical establishment
on the Isle of Wight. The place seemed all that he could wish, the
people in charge kind and sensible, yet still Ashley could not reconcile
himself to this parting from his eldest son. No stranger, he felt, could
really be trusted to care for the boy as meticulously as he had done;
'I have watched every moment, weighed every expression, considered
every thought, and seized every opportunity to drop a word in season.' Having been subjected to this parental vigilance Accy not
surprisingly enjoyed the more casual atmosphere of school, writing
home very happy letters. His father, however, continued to grieve –
'I cannot be reconciled to his absence, I miss him at every turn.'

Bereft of Accy, and beset by 'postmen, knockers, bells, visitors,
business, questions, answers, hopes, fears, doubts, difficulties,'
Ashley fell into the frame of mind when almost everything and
everyone provoked him to acid criticism. His old friend Morpeth
fell from favour for refusing to sign the anti-Tractarian memorial;
the Queen was at fault for 'running about in a more than Elizabethan

progress'; the Duke of Devonshire was censured for spending vast sums on her entertainment whilst refusing 'on the plea of poverty, a farthing to the National Society.'* Worst of all was the behaviour of John Fielden, who with John Walter of *The Times* organised a great meeting at Huddersfield to launch an appeal for funds to pay Oastler's debts and release him from jail. Naturally enough, this meeting was concerned solely with Oastler; Ashley, however, saw in its proceedings a deliberate slight, amounting almost to an attack, upon himself:

> The *Standard* of Saturday last contains extracts from Yorkshire papers with an account of a meeting for the liberation of Mr. Oastler – it was, as I suspected it would be, manifestly of a spirit very hostile to myself, though my name was never mentioned. The whole relief of the factory children, from first to last, *was attributed to him alone,* only once was Sadler mentioned, myself never . . . What on earth have I done to attract so much dislike? . . . Oh, it is clear enough there is a sad jealousy.

It may be significant that in this winter of discontent Ashley first mentions a physical ill which was to trouble him severely, though intermittently, for the rest of his life. On November 9th he records, 'noises in my ears frequent and tedious.' This occurrence of tinnitus, to use the medical term for such noises, is interesting as yet another indication of the probable psychogenic origin of many of Ashley's physical complaints, although the absence of reliable evidence makes even a tentative diagnosis virtually impossible. In an article in *The Encyclopaedia of General Practice* Mr. Harold Ludman describes one form of tinnitus, which may or may not have been the form from which Ashley suffered, as being 'greatly influenced by psychogenic factors such as emotion, worry, or fatigue.' Although normally the cause of tinnitus is a physical one, in certain cases the condition is clearly linked with psychogenic trouble or definite psychogenic disease, most frequently with depression. We do not know whether Ashley suffered from any physical defect which would explain these noises; we do know that he suffered from depression and that in his case the noises were not permanent but intermittent, occurring when he was tired, anxious, or unhappy, and most frequently of all when he was depressed. It seems reasonable, therefore, to suppose that his tinnitus was psychogenic in origin, though such a diagnosis can be no

* The National Society for promoting the Education of the Poor in the Principles of the Established Church.

more than a likely guess incapable of proof. Even if the primary cause of the trouble was a physical one the immediate cause of any specific attack was almost certainly psychogenic. Suffering from acute depression allied to tinnitus and the gastric ulcer or nervous dyspepsia which was to plague him more and more frequently, Ashley was a textbook example of the interaction of psychogenic illness and physical disease.

Ashley's depression and bitterness of spirit were not lessened by the fierce attacks being made on him on the ground of his apparent unconcern with the shocking condition of the agricultural labourers in his native county of Dorset. His most formidable assailant was the popular writer, Harriet Martineau, high priestess of *laissez faire*, who put forward the almost unanswerable statement that whilst Ashley was attacking conditions in the Lancashire cotton industry, where the operatives earned as much as three pounds a week, labourers on his family estates were living in wretched hovels 'in a state of desperate ignorance and reckless despair,' and subsisting on a wage of eight or ten shillings. (On this last point Miss Martineau unaccountably erred in Ashley's favour; some labourers at St. Giles earned no more than six shillings a week.) A similar protest came from an aristocratic Dorsetshire parson, Sidney Godolphin Osborne, whose deep concern for the welfare of the agricultural labourers paralleled Ashley's own concern for the factory children.

Nobody likes to be called a hypocrite. Ashley was in an entirely false position, held responsible for conditions which he was powerless to remedy. Whilst his father lived he could do nothing to improve affairs at St. Giles, nor could he make any public protest without appearing to criticise his father. Family pride perhaps, filial duty certainly, had hitherto kept him silent, though for years he had been deeply troubled by the scandalous state of affairs. Uneasy in conscience, and smarting under repeated attacks, he at last decided to speak out.

On November 30th 1843 he addressed an Agricultural Society dinner at Sturminster Newton, a little market town within a few miles of Sidney Godolphin Ostome's parish of Durweston. He told his audience of landlords and farmers that the county of Dorset was within an ace of becoming a bye-word for poverty and oppression.' Could they, he asked, possibly deny the assertion that 'the wages of labour in these parts are scandalously low, painfully inadequate to the maintenance of the husbandman, and in no proportion to the profits of the soil'? He called for 'a larger self-denial, an abatement of luxuries, a curtailing even of what are called comforts,' on the part of the

richer classes so that the labourers might have higher wages and
healthier homes to live in. Existing cottages he described as 'ruinous,
filthy, contracted, ill-drained, ill-ventilated, and so situated as to be
productive of many forms of disease and immorality.' Instead of
blaming the agricultural population for their lack of morals they
should look to the conditions in which these people were obliged to
live – 'People go to their Boards of Guardians and hear the long
category of bastardy cases, they cry out "sluts and profligates",
assuming that, when in early life these people have been treated as
swine, they are afterwards to walk with the dignity of Christians.'[6]

These were bold words, spoken because Ashley felt in his heart
that he must no longer remain 'lynx-eyed to the conduct of manufacturers and blind to the faults of land-owners,' even though the
erring land-owners included his own father. He had said nothing that
might be construed as reflecting upon Lord Shaftesbury personally,
but as he returned from Sturminster to St. Giles he could not have
been looking forward to a very warm welcome. Not surprisingly,
Lord Shaftesbury vehemently disapproved of his son's speech. The
labourers, he maintained, did very well on six or seven shillings a
week, though he had the grace to add that 'he did not know how.'
He neither could nor would raise wages or improve cottages – 'these
things cost too much.' His son could not but reflect on the nine
hundred pounds spent that very year on a hothouse, and the further
eight hundred on an unnecessary new farmhouse, reckoning up the
number of cottages that might have been put in order for that money.
Ashley's plain speaking had shattered to pieces the new-found relationship between father and son which he had so highly valued; nor
were his Dorsetshire constituents, landlords and farmers for the most
part, likely to be very tolerant of his words. Bitterly he reflected on a
remark about himself which had recently appeared in *The Examiner*,
'This lord must expect, if he go about telling everyone the plain
truth, to become odious.'

Lord Shaftesbury was gracious enough to bear with his son and
his son's family over the Christmas holiday, though for no one was it
an easy or a pleasant time. Ashley passed Christmas Day itself in
'meditative and subdued, but not melancholy mood'; it was to be
the last Christmas he was to spend in his family home during his
father's lifetime.

Chapter 12

CORN LAW CRISIS

When Parliament reassembled Ashley launched a fierce attack on the
British policy in India which had culminated in the annexation of
Scind. During the Afghan War the Amirs, or princes, of Scind had
objected to the action of the British in occupying forts, forcing a
passage through their territory, and exacting a very large sum in
tribute. Sir Charles Napier, Commander of the British forces, was
put in charge of negotiations. 'We have no right to seize Scind,' he
wrote in his diary, 'but we shall do so and a very advantageous,
useful and humane piece of rascality it will be.' An attack on the
British Residency in Hyderabad gave Napier the excuse he needed.
He defeated the armies of Scind at the battle of Miani, clapped the
Amirs into prison, annexed their territory, sending home the punning
despatch *'Peccavi,'** and proceeded to set up a model administration,
greatly to the benefit of the country and its inhabitants.

Ashley's reaction to these events was curiously modern in tone.
Unlike most of his contemporaries, he saw nothing romantic or
admirable in war or military conquest. A few months later he was to
quote de Joinville's description of Mogador after a bombardment by
the French, 'riddled with balls, blackened by fire, deserted and *horribly*
devastated,' with the brief and bitter comment. 'This is glory!'
He had no feelings of superiority over 'native' rulers or people, and
he believed that they should be treated in exactly the same manner
as 'civilised' Europeans. 'If these people are good enough for us to
contract treaties with,' he wrote of the Amirs, 'they are also good
enough to enjoy the observance of them.' Peel took the contrary
view, declaring in the House of Commons, 'I am afraid there is some
great principle at work wherever civilisation comes into contact
with barbarism which makes it impossible to apply the rules observed
among more advanced nations.' On February 8th Ashley rose in his
wrath and castigated Peel's conduct of Indian policy in a speech
which, although it could win him only sixty-eight votes, left many
* 'I have sinned.'

members who voted against him murmuring uneasily, 'we never gave such an immoral vote before.'

In spite of this success Ashley described himself on February 28th as 'very dejected, seeing everything under a black cloud.' He complained of fever and pains in eyes and forehead – 'Ah, but the Ten Hours Bill would be the best tonic!' On February 6th Graham had brought in a new Factory Bill, limiting the hours of work for children under thirteen to eight and for women and adolescents to twelve. On March 15th Ashley moved an amendment to reduce the working hours of adolescents to ten. The debate which followed produced a fierce passage of arms between Ashley and Bright on the subject of an impostor named Dodd, known as 'the factory cripple.' Ashley stated that 'at the very period of life at which, in many other departments of industry, men are regarded as in the prime of their strength, those employed in the cotton industry are superannuated and set aside,' citing the Ashworths as an example of mill-owners who treated their older workmen thus. Bright, who was related by marriage to the Ashworths, retorted that Ashley's statement was based on false evidence produced by Dodd. He pointed out that Dodd had been discharged from employment because of gross immorality, and accused Ashley of deserting Dodd when once Dodd ceased to be of use to him. In reply Ashley admitted that he had been deceived by Dodd but denied that he had in any way behaved unfairly towards that most undesirable character. (In fact, he had at first been completely taken in; on December 14th 1841 he had written 'Cripple Dodd is a jewel, he sends me invaluable information.')

Although Bright's disclosures about Dodd did Ashley some harm, the vote went in favour of his amendment by a majority of eight. The occasion was a significant one; for the first time the House of Commons had approved the Ten Hours principle. Triumph, however, was short-lived. On March 22nd, in the debate on clause eight, the House again voted against the Government figure of twelve working hours, the votes being 186 to 183. Then, by an almost comic chance, Ashley's amendment establishing a ten-hour working period was lost by seven votes, five confused and confusing members voting 'no' in each division. Nonsense had been made of the Bill. Ashley, however, took a philosophical view of this curious mishap, commenting that the House had been very kind and that the cause was 'mightily advanced.'

On March 25th Graham withdrew the Bill. In the course of his speech he described Ashley's proposals as 'the commencement of a Jack Cade system of legislation.' For some reason this reference to a medieval rebel caught the popular fancy; Doyle produced a cartoon showing Ashley as Cade, and Graham, Peel, Stanley and Goulburn as knights in shining armour, whilst Wellington told Lady Wilton that the expression 'Jack Cade legislation' had given 'mortal offence.' In this same letter he also referred to 'the foolish vanity of Lord Ashley.'[1]

In the interval between the withdrawal of Graham's first Factory Bill and the introduction of its successor Peel sounded Ashley as to his willingness to accept the post of Lord Lieutenant of Ireland. At first sight this suggestion looked painfully like a bribe to induce him to abandon the Ten Hours cause. Such, however, was not Peel's intention, nor did Ashley so understand the offer. In putting forward this suggestion Bonham, the Tory Whip, assured Ashley that Peel *'would not even breathe the subject* until after the Bill had been disposed of.' Nevertheless, Ashley felt it his duty to refuse the offer. 'O God, grant that I may never be seduced by any worldly motive to abandon truth and mercy and justice!' he prayed earnestly in his diary, then coming down to earth, he added, 'pray, how could I work the Factory question as Lord Lieutenant of Ireland? Answer me *that.*'

Although it may have crossed Peel's mind that the suggested appointment would be very pleasing to the Protestants, whom he wished to conciliate before bringing in his Maynooth Bill,* Ashley was in fact an admirable choice, probably the best man available for this very difficult and important post. Honest and incorruptible, he inspired confidence wherever he went, and, unlike so many honest and trustworthy men, he was also extremely able. Though upright he was not unbending; throughout the Ten Hours campaign he had shown himself a clever negotiator, willing, if necessary, to make a reasonable compromise. Yet he was a strong man; and the hand of a strong man was badly needed in this crisis of Irish affairs.

Ashley himself was under no delusions as to the difficulties which would face him were he to accept the offered post. 'I cannot even theorise on the proper mode of governing Ireland,' he was to write on September 30th 1845. 'I should require something akin to a revelation for my guidance.' Though admitting to some gratification at the offer, he was in no doubt what course to adopt; the temptation must be resisted. He seems, however, to have left Bonham in sufficient uncertainty to allow of a similar suggestion being made to him the following year. In January 1845 he was asked to consider becoming Irish Secretary and agreed to talk the matter over with Peel, although

* A controversial proposal to give a Government grant of money to the Roman Catholic College at Maynooth.

protesting that he foresaw 'portentous difficulties.' So apparently did Peel, for the suggested conversation never took place. Instead, Bonham asked Ashley if he were indeed serious in his determination not to take office until the Ten Hours Bill had been carried, to which Ashley replied 'that as long as I had the opportunity of asserting this great principle with even a shadow of success, I was so bound.'[2] So, this spring of 1844, instead of taking up residence in Dublin as Lord Lieutenant, Ashley prepared to engage in yet another battle for the Ten Hours Bill.

On March 29th Graham brought in a new Bill which continued to allow a twelve-hour working day for adolescents, a point on which Peel and Graham were determined to fight to the last. On every other count but this Ashley gave full support to the measure, though some of his more hot-headed followers were for total rejection. The Ten Hours principle was rapidly gaining ground, both inside Parliament and out of it. Successful meetings were held in the great industrial towns; and nearly everywhere the local clergy came out in support of this new campaign. By its vote on Ashley's amendment the House had given its approval to the Ten Hours principle; and now, for the first time, leading Whigs declared strongly in its favour, Russell, Macaulay, Grey, and, most important of all, Palmerston.

Palmerston's conversion came about in an odd manner. One of the most hotly-debated points was the number of miles children had to walk daily whilst tending the machines. With the help of a professional mathematician Ashley had assessed the distance at well over twenty miles, a figure which his opponents declared to be a gross exaggeration. During this resurgence of the Ten Hours campaign two delegates, Grant and Haworth, came up to London from Lancashire to lobby Members of Parliament. Boldly approaching Palmerston in his own home, they succeeded in gaining admittance and found the great man 'dressed like a youth of eighteen and lively as a cricket.' He listened incredulously to their description of the heavy labour performed by factory children – 'Oh, the work of the children cannot be as hard as you represent it, as I am led to understand that the machinery does all the work without the aid of the children, attention to the spindles only being required.' Puzzled as to how to convince the noble lord that a little piecer's lot was not exactly a bed of roses, Grant looked about him for inspiration. His eye fell on two large chairs on castors. Haworth and he pushed these chairs into the middle of the room, where they were made to serve as spinning mules, Haworth acting as spinner and Grant as his little piecer. For a while Palmerston watched fascinated, then ringing for a footman he ordered the man to take one of the chairs whilst he himself took the other. Slowly they pushed them up and down in imitation of the movements of the machines. The play went on until Palmerston, exhausted, stopped his 'machine,' exclaiming, 'Surely this must be an exaggeration of the labour of factory workers.' Haworth had come straight from a Bolton mill; unabashed, he rolled up his trousers and showed his knees deformed by the heavy labour of 'pulling up the carriage.' Palmerston was completely won over, convinced that the children walked or trotted a full twenty-five miles a day. From now onwards he was to be a whole-hearted supporter of Factory Reform.

With the feeling of the country so clearly in favour of a Ten Hours Bill, and even the mill-owners coming round to admit the inevitability of such legislation, it is a little difficult to see why Peel remained so firm in his opposition. He felt profound sympathy with the workers, although his habitual shyness and reserve hid this almost painful concern from general view. On one occasion, in private conversation with the Comte de Jarnac, he lowered his guard and spoke with passionate feeling of the millions of human beings doomed 'to an existence of perpetual labour, to profound ignorance, and to sufferings as difficult to remedy as they are undeserved.' Jarnac describes the extraordinarily vivid and moving impression that Peel's words made upon him:

As the great statesman held on his way, those walls around me, all blazing with light, and teeming with the masterpieces of Rubens and Reynolds, seemed to crumble and vanish in a moment before my gaze. And from the dark and dismal abyss which lay beyond them, I saw conjured up before me, the disinherited among men, the outcast masses of humanity, who exist but to suffer and to labour and to curse their fate, and under the weight of whose just and wrathful indignation the most august and venerable Empires of Christendom shall perish in a day.[3]

Peel certainly did not oppose the Ten Hours Bill because he lacked sympathy with the workers, nor was he in theory opposed to legislative regulation of hours and conditions of labour, but he believed that this was not the moment for so drastic a restriction as that Bill would impose. Trade and industry were only just beginning to recover from a very severe depression; he feared lest any interference with the delicate balance of production might cause a further setback, from which the workers would be the first people to suffer.

*Anne, Countess of Shaftesbury, mother of the Seventh Earl,
whom he referred to as 'a fiend'*

Emily Cowper (Minny) as a child.
A portrait by Sir Thomas Lawrence

In early married life. An engravin
by H. Cook from a portrait
by W.C. Ross

Raphael's 'Madonna di Foligno'. Shaftesbury's favourite picture

The Seventh Earl of Shaftesbury. A portrait by George Richmond

Child worker in a coal pit. An illustration reproduced from the First Report of the Commissioners of Mines, 1842

Winching two children up a coal-shaft

The 'One Tun' Ragged School

An engraving showing the interior of a Ragged School

Ragged School and pupils

A typical slum street in which Ragged School teachers were working

'*The Shoe Black's Lunch*'. *A painting presented to
Lord Shaftesbury by the teachers of a Ragged School*

St Giles House, Dorset

A garden party at St Giles.
Lord and Lady Shaftesbury are on the right. D'Azeglio is in the background

Lord Shaftesbury working at his desk in 1884, one year before his death.
A pencil drawing by **J. G. Wirgman**

'*Shaftesbury, or Lost and Found*' by William Macduff.
Painted in 1864

Unlike Peel, Radicals such as Bright disapproved of the Ten Hours principle in theory as well as in practice. On May 3rd a Radical Member called Roebuck, later to be famous as a critic of the conduct of the Crimean War, brought in a motion condemning any interference with the principle of free contracts between workmen and employers. Though the motion was lost, Ashley smarted badly under this sharp attack. 'A night of trouble, rebuke and blasphemy,' was his description of the debate; 'they fired on me without mercy and left me, like Saint Sebastian, shot through and through with arrows.' Roebuck referred to aristocratic land-owners as 'mere Nimrods, spending their lives in the fox-chase,' hardly an accurate description of Ashley himself, who in the whole course of his life never hunted a fox and only once a hare.

On May 10th Ashley rose to move a Ten Hours Amendment to Graham's Bill. With the aid of statistics he demolished the four main arguments put forward by his opponents, who had declared that such a restriction would diminish production, decrease the value of invested capital, diminish wages, and, by raising prices, increase foreign competition. He also pointed to the fact that only seven weeks previously the House had decided in favour of the restriction to ten hours. No new facts had been brought forward to induce Members to change their minds; 'this House is summoned to cancel this vote, not upon conviction but to save a Government.' In his opinion, this amounted to a declaration that Members should 'never exercise a vote but at the will of a Minister,' a situation which he described as 'a despotism under the forms of the constitution.' He ended with a peroration made up of borrowed phrases, but moving none the less, especially when it is remembered what the future held for him and the Ten Hours Bill:

Sir, it may not be given to me to pass over this Jordan; other and better men have preceded me, and I entered into their labours; other and better men will follow me, and enter into mine; but this consolation I shall ever continue to enjoy – that amid much injustice, and somewhat of calumny, we have at least lighted such a candle in England as, by God's blessing, shall never be put out.

Though the House was clearly on Ashley's side, Graham remained adamant, declaring that if the Ten Hour Amendment were carried he would resign. Faced with this threat the Tories came meekly to heel. In spite of strong Whig support the Amendment was lost by a majority of 138. Ashley, however, was not unduly downcast. The Bill itself was saved 'with all its valuable clauses about machinery and female labour,' and passed the House of Lords, in spite of Brougham's vehement protest, 'I feel that this is great nonsense.' Ashley believed that over this measure Peel had behaved in an unfair and personally vindictive manner:

> Peel was unusually offensive and unjust, he misstated every argument and sneered at every good sentiment – logically he was dishonest; morally he was a heathen. Towards myself and my speech he showed more malignity and more unfairness than I have experienced during the whole debate from Bright, or Cobden, or even Roebuck!

A few weeks later Peel again by threat of resignation forced the House of Commons to rescind a vote already given, this time on the subject of the sugar duties. An irrepressible Radical Member called Duncombe, who had often caused Ashley severe perturbation, proposed that the usual words, 'freely and voluntarily resolved,' should in these circumstances be omitted from the preamble to the Sugar Act; and, for once, Ashley found himself in agreement with Duncombe. He had remained commendably calm when the Government had used this strategy of threatened resignation against the Ten Hours Amendment, fearing 'the influence of temper' in a case which touched him personally. Now, however, he felt free to protest in a letter in which he made his disapproval crystal clear. He took this step believing that 'it is right to undeceive a leader who believes, or may believe, that one is an unqualified admirer and supporter.' Peel had little grounds for supposing Ashley's support to be unqualified, and he now naturally assumed it to be totally withdrawn. Ashley replied that he still intended to vote for most of Peel's measures, thus preserving an uneasy *modus vivendi*.

Ashley had one more important speech to make before the end of this session. Since 1834 he had been Chairman of the Metropolitan Lunacy Commissioners, whose powers had been extended in 1842 to cover the whole of England and Wales. The statute under which the Commission had been constituted would expire in 1845; Ashley therefore now brought in a motion 'praying Her Majesty to take into her consideration the Report of the Metropolitan Commissioners in Lunacy,' as the first step towards the passing of a new Act. In his speech on behalf of 'the most helpless if not the most afflicted portion of the human race' he pointed to the scandals surrounding the confinement of single lunatics in private houses, a class of persons unprotected by the existing law. He described the state of affairs existing in many private asylums receiving both pauper and paying patients, where, in spite of the Commissioners' efforts, conditions remained appalling. He urged the building of more county asylums which should be regarded not as places where the insane could be locked away but as hospitals where patients could be restored to health. Perhaps remembering his druidic days, he made a special plea for the building of asylums in Wales – 'the greatest of all cruelties was to send the wretched pauper to a people whose language he could not understand.' Finally, he begged his hearers not 'to run away with the notion that even the hopelessly mad are dead to all capacity of intellectual or moral exertion, quite the reverse; their feelings too are painfully alive, I have seen them writhe under supposed contempt, whilst a word of kindness and respect would kindle their whole countenance into an expression of joy.'[4] That reference to 'respect' contains the secret of Ashley's hold over the derelict and the down-and-out; he was never to fail in respect for the least of God's creatures, be they thieves, chimney-sweeps, drunkards, or raving lunatics.

At the beginning of August, Ashley was at last free to set off for Ryde on the Isle of Wight, with 'bag and baggage, wife and children.' During this holiday he inspected Parkhurst Prison and made the typical comment, 'How ignorant and how criminal is the nation – quite as ignorant and far more criminal than these wretched boys – which permits, by its neglect, these tares to be sown and then tediously labours to uproot them!' He also visited the new royal yacht which he described as 'a floating palace, a thing not seen since the days when Cleopatra descended the Nile':

All this is very well, quite right, the Queen should have such a barge to carry her on the seas, but not very well, not quite right, to enjoy such prodigious ease and splendour at the expense of every comfort, almost every decency, so to speak, nay more, by the absolute privations of the crew – labouring men, who bear Her Majesty in state and safety. The contrast was painful and disgusting.

In September Ashley set out on another tour of the industrial North. As always, he grieved to leave his children – 'sad to have no kids, no reading in the morning' – but he was pleased to have Minny with him and her brother, William. Ashley's feelings towards this brother-in-law were somewhat ambivalent. Like his uncle, Melbourne, William

had an intellectual interest in religion, though he could not be described as a spiritually-minded man._ He investigated, and for a brief
time professed, all manner of beliefs, ranging from what was afterwards known as Irvingism to the Broad Churchmanship of Maurice
and Stanley. By temperament he was light-hearted and inclined to
be amorous. His pretty young wife died tragically within their
first year of marriage. Three months after her death Ashley was
horrified to see the supposedly disconsolate William come down to
breakfast wearing a pink coat and in high spirits at the prospect of
a day's hunting. All through this summer of 1844 William had been
dancing attendance on Caroline Norton, who was believed to be
Melbourne's mistress. 'He goes on retired expeditions with Mrs.
Norton, his master's real or suspected paramour,' Ashley wrote. 'She
may not be so but public decency requires on his part at least more
reserve.' William escaped from Caroline Norton only to be ensnared
by a still more dangerous anonymous lady 'deep in Tractarianism
and certainly clever.' Ashley was much relieved to be assured by
Minny that in this case William had no serious intention of matrimony, realising all too clearly that 'the differences of opinion were
too wide to admit of domestic harmony.' Tractarianism was one of
the few creeds William had never thought to embrace.

In political as well as private affairs Ashley was apt to find his
brother-in-law a little unstable. The two disagreed over measures
such as the Dissenters' Chapels Act and the Act for the admission of
Jews to Parliament. On these occasions Ashley could become sufficiently annoyed to declare that although he was to be personally loved
he was never to be politically trusted. The two men, however, were
warmly attached and were to remain friends for life.

Accompanied by William, Ashley visited Manchester and, a few
days later, rode to Turton to see the Ashworth mills, an expedition
which was in a sense a return visit, Henry Ashworth having already
visited the Shaftesbury estates and commented publicly on the
shocking conditions prevailing there. Ashley was magnanimous
enough to be full of praise for all he saw at Turton – 'the mills are
worth seeing, cleanliness quite astonishing, much discipline and
order, houses for his people in the best state that I ever saw dwellings
for working men, his hands healthier than the generality.'

All mills were not as Ashworth's. At Bolton, Ashley called on a mill-
owner called Bolling, notorious for truck-payment, and inspected
his mill – 'place me rather on the dust heap or in the dung hole than
in his factory!' At Rochdale, finding John Bright himself away,
Ashley thought it more tactful not to ask to see over the mills, a

piece of politeness which he was afterwards to regret. Instead he talked with John's brother Thomas, who 'pounded me for half-an-hour by the clock with Corn Laws and taxation.'

The atmosphere of activity, change and growth typical of the industrial North, which many men found so exhilarating, was to Ashley merely 'a hurry, a rush, a violent and maddened race.' He could not but admire such mill-owners as Richard Birley, 'a sensible man in a mighty business, a striking specimen of the master manufacturing class,' but he had no use for the order of society to which Birley belonged. With unusual foresight he pointed to the two blind spots in the mill-owners' outlook which were in the long run to prove fatal to the cotton industry, the inability to see beyond today's prosperity to tomorrow's depression, and the fanatical belief in Lancashire cotton which made them put all their financial eggs into that one over-loaded basket. The mill-hands were the worst sufferers from the inevitable but unforeseen sequence of boom and recession – 'the masters suffer in their profits but the work-people in their lives.' He believed the masters to be entirely callous towards this suffering – 'They are playing with men as with ninepins, setting them up and knocking them down again' – but he had the justice to admit that his own South country agriculturalists would behave in similar manner were it equally in their interest to do so.

Whilst in the North Ashley took care to steer clear of the Young England group, 'not wishing to enter into competition with Disraeli, John Manners, Mr. Smythe, and make rival speeches over a tea-table.' Although he had come to regard Manners as 'a really well-intentioned fellow,' he yet believed that *The Times'* support of Manners was a deliberate attempt 'to raise up a Tractarian champion for the poor in opposition to myself,' a scheme engineered by an editor whom he described as 'a devilish fellow, a classical Beelzebub.' Hodder writes that 'Mr. Walter, in the columns of *The Times*, gave very material support to the cause.' John Walter had been drawn into the Ten Hour movement through his championship of Oastler and his opposition to the new Poor Law. His support of Ashley personally was much more equivocal, or so it appeared to Ashley himself, who referred to *The Times* as being 'more malignant than ever,' publishing accusations against him which 'could only have been made by a man in whose heart the Devil had attained full power.'

Because they were not welcome at St. Giles, Ashley and his family spent much time this winter at Broadlands, a place where he could never feel really well or happy – 'What waste of time; what killers of precious moments, what ravishers of systematic habits!' He could

only remind himself that 'the dear kind people,' Lord and Lady
Palmerston, were showing him the affection and hospitality denied
to him by his own father, and keep his opinions of their manner
and morals entirely to himself, only lamenting privately in his
diary, 'Woe is me that I am constrained to dwell in the tents of
Kedar!'

As part of his plan for Irish education Peel now proposed to
increase the grant which the British Government already made to the
Roman Catholic college at Maynooth. Though the sum involved
was small the emotions aroused were intense. Gladstone at once
resigned his post at the Board of Trade. He had once written a book
in which he had stated his disapproval of such grants, and although
he had now changed his mind on the subject, he conceived that
honour demanded he should resign, though as a private member he
would vote for the measure. On April 11th he explained this complicated position to the House of Commons. 'Gladstone last night unintelligible to everyone,' Ashley recorded, 'doubled and re-doubled like
an old hare.' In a further effort to explain himself Gladstone wrote
Peel a letter of quite remarkable length and obscurity. It is difficult
not to feel a little sorry for a busy Prime Minister whose party included two such high-minded and indefatigable letter-writers as
Gladstone and Ashley. To Peel their piety was unattractive and their
scruples incomprehensible; it is greatly to his credit that he bore
with them so patiently.

On the Maynooth question Ashley himself took up what he described as 'the highest ground of opposition,' maintaining that to give
any endowment to the Roman Catholic Church was both wicked
and objectionable. His attitude was at least logical, for he had
always believed that the existence of the Protestant Church of
Ireland could be justified on one ground and one only – Protestantism was right and Catholicism was wrong. Feeling as strongly as
he did, he longed yet feared to speak in the Maynooth debate. On
April 18th, overcoming his hesitation, he made one of the most
successful speeches of his parliamentary career – 'Astonishing!
Astonishing! How, why, wherefore, what? I must sing, more than
ever, *Non nobis Domine.*' Even the Maynooth priests listening in
the gallery found something to praise in the studied moderation of his
language, whilst the members of the Young England party commended his powerful and sincere eloquence. With a wistful glance
at what might have been, Ashley was especially pleased that so
many Members should describe his speech as 'the speech of a man
who might be sent for to form a government.'

Special praise came from Disraeli, who was never slow to applaud success:

> Disraeli said to me, 'I think it quite a duty to tell you what an effect your speech has produced.' I thanked him and replied that, standing as I did, these things gave me hearty encouragement. 'Yes,' he added, 'I have long observed your single efforts and I thought it a duty to break the ice and say so.'

Disraeli's attitude towards Ashley's social reforms was never absolutely clear and unequivocal. In his novel *Sybil* he shows real concern for the working classes, yet not till 1850 did he speak in favour of any Factory Act. In a general way he was in sympathy with Ashley's efforts, but his sympathy did not stretch as far as practical support. This spring of 1845 Disraeli's attacks on Peel were so fierce as to shock Ashley, who was certainly no friend to the Prime Minister. In March, on an Anti-Corn-Law motion brought forward by Cobden, Disraeli delivered a speech, described by Ashley as 'very clever and biting,' which left Peel twitching nervously, powerless to conceal his distress and annoyance. 'Were not Peel the most unpopular head of a party that ever existed,' Ashley commented, 'these things would be put down by rebuke in public and frowns in private society.'

Ashley could never approve of Peel himself, but he could, and did, approve some of his measures, such as the 1845 budget:

> Peel's budget last night bold and ingenious and likely to benefit the working man . . . His whole speech and budget was a thing of Free Trade . . . Surely such a budget must produce great and beneficial effects, yet how *could* Peel introduce it?

Ashley himself was in very much the same position as Peel. He had now to answer his own question, 'What is the latitude permitted to public men in change of opinion and action?' For the last three or four years he had seen and acknowledged the fact that the prevailing trend was towards Free Trade, and he had not been altogether disapproving. Because he could not and would not 'roar out about Protection,' his Dorset constituents had become at first suspicious and by now frankly distrustful, so much so that a group of malcontents was already planning to replace him by a more orthodox Tory. His position was the more unhappy because the Lancashire operatives had also become doubtful of his good intentions,

wondering why he did not bring in yet another Ten Hours Bill. He
knew well enough that the time was not yet ripe, but he suffered
none the less. The injustice of their suspicions cut him to the quick –
'No man, living or dead, has sacrificed for them the tenth part of
what I have; and what motive can I have, but their interest, to be
silent even for an hour?'

One small piece of factory reform Ashley did in fact achieve
during this year of 1845. Visiting a calico printing works during his
Northern tour he had been appalled by the working conditions and
hours of the children employed there, and in February 1845 he
brought in a Bill to regulate the labour of children in the calico printing industry. On a fine morning in March he was up early to hear the
birds sing – 'Let everything that hath breath praise the Lord, aye,
children in print-works no less than birds and beasts and creeping
things.' Such a day made him feel that he could gladly abandon his
commitments and settle down to a quiet life in the country; but in
more clear-sighted moments he realised that both his duty and his
happiness lay elsewhere: 'The country is charming, inexpressibly
charming, but I prefer London, and all its sterility of social life, and
gloominess of atmosphere, with its capacity for fruitful exertion.'
The progress of the Calico Printers' Bill caused him 'sad alternations
of joy and fear' before it finally passed the House of Lords in June.

In July two much more important Bills became law. Ashley's
great Lunacy Acts, 'For the Regulation of Lunatic Asylums' and
'For the better Care and Treatment of Lunatics in England and
Wales,' were among the most valuable measures he ever sponsored.
They arose out of the Report of the Commissioners in Lunacy which
he had commended to Parliament the previous year. These Acts
amended and consolidated the existing law, ordered instead of merely
permitting the building of country lunatic asylums, and established
a permanent Lunacy Commission with Ashley as Chairman. They also
established a better method of record-keeping and a more stringent
system of certification to safeguard patients against unwarranted
detention.

In a masterly speech Ashley argued that in spite of the great improvement brought about by the 1828 Act there was still much need
for reform, and cited several particularly horrid cases to prove his
point. He described the plight of a Welsh lunatic girl, Mary Jones,
who had been shut up for more than ten years in a tiny loft with one
boarded-up window which admitted little air and no light. The
room was indescribably filthy and the smell almost intolerable; the
miserable girl could only squat 'in a bent and crouching posture,

which had produced shocking deformity,' and 'her countenance, still pleasing, was piercingly anxious and marked by an expression of despair.' When Ashley spoke of the treatment of lunatics he was speaking from long experience and great knowledge. Since 1828, when he started his life-long work on behalf of the insane, he had visited numerous asylums, both public and private, and dealt with many individual cases. (The next year, 1846, he was to be consulted about the delicate problem of Gladstone's sister, Helen.) Thankless and trying though it was, this was a work in which he found great satisfaction because he could see real improvement resulting from his labours.

The passage of the Lunacy Bills through Parliament caused Ashley much anguish of spirit. He was particularly distressed that one of their chief opponents in the House of Lords should be his own father, 'of course taking the lead in hatred and resistance to anything of mine.' He grew more and more alarmed about the state of affairs at St. Giles, where, reversing the practice of a lifetime, Lord Shaftesbury was granting long leases of farms to dishonest and undesirable tenants and allowing everything to fall into confusion and decay. With all these anxieties pressing heavily upon him Ashley found himself burdened with a sudden increase in his parliamentary work. Eighteen-forty-five was the year of the great Railway boom. Ashley was made chairman of a Parliamentary Committee dealing with railway matters; and so great was the pressure of business that this Committee frequently sat on six days of the week. Ashley's own reaction to railway travel was similar to that of the Roman Catholic priest who, whenever the train entered a tunnel, fell to reciting the *De Profundis*. He saw a railway journey as a subject for earnest prayer: 'We might see and acknowledge that this invention of man had brought with it a vast addition of danger, and magnified, if possible, the necessity of prayer before a journey; thus it is in our own power to sanctify our terrors and make them fruitful.'

Perhaps the most painful of all Ashley's cares was anxiety for his eldest son. The time had come for Accy to leave the pleasant, pious establishment on the Isle of Wight and go to a larger school. Ashley does not seem to have considered sending Accy to Harrow, his own old school. He reflected on Eton, but rejected the idea:

I fear Eton; I dread the proximity of Windsor with all its means and allurements; dread the tone and atmosphere of the school; it makes admirable gentlemen and finished scholars – fits a man, beyond all competition, for the drawing-room, the club, St. James's

Street and all the mysteries of social elegance; but it does not
make the man required for the coming generation. We must have
nobler, deeper, and sterner stuff; more of the inward, not so much
of the outward gentleman.

Ashley decided on Rugby, the school which Thomas Arnold had
made so famous, and which was now, under Arnold's successor, Tait,
flourishing as never before in its history. In Accy's case, however,
the school proved a failure from the first. Within a month Ashley
was asking himself anxiously, 'Have I done rightly in sending my
son to Rugby?' He knew well enough that his hopes and fears for
Accy were much exaggerated – 'I form too high a standard, entertain too sanguine hopes, swallow a camel and strain at a gnat' – yet
he could not rid himself of them. Accy's own letters were unsatisfactory; and soon his tutor was sending home reports complaining of
unpunctuality and carelessness. For the first time Ashley honestly
admitted to himself his disappointment in his eldest son:

> Alas, dear Accy, may God bless and prosper him, and lead him to
> high and fruitful service! But as yet I see only scanty signs of
> such a spirit and capacity. Courteous, liberal, kind, good-tem-
> pered, he adds to these qualities idleness, want of zeal and energy,
> love of pleasure and display, with ready forgetfulness of things
> and individuals. These are not the materials for, I say not a great
> man (I desire not power or renown) but for a useful man; and much
> shall I have for which to thank God if, with such feeble composition
> as this, he does not harass my mature life and grieve my old age.

Ashley's disappointment in Accy was partly compensated for by
his pleasure in his second son, Francis, a boy after his own heart,
'giving signs that he is set for the honour of his Saviour, the benefit of
his generation, and the comfort of his family.' In spite of Accy's
weakness Ashley could still say, 'God has blessed me greatly, wonder-
fully, most undeservedly, in my children.' He could see in them,
and especially in Francis and in young Evelyn or Edy, 'dawnings of
piety, energy, and religious zeal.' In the Ashley family, however,
life with father was by no means an unvarying round of piety and
good works. A seaside holiday was an annual delight, whilst in London
a visit to the Zoo was a favourite excursion (Ashley, like many
another parent, found it a most exhausting one). If a treat had been
promised he took the greatest care to see that the promise was fulfilled at no matter what cost to himself in time, inconvenience or

money – 'Children hold much to such things and the loss of money is of less account than the loss of confidence.' This attitude was the more remarkable in a man as badly-off as Ashley; about this time he congratulated himself that an invitation to Windsor had reached him too late for acceptance, since he could not afford the twenty-five pounds' expenditure such a visit would have entailed.

Such was the dissatisfaction among the North Country operatives that in October Ashley judged it necessary to make another visit to the industrial districts. From Rowton, his first stopping-place, he despatched a letter to his Dorsetshire constituents. The cold wet weather had destroyed all hopes of a good harvest and even in England there was bound to be shortage and distress. In Ireland a worse disaster had occurred; the potato crop had failed completely. Though the full extent of the impending tragedy was not yet apparent, Ashley realised that the Corn Laws were doomed; with famine in Ireland not a threat but a certainty and shortage certain in England also, no statesman could continue to keep the ports closed to cheap foreign corn. Since repeal could not now be avoided Ashley advised his constituents to accept the inevitable and concentrate their attention on making the best terms they could for themselves – 'It is needless to argue the policy or impolicy of such a change; it would rather be wise to consider in what way you can break the force of the inevitable blow.' In his diary Ashley summed up his own situation as he saw it:

> On one side I shall lose, or appear to lose, some electoral support; but that is in fact nothing; the Sturminster speech is the *fons et origo mali*; the farmers will never forgive it. On the other, I have spoken my mind honestly and have [illegible] my own actions by giving them the best advice; and time and our position will [illegible] to desist from a hopeless attempt to maintain the Corn Laws in all their integrity. I have been pained, sadly pained, to follow the rash and obstinate ignorance of the landed gentry; they will find it difficult to sustain their monopoly – it may be the best and most necessary of laws but the thing has gone from them; and they must make the loss as light as they can.

From suspicious Dorsetshire farmers Ashley turned to suspicious North Country mill-hands. Here at least all went well. Distrust and annoyance melted away as soon as Ashley and his critics met face to face. In Bolton he found the operatives 'hearty, in excellent spirits, full of hope, far more so than I am.' He praised the workers for their remarkable restraint – 'no violence of language or action, and no threats, no expressions of vengeance, no bitter accusations, no unhealable wounds' – and pointed to their behaviour as 'a bright example to the whole world of the mode in which people should demand, and will obtain, their inalienable rights.'

On his return to London Ashley fell into one of his deep depressions, cheered only by the birth of a third daughter, Constance, on November 29th. It was becoming more and more apparent that the repeal of the Corn Laws could not be long delayed. At a Cabinet meeting on November 25th Peel proposed immediate suspension. Next day the Whig leader, Lord John Russell, declared himself in favour of total repeal. 'Well done, Johnny!' was Ashley's comment. On December 5th Peel resigned, but when Russell failed to form a ministry he found himself with no option but to resume office. He had come into power as leader of a party pledged to support the Corn Laws; he now saw himself faced with the necessity of forcing their repeal through Parliament against the express wishes of his own supporters.

Ashley's dilemma was similar to Peel's and no less agonising. As a declared Protectionist he had been elected for a constituency where the voters were, almost to a man, hot against repeal. He had now changed his mind. On Christmas Eve he summed up his position: 'It seems that, if I were to vote for abolition, I should vote in a sense diametrically opposite to the sense of their hopes and views when they chose me for their representative, and in a way which, had it then been foreseen, would have, in all likelihood, prevented my election.' Yet neither he nor Peel could possibly acquiesce in the continuation of a policy which they had ceased to approve. Peel was afterwards to write, 'The honour of public men would not have been maintained if a Minister had, at a critical period, shrunk from the duty of giving that advice which he believed to be best';[5] Ashley wrote in similar strain, 'I could not myself coldly persist in a line of conduct which was at variance with my own judgement of what was required.'

Ashley had the alternative, which Peel had not, of retiring from the struggle. Since Russell could not or would not assume responsibility, Peel had to carry on, knowing that he alone could force repeal through a predominantly Tory Parliament. Ashley, on the contrary, was free to resign his seat, little though he wished to do so. His great aim and ambition was to see the Ten Hours Bill become law. After twelve years of struggle and disappointment the House of Commons had at last voted in favour of the Bill's principle; leading figures on both sides of the House had declared their support. Though Ashley had wisely refrained from bringing the measure in again whilst men's minds were so preoccupied with the Corn Laws, already he was looking for a propitious moment for its re-introduction. As early as August he had written, 'it is time to revert to the Ten Hours Bill.' For a long time he had feared that it might not fall to his lot to steer that measure safely through Parliament; the phrase 'it may not be given to me to pass over this Jordan,' had recurred more and more frequently in his writings and speeches. In his mind had been the thought of his father's death and his own relegation to the House of Lords; now, for a different, unforeseen reason, his prophecy was to come true.

The choice before Ashley was the more painful because by resigning his seat he would apparently be aligning himself with those with whom he in fact profoundly disagreed. He had no use for the extreme Protectionists who continued to hold out against any measure of repeal, imagining that they could form a government without Peel – 'Saul was not more demented than these men nor more certainly on the road to destruction.' Much as he disliked and distrusted Peel, Ashley would have been perfectly prepared to support him on this issue had it not been for his duty towards his constituents. And not to his constituents only – he had a duty towards all professedly religious men, in particular towards all Evangelicals. The nation at large had come to regard him as their representative. He must not seem to go back on 'an honourable understanding,' he must be clearly *sans peur et sans reproche* – 'far better that I should suffer any loss than give "occasion to the enemies of God to blaspheme;" and to say that "after all, your religious men, when they come to be tried, are no better than any one else." '

The struggle in Ashley's mind continued all through the holiday season. In these circumstances it is not surprising that he should find Christmas an especially trying time – 'They talk of a merry Christmas; it is never, I confess, merry to me; I am ever beset by melancholy thoughts and hopeless sympathies.' As always, he took refuge in thoughts of the Second Advent, and in Minny's love and loyalty. The passage which Hodder quotes as showing that she was 'with her husband heart and soul in this matter,' is, however, taken out of context.[6] When Ashley wrote 'Ought I not to be deeply grateful to Almighty God that he has given me a wife capable of every generous self-denial and prepared to rejoice in it?' he was thinking of clothes and carriages, not of the Corn Laws. He had just remarked on the worldly behaviour of a bishop's wife who drove about London 'in an equipage which is the talk and admiration of the town,' and

he was thanking Heaven that his own wife chose to spend what little
spare money they had on charitable gifts rather than on splendid
liveries for her footmen.

On January 3rd Ashley received a letter from Farquharson, 'the
King of the Dorset farmers,' and one of his chief supporters, saying
that the time had come to make a stand in support of the Corn
Laws, and adding that in his opinion such a stand would prove
successful. Ashley was shocked to find a man of Farquharson's
position so ignorant of the true facts of the situation, but he nevertheless recognised that his constituents were almost unanimously
of this opinion. When Parliament assembled on January 22nd Peel
announced that he proposed to lower the duty on corn immediately
to a few shillings, and to abolish it altogether within three years.
Five days later he made a still more explicit statement. When, later
that night, Ashley opened his diary, his mind was made up:

I shall resign my seat, and throw up all my beloved prospects;
all for which I have sacrificed everything that a public man values;
all that I had begun, and all that I have designed. Nearly all my
whole means of doing good will cease with my membership of
Parliament. But God's will be done.

On January 30th he introduced a Ten Hours Bill, this time, according to Hodder, 'with every prospect of success.' Ashley himself
recorded that the House, though civil, was 'very cold and comfortless.' In the course of the debate Bright declared that Ashley had
refused to visit the Bright mills, thus deliberately ignoring evidence
which would tell against his own case. Bright then walked out of the
House without waiting to hear Ashley explain that he had not visited
the mills because he did not wish to appear to be spying in the absence
of the owner.

The next day, January 31st, Ashley received another letter from
Farquharson saying bluntly that the farmers would regard any vote
for repeal as a direct violation of election pledges. Immediately
Ashley took up his pen and wrote to apply for the Chiltern Hundreds.
'Am now,' he recorded in his diary, 'for the first time for nearly twenty
years, no longer a Member of Parliament.'

PART THREE

Philanthropy, with a peerage, reduces a man to the lowest point.

Shaftesbury's Diary, May 3rd 1853

Chapter 13

PHILANTHROPIC WORK OUTSIDE PARLIAMENT

Ashley's departure from the House of Commons marks a watershed in his life. Hitherto his ambitions, his efforts, and, most important of all, his plans to help his fellow men, had flowed broadly in one direction; now they were to be turned into another channel. After 1841 he had definitely abandoned the idea of a political career but he still looked to the House of Commons as the place where his real work was to be done. On April 5th 1844 he had written of 'foolish, well-meaning people urging me to go down to the West Riding,' adding, 'my place is in the House of Commons.' So he had always seen it, believing that his chief vocation was to act as Parliamentary spokesman for the poor, the oppressed, and the outcast, who had no votes and could not speak for themselves. Because of his pre-occupation with Parliament he had hitherto been described as a politician; now he was to be called a philanthropist, a term which he himself disliked.

Too much, of course, must not be made of this shift of emphasis. The importance of Ashley's application for the stewardship of the Chiltern Hundreds was, like that office itself, symbolic rather than actual. No one supposed that he would long remain without a seat; he himself confidently expected to return to the House of Commons speedily. He knew, however, that this return could be for but a short time; before very long the death of his old and ailing father must see him removed to the House of Lords. Faced with the necessity of abandoning his seat he had written sadly, 'nearly all my whole means of doing good will cease with my membership of Parliament.' The brief period which he was now to spend without a seat in the House of Commons was long enough to show him that he could do as much good work outside Parliament as ever he could achieve inside it.

On his return to Parliament Ashley was still to remain the great promoter of legislation dealing with social reforms, but from now

onwards he was to find ever increasing interest and opportunities
for service outside the House in what would today be called welfare
work. What he himself wrote of his preoccupation with Ragged
Schools applied equally to his philanthropic work as a whole. 'Expul-
sion from Parliament has led me to this pursuit which I could not
undertake had I remained in the House of Commons,' he noted
on December 8th 1846; 'thank heaven I thus changed my front but
did not retreat from duty.'

Ashley was never one to let the grass grow under his feet. Immediately upon his application for the Chiltern Hundreds he decided
to turn his enforced leisure to good account by seeing for himself
the conditions in which the London poor were obliged to live. Though
extreme poverty and squalor were to be found not only in South
London and the East End but in fashionable quarters such as Westminster and Mayfair, the rich remained in almost complete ignorance
of a state of affairs existing at their very doorsteps. The Victorians
were not squeamish; wives and daughters of country squires and
parsons were very familiar with ragged village children and stinking
cottage homes; the urban slums, however, remained *terra incognita*
to the wealthier classes.

With Southwood Smith, Ashley had already made one or two
'perambulations' of Whitechapel and Bethnal Green; now he set
about a thorough exploration of the hidden and horrible slums
of London. Again with Southwood Smith, or with a City missionary,
he threaded his way through dark, narrow alleys, the walls running
with filthy slime, the pathway an open drain. Determined though
he was to see the very worst, Ashley was unable to force himself
to go beyond the entrance to some of these alleys, so overpowering
was the smell. Behind the crumbling façades of what had once been
respectable houses Ashley discovered insanitary, dilapidated 'rook-
eries' crammed with human beings. At the back of these houses was
a labyrinth of courts opening one into the other. Most courts had
one leaking privy to serve all the surrounding dwellings; some courts
had no sanitary arrangements whatsoever. Time and again Ashley
and his guide found themselves surrounded by ragged and angry
women who supposed these well-dressed visitors to be officials of some
sort. Their cry was always for water, since several courts had none
at all and in others the supply to the one common tap might be cut
off for days and weeks together. They would also beg for the removal
of the piles of accumulated dirt, dung and rubbish. The best streets
were cleaned once a week, second-best once a fortnight, courts and
similar places never.

These filthy, stinking courts were surrounded by decaying cottages and shacks. Inside them was damp, darkness, dirt and foul air. Sometimes there would be a table, two or three chairs, and a communal bed for all ages and both sexes, sometimes no furniture at all and for a bed a heap of rags even dirtier than the floor. These hovels were grossly overcrowded – 'happy is the family that can boast of a single room to itself, and in that room a dry corner.'[1]

One phenomenon especially struck Ashley. In these terrible places there existed a race of beings apparently unknown to the outside world, 'singular children, things *sui generis*, nondescript, unknown and uncared for.' Everywhere he saw them, children begging at street-corners, children squatting on doorsteps, children wading in gutters or clambering up rubbish heaps in search of what they could pick up. Many were illegitimate, others were orphans, none of them had a home, some had no name. At an age when more fortunate children were still in the nursery, these children lived in the only manner open to them – Ashley found a three-year-old keeping itself alive entirely by its own wits – begging, scrounging, stealing. If they could come by the necessary two or three pence they slept by night in a common lodging-house, if not, under arches, in derelict buildings, or, like one enterprising boy, curled up inside a garden roller. 'They lived as the pariah dog lived,' wrote Ashley, 'and were treated much in the same way.'

The modern age has seen hoards of such children wandering over countries devastated by war and famine; Ashley found thirty thousand in the capital city of the British Empire at the height of its prosperity. They aroused his curiosity as well as his pity; he set out to investigate 'their natural history, their haunts, their habits, their idiosyncrasy, their points of resemblance to the rest of mankind, and the part they maintain in the great purpose of creation.' He watched them as they paddled in the stinking river mud at low water searching for corks, coals, sticks or scraps of metal, and listened to their delighted shouts when any such treasure-trove came their way, marvelling that these neglected, starving creatures should be so full of spirits and energy. Most of them ran about half-naked, counting themselves lucky if they possessed a ragged pair of trousers stopping short at the knee or a tail-coat trailing below their heels. All this Ashley described in an article in the *Quarterly Review*, written as if detailing the habits and customs of a hitherto unknown tribe of savages. The tone of his comments shows how strong was his instinctive liking and sympathy for these independent urchins, bold and cheeky as London sparrows, though, sadly, not so plump:

They receive no education, religious or secular; they are subjected to no restraint of any sort; never do they hear the word of
advice or the accent of kindness; the notions that exist in the
minds of ordinary persons have no place in theirs; having nothing
exclusively of their own, they seem to think such, in fact, the true
position of society; and, helping themselves without scruple to
the goods of others, they can never recognise, when convicted
before a magistrate, the justice of a sentence which punished them
for having done little more than was indispensable to their existence.

Ashley's favourite method of dealing with these children was by
the establishment of Ragged Schools. He had come in touch with
the Ragged School movement as early as 1843 when he chanced to
see a notice in *The Times* appealing for help for Field Lane School,
which was situated in a notorious district nicknamed 'Jack Ketch's
Warren' because so many of its inhabitants ended on the gallows.
Charles Dickens, a keen supporter of Ragged Schools, has given a
description of the Field Lane School as it was when Ashley first
visited it:

I found my first Ragged School in an obscure place . . . pitifully
struggling for life under every disadvantage. It had no means; it
derived no power or protection from being recognised by any
authority; it attracted within its walls a fluctuating swarm of
faces – young in years, but youthful in nothing else – that scowled
Hope out of countenance. It was held in a low-roofed den, in a
sickening atmosphere, in the midst of taint and dirt and pesti-
lence; with all the deadly sins let loose, howling and shrieking at
the doors. Zeal did not supply the place of method and training;
the teachers knew little of their office; the pupils, with an evil
sharpness, found them out, got the better of them, derided them,
made blasphemous answers to Scriptural questions, sang, fought,
danced, robbed each other – seemed possessed by legions of devils.
The place was stormed and carried, over and over again; the lights
were blown out, the books strewn in the gutters, the female scholars
carried off triumphantly to their old wickedness. With no strength
in it but its purpose the school stood it all out and made its way.[2]

In origin the Ragged Schools were not part of an organised, con-
certed effort. Schools of this type sprang up wherever and whenever
two or three devoted enthusiasts set to work to meet an obvious need.
Most of them were in city slums but a few were to be found in country

districts. In *The Daisy Chain,* for instance, Miss Charlotte Yonge describes how a fifteen-year-old girl started such a school in a neglected hamlet for children too dirty and ragged to be admitted to the neighbouring National School. Expenses were low, funds almost non-existent. Ethel May of *The Daisy Chain* started with a capital of fifteen shillings and sixpence; Ashley reckoned that a school for two hundred and eighty children, open every evening, could be run on an income of fifty-eight pounds a year. All Ragged Schools were religious in tone; but the type of religious teaching varied from Miss Yonge's Tractarianism to the Unitarianism prevalent in most Bristol schools. Those schools, however, who were later to join the Ragged Schools Union, were exclusively Evangelical or Nonconformist.

That Union sprang from very small beginnings. In April 1844 a clerk, a woollen-draper, a dealer in second-hand goods and a City missionary, four men without money, influence, or position, met together to form an association 'to give permanence, regularity and vigour to existing Ragged Schools and to promote the formation of new ones throughout the Metropolis.' From that resolution came the Ragged Schools Union with Ashley as its president. During his first years of office he visited several schools and took the chair at various meetings, but so long as he remained in the House of Commons he could not devote as much time as he would have wished to this work. Now, temporarily free of parliamentary duties, he made the Ragged Schools his first priority.

The adjective 'ragged' was chosen of set purpose, not as an insult, but as an encouragement to the type of child for whom these schools were intended. That any school should deliberately be given a title apparently so destructive of the pupils' self-respect is clear evidence of the vast distance between that generation and our own. 'We entertain no fanatical passion for the name,' Ashley wrote in his *Quarterly Review* article, 'though we could quote many instances in which some of the most degraded of the race have been invited by the belief that the place and the service were not too grand for their misery. . . . The permanence of the title does not condemn the pupils to the permanence of their condition. The pupils, if improved, are drafted off to better places of. education; but the Ragged School remains for those who are still ragged.'

The Hammonds, disregarding the values and circumstances of the mid-nineteenth century, speak slightingly of 'the pious and dutiful twilight of the Ragged Schools.'[3] If the Ragged Schools were a twilight, the ignorance from which they helped their pupils to emerge was darkness entire. They were places where, to quote the Hammonds

again, these outcast children 'had learned their Bibles, had come
to like clean faces and clean collars, had grown into respectable and
God-fearing men and women.'4 (The Ragged Schools also taught
the children the three Rs, and sometimes gave them the rudiments of
training in a handicraft.) This may seem an inadequate educational
achievement to a generation that sets no undue store by either
cleanliness or godliness, but it represents, not unfairly, the Victorian
ideal. It would be ridiculous to suppose that a Ragged School could
have been run in accordance with twentieth-century ideas, or follow
the same principles as a modern Comprehensive. Of course the Ragged
Schools were paternalistic; nothing else was to be expected in that
paternalistic age. Paternalism was in fact no bad thing for children
who had never known a father's love and care and discipline. These
schools met a need which is now mercifully extinct; they should be
judged by their success or failure in achieving their own objectives,
not by the educational standards of a more prosperous and sophisticated age.

Ashley's passionate preoccupation with Ragged School work –
'If the Ragged School system were to fail,' he was to declare in his
old age, 'I should not die in the course of nature, I should die of a
broken heart' – sprang from that intense love of children which
was one of his most marked characteristics. The company of his own
children was his greatest joy and, more surprisingly, his greatest
relaxation; for him no holiday was really complete without their presence. He could not pass a ragged child in the street without stopping
to speak, and he was a well-known friend to all the village children at
St. Giles. He did his duty sitting on committees, taking Chairs,
and making speeches, but he found his pleasure in the Ragged Schools
themselves, where he took a personal interest in the children and knew
many of them by name. Ashley himself never seems to have connected
his deep and painful sympathy with the sufferings of children with
his own unhappy memories of childhood. The connection may well
have been there, but if so, it went unadmitted and unrecognised.
Though he was usually untroubled by the religious doubt which was
an endemic disease with pious Victorians, suffering childhood presented him with a problem he could not solve. Here, and here only,
was he tempted to question divine providence, as he wrote in his
diary for May 31st 1856 after hearing of a peculiarly bad case of
cruelty to a little girl:

These cases are painful in the extreme, not only because of the
terrible cruelty involved, but because they overwhelm for the

moment one's sense and conviction of a superintending Providence.
. . . The mind shrinks in wonder from the view of protracted tortures inflicted on children of tender years. Why such parents are
allowed to have offspring; why to exercise such power; what the
end to be served in the sorrows of such a young and innocent girl
as this? All these are thoughts full of distress and difficulty.

Next in importance to the provision of Ragged Schools Ashley
placed 'the health of towns and dwellings,' which he described as
'of all *physical* problems the most important by far and exercising
a terrible influence on things *spiritual*.' He was always well aware
of the practical limits of action; now instead of tackling the housing
problem as a monstrous whole he attacked it at one small point where
it was clearly vulnerable to an assault. Of all slum dwellings the
common lodging-houses were the most revolting and the most
pernicious. Dickens describes them thus in *Bleak House*:

These tumbling tenancies contain by night a swarm of misery. As on
the ruined human wretch vermin parasites appear, so these ruined
shelters have bred a crowd of foul existence that crawls in and
out of gaps in walls and boards; and coils itself to sleep, in maggot
numbers, where the rain drips in; and comes and goes, fetching
and carrying fever, and sowing more evil in its every footprint.

The horrific vagueness of this picture is milk-and-water fantasy
compared with the actual facts as Ashley gave them, quoting in
this instance from a report by the town-clerk of Morpeth:

Those [houses] that offer beds have these articles of luxury filled
with as many as can possibly lie on them. Others find berths below
the beds, and then the vacant spaces on the floor are occupied.
Among these is a tub filled with vomit and natural evacuations.
Other houses have no beds, but their occupiers are packed upon
the floor in rows, the head of one being close to the feet of another.
Each body is placed so close to its neighbour so as not to leave
sufficient space upon which to set a foot. The occupants are entirely naked, except for rugs drawn up as far as the waist; and
when to this is added that the doors and windows are carefully
closed, and that there is not the least distinction of sex, but men,
women and children lie indiscriminately side by side, some faint
idea may be formed of the state of these places and their effect
upon health, morals and decency.[5]

A City missionary gave a similar description of the common lodging-houses of London:

> These houses are never cleaned or ventilated; they literally swarm with vermin. It is almost impossible to breathe. Missionaries are seized with vomiting or fainting upon entering them. 'I have felt,' said another, 'the vermin dropping on my hat like peas.'[6]

On his return to Parliament Ashley was to launch a legislative campaign against this scandal, but for the present he could do nothing to regulate or improve the condition of existing houses. He could, however, take a small step towards the provision of new and better ones. In 1842 he had helped to found the Labourers' Friend Society, afterwards known as the Society for Improving the Condition of the Labouring Classes. The object of this strangely named body was the erection of dwellings to serve as models for the commercial builder or landlord. The society did not set out to provide working-class accommodation on any large scale, but rather sought to prove that such accommodation could supply all the essentials for health and comfort and yet be made to yield a reasonable return to the investor. Ashley actively interested himself in the proposal that the society should build model lodging-houses run not as a charity but at a slight profit. Two houses were built, one in Bloomsbury, one near Drury Lane. In 1851 Ashley claimed that the Bloomsbury house could show a profit of six and a half per cent. However, though charging a fee of only fourpence a night, which it was reckoned a working man should be able to pay, it was reported to be of a character and cost well above the means of the people who needed it most.

Ragged Schools and model lodging-houses were by no means the end of Ashley's philanthropic commitments. He was deeply involved not only with the six great Evangelical societies but with innumerable other bodies. Many of these associations would have been content merely to have his name at the head of their notepaper, so great was the prestige attaching to his patronage; but he would never allow himself to take that easy way. For him membership of a society meant not only an addition to his already heavy burden of meetings, Chairs, and speeches, but also the unspectacular, day-to-day work of dealing with individual cases, settling disputes, and battling with financial problems. The amount of work Ashley undertook is staggering. 'I am not roasted whole, but hacked to pieces by engagements, Chairs, committees, etc,' he wrote on May 8th 1847. He would often be faced with the prospect of taking three Chairs in one day as well as dealing with letters and personal interviews. His enormous correspondence was to be a lifelong burden; being unable to afford secretarial assistance, he was obliged to answer every letter in his own hand. Minny would sometimes help with necessary copying but as the mother of nine children* and the mistress of a large house she had little time to spare for such work.

Much of Ashley's time was devoted to a constant battle against 'this frightful heresy, this leprous system' of Puseyism. In June 1846, following the repeal of the Corn Laws and Peel's subsequent defeat on an Irish Coercion bill, Lord John Russell became Prime Minister. Ashley was not likely to find himself much in sympathy with a man who had been heard to remark 'It conduces much to piety *not* to go to church sometimes'; nevertheless, at the end of October he called twice upon Russell to discuss Church appointments and to warn him against the 'soul-destroying heresy' of Puseyism. He left with the comfortable conviction that 'I have, thank God, done my duty, I have testified to this Prime Minister as I did to the last.' Ashley did not believe that this piece of testimony would be any more fruitful than the previous one, but he came away feeling that, man for man, he preferred Whig Russell to Tory Peel.

Ashley was especially grateful to Russell for his support of the Ten Hours Bill. In spite of his absence from Parliament the progress of the Bill remained Ashley's first and overriding concern. Early in March 1846 he visited Lancashire and Yorkshire to explain personally to the operatives his reasons for abandoning his seat and therefore resigning the sponsorship of the Bill. Though he found them sympathetic and understanding he was exhausted by a tour which involved delivering a different speech in a different place every night – 'This is the pertinaceous, unwearied revolution of a steam-engine!' He found speaking particularly difficult because although he was anxious not to lower the spirits of his own supporters he felt it was essential to conciliate the mill-owners: ' "Soft sawder" to the mill-owners, unless it be skilfully applied, is a damper to the men; and a stirrer to the men is a damper to the mill-owners.'

In Ashley's absence John Fielden took charge of the Bill in the House of Commons and on April 29th 1846 moved its Second Reading. During the debates which followed Ashley haunted the lobbies, unable to bring himself to enter the gallery and listen to the speeches. Apparently he still believed that the Bill would affect the working hours of children only. 'Heartless and dishonest men!' he exclaimed

* A fourth daughter, Edith, usually known as Hilda, was born in April 1847.

of Graham and his supporters. 'The whole debate proceeded, and will proceed on a lie, the lie that the Bill is directed to control the labour of grown men!' When the division was taken the Bill was lost by merely ten votes. Some of its supporters urged that the introduction of a new bill should wait until Ashley's return to Parliament; but he himself refused to deprive Fielden of that honour. Through all this trying time he behaved with unfailing selflessness and magnanimity, and only in the pages of his diary did he give way to his natural feelings of disappointment and frustration. At heart he remained convinced that no one appreciated him at his true worth. 'Cobden is to have public thanks and a testimonial for his *labours, perseverance,* and *sacrifice* (!)' he wrote on July 1st. 'Why, what on earth has he lost by his undertaking? I have lost ten times as much and my seat into the bargain by this Corn Law affair – and what do I get?'

Disappointed by the failure of the Ten Hours Bill and beset by family worries, by midsummer 1846 Ashley had reached an acute pitch of nervous exasperation. He delighted much in his sons and missed them sadly on their return to school – 'Their absence makes a void; I feel it for I twaddle much about them' – but he also agonised much over them, and in particular over the beloved Anthony, whose reports from Rugby were far from reassuring. 'Is Anthony a bad boy? Is he a heartless, contumacious boy?' he asked himself anxiously. 'Alas, I see in him many signs of a wilful, selfish spirit; I cannot see many signs of duty and affection to his parents.' Now, as always, he was touchingly anxious to take the prodigal back into favour – 'He has expressed remorse and shed tears; all is well.' Maurice too was causing great anxiety to his parents, though for a different reason. His health was so bad that it was decided to try the effect of treatment at a German spa and a stay in the healthy climate of Switzerland. Accordingly, Ashley, Minny and the four eldest boys left England on July 7th. The experiment was a failure; Maurice became so ill that the party was obliged to return hastily to England before the end of August. To add to Ashley's anxieties came the news that his friend Bickersteth had suffered serious injury in a collision between his carriage and a brick-cart. Displaying an unexpected turn of humour, Bickersteth gleefully pointed out that the bricks had been intended for the building of a Roman Catholic chapel.

The winter of 1846–47 was a particularly hard one which brought much suffering to the poor. 'We have food, a house, clothing, fire,' Ashley wrote on December 5th. 'I can scarcely enjoy the blessings I receive when I remember those who are destitute . . . I redouble my prayer to God for thanks, and for ability to serve *Christus in pauperi-bus.*' In Ireland conditions were appalling. 'People talk of one million people dying in Ireland – is it possible?' Ashley asked incredulously. In all probability a million and a half died before the great famine ended. 'Private subscriptions on foot; they must be promoted, however hopeless of good results on the bodies and minds of the Irish,' Ashley wrote on January 11th 1847. 'The people are actually starving, which takes the question out of the list of things to be considered; you must relieve first and deliberate afterwards on permanent measures.' Convinced that 'everyone, in his own private self-denial, ought to aid the legislative efforts for relief,' Ashley took meticulous care over the small charities and economies which were all he could personally do to help the famine victims. He attended sermons in aid of Irish relief, he held a collecting-plate in Park Street, he forbade the use of flour in his own house except for bread-making, and he entirely prohibited the eating of potatoes, a decree which his servants much resented. On the National Fast Day he gave every member of his household a treatise by Bickersteth as well as a copy of the specially appointed form of prayer, and he allowed nothing to be eaten except frumenty and fish whilst he himself took only a mug of cocoa and a little dry bread.

Meanwhile the agitation in support of the Ten Hours Bill continued. 'I cannot but feel, though only for a moment, how soon the man who has made the real sacrifice and borne the burden of the day, may be displaced from the mind when no longer in sight,' Ashley wrote on hearing of the enthusiastic reception given to Oastler and Ferrand in Scotland, where they were addressing crowded meetings; 'but, if the battle be won, I ought to, and will rejoice.' In January 1847 he himself set out on a tour of Lancashire, addressing meetings at Manchester, Blackburn, Bolton, Bury, Todmorden, and Rochdale. He took Anthony with him, hoping 'to provoke him to emulation and give him a taste for usefulness and kindle the dormant spark of zeal for God's service.' Always a pleasing, well-mannered boy, Anthony behaved admirably and appeared to be much interested.

On January 26th, whilst Ashley was still in Lancashire, Fielden re-introduced the Ten Hours Bill into the House of Commons. 'My duty is clear,' Ashley wrote that same day; 'I must labour and urge and compel, as though I were in Parliament and the measure would be called by my name.' He told the Manchester operatives, 'A rose by any other name will smell as sweet, and so this measure, whether carried to completion by me or by John Fielden, will be equally conducive, under God's blessing, to the moral and physical welfare

of yourselves and your children.' The new Bill was nearly identical
with the one which had been defeated the previous year. Its failure
then had been due to the general preoccupation with the Corn Laws,
and to the desire of many members not to risk putting Peel's government in a minority until repeal had finally become law. Now, under
a Whig government which had openly declared its support for the
Ten Hours principle, the measure stood a much better chance of
success. Ashley, however, not unnaturally worked himself into a
state of extreme nervous tension. 'Intense anxiety about the Factory
Bill,' he recorded on March 1st; 'I dream of it by day and night
and work as though I had charge of the Bill.' In the Commons the
Second Reading was carried by a majority of 108, the Third Reading
by a majority of 63; on June 1st the Bill passed the Lords. Victory
was won at last.

Ironically enough, within two months of the passing of the Ten
Hours Act Ashley himself was returned to Parliament. As early as
October 1846 he had been asked to stand as Tory candidate for Bath
against his old opponent Roebuck. By refusing to give an unqualified
pledge in support of Protestantism he had laid himself open to the
strange accusation of being 'half a Puseyite or half a Papist.' He
had also refused to employ a paid agent or to spend a penny on election
expenses; there was to be no free beer, no processions, no banners,
bands, or party colours. Nevertheless, at the July General Election,
which resulted in an increased Whig majority, he was returned in
triumph at the head of the poll.

In spite of this success the summer of 1847 saw Ashley once again
sunk in depression. He persisted in believing, with no shadow of
reason, that every man's hand was against him. The diary is full of
entries such as the one for August 14th, 'I live in perpetual apprehension lest my many and vigilant enemies should seize any trifling
circumstances and dress them into a terrible accusation.' He was
troubled too by what he believed to be a decay of his mental powers,
apparent, needless to say, to no one except himself, 'an increased
weakness of memory, a greater wish to be silent on all occasions,
none of my former vivacity and imagination.' Even the prospect
of a visit to his favourite Scotland was spoilt by the thought of
parting from his children – 'the flesh creeps when I think of separation.'
This six weeks' holiday, most of it spent at Cumloden in Galloway, in
fact proved to be the very best of tonics. In pleasant, congenial
company, which included Agnes Strickland, the popular historical
writer, Ashley thoroughly enjoyed the scenery, the excursions, the
long, wet walks which ended with laughter and hot toddy. 'I have

been in good spirits since my arrival in Scotland,' he noted on October 9th, 'and have laughed a great deal, perhaps too much.'

On returning to London Ashley took his seat in the House of Commons where he found himself as much overwhelmed by shyness as any new-comer. Part of this feeling was due to his political isolation. 'Place myself where I will I must sit alone,' he wrote on November 30th. 'I cannot join the Whigs; I have no sympathy with the Protectionists; I have almost a sentimental *antipatico* to Peel.' However, he admitted to having 'some success' in the House and on December 16th made a speech on the admission of Jews to Parliament which won him praise from all sides.

At home financial troubles pressed hard upon him. He was still dependent on an allowance from his father only a hundred pounds larger than the one he had been given as an undergraduate at Oxford. 'My own condition is approaching that of a Ragged School,' he wrote with wry humour. With five sons to educate and four daughters to provide for he had no money for luxuries and little enough for necessities. He found riding of great benefit to his health, and in warm weather he longed for the relaxation of an occasional outing in an open carriage, but he could not afford the necessary horses. Worst of all was the discovery that Anthony was in debt to the tune of seventy-five pounds. The boy had been removed from Rugby and sent to a private tutor in Essex where, as usual, he was well-liked for his kindly disposition but regarded as incorrigibly idle and apathetic. Yet he was still the apple of his father's eye – 'he offends me *often* and distresses me *always*, and yet he occupies my heart.'

In January 1848 Ashley and Minny came to a desperate decision; Anthony must join the Navy and go to sea. Life on board ship under naval discipline might perhaps cure his idle habits and arouse his latent energies. Though the scheme was for Anthony's own good and the boy himself seemed to rejoice in the prospect, his father could not endure the thought of the parting – 'I cannot imagine it real, that my own boy, my own first-born, should leave me for three years, never to be seen during that time, and but little heard of, and go to a place ten thousand miles off.' He could not rid himself of irrational fears, imagining his son far away from home and friends, treated unjustly and falsely accused with no one at hand to stand his friend – 'I have more fears than I can define, as many as imagination can furnish.' Anthony sailed at the beginning of April. Affectionate but incorrigible to the last, he delayed till almost too late the sending of the farewell letter he had promised his parents, thus causing them much unnecessary misery.

Hardly had Ashley and Minny recovered from the grief of parting from their eldest child than a tragic blow fell upon them. For some time they had feared that Maurice's mysterious illness might prove to be what was described as brain-fever; now, on Easter Day, the boy fell down in the street in an unmistakable epileptic fit. The doctors warned them to expect many more such seizures, though holding out vague hopes that the trouble might not affect the brain. 'Oh, God,' Ashley prayed desperately, 'if it be Thy pleasure to afflict his body, be gracious in Thy mercy to spare his mind.'

Chapter 14

DIFFICULTIES OVER THE TEN HOURS ACT

The year 1848 was a time of revolution abroad and Chartist disturbance at home. In April Ashley was invited to Osborne where
he was told by the Queen that she and Prince Albert wished to know
'what we could do to show our interest in the working classes, and
you are the only man who can advise us in this matter.'[1] The Prince
agreed to accompany Ashley on a tour of London slums and to
preside at a meeting of the Labourers' Friend Society. Ashley was
convinced that social conditions and not political grievances were
the real cause of trouble. 'A Sanitary Bill would in five years confer
more blessing and obliterate more Chartism than Universal Suffrage
in half a century,' he wrote on April 13th; 'but the world, when ill
at ease, flies always to politics, and omits the statistics of the chimney-
corner, where all a man's comfort or discomfort lies.'

Through 1848, 1849 and 1850 Ashley was much occupied with the
promotion of emigration. He saw here at least a partial answer to
the problem of London's destitute children. Australia in particular
was clamouring for emigrants, prepared to take young people from
fourteen years old and upwards. Why not choose some promising
pupils from the Ragged Schools and send them out to start a new
life in the colonies? In many of these schools boys were taught such
crafts as tailoring and cobbling, skills which would serve them well
in a new country, whilst girls would always be welcome as domestic
servants. The children were willing to go; the colonies were ready to
receive them; the only serious problem was money. On June 6th
1848 Ashley brought in a motion asking for an annual grant from
Parliament. He pointed out that apart from the benefit to the colonies
and to the children themselves the scheme made economic sense.
These children would be saved from a life of crime; money spent on
emigration would be money saved on prison expenditure. He was
granted the small sum of fifteen hundred pounds not as an annual
subsidy but for one year only. A year later he again addressed the
House, describing what had already been achieved and asking for a

renewal of the grant. His plea was refused. Depending solely on what
he could raise by private donations, Ashley continued with his child-
emigration scheme, which grew and prospered with the years, proving
remarkably successful. His personal interest in this work never
slackened; if it were at all possible he would himself say a word of
goodbye to each batch of child-emigrants. It is illustrative of his
profound belief in the importance of individual contacts that in one
farewell address he bade the children not only to bear in mind what
had been said but to 'remember the faces of those who are here
present tonight.' Some of the children wrote letters to 'Most Noble
Lord' telling him how happy they were in their new homes. He kept
track of many individual cases, and delighted to tell how well his
girls and boys had done. Most of the boys went to Australia, but in
later years girls were more often sent to Canada under the auspices
of a Miss Chisholm, a Roman Catholic lady whose co-operation with
him called down upon Ashley's head the wrath of his more bigoted
fellow Protestants.

Ashley's schemes for emigration were not confined to Ragged
School children. In July 1848 he had the strange experience of
addressing a gathering of two or three hundred thieves. 'His Lordship
wants to know the particular character of the men here,' a City
missionary announced to the meeting. 'You therefore who live by
burglary and the more serious crimes will go to the right, the others
to the left.' About half the men moved to the right as admittedly
dangerous criminals. Several men told their personal stories, speaking quite openly, before Ashley rose to talk to them of self-help,
mutual aid, and, of course, prayer. Afterwards he admitted to some
sympathy with a much-convicted burglar who remarked, 'My Lord
and gentlemen of the Jury, prayer is very good but it won't fill an
empty stomach.' Ashley then put forward the practical plan of
emigration. The men showed great interest, and a dozen of them
did in fact leave England for Canada within the next six months, to
be followed by other emigrants of similar type.

In November 1848 came the death of Minny's uncle, Lord Melbourne. Lord David Cecil thus describes his end:

In the pale light of the autumn day his countenance, still beautiful
in spite of the ravages that time and suffering had wrought upon
it, wore an extraordinary look of contentment and peace.[2]

Ashley's account is somewhat different in tone:

He died and gave no sign; all *without* was coldness and indifference; God only can discern what was within. Those who stood around his bed were either ignorant or thoughtless . . . It was not the death of a heathen; *he* would have had an image or a ceremony. It was the death of an animal.

All through the early months of 1849 Ashley was plagued by ill-health which seems to have been mental rather than physical in origin. His symptoms were peculiar: 'Sadly, sadly nervous last night; feel as though I were sometimes very long, sometimes very light, alternately a telescope and a feather.' By Easter, however, he was once more on the upward swing of the pendulum. On May 19th he recorded an approach made to him through his brother William by Lord Stanley, offering him the Home Office with the leadership of the House of Commons when the Tories should return to power. As there was no immediate prospect of this the offer can scarcely have been intended very seriously.

Stanley may have thought that the passing of the Ten Hours Act had removed Ashley's objections to taking office. Unfortunately that Act was not working satisfactorily. Many, though not a majority, of the mill-owners were evading the law by working a relay system, an arrangement much disliked by the operatives, because although it allowed them their statutory free time it obliged them to take this in brief, broken periods of no use either for rest or recreation. In the industrial districts agitation was once more astir. Oastler now lived in Fulham; and although he went North to take part in the revived campaign the leadership was passing to the Radical Stephens, who was always mistrustful of Ashley. On April 5th Ashley noted in his diary that the Ten Hours Act was in jeopardy, adding the gloomy remark, 'here is fresh toil, fresh anxiety.' Fielden, to whom had fallen the final glory of that Act's passing, was no longer in Parliament; already a very sick man, he was to die within six weeks. The burden was once more on Ashley's shoulders, much as he might dislike the thought. His interest had drifted away from factory legislation to Ragged Schools and other philanthropic and religious concerns. In September 1848 he had joined the Board of Health and begun a new and absorbing struggle for sanitary reform. All these interests, combined with his parliamentary work and the business of the Lunacy Commission, filled his time to overflowing. His doctors, and Minny also, were insisting that unless he gave himself more time for relaxation he risked serious damage to his health. Instead, he was now asked to take up again a difficult and demanding work which he had thought finished, a battle which he had believed won.

At this moment of stress and disappointment Ashley was struck by an unexpected and bitter personal tragedy. His second son, Francis, had not followed Anthony to Rugby but had been sent to Harrow, his father's old school, where he was making a great name for himself. Late on the evening of May 19th Ashley heard that the boy was seriously ill with pleurisy. He hurried down to Harrow to find Francis in a high fever, but 'calm, composed, and cheerful.' Ashley's account of his son's death-bed is lit with a curious glow which can only be described as joy. This was not 'the death of an animal,' as Melbourne's had been, but of an intelligent, affectionate boy, fully conscious of his danger and facing it with courage and a great hope. 'His voice and manner throughout his whole illness were so to speak sublime; he retained his infantile simplicity and yet he was above himself,' Ashley was to write of his son. 'His heart was unlocked and all its treasures displayed.'

On May 24th, leaving Francis a little better, Ashley went up to London to present the Home Secretary with a petition against relays. On his return to Harrow he found his son once again desperately ill. For a few days hope alternated with alarm, until by June 1st the worst seemed to be over. That evening Ashley and Minny were congratulating themselves on what they believed to be signs of real improvement when they were suddenly called to the sick-room. In a moment or two all was over; Francis was dead.

It was the moment of sunset; and the beauty of the summer evening gave a strange comfort to Ashley, who all his life shrank with a peculiar horror from death in the dark night. With Minny he found some relief in going over and over their son's sayings and doings during those last days – 'sometimes in talking of these things we mount almost to joy.' The shock had nevertheless been extreme. Ashley's nerves were shattered. 'Small things throw me into a flutter'; a footstep, an unexpected letter, a knock at the door, filled him with panic. With terror he looked at the children who remained to him. Vea was sickly, apparently threatened by 'a decline'; both Mary and Conty were in bad health; Maurice was subject to ever more frequent fits. A pathetic entry on July 23rd shows with what care and anxiety Ashley watched over this epileptic child:

We have tried an immense variety of physicians, we have expended hundreds of pounds (how shall we ever repay them?) and he is far worse. He must not be left for a moment; he now goes down like a shot; he fell yesterday in the Park and I trembled lest a vast crowd should be gathered. Sent away the children and sat by his side as though we were only lying on the grass, and by degrees he recovered and walked home.

The doctors now decreed that Maurice must be separated from his brothers and sisters and sent away from home to lead an absolutely quiet and retired life. Sadly Ashley accepted their verdict, and with it, of course, yet another addition to his financial burdens. A little consolation came with the birth of a sixth son on August 8th, 'my Seth,' as Ashley would often call this boy, remembering the son given to Adam in place of the dead Abel. At first, however, baby Cecil, a delicate and sickly child, gave little pleasure to his parents but rather added to their anxieties.

Tired and preoccupied by these family troubles, Ashley was obliged to take up once more the fight for the Ten Hours principle and to make decisions of vital importance to that cause. The mistakes he made in coming to those decisions and his unfortunate handling of the whole situation can only be understood if seen against the background of his private life. Here was a highly sensitive man, shattered by the sudden death of his most promising son, faced with the tragic fact that another son was an incurable epileptic, in constant nagging anxiety for the health of three more of his children, plagued too by insoluble financial problems, and himself on the verge of nervous collapse. 'I may fairly say that since August 1848 I have hardly had a day of my former freedom from bodily troubles,' he wrote on November 2nd 1849; 'it seems that a real change has occurred in my nervous condition.' A tight weight seemed to press on his neck 'as if I wore an iron collar'; the slightest emotional strain made 'my head and my body ring like metal.' The noises in his ears had reached an unprecedented pitch – 'my ears more terrible than ever before; they almost make me frantic; Oh, God, have mercy upon me!'

Only a week after Francis' death the trouble began. The *Manchester Guardian* reported a meeting between a deputation from the mill-owners and the Home Secretary, Sir George Grey, at which Grey was said to have agreed to legalise the relay system. Members of the deputation had also called on Ashley who, according to The *Guardian,* had declared himself in favour of a ten-and-a-half hours day. The mischief was done. In vain did Ashley write to The *Guardian* protesting that the report was inaccurate. He admitted to receiving two members of the deputation who had shown him, unofficially, a plan approved by the masters:

> I told them the law was now the property of the factory workers; that I could not say ay or no to the proposition; that it was for the operatives to determine whether they would surrender the whole, or any part of it, or stand upon their full rights. I added that so far as I was concerned, I should be ready to consider the proposal of ten hours and a half of labour (provided that labour was taken between the hours of six and six) and probably accede to it, if such were the views of the workers in factories.[3]

For the first time the North learnt that Ashley was prepared to compromise. Useless to point out that he would do so only with the full consent and approval of the operatives; to the Northerners 'Ten hours and no more' was as the Ark of the Covenant. He who touched it, even from the best of motives, committed sacrilege and deserved to come to a sticky end, like the well-intentioned Uzzah.* So great was the outcry that Ashley was forced to abandon all thought of making an immediate bargain with the mill-owners, though in his heart of hearts he believed a compromise solution to be inevitable. All through the summer and early autumn, whilst Ashley's energies were engrossed by the day-to-day struggles of the Board of Health against the cholera epidemic, the North was ringing with demands for the Ten Hours Act and no compromise. Stephens was particularly bitter, ranting against 'the unsteadiness, time-serving and tergiversation of such men as Lord Ashley,' adding for good measure the adjectives 'inglorious, inconsistent, miserable, contemptible.'[4] In September the Fielden Society was founded 'for the protection and enforcement of John Fielden's Ten Hours Act,' its very name an insult to Ashley and a belittling of his seventeen years' work for the cause.

'Mr. Oastler and Mr. Stephens have seized the opportunity to revile me and to place themselves at the head of the operatives, but I rejoice to say that the operatives will neither believe them nor accept them,' Ashley wrote on October 4th. He was wrong. The whole Ten Hours movement, operatives included, was now divided into two opposing camps. On the one hand was John Fielden's nephew, Sam, with Oastler, Stephens, and their followers, crying out against 'friends of compromisers and traitors' and the more extreme among them threatening strike action; on the other were Ashley's own

* II Samuel, Chapter 6, verses 6–7.

supporters, organising themselves none too efficiently behind the existing Central Committee of the old Short Time Committees. Ashley himself was too tired and too disillusioned to wish to take any part in the struggle. His heart was no longer in the matter:

Mr. Oastler and the crew of them (I can use no milder term) are denouncing and reviling me in every society, by day and by night, in speeches and on paper, as a traitor and a thousand other things to the Ten Hours Bill. God knows my sincerity, my labours, vexations, losses, injuries to health, fortune, comforts, position, in the cause. It is true I told the work-people I would assent (if *they* would assent) to the concession of half-an-hour provided they received in return the immediate and final settlement of the question, and the limitation of the range from fifteen to twelve hours, a concession which the masters alone could make. Here is my offence, and I am too busy, and also too tired, to begin a controversial defence. Like Hezekiah, I spread it out before the Lord.

Ashley believed, and rightly, that an extra half-hour's work a day was a lesser evil than the relay system. The one essential was to make sure that all work was done within a fixed range of twelve hours – say, from six in the morning to six at night – thus making relays impossible. Of their own will the mill-owners would never agree to this limitation unless the Ten Hours men were prepared to make some concession in their turn, which the followers of Oastler and Stephens would never do. A faint hope remained that the law might compel the owners to submit. All those concerned were now waiting impatiently for the result of a case in the Court of Exchequer. A factory-inspector had summoned a mill-owner for working his hands in relays, maintaining that the Ten Hours Act had made the relay system illegal; and the mill-owner had appealed from the verdict given against him by the magistrates. On February 8th 1850 Baron Parke delivered his judgment; whatever may have been the intention of the framers of the measure, relays were not forbidden by the letter of the Ten Hours Act and were therefore lawful practice.

The blow was a bitter one. 'The work to be done all over again,' Ashley commented, 'and I seventeen years older than when I began.' In an attempt to bring the two sides of the Ten Hours movement together to formulate a common policy a conference was called to meet at Manchester on February 17th, and Ashley was invited to attend. He did not do so; and in his letter of reply, though declaring himself ready to renew the struggle, gave no explanation for his absence. Whatever his reasons – and they may have been imperative ones – here was a missed opportunity. He had not visited the North since the renewal of the Ten Hours campaign and he was sadly out of touch with local feeling. In his absence the conference discussed the question of the Parliamentary leadership with much bitterness. Though feelings ran high against Ashley, a compromise solution was at length agreed upon, appointing a triumvirate of leaders consisting of Ashley, Lord John Manners, and the Dorset member, George Bankes. Ashley's supporters should now have left well alone; instead they called another packed conference, admitting only invited delegates, who duly appointed Ashley as sole leader. The Ten Hours movement was split from top to bottom.

Two days after this second meeting another personal blow fell on Ashley with the death of his dear friend and counsellor, Edward Bickersteth. Where the Ten Hours Act was concerned he was now faced with two alternatives. Either he could bring in a new bill amending the Act by prohibiting relays or he could make a compromise with the mill-owners. On March 14th he asked leave of the House to bring in an amending bill which he promised would contain no new matter whatsoever apart from the prohibition of relays. He then set about the business of drafting such a bill, but although he had the assistance of various lawyers and Parliamentary draftsmen the harder he tried the more difficult the task appeared to be. To construct a watertight clause prohibiting relays and admitting of no evasion seemed a near-impossibility. The Lancashire men, failing to understand his position, now drafted a stringent clause, watertight indeed, but containing a mass of new matter. Ashley pointed out that the House would almost certainly throw out such a clause as being 'contrary to my statement that I would not swerve by a hair's breadth to the right hand or the left but simply touch what was disputed.'[5] He nevertheless declared himself ready to abide by the decision of the Central Committee, and when that Committee unanimously voted in favour of the new clause he gave notice of moving it in the House. Privately he was convinced that Parliament would never pass such a measure and that the only possible course was to strike a bargain with the owners, accepting the ten-and-a-half hours day in return for the total and irrevocable abolition of relays.

On May 3rd Sir George Grey announced that the Government would accept just such a compromise. 'I am sure they are the best terms that ever will be offered,' Ashley wrote on May 7th, 'and that probably this is the last time of their being offered.' That same day he wrote a letter which, by inexplicable mischance or misjudgement, appeared in *The Times* before and not after it had been read by the members of the Short Time Committees to whom it was addressed. The exact text of the letter is important:

Gentlemen, It has become my duty to state to you, without further delay, the course that I would advise you to pursue in the present position of the Factory Bill in the House of Commons.

I am bound to act as your friend, and not as your delegate; and I counsel you, therefore, to accept forthwith the propositions made by Her Majesty's Government as the only means of solving the difficulties in which we are now placed. I wish most heartily for your sakes that they contained an unqualified limitation to ten hours daily; but I am induced, nevertheless, for the following reasons to give you that counsel:- 1. The dispute is now limited to a struggle about two hours in the week – whether the aggregate toil should be 58 or 60 hours; the Government plan requiring the two additional hours but giving an equivalent in exchange. 2. The plan imposes a most important and beneficial limitation of the range over which the work may be taken, reducing it from 15 to 12 hours in the day, thereby preventing all possibility of shifts, relays, and other evasions – a result which cannot be obtained by any other form of enactment. This has always been my strong conviction, and I carried the question by the separate divisions in 1844. 3. It secures to the working people, for recreation and domestic duty, the whole of every evening after six o'clock. 4. It provides for a later commencement of work by half an hour in the morning. 5. It ensures extra leisure time on every Saturday. 6. Because this arrangement would secure, I believe, the co-operation of the employers – a matter of no slight importance in the good working of any measure, and essential to the harmony and good feeling we all desire to see in the vast districts of our manufactures.

But there are other reasons, drawn from the embarrassments of our present position. I have already described to you in a former letter the necessity I have been under (after making many essays and taking many learned opinions) of introducing a clause to prohibit relays which contains new matter and imposes fresh restrictions. This unavoidable step on my part sets at liberty many members who considered themselves engaged to maintain the honour of Parliament, and thus endangers the success of the measure ultimately, and certainly the progress of it in the present session. Its progress, even were the bill unopposed, would be difficult under the heavy pressure of public business; but, opposed as it would be, postponement would be inevitable. Now, I greatly fear delay; I refrain from stating my reasons; but, I repeat, I greatly fear delay, as likely to be productive of infinite mischief, and which may possibly completely alter your relative and actual position.

I have tried to discover the bright side of postponement, but I cannot conceive any advantage in it whatsoever. You will stand no better in the next session than you do in this; you may possibly stand worse.

The two hours are, I know, your unquestionable right; but, on the other hand, the range of 15 hours is the unquestionable right of the employers; the exchange they offer is fair, and the gain is on your side.

In giving this counsel, I know that I shall be exposed to sad misrepresentations; but it is my duty not to do that which will secure applause to myself, but that which will secure protection to your families and children. I should be overjoyed to obtain for you the full concession of the two hours in the week, but such an issue seems in my mind next to impossible; and in the protracted struggle to reach the ten, you incur the hazard of being brought to eleven hours. Postponement must follow conflict; division among the operatives will follow postponement; and when once you are a divided body your cause will be irretrievably lost.

It will be necessary to insert the word 'children' into the clause introduced by Sir George Grey, in order that the youngest workers may be sure to enjoy the benefit of the close of the daily labour at 6 o'clock.

With this view I shall accept the amendment proposed by the Minister, in the humble but assured hope that the issue will be blessed to the moral and social amelioration of your great community.[6]

'I am bound to act as your friend and not as your delegate' – in that sentence lay Ashley's fatal mistake. The Northern men were not looking for a paternalistic friend to act in what he considered their best interests; they wanted a mouthpiece for their own views. Previously Ashley had recognised and respected this attitude; as recently as April 27th he had asked for their opinion of the new clause and had acted in accordance with it against his own judgement. Now, without warning or consultation, he had taken the whole responsibility upon himself and had gone against their expressed wishes.

At first Ashley was under no delusions as to the reception of his decision in favour of a ten-and-a-half-hours day. 'Expect from the manufacturing districts a storm of violence and hatred,' he wrote on May 8th. The storm, however, did not break immediately. 'Hear, in the main, very good accounts of the effects of my letter to the operatives,' he wrote on May 18th at Brighton, where Minny had insisted that he should go for a brief holiday; 'am assured that all the *thinking* portion is with me.' He added with a touch of irony, 'In truth they show it by their silence.' Those who disapproved were not to remain silent for long. The North blazed with fury. 'Talk of the treachery of others,' Oastler exclaimed, 'Lord Ashley has betrayed the poor.' Stephens railed against his 'mask of affected sympathy' and accused him of 'unparalleled baseness.' A Halifax newspaper referred to his 'betrayal of the cause,' and a meeting at Manchester passed a resolution deeply deploring 'the infatuation which led to the cause of the factory workers being entrusted to Lord Ashley.' Both at this meeting and at one held at Bradford it was decided to adopt a new leader in the person of Lord John Manners, who had come out unequivocally in favour of a ten hours day.

The worst was yet to come. At the very last moment the workers were to be cheated of the prize for which Ashley had sacrificed both popularity and reputation. The Government bill introduced by Sir George Grey enforced a fixed range of twelve hours for the work of women and young persons but made no mention of children. As his letter of May 7th makes perfectly clear, Ashley intended to remedy what he believed to be a mere oversight. On June 6th, when he moved the necessary amendment to include children in the restrictions, to his surprise he found himself opposed by Grey and in consequence lost his motion by thirty votes. A week later he again moved that children be included, and this time lost by a single vote. All hope of a ten-and-a-half hour day for men had vanished, because the failure of his amendment meant that after women and young persons had left the mills, men could still be kept at work aided by relays of children. As Disraeli declared in the first speech he had ever made in support of factory reform, the Government had taken advantage of a technical flaw in the Act to deprive the workers of the fruits of their hard-fought struggle 'not on the merits of the case but by acts which an attorney would despise.' Ashley himself, faced by this piece of trickery, declared his alliance with the Government to be at an end and reserved to himself to vote as he chose on Grey's bill. In the end he abstained from voting, a reasonable course in the circumstances but one which was inevitably misinterpreted by his detractors. The Bill, as it became law in August, made two useful advances by imposing an effective limitation on the working hours of women and young persons, though not children, and in enforcing a Saturday half-holiday. Three years later, when Palmerston was Home Secretary, an amending act was passed including children within the regulations, thus bringing the practice of relays to an end and, in effect, securing a ten-and-a-half hour day for all workers.

The furious reaction against him Ashley attributed simply to the fact that he had abandoned the ten-hour-day in favour of ten-and-a-half, 'I won for them *almost* everything, but for the loss of that very little they regard me as an enemy.' He never realised how much anger and annoyance he had caused by his high-handed assumption of sole responsibility, his failure to consult the Short Time Committees, his error in allowing the letter announcing his decision to appear first of all in the press. The fact that his decision was the only right and sensible one merely inflamed matters more; the independent-minded Northerners could not stomach his bland assumption, 'I know what is good for you better than you do yourselves.' If he had not been tricked of the final reward he would in fact have made an excellent bargain for the operatives; the abolition of relays was of far greater importance to them than the extra half-hour's work. Of course Ashley was right and the Northerners were wrong; but somehow their attitude is the more sympathetic. The main outcry came not from Yorkshire but from Lancashire; then, as always, Lancashire men were both tough and romantic. Like the martyrs, they were tough enough to be prepared to die and romantic enough to die for a symbol, a grain of incense, something altogether unimportant except to the eye of faith. To them 'ten hours and no more' was just such a symbol. Ashley had not understood the North.

Posterity probably grieves more for him over this sorry ending than ever he grieved for himself. His diary shows him to have been both hurt and angry; but he did not write passage after passage raging against Oastler and Stephens as once he had raged interminably against Graham and Peel. The matter was no longer of first importance to him. He had lost interest in factory acts and factory children, and he turned with some relief to more congenial subjects. At the height of his unpopularity over the ten-and-a-half-hours compromise he must needs, with almost masochistic zeal, introduce into the House of Commons a motion to put a stop to all Sunday work in Post Offices. The fate of this motion seems to have interested him more than the fate of his Factory Bill amendment, which was debated a week later. By some freak of chance this most unpopular proposal passed the House of Commons. For three weeks England was without a Sunday post; then the Government bowed to the storm and rescinded the order – 'all this because certain aristocratic people will not have their gossip in the country on Sunday morning.' Not content with the hatred of the operatives, Ashley had now made himself thoroughly unpopular with the upper classes. 'The Factory Bill and the postal resolution taken together have brought on me a variety, universality, and bitterness of attack quite original,' he wrote on June 22nd 1850.

Very soon, however, Ashley came back to popularity on a flood-tide of Protestant fervour. On October 7th 1850 Cardinal Wiseman issued his foolish and provocative pastoral letter, 'from out the Flaminian Gate,' announcing the establishment of a Roman Catholic hierarchy in England, the bishops to bear territorial titles. A month later Lord John Russell replied with his equally foolish and provocative 'Durham Letter,' attacking not only the Roman Catholics but also the Tractarians. Ashley rushed into the fray in defence of outraged Protestantism. On December 5th he took the chair at a meeting held, appropriately enough, in Freemasons' Hall, 'to protest against the insolent and insidious attempt of the Bishop of Rome.' 'We own, under God, no rule in these kingdoms but that of our beloved Queen', he thundered; 'and, God helping us, none other shall be planted here.' 'Do you know what Canon Law is?' he demanded. 'It is a law incompatible with the civil law of this realm; it elevates the Pope as God.' From the intolerable claims of the Papists he turned to the intolerable practices of the Puseyites, whom he castigated for their adoption of popish rites and ceremonies. Nor was this the sum total of their offending – 'When to these they add the teaching of false and heretical doctrines; when they add the practice of auricular confession, the most monstrous, perhaps, of all the monstrous practices of the Roman system, who can wonder that the appetite of the Pope was whetted, that his eyes were blinded, and that he believed the time was come for once more subjecting this Protestant land to his odious domination?'[7] At the end of this speech the whole audience, ladies included, rose to their feet and shook the room with thunders of applause.

The hardening of Ashley's Evangelical zeal into something very near bigotry seems to date from this period and may be due to the influence of Alexander Haldane, who took Bickersteth's place as his chief counsellor and friend. Though a cultivated and highly intellectual man, as might be expected of the uncle of Lord Haldane of Cloan and the scientist J. B. Haldane, Alexander Haldane was narrow-minded and bellicose, entirely lacking in Bickersteth's kindly spirit. He came of an ancient Scottish family with a long tradition of fervent Evangelicalism. Ashley knew him as the owner of the extreme Evangelical paper, *The Record*; but not till 1845, when Haldane wrote a letter of condolence on Francis' death, did the acquaintance ripen into friendship. Hodder had access to the voluminous correspondence between Ashley and Haldane, but, most unfortunately, he quoted very sparingly from these letters, which have since disappeared. Their loss makes it impossible to study this important relationship in any detail. It is certain that Haldane had a great influence over Ashley; it is probable that this influence was not altogether for the good.

Perhaps it was this spirit of bigotry, or perhaps it was merely their unfortunate choice of name – Ashley always disliked and distrusted any form of Socialism – which blinded him to the merits of a group of fellow Protestants as devoted as ever he himself was to the cause of social justice and reform. 'What is all this that we read and hear from Messrs Maurice, Kingsley, and Co; liberty, equality, fraternity (brotherhood, they call it) on the principle of the Gospels!' he wrote scathingly on July 1st 1851. If Ashley could have brought himself to try to understand the Christian Socialists and to co-operate with them, the Church might have made a considerably greater impact upon the Victorian working-classes.

On Christmas Day 1850 Ashley looked back over his past life and summed up the results of this survey under three heads: 'What have I gained for the public? What gained for the cause of our Blessed Master? What gained for myself?' Under the first heading he listed Ragged Schools, Factory Acts, sanitary reforms, and the like. His entry under the second heading was less obvious:

> Perhaps we may rejoice in an awakened attention, though but partially so, to the wants and rights of the poor; to the powers and duties of the rich; perhaps, both in Parliament and out of it, in a freer, safer use of religious sentiment and expression; perhaps in an increased effort for spiritual things, and in greatly increased opportunities for doing and receiving good. This, alas, is not the thing itself, but only the means to it.

For himself he claimed to have gained 'peace of mind but nothing else.' Thus so strangely do men misjudge themselves; Ashley credited himself with the one thing he was never to attain.

Chapter 15

THE BOARD OF HEALTH

From 1848 to 1854 Ashley was deeply involved in work which, un-popular with his contemporaries and all but forgotten by posterity, was yet of vital importance to the well-being of this country. Perhaps because there is so little of charm or romance to be extracted from the subject of sanitary reform Ashley's efforts in that direction have gone almost entirely unhonoured and unsung. Hodder, for instance, treats the subject in so slight and superficial a manner that in the index to his book the name Chadwick does not occur.

The six years which Ashley spent at the Board of Health form an episode complete in itself and are therefore best treated as a separate entity apart from the chronological story of his life. One small but important point should be made at the very beginning. The words 'sanitary' and 'sanitation' have slightly changed in meaning during the past hundred years. Today they have an exclusively cloacal connotation; but the Victorians used them in the wider sense of the dictionary definition, 'of the conditions which affect health, especially with regard to dirt and infection.' If, for instance, in such phrases as the title of John Simon's well-known book, *English Sanitary Institutions,* published in 1890, the words 'public health' are substituted for 'sanitary,' the modern reader will gain a better idea of the importance and scope of Ashley's work in this field.

The man who played the chief part in exposing the scandal of the appalling sanitary conditions existing all over the British Isles was that devoted but prickly character, Edwin Chadwick. He had been partially responsible for the 1838 Report of the Poor Law Commissioners which had first drawn attention to this problem and had himself drafted the 1842 Report on the Sanitary Condition of the Labouring Population of Great Britain, the foundation-stone of all subsequent reform and a document described by Ashley as 'almost the boldest ever produced by a subordinate department.'[1] Chadwick had first made his name – where the general public was concerned, lost his name might be more accurate – as the man chiefly responsible

for the new Poor Law of 1834. Ashley had come across him as one
of the three Commissioners appointed under the 1833 Royal Commission on the Employment of Children in Factories. Although
Ashley had strongly opposed the appointment of these Commissioners
he had been very favourably impressed by their Report. On many
matters Ashley and Chadwick were completely out of sympathy.
In all his work in the cause of sanitary reform Ashley's declared
intention was 'to Christianize' the condition of the working classes.[2]
Chadwick was moved by no such religious motive; a Radical and a
Benthamite – for a time he had worked as Bentham's secretary – he
sat very loosely to all conventional creeds. He was, moreover, an
extremely difficult person to work with, tactless, overbearing, as
quick to take offence as Ashley was but far more prone to show his
annoyance. Yet the two men worked together in almost perfect
harmony, and after the collapse of the Board of Health they remained personal friends for life. Ashley could tolerate aggressiveness,
arrogance and a lack of consideration for other people's feelings
because he saw these faults as the reverse side of Chadwick's good
qualities, his energy, his single-mindedness, and his undoubted
ability. What he could not stomach was lack of zeal, and in Chadwick
he found a colleague even more zealous than himself.

In 1844, following the publication of Chadwick's 1842 Report, a
Commission on the Health of Towns exposed the shocking deficiencies
of the drainage and water-supply systems in fifty of Britain's largest
and most important cities. One result was the foundation of the Health
of Towns Association, with Ashley as a founding member and Chairman of the London branch. In 1847 he was appointed a member of
the newly-formed Metropolitan Commission of Sewers, the first
body ever to assume responsibility for the planning and construction
of public works for the whole of the London area outside the City.
Meanwhile, various measures dealing with sanitary reform had
been brought before Parliament but all of them for different reasons
had been either defeated or abandoned. In February 1848 Morpeth
introduced a Public Health Bill, a revised version of one he had failed
to carry the previous year, its main object being to set up a central
body to deal with all sanitary matters. The measure was hotly debated
in both Houses. On May 28th Ashley spoke in its support, urging that
such a scheme would be of the greatest possible benefit to the very
poor and a step towards 'the recognition of their right to be placed
on a level with sentient and immortal beings.' In August the Bill
became law and Ashley found himself a member of the newly-estab-
lished Board of Health.

As promoter of the Public Health Act Morpeth was appointed the Board's President. 'It will be no small gratification to me, after many years of political difference, to be at last associated with the friend of my youth in a labour for the happiness of the nation,'[3] Ashley wrote to him on September 9th. Since Morpeth was also First Commissioner of Woods and Forests, a body roughly corresponding to the modern Ministry of Works, the Board was incongruously attached to that department. All was to go well so long as Morpeth remained in control; it was, however, clear that once he retired trouble was bound to occur, since the next Commissioner of Woods and Forests would be unlikely in the extreme to share his interest in sanitary matters. The other members of the Board were Doctor Southwood Smith, a man well known and well liked by Ashley, and, of course, Edwin Chadwick.

It is impossible not to suspect that one of the reasons for Ashley's appointment was a wish to improve the Board's image with the public. A Board of Health without Chadwick would have been inconceivable, but a Board of Health with Chadwick was certain to be heartily disliked from the moment of its inception. An unattractive personality, a bad speaker and a prodigious bore, Chadwick's faults of temper and temperament combined with his connection with the hated Poor Law to make him the most unpopular man in Great Britain. Ashley, on the contrary, was handsome, aristocratic, and by now genuinely eloquent. In spite of his own conviction to the contrary, he was a popular character, revered and respected even by his opponents. This glamorous lord might serve to turn the public gaze away from the unglamorous and execrated figure of Edwin Chadwick. As for Chadwick himself, he was genuinely delighted by Ashley's appointment, which, he declared, 'affords to the country a guarantee of earnestness, sympathy for suffering, singleness of purpose in labouring for its relief.'[4] Ashley was the only unpaid member of the Board, but he was nevertheless to work almost as hard as Chadwick himself. Although his main function was to act as the Board's Parliamentary spokesman, he took his full share in the daily work at its headquarters at Gwydyr House, in times of crisis sending Chadwick two, three, or even four notes a day dealing with matters of urgency. When pressure of work was acute the Board would meet as often as five or six times a week, and never did Ashley miss a meeting if he could possibly avoid doing so.

A sinister threat to the nation's health sent the Board off to an unexpectedly good start. The debates on the Public Health Act had been held under the shadow of an impending cholera epidemic.

By September 1848 the disease had definitely declared itself. Remembering the horrors of the 1831 outbreak, people were unusually willing to submit to drastic and unpopular sanitary measures, provided only that these offered some sort of protection against the infection.

During the first year of the Board's existence much of Ashley's time and energy was devoted to work connected with the cholera epidemic. The preventative measures taken by the Board appear both inadequate and irrelevant when seen in the light of modern scientific knowledge. Men who did not know that germs existed could not be expected to realise that the cholera germ was water-borne or that cholera itself was a specific disease, not an acute form of typhus or ordinary diarrhoea. The Board was hampered not only by this unavoidable lack of scientific knowledge but by its own terms of reference, which obliged it to work through the local Boards of Guardians, and by the penny-wise policy adopted by the Treasury. The Board could and did order the inspection and cleansing of filthy houses and courts, the removal of refuse, the lime-washing of interiors, and a house-to-house visitation to seek out and treat persons in the early stages of cholera, but it had no power to force the Guardians to carry out its instructions. Meanwhile, the Treasury refused to sanction the appointment of more than two general Medical Inspectors to deal with the whole of Great Britain. (Ashley himself regarded the Treasury Secretary, William Goodenough Hayter, as one of the Board's very worst enemies.) Fortunately, the two doctors chosen as Medical Inspectors, John Sutherland and R. D. Grainger, were dedicated enthusiasts for the cause of sanitary reform. Everyone connected with the Board in these early stages was remarkably devoted and hardworking. 'Chadwick and Southwood Smith may feel, but do not *know* fatigue or satiety in business when necessity urges or duty calls,' Ashley wrote. 'As for the staff of the Board, miserably paid as they are, with scanty hopes of preferment, or even of continued employment, I am unable to speak with adequate praise.'

During the autumn of 1848 the pressure of business was such that the Board met every weekday. By January 1849 Ashley himself was so exhausted that he was obliged to take a brief holiday. When spring came the cholera appeared to be subsiding. The lull, however, was merely temporary; in June the disease broke out more virulently than ever, and by the end of September deaths in London had reached the record total of 2,298 in one week. From August 1st to September 11th Ashley remained in London, constantly occupied with the Board's efforts to deal with the epidemic. Everyone who could possibly do so had fled to the country, away from the threat of infection. 'Labour and anxiety at the Board of Health very great,' Ashley noted on September 7th. For a week or so he was alone at Gwydyr House fighting the battle single-handed, the secretary Henry Austin, the assistant-secretary Alexander Bain, Southwood Smith and even the indefatigable Chadwick having all collapsed under the strain. At this juncture, with the cholera at its height, Hayter refused to sanction the appointment of extra medical superintendents to deal with the emergency in London, where the crisis was particularly acute. On hearing of his refusal Ashley himself immediately rushed over to the Treasury, but finding no one there competent to deal with the matter he decided to appoint the necessary superintendents on his own responsibility, an action which, six months later, called down upon him a severe rebuke.

Because of Ashley's sensible if high-handed action the Board now had a more or less adequate staff to deal with the emergency in London and to carry out a system of house-to-house visitation which in the course of eight weeks led to the discovery and treatment of over 45,000 cases of real or suspected cholera. The disease was already beginning to subside, and by the end of October it had ceased altogether. At first Ashley feared that its lessons would go unheeded – 'Will there, or will there not, be a prayer of thanksgiving, a day of thanksgiving, or any recognition whatsoever of God's exceeding and undeserved goodness? Will there be any bounty to the poor, any labouring for their permanent welfare, any flow of zeal or money? I trow not.' Everyone, however, was not so ungenerous or ungrateful as Ashley had supposed; Lord John Russell, for one, sent him fifty pounds towards a thanksgiving fund, adding that 'If you will take orders I will make you the next bishop.'[5] One immediate result was the foundation of the Epidemiological Society to study the causes and prevention of epidemic disease, a powerful body with many leading scientists among its members and Ashley himself the President. He came to admit that the cholera had opened men's eyes to the pressing need for sanitary reform and for improvements in the living conditions of the poor – 'Terror is doing the work of compassion; one might really have a day of thanksgiving as much that the cholera came as that it has gone away.'

All the extra work involved by the cholera epidemic had not prevented the Board from setting about its more permanent duties. These could be summed up as the inspection and improvement of especially insanitary areas in the country at large and the provision of a proper drainage system, a healthy water-supply, and better burial

facilities for London in particular. Ashley was particularly concerned with the last two schemes. For the next few years the macabre
but essential business of burial became one of his chief preoccupations.
To take up such a subject might in itself be described as an heroic
act of self-abnegation. 'We can never be sufficiently obliged to him
for undertaking a task which, beside its immediate disagreeableness,
associates his name with all that is shocking and repulsive,'[6] the
Editor of *The Times* wrote of Ashley's efforts to reform common
lodging-houses. The remark could be applied more appositely to his
concern with cemeteries and corpses. Though it is not altogether fair
to suggest as Mr. R. A. Lewis does in his biography of Chadwick,
that Ashley delighted in 'the satisfaction of doing good conspicuously,'[7] he himself admitted to a craving for applause and approval.
Now, simply from a sense of duty, he took upon himself the task of
promoting a reform which had no popular appeal but rather the
reverse. The subject is one which the living naturally shun; the dead,
for their part, cannot rise up and call the reformer blessed. When
Ashley was deprived of the Parliamentary control of two measures,
the one dealing with water-supply, the other with interments, he
lamented sadly, 'I had hoped that my name (is this an illegitimate
desire?) would be inseparably connected with these reforms.' Few
indeed are the politicians who would wish to have their name inseparably connected with funerals.

As part of the fight against cholera Chadwick and Ashley had
sought to remedy the insanitary condition of London's graveyards.
A Cruikshank illustration to *Bleak House* depicting one of these
grisly places is sardonically entitled 'Consecrated Ground.' Dickens'
sense of the macabre is sometimes called strained or exaggerated;
but in this case the horrors he described were a commonplace of London
life. Every time, for instance, that Ashley went to the Houses of
Parliament, he could see and smell the nastiness of the churchyard
of St. Margaret's, Westminster. During the epidemic the Board of
Health had ordered the closing of some half dozen of the worst
burial-yards, only to be met by fierce opposition from such interested
parties as parsons, vestry meetings, and Boards of Guardians. Ashley
was all for standing firm. 'We must refuse at once to receive any
deputations or committees or any form of resistance to our graveyard
order,' he wrote to Chadwick; 'the necessity is immediate, urgent,
paramount to all law, right, or interests.' He ended with a declaration
seldom made by anyone in official position: 'I will take any amount
of responsibility.'[8] Twice the Board summoned recalcitrant parish
authorities before the magistrates, and twice the magistrates dis-

missed the Board's case. Their decision merely stiffened Ashley's conviction that the Board had acted with both wisdom and courage.

The plan devised by Chadwick to remedy this state of affairs amounted to the nationalisation of the business of burial as far as London was concerned. A Burials Commission was to take over the work of private undertakers, to close all overcrowded graveyards, and to control seven or eight publicly-owned cemeteries on the out-skirts of London. Chadwick's written draft included such unexpectedly imaginative touches as a cemetery church crowned by a dome of stained glass and approached through avenues flanked by giant statues. This scheme, considerably pruned by the tactful Morpeth, formed the basis of an Interments Bill which Ashley confidently planned to pilot through the House of Commons. 'If you and the Government have ordinary pluck we shall have the noblest interment Bill that ever was propounded,'[9] he wrote on November 19th 1849 to Carlisle, as Morpeth had now become, following his father's death. In January 1850, however, Ashley was informed that the Whig Government intended to keep the measure in its own hands.

This bitter blow was followed by a worse shock to his personal pride. Now that he had come into his inheritance Carlisle needed more leisure for his private affairs; in March 1850, therefore, he re-tired from the Commissionership of Woods and Forests and also from the Presidency of the Board. Ashley wrote a warm farewell to his old friend:

Your other colleagues will feel, as keenly as myself, the severance of the tie that has bound us in perfect harmony since the day we began our operation. It will not be easy, if it be possible, to replace you at the Board; there is needed not only ability but zeal in the cause, and many of the qualities that adorn and endear the private gentleman.[10]

Carlisle's obvious successor would have been Ashley himself; instead Russell appointed Lord Seymour, eldest son of the Duke of Somerset. Ashley promptly resigned, rightly aggrieved because 'they have put a man my junior in everything over my head and made me second to him in the House of Commons.' Russell, however, per-suaded him to withdraw his resignation, promising him in return the Parliamentary sponsorship of the Metropolitan Water Supply Bill, another of Chadwick's far-reaching schemes.

Russell himself seems to have had misgivings as to the future of the Board under Seymour. On August 14th 1850, Ashley wrote

Carlisle a letter in which he clearly foresaw a clash between Chadwick and the new President:

> Our Doctor [Southwood Smith] . . . is strangely discomfited by a sentence in Johnnie's letter urging peace, harmony, co-operation, etc, etc, with Seymour. Why, what has passed? You know that, during your time, there never was so united and undisputing a Board as ours. If Seymour finds anything go wrong, the fault will be with himself. Alas, there are some men who are so constituted that they cannot speak or write to a Chief, a Secretary, or a Clerk, without giving pain, or at least, 'rubbing the hair the wrong way.'[11]

One of Ashley's most important functions at the Board of Health had been to exert a soothing and moderating influence on Chadwick. By what he himself described as delicate hints he tried, with some success, to induce Chadwick to behave in a less autocratic manner and to adopt a more conciliatory tone. 'Our friend's infirmity is being a little disposed to use authority instead of persuasion; and this infirmity has been lately fretted by personal collisions,'[12] he had written when Chadwick was engaged in a dispute with the Commissioners of Sewers. Now that Seymour had taken the place of the ever-tactful Carlisle he rightly feared that these 'personal collisions' would become much more serious and frequent.

Deprived of the control of the Interments measure Ashley now turned his energies to the business of the Water Supplies Bill. In 1848 London's water, both for washing and for drinking, was drawn from the Thames, a river which also received the whole of London's sewage. One of the nine London water companies actually pumped its supply from a point opposite the outflow of the Ranelagh sewer. Chadwick devised a plan by which a single authority was to supply London with pure soft water from gathering-grounds in the Surrey countryside. For Ashley a ramble over heaths and commons in search of suitable springs made a pleasant change from the 'perambulations' of slums and graveyards which the Board's business usually entailed. So interested was he that he spent part of his Scottish holiday inspecting similar gathering-grounds proposed for Glasgow's water supply. Everything seemed set fair when one day in December 1850 Seymour descended on Gwydyr House, a building he entered as seldom as possible. The Board, he announced, was acting without his authority or that of the Treasury; all research and planning of a new water-supply must cease forthwith.

Ashley had never had a good opinion of this deliberately obstructive President. 'I more than distrust Seymour,' he had written on November 7th, and later he was to complain that 'Seymour's insolence at the Board of Health, (which he never attends) is intolerable.' Now he arose in his wrath. Why, he demanded, had the President not called his colleagues together and asked them for an explanation before delivering so sharp a rebuke? The Board, replied Seymour, had not informed him of their plans although the Treasury had given 'explicit directions' that schemes involving expenditure must first be submitted for his approval. Ashley retorted that no trace could be found of those explicit directions – 'I asked you before and I now ask you again, "When was the order given? What was it; was it by word of mouth or in writing, where is it now to be found?" ' Driven into a corner, Seymour was forced to admit that the order in question really amounted to no more than an 'understanding.' Ashley now produced two letters, written only six months previously, which proved conclusively that Seymour had been informed of the proposed survey of gathering grounds and had replied that he could see no objection. 'Such is the haste and want of consideration with which you attack your colleagues,' Ashley concluded.

He had indeed won the immediate battle, but he had not won the war for London's water-supply, nor had he endeared himself to Seymour, who from now onwards treated him with undisguised hostility. Meanwhile, at the Home Office he was kept waiting week after week for an answer to his query as to whether the Government did or did not intend to proceed with Chadwick's scheme. 'The shuffling Sir George Grey on the water question will compel my retirement,' he wrote on January 15th 1851. Only his conviction that of all necessities of life water was the one most essential to the poor kept him from throwing up the business in disgust.

The appointment of Seymour, 'the President who cannot preside,' had indeed proved a fatal blow, his declared intention being 'never to act until he was obliged and then to do as little as possible.'[13] The Board was now a mere shadow of its former self. Not only had Carlisle gone but the two secretaries, Austin and Bain, had both resigned, worn out by sheer pressure of work. Chadwick, Southwood Smith and Ashley were left to carry the whole burden, hindered rather than helped by the vagaries of Austin's successor, Tom Taylor. The gifts which had brought Taylor success as a writer of farces and a contributor to *Punch* hardly sufficed to make him an efficient secretary to a Board of Health.

At this time of disappointment and frustration Ashley at least had the satisfaction of carrying through Parliament two measures closely connected with public health. In April 1851 he introduced two bills, one to allow local authorities to build lodging-houses, the other to provide for the registration and inspection of all common lodging-houses. He achieved the unusual feat of piloting these measures through both Houses of Parliament, his father dying in June after the bills had passed the Commons but before they had been introduced into the Lords.

Ashley is henceforth to be known as the Earl of Shaftesbury. His transference to the Upper House was as disastrous to the Board of Health as it was distasteful to him personally. Seeking to console him over this unwelcome promotion Chadwick wrote to point out that he would still be able to initiate legislation, that he would probably have an increased influence on public opinion, and that his health would have made it difficult for him to keep the late hours so often necessary in the House of Commons. (Shaftesbury's diaries of this period are more than usually full of complaints of noises in his ears, always with him a sign of general ill-health.) The Board had now no spokesman in the Commons except Seymour, who openly sided with its opponents. In August 1850 the Metropolitan Interments Act had become law, only to meet with strong opposition from the Treasury, and from Hayter in particular, who was determined to prove the measure unworkable. Seymour unashamedly backed the Treasury against his own Board; so too did Shaftesbury's old enemy, John Bright, who put forward an argument particularly telling in an age all too familiar with jobbery. In this attack on Chadwick, Bright made a sideways thrust at Shaftesbury himself:

Whenever he [Chadwick] had a Board with such people as Lord Shaftesbury sitting on it he would be certain to pull the wire. And he did pull the wire, for if they granted the sum now asked for,* Mr. Chadwick would become the arbitrary disposer of more patronage than was in the gift of officers filling the highest situations in the Government.[14]

In the face of such opposition the Interments Act was abandoned and a less far-reaching measure introduced into Parliament as a substitute. The grand design for 'the noblest system of extra-mural interment the world ever knew'[15] was itself dead and buried.

Anxious to salvage what he could from the wreckage, Shaftesbury begged the intransigent Chadwick to accept the new attentuated

* A grant to buy land for two cemeteries.

scheme as the only alternative to no scheme at all. 'There is no use, I am sure, in fighting against power unless we have something on our side to appeal to,' he wrote on December 7th 1851. 'You particularly and the Doctor cannot *long* resist and retain your positions, and we shall then lose *all* by endeavouring to save *half*. We shall never bring the Government again to *our* scheme, and it will be therefore our wisdom to accept *theirs*, throwing the whole responsibility on those who command this course.'[16]

Chadwick's plan for London's water-supply went the same way as his plan for London's burials. In spite of Russell's promise to Shaftesbury, which alone had kept him from resignation on Seymour's appointment, Sir George Grey, as Home Secretary, took the Water Supply Bill into his own hands. In any case, it was not the kind of measure Shaftesbury would have wished to sponsor. Even this inadequate bill met with such a poor reception in the Commons that it was quietly withdrawn. Another one of the Board's schemes for reform had come to nothing; and as late as 1886 Londoners were still drinking Thames water.

Russell's resignation and the formation of Lord Derby's ministry in February 1852 meant the substitution of Lord John Manners for Seymour. The Board's new President, though less offensive, was no more zealous than the old one. The Tories had no intention of concerning themselves with anything so unpopular as sanitary reform nor did the change back from Tory to Whig following Derby's defeat in December of the same year raise Shaftesbury's hopes for the future of the Board. 'What shall we gain by a return to our old masters?' he wrote to Chadwick on December 18th. 'Seymour will be no better than John Manners as John Manners proved to be no better than Seymour . . . All are nearly alike. Public men know nothing, wish to know nothing, hate to be told anything which does not openly and directly affect their political position and safety.' He contrasted the apathy towards public health in free and democratic England with the interest shown by the despot of France – 'The Emperor is laying about him famously in Paris; he has declared war on all courts, alleys, lanes and culs-de-sac.'[17]

The new President of the Board was not to be Seymour but the Radical Sir William Molesworth, of whom Shaftesbury wrote, 'he has inherited the spirit of his predecessor of the Woods and Forests and has entered into all the enmities against us.' The only ray of light in the general gloom was the appointment of Palmerston as Home Secretary. Here at last was a powerful man in a key position who might be prepared to come forward in support of the Board, if only because he liked and respected Shaftesbury personally. Though his name is more commonly associated with the Foreign Office, Palmerston proved an active and efficient Home Secretary, where sanitary reform was concerned definitely on the side of the angels. His biographer, Mr. Jasper Ridley, says of him, 'he entirely accepted the doctrine that public health should be administered by Boards staffed by Government officials with compulsory powers,'[18] a point of view much in advance of general opinion in his own day. Shaftesbury himself was to write that he had never known any Home Secretary equal to Palmerston 'for readiness to undertake every good work of kindness, humanity and social good, specially to the child and the working class; no fear of wealth, capital, or electors; prepared at all times to run a-tilt if he could do good by it.'

In Palmerston's support lay the only hope for the Board's survival. Luck, however, was against him. When he took office an epidemic of typhoid fever was raging in Croydon which was to do serious if unmerited damage to the Board's reputation. Chadwick had pinned his faith to a system of piped, water-borne drainage. Such a system had just been installed at Croydon with considerable flourish of trumpets, only to be followed by the worst outbreak of fever the town had ever known. The misfortune was one of the inevitable growing-pains of any new invention; investigation was to show that the fault lay with inefficient, dishonest contractors rather than with the system itself. Chadwick's many enemies were none the less provided with a splendid stick with which to beat the Board, and beat they did, without justice or mercy. Never one to submit meekly, Chadwick prepared a most belligerent Report. Shaftesbury, however, was too wise to assent to the publication of this provocative document. He had already begged Chadwick to take care to use 'the most conciliatory tones,' and now he spoke out bluntly in condemnation of the Report – 'The language is frequently personal and betrays feelings which will be commented on; and it does not wear, to my eye at least, the air and manner of an official document.' He begged Chadwick to think again – 'The reply, if sent out as I have it before me, will be absolutely the ruin of the Board. You, I and the Doctor, we three would, by our own act, be cast down, bound hand and foot, into the burning, fiery furnace.'[19] Thus admonished, Chadwick, who would take from Shaftesbury what he would take from no one else, agreed to suppress the Report.

Shaftesbury knew his colleague's failings only too well, but he also took some blame to himself. 'Doubtless we have not always been on our guard and Chadwick certainly has added to former unpopularity a fresh supply drawn from overbearing manners and modes of action too doctrinaire,' he wrote on August 8th 1853, adding the admission, 'I myself have been imprudent.' He was pleased to see Palmerston enforcing several measures recommended by the Board, though he must needs draw a comparison between the Home Secretary's effortless success and his own long, fruitless labour: 'We unfortunate people, having borne the burden and heat of the day, having stirred the public attention, having incurred all the odium, receive no support from the Government and consequently fail. He, having borne and done nothing of the kind, but being the Secretary of State, succeeds!' He reflected morosely, 'Success is not what you do but what people say of it; and they are nearly always too ignorant to judge rightly.'

At the beginning of August, Sir William Molesworth, who should have been the Board's most determined champion, rose in the House of Commons and pointed out, amid cheers, that unless the Act of 1848 were renewed the Board's existence would terminate the following year. This act of treachery enraged Shaftesbury – 'A more bitter and cruel insult could not have been passed on men who have laboured earnestly for four years and have produced many great and beneficial results.' At this critical moment, when the future of the Board hung in the balance, cholera broke out again, the first cases occurring on Tyneside in September 1853. On December 5th Shaftesbury wrote to Palmerston pointing out that the members of the Board had fought the 1848–49 epidemic with great zeal and devotion and a fair measure of success, and urging that it would be madness to replace them now with new, untried men experimenting with new, untried methods.[20] Six weeks later he wrote again to say that if he were asked his opinion as to the future constitution of the Board he would have no hesitation in stating that to ensure the best possible service to the public the Board's present constitution must remain unchanged – 'We shall never find men to replace Chadwick and Southwood Smith, in whom great knowledge, experience and indefatigable zeal are combined.' The suggested alternative of a President changing with every change of Government and assisted only by two secretaries he dismissed as unworkable. He begged that if the Board were indeed to be disbanded it should at least be allowed to remain in existence for the full statutory period so that 'no unnecessary pain would be given to men who have toiled most vigorously in the service of the country and have received in the way of thanks and respect as little compensation as ever fell to the lot of any *"set of philanthropists"*.'[21] (The word philanthropist was beginning to sound unpleasantly in Shaftesbury's ears.) He himself was not entirely pessimistic. 'Great, well-founded hopes of sanitary triumphs in the zeal, energy, and judgement of Palmerston,' he wrote on December 14th; 'relied too, humanly speaking, on his aid to save the Board of Health from *immediate* destruction.'

In the early summer of 1854 the Board was under fierce attack in the Commons, its chief and most deadly opponent being its former President, Seymour. Now that Shaftesbury had been removed to the Upper House there was no one in the Commons capable of replying to this onslaught. On July 12th Shaftesbury thus described the Board's position:

The Board of Health is in a state of siege, and all the barbarians of the North and South, both in and out of Parliament, the Press, *et hoc genus omnes*, are lashed into a paroxysm of virulence and falsehood against Chadwick and Southwood Smith. The language of Sir Benjamin Hall* and especially of Lord Seymour, is as bitter in tone and as false in statement as though Satan himself had spoken it . . . The articles in *The Times* are in the highest style of that fiendish and ingenious paper. I suspect that Sir William Molesworth, who covets the absolute headship of the Board for himself, and the patronage and places in it for his electioneering friends in Southwark, instigates the articles. Myself ignored as a thing of naught, a cypher at the Board, etc, etc. Palmerston very well-disposed, but it requires something superhuman to protect the Board now. Such is the result of four years of intense and gratuitous labour.

Palmerston had already brought in a bill prolonging the life of the Board and attaching it to the Home Office instead of to the Woods and Forests. In the face of Seymour's attack it now seemed impossible that this bill should pass the House of Commons. Palmerston, who was nothing if not a realist, saw that the last faint hope for the Board's survival lay in jettisoning Chadwick. To this Shaftesbury would not agree. Though he had always admitted to himself that Chadwick was at one and the same time the Board's greatest asset and its greatest liability, he could not be disloyal to a friend. He replied to Palmerston's suggestion by declaring that if Chadwick went he must go also, since all members of the Board were equally responsible for its actions and policy. When Palmerston rose in the

* Benjamin Hall, M.P. for Marylebone, referred to 'the mischievous vagaries of these two persons.'

House of Commons to move the Second Reading of his bill he had in his pocket not only Chadwick's resignation but also the resignations of both Shaftesbury and Southwood Smith. The bill was defeated, the Board disbanded, and the work of sanitary reform set back for a generation.

When Shaftesbury spoke at the farewell dinner to the Board he quoted in his speech St. Paul's words from the second Epistle to the Corinthians, 'We are troubled on every side, yet not distressed, we are perplexed but not in despair, persecuted but not forsaken, cast down but not destroyed.' The concrete results of six years' work were small indeed. A few insanitary areas had been cleaned; a few local schemes for drainage and water-supply set in motion; all larger plans of reform had come to nothing. Yet those six years were emphatically not time wasted. For the very first time a statutory body had assumed control of sanitary affairs; for the very first time politicians and people alike had been brought to acknowledge that public health was a matter for public concern. Henceforward the business of government must include sewers and housing and the prevention of disease no less than treaties and tariffs and electoral reform. The earliest, almost imperceptible step had been taken in the direction of the modern Welfare State; a new chapter of history had begun.

For this alteration in the climate of public opinion all the members of the Board were collectively responsible. Shaftesbury's individual achievement was to change the attitude of the churches and Christian people in general towards sanitary questions. In his preface to the 1965 reprint of Chadwick's great sanitary Report of 1842, Mr. M. W. Flynn points out that the Evangelical pioneers of social reform, characters such as Wilberforce or Elizabeth Fry, took no interest in sanitary reform because they did not believe it to be in any way connected with morals or religion. Shaftesbury was wise enough to realise that public health is a subject which must concern every Christian. He saw clearly that people obliged to live in sub-human conditions could not be expected to live according to ordinary human standards, much less according to the super-human standards demanded of Christians. He knew, for instance, that it was useless to preach chastity to boys and girls living in overcrowded cottages and forced to sleep side-by-side in the same room, and in his Sturminster Newton speech of 1843 he had laboured to make this point clear:

There is a mighty stir now made on behalf of education, and I thank God for it; but let me ask you to what purpose it is to take a little child, a young female, for instance, and teach her for six hours a day the rules of decency and every virtue, and then send her back to such abodes of filth and profligacy as to make her unlearn, by the practice of an hour, the lessons of a year, to witness and oftentimes to share, though at first against her will, the abominations that have been recorded. Gentlemen, if you desire to have a moral and well-conducted people, you must do your best to place and keep them under such circumstances that they may have the means and the opportunity to bring into action the lessons they have been taught, the principles they have acquired.[22]

In the mid-nineteenth century few people understood that religion must be involved with slum-clearance and sanitation as well as with churches and schools, a truth now so obvious as to be a truism but then an idea which was new, startling, and almost revolutionary. Even Shaftesbury himself, on inheriting the family estates, as a matter of course restored the church before repairing the labourers' cottages, though he saw clearly enough that duty towards one's neighbour included a duty towards that neighbour's housing. He had professedly undertaken his work at the Board of Health 'to the glory of God's own name as well as to the permanent welfare of our beloved country.'[23] That the leading English Evangelical – some of Shaftesbury's contemporaries would have gone so far as to describe him as the leading English Christian – should believe that it was his religious duty to devote himself to such matters as drains and dung-heaps, overcrowding, infection and water-supply, went far to convince other Christians that it was part of their religious duty to do likewise.

Chapter 16

EARL OF SHAFTESBURY

Shaftesbury's succession to the earldom in June 1851 brought with it a great change both in his public and his private life. His political position was fundamentally affected. In the spring of this same year, walls had been chalked with 'Ashley for Premier.' He had long ago abandoned any such ambitions, but he had remained deeply interested in politics and convinced that his political usefulness depended on his membership of the House of Commons. Now of necessity he must take his seat in the House of Lords. The diary for June 24th gives a somewhat ungracious account of his reception there by his peers: 'My greetings yesterday in the House of Lords reminded me of the chapter in Isaiah when the King of Babylon goes down to Hades, "Hell from beneath is moved at thy coming; art thou become as one of us?" ' He was nevertheless pleased to be told of the general belief that his presence in the House of Lords would serve both to rouse and to popularise that assembly. He had always been anxious to see the Upper House restored to life and activity, and in November 1849 he had sent Russell some *Notes on Peerages,* suggesting that grants of peerages should be extended to include suitable men in trade and commerce, and pointing out that such a proposal would come better from Russell than from many another Prime Minister – 'Sprung from one of the oldest and greatest of our noble families, you could say and do things which might be carped at in others.' The covering letter sent with these notes opened with the characteristic phrase, 'It is quite manifest that you hold my opinions, ecclesiastical and religious, in supreme contempt.' 'I do not hold your opinions, ecclesiastical and religious, in supreme contempt,' Russell replied, equally characteristically, 'but I must reserve *some* liberty of judgement to myself.'[1]

Now Shaftesbury approached Russell again, this time suggesting that the parliamentary franchise should be extended by altering the property qualification to cover other forms of property as well as land or buildings:

There can be no reason why the suffrage should be limited, in these days, to the occupation of a house, or the tenure of a piece of ground. Moneyed persons, fundholders, annuitants, etc. have just as deep an interest in the welfare of the country as all the other classes, and yet many of them are shut out.[2]

He also proposed a reform in the system of dealing with business in the House of Lords urging the necessity to put a little more life into proceedings there. 'I do not like,' said Russell, 'an active House of Lords,' and received the tart reply, 'Then you will have none whatever.'

Where Shaftesbury's private affairs were concerned his inheritance left him as poor, perhaps even poorer than before. At St. Giles everything was chaos – 'What incredible waste! What sums have been lavished, what wealth tossed away!' He had inherited a mass of debt which, added to his own considerable liabilities, amounted to some £100,000 – 'debt, debt, debt, a mountain that faith can hardly remove.' No ready money was available for necessary expenditure on the estate, which was in shocking condition, farms under-cultivated, cottages overcrowded and ruinous, labourers brutalised and neglected. Characteristically enough, Shaftesbury's first action was to order the local tap-room to close at nine o'clock each night, his second to appoint a scripture-reader, whose salary he could ill afford to pay. He also embarked on a campaign to put down truck-payments by the farmers, 'that hard, ignorant, selfish race,' but he could do nothing about the most serious evils – 'Alas, alas, I am powerless; I can neither build cottages nor dismiss the farmer from his land without money to fall back upon.'

Though Shaftesbury delighted to be in possession of his family home, with its 'wide and joyous gardens,' his pleasure in it was spoilt by the necessity of spending large sums of money on repairs to the house, which was in a dangerous condition, the walls sinking and the roof threatening to collapse. First, however, he would deal with the church, which he did immediately and to some effect. By the New Year of 1852 he could report that 'it is made to look like a church and has ceased to have the appearance of a ball-room.' Clearly, the process of gothicising the eighteenth-century interior was well under way. Meanwhile, he must borrow from the bank, sell land, pictures, and family plate in order to meet essential expenditure.

All the time he was busy on these improvements and restorations at St. Giles, Shaftesbury was haunted by fears for the future of the place when it should pass, after his own death, to his eldest son and successor:

If I set an example, will he follow it? If I toil, and, by God's
blessing, effect a moral, physical, financial restoration, will he
maintain it? Or am I only fattening the property for the Jews?
. . . Will God or 'Society' be henceforth in the ascendant in my
much-loved home?

Much to his father's delight, at the beginning of December Anthony
had returned home from his long voyage, apparently greatly improved – 'What a vigorous frame! What a picture of health! How
simple, dear, and affectionate! How ready to conform to our wishes,
and to make them his own!' He was, however, again in debt; and
when his commanding officer's report arrived it was unfavourable.
This time Shaftesbury all but admitted to despair over his son and
heir, whom nevertheless he loved most heartily – 'Dear, darling,
affectionate boy, his very weaknesses are amiable.'

One curious and interesting episode of the year 1851 is not recorded
by Hodder. In November, Shaftesbury visited Lancashire, 'to see
my old friends the operatives and thank God with them for the success
of the Ten Hours Bill.' (He would have been more accurate had he
written 'ten-and-a-half.') Only eighteen months previously he had
been execrated as a traitor; now he was everywhere received with
affection and enthusiasm. Not only the operatives but the owners
also gave him a most warm reception; Edmund Ashworth, brother to
his old opponent, went so far as to ask him to dine. The next year,
1852, he again visited the North, and again the operatives greeted
him enthusiastically, numbers of them pressing around him to shake
his hand – 'I love the ready, earnest affection of these Lancashire
people.' Perhaps he had been right in supposing that, although they
had remained silent in the hour of trouble, the wiser heads among
them had always been on his side.

The year 1851 had ended with Palmerston's dismissal from the
Foreign Office, an event which angered and distressed Shaftesbury
considerably:

This is clearly the result of the long-cherished schemes of the
Queen and Prince to get rid of Palmerston; and he, no doubt, has
aided it by his own incaution. If this inter-meddling of the Royal
Pair be not checked, if Albert is to preside at the Foreign Office,
it will go hard with the Crown. Albert is utterly unEnglish and
the Queen follows him.

Two months later Palmerston had his 'tit-for-tat with Johnnie

Russell' by moving a hostile amendment to the Militia Bill and winning it by a small majority. Russell resigned, to be followed as Prime Minister by the Earl of Derby, as Stanley had now become. Shaftesbury immediately called on Derby to give him the benefit of much advice on political questions.

Shaftesbury himself was chiefly occupied with two battles, the old one against Tractarianism and a new one against American slavery. In the early summer of 1852 he accused the Tractarians of 'tenderness towards infidelity' because no Oxford man among them had come forward with an answer to J. A. Froude's novel, *The Nemesis of Faith*. As a leading Tractarian and an Oxford professor, Pusey replied to this accusation in a long and tedious correspondence which unfortunately found its way into the newspapers. More important was Shaftesbury's opposition to the revival of Convocation, a favourite idea with the Tractarians. This purely clerical assembly was an offence to all his notions of Church government, which he summed up in a single sentence: 'I am more and more of the opinion that ecclesiastical affairs of all kinds (leaving aside the purely spiritual) should be left to lay persons.' On November 5th 1852 Convocation met for the first time since 1717. *The Record* immediately announced the holding of a protest meeting, with Shaftesbury, of course, in the chair. On November 8th Gladstone wrote to Shaftesbury not to suggest that he should withdraw his opposition to the revival of Convocation but to ask him to co-operate with any attempt that might be made to give the Church of England some reasonable form of self-government.[3] This wise and tactful letter had its due effect upon Shaftesbury, who was careful to stress in his speech to the protest meeting his strong approval of 'a form of Church government upon a reasonable and moderate basis, in which the laity of the Church will have not only a great, but a dominant share.'[4]

Shaftesbury's interest in the negro slaves in America had been aroused by a reading of *Uncle Tom's Cabin*, 'that marvellous book, that singular and unprecedented compound of angelic genius and infantine simplicity.' With the Duchess of Sutherland he helped to organise British support for the Abolitionist cause. He joined what he described as 'the Nigger Committee,' he started a scheme to evangelise fugitive slaves, he drew up an address from the women of England to the women of America protesting against their acquiescence in 'that awful system.' One salient characteristic of American womanhood has not altered since Shaftesbury's day: 'the American ladies may have very pretty feet,' he conceded, then spoilt the compliment by adding 'but they have very bad logic.' Shaftesbury's

distrust and dislike of America was as strong as ever. 'I look to the
United States with great apprehension,' he wrote on August 26th
1853; 'her fierce democratic spirit is throwing down the old barriers of
non-intervention and seeking to be a busy-body in the affairs of
Europe. Her mission, certainly her desire, seems to be conquest,
bloodshed, and, strange to say, extension.'

He was, however, to meet and highly approve one very famous
American. When Harriet Beecher Stowe, author of *Uncle Tom's
Cabin*, came to England in the spring of 1853, Shaftesbury recorded
his admiration of 'the soft, earnest simplicity of her manner and
language.' He took her to inspect a model lodging-house, and he
went so far as to invite her with her whole party to dinner in the
great house in Grosvenor Square which was now his London home.
Although this particular occasion went off very well the ordinary
Society dinner-party had become a penance to him. 'Ought neither
to give or to receive dinners,' he wrote on May 24th after dining with
Lord Aberdeen; 'am wholly unfit for social purposes; whilst others
descant on pictures and new publications, etc. I have nothing to
say.'

In the later summer of 1852 and again in 1853 Shaftesbury spent
some weeks at Ems drinking the waters. These visits to German
spas, from now onwards a regular part of his annual routine, were
undertaken partly for health reasons, partly to give pleasure to
Minny, who delighted in holidays abroad. Shaftesbury himself,
who was sceptical of the benefits received and would have preferred
a trip to Scotland, found the visits very tedious. The 1852 holiday
was spoilt by the arrival of bad news from St. Giles. The cottages
there which he let at a rent of £3 a year had cost £400 to build, and
so, in an attempt to save money he had decided to try the experiment
of making his own bricks. He had had kilns constructed and engaged
a manager recommended to him by Edwin Chadwick. This man,
however, proved incompetent; and whilst the Shaftesburys were at
Ems the kilns burst, the bricks were destroyed, and the whole wildcat
scheme ended in heavy and profitless expense.

When the burden of the St. Giles estates had first fallen upon him
Minny had, as usual, been her husband's greatest help and support.
On his visit there at the time of his father's death he had found a
bust of her sculpted in her youth, and had kissed the marble lips –
'my precious wife, just as beautiful to me now, though twenty years
have passed.' Now, a year later, a temporary coldness had fallen
between husband and wife. Although the diary is very reticent on this
subject (several passages have been cut out), here and there are

hints of something seriously amiss. 'No sympathy, no community
of ideas, views, duties, no unison of moral sentiments; might as well
be alone; none to share the mind, the soul, the heart' – so runs the
entry for June 10th 1852. Minny, it seems, was in rebellion against
her husband's relentless round of religious practices – 'On Sunday last,
one chapter formally asked, and so formally given, the first in many
weeks. Who "spoke often to one another?" Not *we*, I trow.'

In his need for affection and sympathy Shaftesbury turned to his
favourite daughter, seven-year-old Conty – 'What a child, what a
precious creature!' He found cause for satisfaction too in Edy and
Lionel. Both boys were doing remarkably well at school and, better
still, giving promise of growing up into good Evangelicals. Maurice
was at Lausanne, in the care of a Swiss Protestant family, with whom
he appeared comfortable and content, although rapidly deteriorating
both physically and mentally. In spite of the heavy expense of travel,
Shaftesbury made frequent journeys to Switzerland to see his son,
and also endeavoured to make some permanent financial provision
for this invalid boy whose future troubled him greatly. Anthony
was now with his ship in the Mediterranean. In December 1852 his
parents arranged to spend some time with him at Nice 'to endeavour,
by renewed intercourse, to do him good and maintain our influence.'
They extended their journey to Northern Italy, where Shaftesbury
combined business with pleasure, visiting a lunatic asylum and hope-
fully arranging for a distribution of bibles among the benighted
Italian papists.

During this trip abroad news reached him of a change of ministry
in England, where a coalition of Whigs and Peelites under Aberdeen
had replaced Derby and the Tories. 'Graham, Newcastle, Gladstone,
my greatest enemies and most spiteful opponents, are again installed
in power,' he commented morosely. Even now he could not rid
himself of regrets for what might have been. 'Within the last two years
two governments have been formed and neither has invited my
co-operation,' he wrote on January 3rd, forgetting that whatever
might have been expected of Derby, Aberdeen could hardly be expected to press office upon a man who was neither a Whig nor a
Peelite.

In this year of 1853 Shaftesbury's parliamentary efforts centred on
two social problems, destitute children and housing. The homeless
children of London learnt to beg and pilfer as soon as they could walk.
When they grew a little older they became a serious menace to respectable citizens and almost inevitably they ended as thugs and
criminals. Somehow or other they had to be taken off the streets

and removed from the corrupting influence that surrounded them. In July 1853 Shaftesbury brought in a Juvenile Mendicancy Bill empowering the police to take up children found begging in the street and bring them before the magistrates, who could then order them to be removed from the custody of their parents, if they had any, and placed in the comparative moral safety of the work-house. The Bill came in for much well-founded criticism and was finally thrown out by the Commons. The subject bristled with obvious difficulties; but one difficulty Shaftesbury could not have been expected to foresee. In the course of his speech in support of the Bill he chanced to mention a court judgment depriving Lord Mornington of the custody of his children, whereupon that outraged nobleman challenged him to a duel. Being no fighting man, Shaftesbury very properly referred the matter to his solicitors.

The winter of 1853 was overshadowed by the ever-increasing threat of war in the Near East. In October fighting broke out between Russia and Turkey. In January 1854 the combined French and British fleets sailed through the Dardanelles into the Black Sea. Anthony's ship was with this force; and Shaftesbury trembled to think of his son in danger. On March 27th England and France declared war on Russia.

According to Hodder 'war in a Christian spirit presented no anomaly to the mind of Lord Shaftesbury,' nor, he might have added, to the minds of most of Shaftesbury's contemporaries. He might have felt some qualms about a war in support of Moslem Turkey against Christian Russia had he not conveniently remembered that the Czar had suppressed the Russian branch of the Bible Society and therefore did not deserve to be classed as a Christian monarch. He had doubts too about the religious views of England's ally, Napoleon III, and took advantage of the alliance between the two countries to write the Emperor a polite but firm letter reproaching him for denying full religious liberty to the French Protestants.

'Ah, Lord,' Shaftesbury wrote on March 29th, 'we have not begun this fearful struggle in pride, covetousness or ambition, but to maintain order, justice, right, to resist encroachment of a cruel, aggrandising power, and prevent the might of religious despotism over millions of eastern Christians.' Very soon he began to wonder whether this righteous war was being conducted in a properly efficient manner. Going down to Dover to meet Anthony, who was transferring from the Black Sea Fleet to the Baltic, he watched the troops embarking on overcrowded, insanitary transports, and trembled at the possibility of a fire on board or an outbreak of cholera. The Army's de-

parture gave him other reasons for dismay. 'I wish the feast given
to Sir Charles Napier before his departure had been less jocose,'
he wrote on March 12th; 'surely when ten thousand men are going
to a war, to slay or to be slain, we should send them forth with
prayer and hope, not with wine and laughter.' Similarly he was to
complain that Lord Raglan, the Commander-in-Chief, never thought
in his despatches to give grateful thanks to the Almighty when
victory came his way – 'Is he thinking more of the clubs of St. James's
than of the Heavenly Host?'

The year 1854 was for Shaftesbury an even busier time than usual.
'Oftentimes do look at a book, and wish for it as a donkey for a carrot,'
he wrote on May 15th, 'but I, like him, am disappointed.' At St.
Giles he was hard at work doing what he could for the improvement
of the place and its people, providing allotments, cricket grounds,
evening lectures, and, as far as his means allowed, new cottages.
Financial problems were particularly pressing; because of the war
taxation had increased and mortgage rates risen, whilst for the same
reason he was finding it impossible to get a good price for the pictures
he had put up for sale. Heavily in debt himself, he was deeply disturbed by Anthony's extravagance and lack of financial sense. On
May 26th he described himself as 'much dejected by disappointments
actual and prospective; by sorrows, unshared; by want of co-operation;
by suffering seen, and not alleviated; by evils foreseen and not prevented, by reality and imagination.'

Public affairs were no less trying than private ones. 'Great anxiety
about Bill for relief of Chimney Sweepers,' he wrote on May 2nd;
'have suffered actual tortures through solicitude for prevention of
these horrid cruelties.' The Bill's rejection by the House of Lords
was a bitter grief to him. Meanwhile the Board of Health was in its
death agony. In the House of Commons Lord Seymour, once that
Board's President and now its worst enemy, was attacking it in language 'as bitter in tone and as false in statement as though Satan
himself had spoken it.' Since he was no longer in the House of Commons Shaftesbury could make no immediate reply to these venomous
attacks, which touched not only the Board but his own personal
honour. 'Lord Seymour had it all his own way because there was no
one at hand to answer or even question him,' he wrote on July 31st.
'He is either a frightful liar or afflicted in his memory; he swears that
I did not appear at the meeting on January 30th though four persons
swear that I did, and the Minister confirms their statement and mine.'
On August 3rd he replied to Seymour's charge of falsehood in a
manner which satisfactorily established the truth of his own statement

but did nothing to alter the feeling of the House against the Board itself.

Smarting under personal attack and deeply distressed by the fate of the Board of Health and of the Chimney Sweeps Bill, Shaftesbury allowed his feelings to get the better of his judgement. For once in a way he lost patience with Palmerston, whom he blamed for many of his recent failures. Palmerston had wrecked the Public Health Bill through his self-confidence; he had abandoned the Juvenile Mendicancy Bill 'to please the Irish tail'; he had arrived late for the Chimney Sweep debate, and now, having particularly asked if he might take charge of a Nuisances Removal Bill, 'he is preparing, I see, to make a surrender of it, and then he will rub his hands and say Ha! Ha!.' Shaftesbury was indeed out of spirits and temper.

The winter of 1854–55 was an exceptionally hard one; and the suffering of the troops in the Crimea was extreme. Shaftesbury had once written of Lord Raglan that 'a nobler specimen of a soldier and a gentleman has never existed'; now, however, he held Raglan, as Commander-in-Chief, responsible for the appalling state of affairs:

> He does not exercise, like his great master, the Duke, all the energies and calling of a General. The truth is that a man of sixty-four years of age, after forty years of peace, who never commanded even a regiment, and who has passed all his life, after the crude and inexperienced period of four-and-twenty, at a desk as Secretary, is not fit, on the sudden, to assume command of a large army. He sits too much on his tail, engaged as at the Horse Guards, in writing, and seldom shows himself to the troops. All this mismanagement, loss, neglect, suffering, have been perpetrated under his eyes, and reported to his ears; and if he be not like Gallio and really do care for these things, he may have the merit of sympathy, but he must bear the charge of incompetency.

While the war lasted Shaftesbury raged more than usually fiercely against 'that iniquitous paper, *The Times*,' but he had the grace to praise it with the press in general for the exposures of 'the follies, cruelties, sins, negligences and ignorances of our Crimean authorities.' Once people were aware of the unnecessary sufferings endured by the troops a wave of indignation swept the country. On January 25th 1855 Shaftesbury's old opponent, J. A. Roebuck, moved in the House of Commons for a committee of enquiry into the conduct of the war. When this motion was carried by a majority of 148 Aberdeen resigned.

To find a successor to him was not easy. Shaftesbury referred to 'the bitter resentment of baffled Coburgs' when the Queen, whose dislike of Palmerston was common gossip, ignored his claims to the Premiership, and sent first for Derby, then for Lansdowne, then for Clarendon, then for Russell, a character who in Shaftesbury's mind had taken Peel's place as Public Enemy Number One, 'a low trickster and intriguer, a man full of self-seeking, a cuckoo wanting everyone's place, and a fox, sly and unscrupulous in obtaining it.'

Palmerston it was, however, who ultimately became Prime Minister on February 5th 1855, to the delight of the nation at large and of Shaftesbury in particular. When forming his Ministry one of Palmerston's first acts was to offer Shaftesbury a seat in the Cabinet as Chancellor of the Duchy of Lancaster. As usual on such occasions Shaftesbury made a great show of reluctance, whereupon Palmerston placated the Whigs by giving the post to Carlisle. Three weeks later the resignation of the Peelites, Gladstone, Graham, and Herbert, necessitated an early re-shuffle of the Cabinet. Shaftesbury was again offered the Duchy of Lancaster and again declined, much to Palmerston's irritation and annoyance.

During the first days of March, at the very height of this Ministerial crisis, Shaftesbury received an unexpected visit from a very remarkable American woman. Single-handed, Dorothea Lynde Dix had fought to improve the condition of lunatics in America and to bring about the same reforms which Shaftesbury and the Lunacy Commissioners had achieved in England and Wales. Scotland, however, had always lain outside the sphere of their jurisdiction. Conditions there were appalling, as Dorothea Lynde Dix discovered during a visit in the early months of 1855. Though a foreigner, she felt no qualms about interfering. Telegraphing to make an appointment with Shaftesbury, whom she had never met, she made a hurried night journey from Edinburgh to London to beg for his assistance in obtaining a Commission of Enquiry. The result of that Commission was a great improvement in the treatment of lunatics in Scotland, and an approximation of conditions there to those already existing in England and Wales.

Meanwhile, Shaftesbury's second refusal of Palmerston's offer had led to a serious family row. Though most of the references to this quarrel have been cut out of the diary, papers now at St. Giles show Shaftesbury to have been in a particularly exasperated and exasperating mood. His reaction to Palmerston's well-meant offer is so extraordinarily suspicious as to suggest at least a temporary lapse from mental balance:

They [Palmerston and Lady Palmerston] will never forgive it; and I am convinced that they have other views than my simple adhesion. *They have heard the views of many*; 'This man may be troublesome, get him into the Cabinet on terms which will excite the suspicion of his friends, and he will be neutralised for ever.' How else can I account for the extreme passion they have both shown?

It is almost unnecessary to point out that no such tortuous ideas had ever entered Palmerston's mind or that of his wife. Everyone was genuinely anxious that Shaftesbury should at last receive his political deserts and be promoted to that Cabinet office which had eluded him for so long. Minny begged him not to refuse, pointing out 'how *much more* weight everything has coming from a Cabinet Minister'; Lady Palmerston wrote telling him how many people, the Queen included, wished to see him at last in the Cabinet. At this point tempers seem to have snapped. Shaftesbury's reply to his mother-in-law's perfectly calm, polite, and affectionate letter presupposes a family quarrel, although in his over-strained, nervous state he probably exaggerated its importance and intensity. His letter to Lady Palmerston is dated March 12th:

It is utterly impossible to express the grief and agony that I have undergone and am still undergoing. This affair has completely broken up my private and domestic peace; I cannot hope to retain the affection and goodwill I have hitherto enjoyed from you and Palmerston. Minny shares all your opinions and feelings, and applies, with equal severity, the same language as yourself . . . It is, of course, a great sacrifice to me to decline such an offer and close up the prospects of so much agreeable occupation and honour, but the disruption of family ties is much worse, and I feel that though they may be patched up, they can never be restored as before.[5]

Needless to say, 'the disruption of family ties' proved to be a merely temporary disturbance. Lady Palmerston replied with a charming and conciliatory letter beginning, 'Your letter was so kind and amiable and affectionate that it made me cry.'[6] Shaftesbury's objections had been on the score of the Maynooth Grant, the Jewish Disability Bill, and various measures affecting Sunday Observance, none of them issues of any importance or interest to Palmerston. He tactfully agreed to make concessions, particularly on the subject of the Maynooth Grant, which, though a matter now all but forgotten by the general public, remained a great stumbling block to the Evangelicals. Shaftesbury, with what appears to have been quite genuine reluctance, now at last agreed to take office, but only if no other suitable person could be found to fill the post. He was actually dressed and ready to set out for Buckingham Palace to kiss hands on his appointment when he was reprieved by the last minute substitution of Lord Harrowby – 'It was, to my mind, as distinctly an act of special providence as when the hand of Abraham was stayed and Isaac escaped.'

Chapter 17

BISHOP-MAKER

Though Shaftesbury held no official post in Palmerston's ministry he occupied a position of considerable influence and importance behind the scenes, in particular where ecclesiastical or public health matters were concerned. The appalling sanitary conditions in the Crimea and in the military hospitals at Scutari were the cause of much unnecessary sickness and mortality among the troops. On February 15th 1855 Shaftesbury called on Lord Panmure, the newly-appointed Secretary for War, to urge on him 'my scheme for a Sanitary Commission to proceed, with full powers, to Scutari and Balaclava, there to purify the hospitals, ventilate the ships, and exert all that science can do to save life where thousands are dying, not of their wounds, but of dysentery and diarrhoea, the result of foul air and preventable mischiefs.' Knowing that Shaftesbury had Palmerston's support, Panmure acted immediately on this suggestion. Three Commissioners were selected, Doctor John Sutherland, one-time inspector with the Board of Health, Doctor Hector Gavin, and Herbert Rawlinson, a civil engineer. Shaftesbury issued them with very explicit instructions, written in his own hand. Mrs. Woodham Smith suggests that Florence Nightingale, who had arrived at Scutari the previous November, had a hand in their composition – 'Her name did not appear, but the urgency, the clarity, the force-fulness of the instructions are unmistakably hers.'[1] Though the style of the instructions certainly resembles Florence Nightingale's, on occasion Shaftesbury's tone could be every wit as urgent, as clear, and as forceful as hers. A paper at St. Giles, written in Shaftesbury's own hand, gives an account of the whole proceeding:

It was Doctor Hector Gavin, good and kind man, who was afterwards killed accidentally, who suggested to me the Sanitary Commission . . . I urged on Panmure the appointment of such a Commission. He assented, and desired me to draw up the instructions. I did so.[2]

It is not impossible, however, that these instructions were based
on letters from Florence Nightingale describing the state of affairs
and outlining the measures which she wished to see adopted. Though
no such letters survive she may well have written to Shaftesbury
both as a prominent authority on sanitary matters and as a personal
friend. The two had known each other for some time, the Nightin-
gales being Hampshire neighbours and friends of the Palmerstons.
Shaftesbury recorded with pride that Florence Nightingale said to
him, 'that Commission saved the British Army.'[3] He was not to know
that she also said, 'Lord Shaftesbury would have been in a lunatic
asylum if he had not devoted himself to reforming lunatic asylums.'[4]

   The Commissioners went to work as promptly as even Shaftesbury
or Miss Nightingale could have wished. As early as March 19th
Dr. Gavin was writing a long letter to Shaftesbury describing the
appalling conditions at Constantinople and Scutari. 'There is not that
energy and decision at work which should characterise Englishmen,'
he commented justly, and again, 'Your Lordship would wonder how
men in their sober senses could do the absurd things which seem to be
common here.'[5] When, three months later, Dr. Sutherland wrote to
Shaftesbury reporting on the situation at Balaclava, conditions there,
though far from perfect, were already greatly improved as a result
of the Commissioners' efforts. Nothing could wipe out the unnecessary loss and suffering that had already occurred, but at least
the Army was saved from complete catastrophe.

   Most people would count the work of this Commission as the
most important result of Shaftesbury's unofficial co-operation with
Palmerston. He himself, however, set more store by his position as
'bishop-maker,' as Bishop Samuel Wilberforce rather ruefully called
him. ('Soapy Sam' stood no chance at all of promotion whilst Shaftesbury remained in control.) Shaftesbury had always hankered after
a share in the business of ecclesiastical patronage – 'these appointments make my mouth water,' he had written as long ago as 1845 –
but he certainly did not expect Palmerston to consult him on that
matter. 'I much fear that Palmerston's ecclesiastical appointments
will be detestable,' he wrote to Evelyn on February 28th. 'He does
not know, in theology, Moses from Sidney Smith. The Vicar of
Romsey, where he goes to Church, is the only clergyman he ever
spoke to; and as for the wants, the feelings, the views, the hopes and
fears, of the country, and particularly the religious part of it, they
are as strange to him as the interior of Japan.'[6] Palmerston was
indeed an ecclesiastical ignoramus, but he had the good sense to
seek the advice of people better informed. Nothing was more natural

than that he should take counsel with Shaftesbury, a devout Christian deeply versed in Church affairs, and a member of his own family whom he both liked and respected.

Shaftesbury was Palmerston's chief ecclesiastical counsellor; we have his own word for it that he was consulted over every piece of patronage, excepting only one small, insignificant appointment. He was, however, by no means all-powerful. Palmerston was not a man to abrogate his rights and responsibilities; the final decision was always his own even on questions in which he took very little personal interest. Before making an appointment he took advice from other people as well as Shaftesbury, chief among them being William Cowper, who was at this period going through a Broad Church phase. 'William Cowper has got the ear of Palmerston (always ready to be tickled by liberal flourishes) and neology will carry the day in every future appointment,' Shaftesbury wrote gloomily on May 31st 1856. He even went so far as to refer to 'the influence of Mephistopheles, who is ever at Palmerston's elbow.'

These forebodings proved to be quite unjustified. Of the eleven clerics appointed to bishoprics, deaneries, or professorial chairs during Palmerston's first ministry, six were Evangelicals, two were moderates, and only three were Broad Churchmen. Of these three one was appointed at Queen Victoria's personal request. As a general rule Palmerston did not give undue heed to royal recommendations; 'unless they be really good men,' he would remark, 'I shall not pay any attention.'[7] To his credit be it remembered that he refused to make ecclesiastical patronage a political affair; 'if a man is a good man I don't care what his political opinions are'[8] was another one of his sayings. Nor did he favour his family or acquaintances; of all the men he advanced only one was chosen as the son of an old friend.* Pusey was the last person likely to approve of the general trend of the Palmerston-Shaftesbury appointments, yet even he declared that now for the very first time ecclesiastical preferments were made for religious rather than political reasons.

In a letter to Queen Victoria Palmerston described the qualities which he considered desirable in a bishop:

> Their chief duties consist in watching over the clergy of their diocese, seeing that they perform properly their parochial duties, and preserving harmony between the clergy and the laity, and softening the asperities between the established Church and the Dissenters. For these purposes it is desirable that a bishop should

* T. Garnier, appointed Dean of Ripon, 1859. Dean of Lincoln, 1860.

have practical knowledge of parochial functions, and should not
be of an overbearing and intolerant temperament. His diocesan
duties are enough to occupy all his time, and the less he engages in
theological disputes the better. Much mischief has been done by
theological bishops. [9]

Such an attitude played straight into Shaftesbury's hands. As
Professor Chadwick puts it, 'Cavalier Palmerston wanted simple,
· godly, non-theological bishops; Roundhead Shaftesbury wanted
Evangelical bishops; most Evangelicals were simple and godly.' [10]
And, it might be added, Roundhead Shaftesbury had always disapproved of theological bishops as much as ever Palmerston did.
His thoughts were not with the Universities or the House of Lords,
but with the neglected, untaught multitude of the very poor – 'to
these people the power of preaching is just the same as it ever was,
provided it comes from a truly pious man, who appeals to the heart,
and preaches the simple truths of the Gospel.' [11] But he knew that the
poor, ignorant and illiterate though they might be, could not be
fobbed off with the second-rate – 'I know they will either have
religion of the best quality or not at all.'
Unfortunately this was just what Shaftesbury could not provide.
Pious Evangelicals there were in plenty, but few or no first-class men
among them. However, he saw to it that what was lacking in quality
should be made up in sheer quantity. During Palmerston's two terms
of office more Evangelicals were appointed to important positions
in the Church than in any comparable period either before or since.
Because Evangelicals were unpopular in high places they had always
been inadequately represented on the bench of bishops. The appointment of 'the Shaftesbury bishops' as they were commonly called,
went some way towards remedying this injustice. In his essay on
The Evangelical Party in the Church of England, Mr. Hardman writes
'For the first time in the history of the party, it was placed numerically
in a position of respectability among the bishops and in the Church
as a whole.'
During Palmerston's first ministry Shaftesbury's attitude towards
ecclesiastical patronage can best be described as a determination
to make hay whilst the sun shone. Palmerston was an old man and
his tenure of office appeared uncertain; Shaftesbury therefore determined to promote as many Evangelicals as possible in the short
time that might be available to him, hoping thus to 'lay such a foundation that we might hereafter stand a few shocks of vicious appointments.'

Ironically enough, because of the poor quality of the available Evangelicals, the most interesting appointments were those of two Broad Churchmen, Arthur Penrhyn Stanley and A. C. Tait. Stanley was appointed Regius Professor of Ecclesiastical History in 1856; the real difficulty was not to arise until his further appointment to the Deanery of Westminster during Palmerston's second adminis‐tration. Shaftesbury increasingly distrusted and disapproved of Stanley, but he regarded Tait as the best of the Broad Churchmen. In the spring of 1856, whilst Tait was Dean of Carlisle, five of his little daughters died within a month of each other in a scarlet fever epidemic. Touched by this tragedy, Queen Victoria asked that he should be moved as soon as possible from a place of such unhappy memories. Shaftesbury suggested the vacant see of London, although personally he would have preferred to see Tait promoted to a less important bishopric. His doubts seemed to be justified when the new bishop appointed Stanley as his Examining Chaplain. Immediately Shaftesbury wrote a letter of peremptory protest to Lady Wake, Tait's sister and his own personal friend:

You spoke to me about your brother; and it was in no slight mea‐sure owing to your representation of 'what was in him' that I urged his name on the consideration of the Minister.

I had my fears, I do not disguise it of the Arnold school;* but I felt sure then, as I feel sure now, that he was very much the best of that section. Now I will tell you what has alarmed me. Pray read this extract from a letter.

'Dr. Tait has appointed A. P. Stanley to be his Examining Chaplain!' The letter proceeds, 'the views of Mr. Stanley on Inspiration are shocking; he is moreover much inclined to combine ritualism with latitudinarianism, and the appointment will effectu‐ally dim the lustre of the choice made by Lord Palmerston.'

Hear me; I myself would have appointed Stanley a Dean; I like much that he has written; but as for 'Examining Chaplain', avert it for Heaven's sake. The writer adds, *'Mr. Stanley takes it to oblige the Bishop.'*

Pray let me say that the Bishop knows not the gulf he is opening for himself in the distrust, the suspicions, the covert, the manifest opposition I fear he is preparing hereby among his clergy, aye, and his laity. Can you interpose as a Guardian Angel?[12]

* 'The Arnold School' was a name often given to the Broad Church party. Tait followed Arnold as Headmaster of Rugby; Stanley went to school there.

Politely but firmly Tait made clear that he would stand no such interposition. Meanwhile Shaftesbury, who had been delighted by a sermon preached by Tait on the subject of the Second Advent, wrote to tell Lady Wake that his apprehensions had been quieted. From now onwards he was always to like and respect Tait, who was later to become Archbishop of Canterbury.

The letter which Shaftesbury quoted to Lady Wake had been written by Alexander Haldane, who was his own chief counsellor in the business of ecclesiastical patronage. Haldane's influence was such that a Tractarian newspaper described Palmerston as 'the *Recordite** Premier, whose reign has been to the Evangelicals like the reign of Julian the Apostate to the expiring paganism of Imperial Rome.'[13]

His influence in patronage questions was not the end of Shaftesbury's concern with ecclesiastical matters during this period. In 1855 he had secured the passing of a Religious Worship Act, which repealed an act of George III forbidding more than twenty people to assemble for worship in a house or similar building. As amended in 1856 this Religious Worship Act made it possible to hold special services in Exeter Hall which were attended by thousands of poor Londoners. These services met a great need at a period when, in parish churches, all the good seats were reserved for rent-paying pew-holders, whilst the simple prayers, Bible-reading and hymn-singing appealed to the uneducated and illiterate who found the Prayer Book service hard to understand. When it became necessary to leave Exeter Hall and find other quarters Shaftesbury discovered that the only available places in the poorer districts were the theatres and music-halls. He felt no qualms about holding a religious service in a theatre, an idea which many conventionally pious people found intensely shocking, but on the contrary, he took a special pleasure in attending these services, often reading the Bible lessons himself.

During this year of 1856 Shaftesbury was also much occupied with the question of Sunday observance. Today the strict observance of Sunday is a thing unknown and therefore almost incomprehensible, but a hundred years ago it was a practice taken completely for granted. Sabbatarianism was not Shaftesbury's private quirk, or even a peculiarity of Evangelicalism; it was common ground for all sections of religious opinion, including English Roman Catholics, though not, of course, their continental co-religionists. Only the Tractarians allowed some slackening of the rule; Keble, for instance, went so far as to encourage the playing of cricket after Sunday

* A reference to Haldane's ownership of *The Record* newspaper.

evensong. A day of rest dedicated to God was not necessarily a dreary time. Many people still alive can remember using the term, 'Sunday best,' to describe the dress worn for special occasions, something altogether prettier, smarter, and more desirable than everyday wear. The Victorian Sunday was not all gloom; solemn indeed it was, but a solemn feast-day.

For the poor, however, the solemnity tended to swamp the festivity. They could afford no 'Sunday best,' and, with sports and games forbidden, and all places of amusement, even museums and picture-galleries, closed against them on their one leisure day, they saw their precious free time run aimlessly to waste. When Shaftesbury, whom they had always regarded as their champion, strongly opposed the Sunday opening of the Crystal Palace and the British Museum they turned against him in wrath and indignation. The strongest feelings of all were aroused when he succeeded in banning performances by military bands in the parks of a Sunday. Permission for such performances had only been granted the previous year, and the innovation had proved extremely popular. Feeling ran so high that for two Sundays in succession Shaftesbury thought it advisable to barricade his Grosvenor Square house against a possible outbreak of mob violence, which, however, did not materialise.

Shaftesbury's sabbatarian principles were primarily based on what he believed to be duty towards God, and not on duty towards man. He was convinced that the fourth commandment was to be taken literally, and that God had laid absolute claim to one day in seven. He was, nevertheless, also acting in what he believed to be the best interest of men, and especially of the poor. Experience taught him that a restful Sunday was essential to his own health and happiness. Long ago he had commented, with unusual profusion of underlining, on Peel's attendance at Sunday dinner parties:

How *can* he do it? Does he not desire . . . one day of calm repose, of rest and refreshment of spirit? *My* spirits are far less exhausted, and *my* time far less occupied, and yet (setting aside the sanctity of the day) I could not surrender the Sabbath. *I could not do it.*

For the sake of the workers he was genuinely anxious that the Sunday cessation from work should be complete and that postmen should not be expected to deliver letters nor bandsmen play their fifes and drums on their one day of rest. But, though he would not compromise with what he believed to be both a divine ordinance and a human necessity, Shaftesbury fully understood and sympathised with the

arguments behind the popular outcry. His remedy was not to provide
recreation on a Sunday but to provide the workers with time for
recreation on a weekday. On March 25th, addressing the Young Men's
Christian Association, he declared, 'I must say that all those who have
concurred with me in opposition to the motion for opening places
of amusement on the Lord's Day, are bound to go along with those
who entertain the opinion that I do – that if we refuse to give them
that form of recreation on the Lord's Day, we are bound to do what
we can to give them some form of recreation on some other day.'[14]
A month later he implemented his own words by taking the chair at a
large public meeting called together to demand a weekly half-holiday
for all working people.

Where foreign affairs were concerned Shaftesbury was chiefly
preoccupied with events in the United States, where, to quote Professor Morison, 'Kansas had become the theatre of cold (and not so
cold) war that led to the Civil War.'[15] America had always both
horrified and fascinated Shaftesbury; now his newly-awakened
concern for the Anti-Slavery movement made him take a deeper
interest than ever in American affairs. The diary entry for August
12th 1856 is typical of his attitude:

America is to me the most embarrassing contemplation that times,
past or present, bring before me. It baffles my judgements, disturbs my faith, and leaves me at a nonplus as to the character
of right and wrong, of wisdom and folly, in the conduct of men and
nations. A people of democratic freedom and license keeps in
subjection the most servile, cruel, and degrading, in slavery the
most frightful, some millions of their fellow men. They have
systemised the whole thing by laws federal and local . . . This would
have been hideous and disgusting in ancient Rome, in Bechuana or
the Fiji Islands; but what is it in a country which calls itself
Christian? Which has the light of the Bible? Which has declared
the equality of all mankind? Yet the people thrive, thrive beyond
precedent.

The other two great issues of 1857 and 1858 were Chinese and
Indian affairs. Shaftesbury's attitude towards these questions show
how weak was his connection with the official Tory party. He had in
fact dropped all party ties and become simply a personal supporter
of Palmerston. In the House of Lords he kept a permanent seat,
never crossing from side to side with any change of government.
In the autumn of 1856, following the seizure by the Chinese of the

Arrow, nominally a British ship but actually owned by a notorious Chinese pirate, the Hong Kong authorities ordered British warships to bombard Canton. When this news reached Palmerston he found himself in the same position as Peel in 1840. Though aware that the action of the Hong Kong authorities was both morally and legally wrong, he decided, as Peel had decided before him, that it was his duty to support the men on the spot. In his turn, Shaftesbury decided to support Palmerston. The war of 1857 was not so obviously iniquitous as the war of 1840, its ostensible object being the protection of British shipping, not the promotion of the infamous opium trade, which was none the less encouraged by the Hong Kong authorities, whom Palmerston now upheld against the Chinese. On March 9th 1857 Shaftesbury rose in the House of Lords to denounce that trade as a great national sin, yet only four days earlier, when Palmerston had been defeated on a vote of censure condemning his Chinese policy, he had stigmatised Palmerston's opponents as 'corrupt, unjust, ungrateful.' The following year Shaftesbury was to bring in yet another motion condemning the opium trade, but now he was unswervingly on Palmerston's side, although it was clear that Palmerston's policy gave at least a tacit support to that trade. Shaftesbury saw Palmerston as God's chosen instrument. For him the supremely important thing was the appointment of Evangelicals to church offices – 'If Palmerston will give us good men God grant that he will stay; if bad, or inferior ones, Derby or anyone might be as good a minister as he.' The diary entry for March 4th 1857, written after Palmerston's defeat by a Tory-Peelite coalition, clearly shows Shaftesbury's fanatical obsession with this subject:

> To my own influence (should Palmerston continue in power) I foresee the termination. They will say that my advice led him to the nomination of the several clergymen; that this exasperated Gladstone and gave rise to the effort and the coalition; and that Derby's party, many of whom had professed a resolution to keep Palmerston in office, had deserted him and their promises; that, in short, my counsel had done more harm than good. And yet, has he not prodigious strength in the country? Has he not acquired by this means a popularity such as no Minister has heretofore enjoyed? Nevertheless I have done right, I have done right, I have done right.

Of course neither Gladstone, Derby, nor Palmerston himself thought to connect his parliamentary defeat on the Chinese issue with the Evangelical nature of his ecclesiastical appointments. Nevertheless, when Palmerston decided on a dissolution and a General Election fought on the simple issue, 'Are you, or are you not, for Palmerston?' which resulted in his return to power with a large majority, Shaftesbury persisted in believing that this happy result was chiefly to be accounted for by the Evangelical nature of Palmerston's Church patronage. 'Many causes have contributed to this state of opinion,' he wrote on March 17th 1857, 'nothing *to the twentieth degree* as much as his Church appointments; all admit this and wonder at it.' In fact, except on the bench of bishops itself, the appointment of 'Shaftesbury's bishops,' could not affect Palmerston's popularity one way or the other; the British voter cared for none of these things.

When news of the outbreak of the Indian Mutiny reached England in June 1857, Shaftesbury's first reaction was a remarkably sane and sensible one. 'Endless rumours, one more terrible than another, but in fact based on imagination deceived or diseased,' he wrote on July 21st. 'But every private letter reveals the neglect, ignorance, and bad conduct of successive authorities, the, one cannot deny, many practical and speculative (the speculative oftentimes more harassing than the practical) grievances of the native troops.' Later, he swung round and joined loudly in the clamour for the severe punishment of those whom he described as 'these frantic worshippers of the devil in Hindustan.' It is more pleasant to remember his charitable reaction to one small episode which became part of Mutiny folklore. At Jhansi, a Captain Skene, after holding out heroically against the mutineers, first shot his wife and then shot himself. Shaftesbury was not the stern bigot that some have made him out to be, and he was always especially tender towards suicides. 'Was this permissible?' he asked himself. 'I cannot answer in such words, but I can say how deep is my conviction that God, in a case like this, will not be "extreme to mark what is amiss".'

In February 1858 a Tory government under Derby came into office. Palmerston's return to power had been short-lived. Following an attempt to kill Napoleon III with a bomb manufactured in London, Palmerston had brought in a Conspiracy to Murder Bill, which was defeated in the House of Commons, whereupon he immediately resigned. 'Now the Bishop of Oxford [Wilberforce] will be in the ascendant,' Shaftesbury moaned, 'now Tractarianism, Popery and ecclesiastical despotism will rule the roost.'

From Shaftesbury's point of view Derby's brief period in office was chiefly notable for a dispute over Indian policy. Lord Canning,

Governor-General of India, issued a proclamation confiscating the property of the nobles of Oudh as punishment for the part they had played in the Mutiny. Lord Ellenborough, the Conservative President of the Board of Control in charge of Indian affairs, wrote a dispatch condemning Canning's proclamation. Shaftesbury, who detested 'that Babylonian satrap, Ellenborough,' disapproved strongly of this dispatch as tending to weaken the authority of the Governor General at a crucial moment. Availing himself of the permission once given him by the Prince Consort to write personally about any matter of special importance, he now wrote to the Prince protesting that 'the public attack now made on Lord Canning is coarse, inhuman, and deeply perilous to the stability of Her Majesty's Empire in the East,' and urging that this issue ought not to be made the pretext for a General Election.[16] On May 14th, in a most telling speech, he moved a vote of censure in the House of Lords which was only lost by nine votes. The prospect of a Conservative moving a vote of censure against a Conservative government was not unnaturally a source of surprise to many people. By this action Shaftesbury made clear once and for all his actual if not his nominal freedom from the bonds of party allegiance.

On February 28th 1859 Derby brought in a Reform Bill. 'It is less than I expected,' Shaftesbury wrote of this measure, 'and saving that a Conservative party ought never to have "touched the accursed thing," it is well enough.' The Bill was, however, defeated; Derby fought a General Election, and finding himself in a minority resigned after a defeat on a vote of confidence. Palmerston was back again in power with Shaftesbury at his side as bishop-maker. Two years previously he had written of 'that wonderful man Palmerston at past seventy strong as a horse, lively as a kitten, sitting up all night in the House of Commons, all the while vigorous, cheerful, ready.' Now again he could say, as he had said then, 'It is the finger of God.'

It must never be forgotten that underneath Shaftesbury's pre-occupation with political and ecclesiastical matters there always ran two ceaseless undercurrents, the one of philanthropic business, the other of private anxiety. Year after year, for instance, came the ever-increasing burden of the work he always referred to as 'the May chairs,' when, during the month of May, he must take the chair at the meetings of various Evangelical societies. His diaries for the years of Palmerston's first ministry are filled with references to time devoted to Ragged Schools, soup kitchens, reformatories, refuges for the homeless, and innumerable other schemes to help those whom he aptly described as 'nobody's people.' Perhaps most important of all was his unending, thankless, unspectacular work as Chairman of the Lunacy Commissioners, who at this time were under constant attack from a body known as 'The Alleged Lunatics' Friend Society. Public opinion was much exercised over the possibility of a sane person being unjustly certified as insane and put away in an asylum. This agitation was in fact out-of-date, since the chance of such a happening had been greatly lessened by the passage of Shaftesbury's 1845 Lunacy Acts; but the alarm was not to be quieted. In the spring of 1859 a Select Committee was appointed under the chairmanship of Spencer Walpole to consider this question and other matters connected with lunacy. Shaftesbury of course was to be the chief witness. In his evidence he strongly opposed the demand that certification should be made more difficult by insisting on the signature of a magistrate as well as the two medical men already required by the existing law. He was against any further delay in the process of certification because he believed early treatment to be essential if there were to be any hope of a cure:

> You must be careful, while you are endeavouring to protect the patient, that you do not throw too great impediments in the way of his being put under proper care because if you wait until the symptoms are so clear and so developed that there can be no doubt about it, then you will have waited till such a time that the man is probably become an incurable patient.

He declared that in all his long experience he had known at most only one or two cases in which a person had been confined in an asylum without sufficient grounds for such a proceeding. He urged that the Commissioners should be given more rather than less power, that asylum doctors and nurses should be paid better salaries, that all pauper lunatics still remaining in workhouses should be moved into asylums, and that the law should be extended to give proper protection to single patients in private houses who were often grossly ill-treated or neglected. Questioned as to the causes of lunacy, he stated that he believed drunkenness to be one of the most important, and he strongly denied that 'religion, taken as pure gospel, has had the slightest effect in producing any aberration of reason whatsoever.' He made the odd suggestion that the supposed increase in the rate of lunacy might be connected with the increase in railway travel, a form of transport which he described as leaving the nerves 'in a state of simmer.'

The Committee reported in favour of making a magistrate's signature compulsory on a certificate of lunacy, a recommendation which was not put into practice, chiefly because of Shaftesbury's determined opposition to such a requirement. Otherwise they endorsed all his recommendations and confirmed his view that 'instances are extremely rare in which, under the present law, the confinement is, or has been unwarranted.'

Shaftesbury's experience with the Lunacy Commission had made him particularly fearful for his own epileptic son, Maurice – 'I know well the sufferings of an unhappy creature so afflicted when removed from the vigilant eye of personal and parental affection. What will become of him if Minny and I are removed?' In the summer of 1855 the annual cure in Germany had been interrupted by an urgent summons to Lausanne, where Maurice had been taken dangerously ill. Travelling as fast as possible, Shaftesbury and Minny reached Basle only to find a telegram telling them that Maurice was already dead. Here Minny had to be left behind, too ill and exhausted to travel further, whilst Shaftesbury went on alone to attend the funeral, grieving bitterly that he had come too late to see his son alive. On the return journey he too fell ill, spending several days in extreme discomfort in a miserable inn, unable to send word to Minny, who waited in acute anxiety, fearing that he had been struck down by the prevalent cholera, which, a week or so later, killed her brother-in-law, Lord Jocelyn.

Shaftesbury's family were not merely an anxiety to him; they were also a considerable financial burden. Vea's coming-out in January 1856 was noted as an extra and very unwelcome expense. The greatest cause of financial troubles was, of course, Anthony. Years later one of Anthony's daughters was to describe him as 'a take-it-easy, and if-you-can't-take-it-easy, take-it-as-easy-as-you-can, sort of person.'[17] Between Shaftesbury and such a son there could be no real understanding, but there could be, and was, a genuine, hearty love. In November 1856 came bitter trouble; Anthony was arrested for debt. Somehow or other Shaftesbury managed to borrow the £500 necessary to free him. Once again Anthony was overcome by genuine remorse and misery; once again his ever hopeful father forgave him, thanking God for 'this dawn of new views and new feelings.' It is impossible not to feel sorry for this young man of naturally expensive tastes who at least had the grace never to reproach his parents because, of necessity, they kept him short of money. Now he made a great effort at improvement, so much so that his father set about the business of finding him a Parliamentary seat as 'one of the secondary means to rescue him.' In the General Election of 1857 Anthony won a seat at Hull, greatly aided by the canvassing of his brother Evelyn, always the efficient, helpful member of the family. Shaftesbury was even more delighted when Anthony appeared on the platform at a meeting of the Ragged Schools Union, and spoke 'with propriety, simplicity, good taste and promise of future excellence.' Three months later he married Harriet, daughter of the Marquess of Donegal, a girl almost unknown to Shaftesbury and Minny, but believed by them to be 'good, steady, sensible, right-minded to the highest degree.'

Misgivings over his heir soured any pleasure that Shaftesbury might find in such improvements as he could make at St. Giles. 'Love the dear old Saint,' he wrote on May 17th 1856, 'but painful to be there. Foolish expenses incurred; heavier ones inflicted by fraud; insufficiency of means to live there in any comfort; no money to do what is required; sad conviction that, if any good be done, dissipation or neglect in those who come after me will undo it all.' The estate and its people were of constant concern to him; page after page of the diary is filled with the doings, or, more frequently, the misdoings, of such characters as the village parson, schoolmistress, or policeman. Meanwhile the country neighbours, in the manner of country neighbours everywhere, raised an outcry on the sacred subject of preserving foxes. It was not altogether surprising that Minny should take a dislike to St. Giles, seeking to spend as little time there as possible, an attitude which deeply grieved her husband, to whom his country home was still 'a charming spot where all save the spirit of man is divine.'

Charming though it might be, St. Giles was an extremely expensive place to maintain. Shaftesbury was so short of money that he was finding it difficult even to pay the labourers' wages. In these circumstances it is hard to see why he should have embarked on an extensive scheme of renovation and improvement in the great house itself. He was constantly bemoaning his inability to build decent cottages for his tenants, constantly protesting that he was spending no more on his own house than was absolutely necessary to prevent it from falling altogether into ruin. Why then did he employ the fashionable architect Philip Hardwick to add two towers, to rebuild an attic storey said to contain some forty rooms, and to install a system of central heating which, needless to say, went wrong immediately? Some of these alterations were paid for by his sister, Caroline Neeld, a rich and childless widow who had already paid for the building of several new cottages. Yet, even though Caroline made herself responsible for part of the expense, the puzzle remains unsolved, since Shaftesbury would still have to find a sum of money far in excess of his financial resources.

In spite of debts and difficulties, life at St. Giles was very pleasant to Shaftesbury. He believed his native air to be the best of all tonics, and after a stay in Dorset he would actually admit to feeling 'vivacious.' Hating London parties as he did, he immensely enjoyed village festivities. On October 29th 1856, after an appropriate service in the village church, two hundred and fifty people sat down in the coach-house of the great house to 'a noble feast, excellent in kind, abundant in quantity.' The previous day an even larger number of labourers and tenants from outlying villages had enjoyed a similar feast, 'equally successful in the solid parts, though less so in the spiritual.' Meanwhile the great house was filled with a party of foreign diplomats, 'all this to help my mother-in-law in her necessary duties.' The Russian, the French, and the Portuguese ambassadors, with other notabilities, greatly enjoyed this opportunity to witness an English Harvest-Home.

House parties on this scale were rare events. Guests were usually limited to a few congenial friends such as Haldane, Sutherland, Southwood Smith, 'sagacious and agreeable, with whom one can hold religious talk.' Wishing to give his children 'a rallying-point and a home and to make them love it,' Shaftesbury would occasionally arrange a great family gathering, though he found such parties intolerably expensive. By 1859, the year that Palmerston came back to power, financial affairs were so bad that it was found necessary to close the house altogether for a while, though Shaftesbury could never bring himself to do so permanently.

Chapter 18

RELIGIOUS CONTROVERSY

As 'bishop-maker' during Palmerston's second term of office Shaftesbury pursued a slightly different policy to the one he had followed from 1855 to 1858. Then he had sought to give promotion to as many Evangelicals as possible; now, at Palmerston's expressed wish, he deliberately widened the field of choice. 'I should like to be a little cautious in the selection of bishops,' Palmerston said to him, 'so as not unnecessarily to vex my colleagues, some of whom are very high. It is a bore to see angry looks.'[1]

The 'very high' members of Palmerston's Cabinet were the three Peelites, Gladstone, Herbert, and the Duke of Newcastle. Though Palmerston once remarked, 'Gladstone has never behaved to me in such a way as to demand from me any consideration,' he had none the less thought it advisable to set aside Shaftesbury's candidate for the see of Chester and appoint the High Church Dr. Jacobson at Gladstone's personal request. He had however been at pains to explain the situation to Shaftesbury and to ask for his opinion of Jacobson – 'I will not do it unless you assure me that the Doctor is a proper man.' Two other requests from Gladstone were refused; nothing would have induced Shaftesbury to agree to the appointment of R. W. Church, historian of the Oxford Movement, as Tractarianism was now called, to a Regius Professorship, or the High Church Samuel Wilberforce, the ablest man on the bench of bishops, to the Archbishopric of York.

Shaftesbury blamed the influence of Gladstone and his friends for what he described as Palmerston's vacillation and timidity – 'he pauses and hesitates and delays like a young lady who cannot make up her mind' – but he was fair-minded enough to recognise the difficulties of Palmerston's position. A private patron could appoint the man whom he believed best, but a Prime Minister had to take into account not merely the wishes of his colleagues but the views of the nation at large. He could not afford to give marked preference to one school of thought but must maintain a balance between the various parties in the Church. Shaftesbury admitted that it was impossible for Palmerston to appoint too many 'worthy, qualified, even first-rate men, if they were altogether unknown, without a ready answer attached to their names should a question be asked'; and most Evangelicals were unknown men. Shaftesbury therefore decided that his policy must be to put forward 'good, but not the best, men,' the best being, of course, the extreme Evangelicals.

Even though Shaftesbury made his recommendations on this broader basis, the fact remains that of the eighteen men who received high preferment during Palmerston's second Ministry eight were definite Evangelicals. (It is interesting to note that two of them, Baring and Villiers, were well known as Millenialists.) Ellicott, Browne, and Jacobson were High Churchmen, but none of these three could possibly be described as Tractarian. As might have been expected of avowedly compromise appointments, the remainder were somewhat undistinguished moderates. The three appointments to Archbishoprics, Longley to York in 1860 and to Canterbury in 1862, and Thomson to York, were of this nature, though Shaftesbury himself counted Longley as High Church and Thomson as Broad Church. The Broad Church party came off very badly, the only Broad Churchman to receive preferment being Stanley, who would never have been appointed had Shaftesbury had his own way. As a general rule he was scrupulous to avoid asking for preferment for his own personal friends, but in 1863 he had set his heart on seeing Alexander McCaul, a great worker among the Jews, given the vacant Deanery of Westminster. Palmerston, however, showed him a letter from Queen Victoria asking 'almost in a tone of supplication' that Stanley be appointed, urging the Prince Consort's attachment to him and the fact that he had been chosen as travelling companion for the Prince of Wales. Shaftesbury saw at once that it would be impossible for any Prime Minister to refuse such a request. 'Were the decision in my hands I should reject the man,' he told Palmerston, forgetting that not so long ago he had told Lady Wake that he would willingly appoint Stanley to a deanery, 'but I cannot call on you to take the step.' So, in Shaftesbury's own words, 'Dr. Stanley entered on his infidel and mischievous career at Westminster, corrupting society by the balmy poison of his doctrine, betraying in every word of his mouth and every stroke of his pen "the Son of Man with a kiss".'

Although in this instance he had agreed to fall in with her wishes, Shaftesbury much disapproved of Queen Victoria's interference in matters of ecclesiastical patronage. He objected to what he believed to be Stanley's undue influence – 'the Queen shares his views, feelings and opinions; the Dean will rule all things.' These fears were increased when, in the year of his appointment to Westminster, Stanley married the Queen's favourite Lady-in-waiting, Lady Augusta Bruce. 'Dr. Stanley has determined, aided by his "better self", to have the appointment of all the preferment in the kingdom,' Shaftesbury wrote to Palmerston on April 29th 1864, 'and unless you resist him he will carry through our most *unconstitutional* Queen all matters just as he chooses.'[2]

Yet, in spite of Dean Stanley's machinations, and in spite of the necessity to promote a few clerics who were not thorough-going Evangelicals, Shaftesbury could look back on his work as bishop-maker as being, at least in his own estimation, one of his more satisfactory achievements. To few people is it given to see their most improbable wish fulfilled. Shaftesbury had always longed for but never expected to have some say in the matter of Church patronage; in his wildest dreams he could never have supposed that his would be the most important voice in the appointment of three archbishops, sixteen bishops, thirteen deans, and a number of smaller fry. The Evangelical tone of these appointments might have been expected to produce a revival of Evangelicalism. Shaftesbury's tragedy lay in the fact that when the longed-for opportunity came his way he was unable to profit fully by it because of the poor quality of the available material. Episcopal bricks had to be made without straw. Had there been even one Evangelical of the calibre of the Broad Churchman Tait or the High Churchman Wilberforce to be appointed Archbishop, or had there been a fair sprinkling of able men to fill lesser sees and to exercise some influence in the Church, the era of the 'Shaftesbury bishops' might have marked the opening of a golden age for Evangelicalism. Nothing of the sort occurred; instead, Evangelicalism continued to decline, as Shaftesbury himself saw all too clearly. 'The Evangelical body, once so powerful, is in fact disappearing,' he wrote on April 16th 1865.

He had none the less done the very best that was possible with the material at his disposal. If none of his appointments were outstanding, none were definitely bad. Neither Baring nor Villiers were really worthy of a place on the distinguished roll of Bishops of Durham. (The *Guardian* described Villiers' appointment as 'a rise in life for a man of good family, no acquirements, and inferior capacity.') Otherwise, the Shaftesbury bishops were, on the whole, good Christian men who did their duty conscientiously in their dioceses and made little stir in the world at large. Their influence might have been greater had the mortality among them not been so surprisingly high. To make any impact at all upon the life of the Church they had at least to stay alive, but this they somehow failed to do. Of the bishops, Longley, Wigram, Waldegrave and Villiers were all dead by 1870; so too was Dean Goode, the best theologian among them. Ten years after Palmerston's death only four Shaftesbury bishops survived.

Even if they had been longer lived, none of these men would have been capable of taking Shaftesbury's place as leader of the Evangelicals, a title which he was always at pains to disclaim. The Evangelical group was in fact so loosely knit that it hardly deserved the name of a party. Evangelicals were essentially individualistic; they set no store by corporate Christianity. Here lay part of their quarrel with the men of the Oxford Movement. 'Our struggle with such men as Lord Shaftesbury is for our existence as a *Church*,' Samuel Wilberforce once said to Hook, the famous High Church Rector of Leeds; 'they believe only in separate spiritual influences on single souls.' Such people did not take kindly to organisation or leadership of any sort. But if Shaftesbury could not be correctly described as the leader of the Evangelicals he was certainly the most conspicuous and the most articulate figure amongst them, and as such he was to play a vitally important part in the religious controversies of the next decade.

In these controversies Shaftesbury could expect no help from the men whom he himself had selected for high office in the Church. Hitherto his battle had been with the Tractarians; now he was to fight on another front, against the exponents of 'neology,' a term which the Oxford Dictionary defines as 'a tendency to, or adoption of, novel or rationalistic views.' This convenient word was used by Shaftesbury to cover the new biblical criticism, the new theology, the new science, and any attempts to re-state Christianity in nineteenth-century terms, as for instance the biographies of Christ written by Strauss and Renan. In this struggle Shaftesbury needed the assistance of learned men and able writers, yet he himself had deliberately put forward unlearned men for high ecclesiastical office. Good scholars were chiefly to be found among the High Churchmen or the Broad Churchmen, not in the ranks of the Evangelicals; even Payne Smith, the Evangelical appointed to the Regius Chair of Divinity, could in no way rival Pusey's vast learning or lay claim, as Pusey might, to a real and extensive knowledge of the new theology. And if the Evangelicals were lacking in the learning which made the matter of controversy they were equally deficient in manner, since their pietistic style and peculiar turn of expression made their writing unattractive and unacceptable to the majority of educated readers.

'For many years, and especially from 1860 to 1866,' Hodder writes, 'there was hardly a day when, either by lip or by pen, Lord Shaftesbury was not protesting against attacks on the orthodox faith.' Perhaps Hodder should have remembered Bishop Warburton's remark to Lord Sandwich, 'Orthodoxy is my doxy; heterodoxy is the other man's doxy.' The orthodox faith was understood differently by Shaftesbury and by Pusey, who yet combined together to fight neological theories which today do not seem so very unorthodox after all. The struggle centred round three books, *Essays and Reviews* (1860), Colenso's *Critical Examination of the Pentateuch* (1862), and Seeley's *Ecce Homo* (1865). The controversy over a fourth, even more important book, Darwin's *Origin of Species*, falls into a slightly different category.

Essays and Reviews was a collection of essays by several authors, the moving spirit among them being Benjamin Jowett, the famous master of Balliol. Jowett's father, a Yorkshireman and a furrier by trade, had been one of Shaftesbury's paid helpers in the Ten Hours campaign, and it was Shaftesbury who had helped two of Benjamin's brothers to commissions in the Indian Army. The Introduction to *Essays and Reviews* described the book as 'an attempt to illustrate the advantage derivable from free handling, in a becoming spirit, of subjects peculiarly liable to suffer by the repetition of conventional language and from conventional methods of treatment.' As such, it not surprisingly gave great offence to conventional Christians, who considered the spirit in which it was written to be anything but becoming. The points chiefly at issue were the nature of biblical inspiration and the doctrine of eternal punishment, two of the essayists being prosecuted for their views on these subjects. In the ecclesiastical courts matters moved very slowly; not until 1864, four years after the book's publication, did the Judicial Committee of the Privy Council, the supreme Court of Appeal in such cases, issue the judgment which, in the words of a mock epitaph on Lord Westbury, the presiding judge, 'dismissed Hell with costs and took away from orthodox members of the Church of England their last hope of everlasting damnation.'

Opposition to this judgment drew together such unlikely allies as Shaftesbury, Pusey, and Bishop Wilberforce. Shaftesbury had never liked Wilberforce, for whom his favourite adjective was 'satanical.' In his turn Wilberforce had but little use for Shaftesbury, to whom he nevertheless now wrote asking for his co-operation 'in resisting this flood of rationalistic infidelity.' His appeal seems to have gone unanswered; in all probability both the temperamental differences and the divergence of views between the two men would have proved too great to allow of any effectual alliance.

Matters were different where Shaftesbury and Pusey were concerned. Between the cousins there had always been affection, though not agreement. When a letter appeared in *The Record* in which Pusey appealed for combined action by Evangelicals and High Churchmen against the neologians, Shaftesbury seized the opportunity to write a conciliatory letter in which he described himself and Pusey as fellow-collegians and old friends, unfortunately separated for many years by 'time, space, and divergent opinions.' In his reply Pusey welcomed this renewal of old friendship and declared himself to be 'of one heart and one mind with those who will contend for our common faith against this tide of unbelief.'[3] In their combined attack on neology Shaftesbury worked harmoniously with Pusey, greatly disapproving of the intolerance of his fellow Evangelicals who refused to do likewise. To their great credit be it remembered that at the height of the struggle both men made themselves very unpopular with their own supporters by insisting that their chief opponent should not suffer an obvious injustice. A dispute had arisen over the endowment of the Chair of Greek at Oxford, which was held by Jowett. Both Shaftesbury and Pusey maintained that Jowett's religious views were no ground for refusing him a proper salary for the work he performed as professor of a subject unconnected with religion. 'Heaven knows I loathe the theology of Dr. Jowett,' Shaftesbury wrote to the High Church Archdeacon Denison, 'but we shall not put him down by dishonouring his Chair.'[4]

Though Shaftesbury's opposition to *Essays and Reviews* was ostensibly concerned with biblical inspiration and belief in Hell, his real quarrel with that book was more widely and deeply based. The religion of *Essays and Reviews* was a system of belief and practice which fitted in easily enough with the ideals and behaviour of educated, cultured people. But what of the uncultured man of no education, the thief, or the Ragged School child for whom Shaftesbury cared so profoundly? For him 'this sublime statement of the normal feelings of a gentleman,'[5] to quote Mr. Cockshut's witty comment in *Anglican Attitudes*, was inevitably hollow and meaningless, a thing, in Shaftesbury's own words, 'cold, comfortless, and earthy.'

On any question touching the Bible Shaftesbury might be expected to take up an absolutely unyielding position, an attitude which explains his objection to Colenso's *Pentateuch*, a book which he was not altogether wrong in describing as 'puerile and ignorant.' His loud protests when Bishop Grey of Capetown ejected Colenso from the see

of Natal may have been due to the fact that Grey was a staunch
Tractarian.

Shaftesbury's objection to the third book, *Ecce Homo,* is more
important because it was based on an interpretation of the doctrine
of the Atonement which was fundamental to his view of Christianity.
The point is very clearly set out in a letter to his old friend, the
Duchess of Argyll, dated January 23rd 1864. Though the letter is
actually concerned with the preaching of Dean Stanley, Shaftesbury's
remarks apply equally well to the neological school as a whole and
to *Ecce Homo* in particular. After attacking the new biblical criticism
which, he maintains, leaves the Bible as 'a volume so inspired that
no one can say, or even conceive, when, how, and in what parts,
and to what extent, it speaks the mind of Almighty God,' he comes
to the real heart of the matter:

> If Dr. Stanley's theology is to be the theology of mankind it will
> bring our blessed Lord to the same level with them, and His
> ministry will have done no more for our race than Plato did for
> the Greeks, Cicero for the Romans, and Confucius for the Chinese.
> Those who complain of Dr. Stanley complain not so much of what
> he says as of what he does not say; not so much of what he states
> as of what he omits to state. They may be in error, but they think
> that the Gospel talks much of 'original sin'; of man's utter corrup-
> tion; of his fearful condition of lying under God's just wrath;
> of his unqualified inability to do, or even to think, a good thing of
> himself; of God's justice which demands an expiatory sacrifice;
> of Blood (such as no few men of that school call 'a religion of the
> shambles'); of the incarnation of His beloved Son to offer that
> Sacrifice; of a constant, indwelling sense of sin, of heart-felt
> sorrow for that sin, and of the only cure for it, the *personal* in-
> fluence of the Holy Ghost.

Shaftesbury cites St. Augustine in support of this point of view –
'I and others may give our adhesion to the Bishop of Hippo as you
give yours to the Dean of Westminster!' – before summing up the
gravamen of his charge against Stanley and the neological school
in a single sentence:

> Christ and His Apostles assert the full necessity and merit of an
> expiatory sacrifice to wipe away sin; the School, in cold and cal-
> culated homage, allow Him no more than the virtue of unprece-
> dented generosity, unparalleled self-sacrifice.[6]

Here Shaftesbury is maintaining the classic Evangelical position. The language is difficult, especially to the twentieth-century unbeliever; as Lord Hailsham writes, 'Shaftesbury's religion was narrow, and represented, in its strictest aspects, a phase of opinion almost unrepresented in the modern world.'[7] The doctrine of the Atonement is not easily understood by the non-Christian; since the days of St. Paul it has been 'to the Jews a stumbling-block, to the Greeks foolishness.' Yet, though the modern Christian might express his belief in terms less crude than those in use among Victorian Evangelicals, in his heart he knows, as Shaftesbury knew, that the Cross is central to Christianity.

The absence of the Cross was the core of offence in *Ecce Homo*, which Shaftesbury publicly denounced as 'the most pestilential book ever vomited from the jaws of Hell.' What annoyed him far more than the outcry which quite rightly greeted this outrageous remark was the author's boast that the unsolicited advertisement had sold ten thousand copies and put one thousand pounds into his pocket. *Ecce Homo* was published anonymously, the author being Seeley, son to Shaftesbury's old friend, the Evangelical publisher, Robert Seeley. A modern reader would find this most pestilential book a curiously mild and inconclusive piece of work. Seeley does not question either the text or the authority of the Gospels, and he specifically asserts his belief in miracles. *Ecce Homo* is not a *Life* of Christ; the Introduction describes it as an attempt to answer the question, 'What was Christ's object in founding the society which bears his name, and how is it adapted to serve that object?' Seeley planned another book, which remained unwritten, to deal with 'Christ as the author of modern religion and theology.' It is therefore unfair to judge of *Ecce Homo* as a finished whole; the book gives, and is intended to give, only one side of the picture.

Because it is primarily concerned with Christian morality, *Ecce Homo* almost entirely ignores the supernatural element in Christianity. The chapter entitled 'Christ's Credentials' makes no mention of any claim to Godhead. One small slip is significant: Seeley describes the injunction to love one's neighbour as oneself as 'the first and greatest commandment.' For the love of God enjoined by the actual first commandment he substitutes what he describes as 'the enthusiasm of humanity,' a sentiment seldom if ever experienced by Shaftesbury the philanthropist. One of the few references in *Ecce Homo* to Christ's crucifixion is a passage describing the Apostles' teaching:

Christ's voluntary surrender of power is their favourite subject, the humiliation implied by his whole life and crowned by his death. This sacrifice, which they regard as made for *them*, demands in their opinion to be requited by an absolute devotion on their part to Christ.

This unobjectionable, colourless statement is poles apart from 'the religion of the shambles' referred to by Shaftesbury in his letter to the Duchess of Argyll, a disparity which goes far to explain why he attacked *Ecce Homo* with a ferocity he never bestowed upon *Essays and Reviews*.

It must be admitted that Shaftesbury's reaction to the new criticism and the new school of theology was essentially and unashamedly obscurantist. For him religion was an affair of the heart, and not at all of the head. Believing therefore that intellectual enquiry into religious matters was at best useless and at worst sinful, he refused to admit the validity of the findings of any such enquiries. His attitude towards the new science was slightly more enlightened. *The Origin of Species*, regarded today as by far the most important of these controversial books, caused less shock to Shaftesbury and his contemporaries than did *Essays and Reviews* and *Ecce Homo*. On first sight the theory of evolution did not seem to strike a very serious blow at religious faith; as Professor Chadwick puts it, 'the Christian could jettison the doctrine of special creations without any sense of loss.' To quote again from the same authority, 'the conflict was not ultimately over the theory of evolution or any other scientific theory, but over the freedom of the scientist to be a scientist.'[8] The scientists claimed the right to pursue their investigation of physical phenomena even if their findings should prove incompatible with the statements of biblical revelation; conservative Christians held such conclusions to be wholly inadmissable on the simple grounds that revelation could not err.

Shaftesbury's youthful interest in science had given him at least a slight insight into the scientific mind, a slight sympathy with the scientific ideal. The exceptionally gentle and charitable tone of a letter to Richard Owen, a scientist whose attitude towards the theory of evolution was extremely ambiguous, shows how much more reasonable was Shaftesbury's reaction to the champions of the new science than to the champions of the new biblical criticism and the new theology. In a speech at Exeter Hall he had criticised one of Owen's lectures; and Owen had written replying to his criticism. Shaftesbury's answer to this letter, though very long, must be quoted almost in full since it explains more clearly than any summary could his attitude towards scientists and science in general. It is dated Easter Sunday, March 27th 1864:

Before I go to Church on this most holy day I must acknowledge the most acceptable letter I received from you last night, and say how heartily I thank you for so friendly, and so Christian, a communication; and secondly, how truly I shall think of you (afar in body, though, I am sure, not in spirit) at the common table of our blessed Lord. So much for the moment; I shall proceed afterwards.

I am returned; and safely may I say that you and your appeal were not forgotten. Now let me explain –

I cannot wonder that, my speech having arisen upon the events that grew out of the lecture, all my observations should have been assigned to that, and to that alone. The fault is mine in having omitted to draw the line of distinction, and state where I was thinking of *you*, and where of *others*. I never imputed to you, God forbid that I should ever imagine I had ground to impute to you, the reckless audacity, the scientific conceit, the saucy ignorance of Professor H. Professor G. Sir C. this and Doctor that; you are as far above them in judgement, earnestness, and good taste, as you are in real and substantial knowledge. When I spoke of flint-heads, javelins, etc. I was thinking of the *Divines balestres et hoc genus omnes* of science, not by any means, believe me, of that Professor whom I had regarded (and shall I not ever have reason to regard him?) as not only one of the most accomplished but as one of the most Christian of men.

But my difference with you lies here. I spoke with distrust, and even (so far did I presume) with censure, of an essay that, addressed to a mixed assembly of young men, some of very tender years, threw broadcast, and without explanation or guidance, doubts and difficulties to be entertained respecting the plain, literal, historical reception of the Word of God. You raised perplexities that you never can unravel; you converted, in many, a child-like simple belief into a mental state of uncertainty and distress, and spoke to young minds, and young hearts, of 'a symbolic text' leaving them (for no rule of discernment was laid down) to call by that name, as their vanity or their passions may dictate, any or every part of the sacred Scriptures.

Was this, my dear friend, the teaching of a 'master in Israael'? Scores may have gone away, shaken in faith, and crushed by doubts, of which they may never have the desire or the opportunity of solution.

Again, I thought it unwise, had it been anyone but you, I should have said 'wicked', to speak so lightly of 'ists and isms'. Why snap asunder the strong and beneficial restraints of specific views and dogmatic teaching? Why make a man disdain the Creeds and Catechisms of his early years? Why urge him (for such is the practical result) to cast aside the words and prayers of a devout, though, it may be, a precise Mother? The religion that a man has learned at his mother's knees is his viaticum for time and eternity.

You observe that 'the cheers of your auditory at Exeter Hall were as freely given to myself uttering there what you rebuke' – No, my dear friend, it is not so. Those who cheered *you* did not cheer *me*. But there we had the first proof of the evil effect of this essay. It has engendered, or at least called forth, a controversial and polemical spirit. Some are now for the modern lights, some for the ancient theology; some would stand in the old paths; some will walk in the new. These associations will not, I fear, be carried on much longer in the unity of the spirit and the bond of peace, but will become schools of dissension and debate, or sink into a cold uniformity by the secession of half their members.

And for all these sad issues your great and good name will be quoted in authority.

May I dare to say how I would teach science in conjunction with the Bible? I would check no enquiry; I would suppress no fact; nor shrink from any just inference. I would offer no shifts, nor suggest such weak and fanciful explanations as have increased rather than have abated, doubt. Take, for instance, your own doubts of the Serpent. I would tell my pupils that I received the narrative as literally and historically true, but that, beyond question in our present state of knowledge, it passes our comprehension. I would not disguise that there was difficulty in reconciling it with the actual results of scientific research, but that we must have patience, dive deeper, learn more, and believe that the Book of Revelation and the Book of Science will ultimately be found to be in perfect harmony.

Meanwhile, let not you and I be divided in this awful matter. I must hope, nay believe, that our ends are the same. I am convinced that the heart is everything, and the intellect scarcely anything in the great pursuit of salvation. This is, to my mind, one of the most beautiful and unanswerable proofs of the divine origins of the Gospel. You may to some extent differ from my view, and act accordingly. Yet be assured that the prayer you have secretly breathed this day, 'God be merciful to me, a sinner,' is worth all your stores of science, and all your high efforts of intellectual power. Seldom have I ever, on so short and scant an acquaintance, admired and loved a man as I admired and loved you. I looked on you as a rich, choice, and lovable spirit; and I look on you so still.

God grant that we may ever exchange these expressions of kindness; and you be to me, as I am to you, your sincere friend.

Shaftesbury[9]

This letter makes clear three important points: Shaftesbury's reluctance to condemn the new science out of hand as he had condemned the new biblical criticism and the new theology, his profound mistrust of intellectualism when applied to religion, and his conviction that, all truth being one, some day, somehow, the discoveries of science and the assertions of revelation would be found to be in complete agreement. The contradiction between science and religion left him comparatively unperturbed. Time, he believed, would resolve the difficulty, as indeed it has, though not quite in the manner he expected. Shaftesbury supposed that further scientific discoveries would re-establish the literal truth of the biblical statements. 'Science, in a more extended compass, long, very long before it is perfect, will be the surest, stoutest, and most irresistible "Apology for the Bible" in the whole history of facts and arguments since controversy began,' he wrote on August 30th 1863. 'It will prove the Mosaic creation; the authenticity of the Pentateuch; it will establish the Deluge and Noah's Ark.' In fact, since Shaftesbury's day the findings of science have led to a re-assessment of the real meaning and value of the biblical narratives and a more informed approach to them on the part of the believer. Science has not re-established the literal truth of the story of the Flood, but rather, it has helped men to realise that belief in Noah's Ark is not an essential article of the Christian creed.

Because he was certain that science would ultimately prove a support rather than a threat to religious faith, Shaftesbury wished to give unlimited freedom to the scientists and even to provide financial endowment for scientific research. Again and again he urges these two points. A further passage from the entry of August 30th is typical of many other passages in his diaries and letters:

Were I wealthy and powerful I would . . . give enormous sums for the advancement of science. I would make no conditions, I would abstain from all interference. I would make the promotion of it various and rapid. I would hugely reward men without reference to their theological views; I would render, under God's blessing, the scientific and intellectual, and even the malignants and infidels, pioneers for the truth. They should, unknowingly and unwillingly, build up that faith they sought to destroy.

Though to the scientists themselves Shaftesbury's support of scientific research and experiment might have seemed the worst treason of doing the right thing for the wrong reason the fact remains that he was prepared to give them the complete freedom of investigation for which they were fighting. Such an attitude was at least more sensible, and be it said, of more practical help to the scientists, than the ostrich-like behaviour of those timid Christians who sought to muzzle all scientific enquiry.

Chapter 19

PALMERSTON'S SECOND MINISTRY

Palmerston's second Ministry was an important period both in Shaftesbury's private and public life. Unfortunately, his diary entries for these years of 1859 to 1865 are tantalisingly few. He says nothing, for instance, of the extraordinary suggestion that he might become King of Greece. The difficulty of filling the vacant Greek throne was much exercising the minds of European statesmen. Writing to Queen Victoria on January 15th 1863 about this subject, King Leopold of the Belgians, who had a finger in most dynastic pies, told her that 'even an English nobleman, perhaps Lord Shaftesbury,' had been suggested.[1] The new King of Greece was in fact to be Prince William of Denmark, brother to the Princess Alexandra who this same year of 1863 married the Prince of Wales. The Princess was one of the few members of the Royal Family whom Shaftesbury always approved. He admired her beauty, describing her as looking 'as lovely as a woman could,' and when the Prince's behaviour was causing scandal he wrote, 'If once the people of England are certain that he is unfaithful to the Princess, whom they have adopted as a daughter, he will no more mount the throne than he will ride Bucephalus.'

In the foreign affairs of this period Shaftesbury's chief concern was with Italy. He had a close personal link with the leaders of the *Risorgimento* through his friendship with the Sardinian Minister in London, Emanuele d'Azeglio, nephew of the statesman and author Massimo d'Azeglio, a friend and fellow-worker with Cavour. Occasionally Emanuele d'Azeglio used Shaftesbury as a channel for private communication with Palmerston. On December 27th 1861, for instance, Shaftesbury passed on to Palmerston the substance of a confidential despatch from the Sardinian Premier, Ricasoli, on the subject of the recognition of the Kingdom of Italy and the intrigues of Napoleon III. The relationship between Shaftesbury and d'Azeglio was, however, more of a personal than a political affair; d'Azeglio was a family friend, 'quiet, happy, domestic, and comfortable as a house-dog.' A frequent guest at St. Giles, he would often join the family on their continental travels, sometimes, if Shaftesbury were detained in England, acting as escort to Minny and her daughters. To Minny herself he was deeply and chivalrously devoted; no evidence remains to show whether she in any way returned his feelings. In the grounds of St. Giles there still stands a solitary stone-pine, last survivor of a present of trees he brought her from Rome.

So keenly interested was Shaftesbury in the fight for Italian freedom that he wrote a letter to *The Record* urging all those who 'took an interest in the blessings of civil and religious liberty to come forward and express their sympathy with this just and noble cause,' later repeating these words in a speech to the Bible Society.[2] The fact that he thus chose to appeal to the extreme Protestant section of opinion shows how closely his enthusiasm for Italian liberty was connected with his hatred of popery. When, in the spring of 1859, Massimo d'Azeglio arrived in London on a special mission Shaftesbury broke one of his most stringent religious rules by dining out on Maundy Thursday with the Foreign Secretary, Lord Malmesbury, in order to meet d'Azeglio, and gave a dinner himself on Easter Eve at which he introduced d'Azeglio to John Delane, Editor of *The Times*. He justified this unprecedented burst of party-going in Holy Week by explaining that 'ten thousand misconceptions may thus be removed, and ten thousand truths established towards the defence of Sardinian freedom and the maintenance of European peace.'[3]

In August 1859 Shaftesbury was in correspondence with the French ambassador, de Persigny, who questioned him as to English public opinion on the subject of Napoleon III's Italian policy and in particular, the French occupation of Rome – '*J'ai toujours remarqué que personne n'appréciait mieux que vous le véritable sentiment publique en Angleterre.*'[4] The fact that a foreign diplomat should seek such information from a person who held no official position whatsoever goes far to prove Shaftesbury's right to speak in the name of those whom he described as 'the people of England, from whom I separate altogether the diplomatic officials, a few journalists, and a few fine folks in London.'[5]

To Palmerston also Shaftesbury assumed this role of spokesman for the people of England on the subject of Italian liberty. In a letter dated January 17th 1860 he described the popular reaction to the proposal that France should annex the Sardinian territories of Nice and Savoy in return for French support for any plan for the unification of Italy:

> The rumours are again rife that the Emperor of the French demands the surrender of Nice and Savoy.

To say nothing of the discredit that will attach to him for such a stain on his intervention on behalf of Italian liberty, and the suspicion that other motives than those of generosity prompted him to action, I cannot refrain from observing to you how deep will be the public feeling in this country if the Government, directly or indirectly, openly or tacitly, approve such a proceeding; nay, if they do not protest against it.

1. The country will consider the act as a return to the old system of dealing with nations like flocks of sheep, and handing them over as articles of barter and exchange.
2. It would be the surrender of a *free* people to a despotic rule; of a people in enjoyment of *religious liberty* to an empire where it is professed, and violated.
3. It would beget in all minds an apprehension that this was a revival of the French policy to attain 'natural boundaries'. The acquisition of Savoy might be followed by an effort to effect the acquisition of the Rhine.
4. It would render your administration unpopular to the greatest extent.

Pray consider this.[6]

Shaftesbury also wrote to Cavour to protest, although vainly, against the proposed annexation.

In the autumn of 1859 a group of Italian Liberals proposed the formation of a committee of English supporters of Italian liberty with Shaftesbury as Chairman. Though the scheme itself came to nothing, two letters which Shaftesbury wrote to the press on the subject brought him to the notice of Garibaldi, who thanked him warmly for his support and sympathy. In reply Shaftesbury invited Garibaldi to visit England, a plan which was not to materialise for another four years.

The American Civil War provided the other great topic of interest in foreign affairs during Palmerston's second Ministry. Shaftesbury, who was both shocked and fascinated by everything American, devoted a special notebook to this subject.[7] His comments, however, are only interesting as showing how wide of the mark he could be in both his judgements and his predictions. He believed, for instance, that North and South could and should separate. 'A quiet and peaceable severance would prove best for America and the world,' he wrote in May 1861; 'the severance will take place at last.' Somewhat surprisingly, he regarded the Confederate general, Stonewall Jackson, as 'the greatest man since the days of Washington and in many respects much above him' – this presumably because Jackson was frequently to be found on his knees in his tent, 'wrestling with the Lord.' He disapproved of Abraham Lincoln, even going so far as to accuse him of doing 'all in his power to intensify and extend the horrors of this war.' After Lincoln's assassination he wrote, 'the extreme character both in quality and amount, of eulogiums on President Lincoln is absurd in itself and will be hurtful to his memory,' adding, a few days later, that Lincoln had enjoyed 'power like the Emperor of Russia and used accordingly.' Almost his only favourable comment concerned the war's final scene at Appomattox: 'Lee has surrendered, wisely and humanely; Grant has been, for the first and last time, a gentleman.' In April 1868 he ended his notes with the remark, 'This strange and fearful people are engaged now in the impeachment of their President.'*

Where his private affairs were concerned Shaftesbury was at this period in much distress over his children. His younger sons were growing up, and, as sons will do, separating themselves from their parents. Though Shaftesbury admitted that such behaviour was only natural and to be expected he found it impossible not to feel hurt when 'my boys listen to my remonstrances, return to their cigars, and respectfully laugh me to scorn.' He was also disillusioned and distressed by the character of his daughter-in-law, Harriet. A month or so after her marriage he had described her as 'a joy and a comfort to the house, lively, good-tempered, easily pleased, full of social sense and very affectionate.' Two years later he was complaining that he had been completely deceived in her and that he could foresee 'nothing but shame and sorrow for the marriage.' In Harriet's defence it should be pointed out that Shaftesbury was not the ideal father-in-law for a lively girl with a taste for social gaieties. Her behaviour during the 1860 Ascot week caused him particular perturbation:

> She went to Ascot races in a crowded carriage called 'a drag'; she descended from it on the race-ground; and before all the assembled mobs of every species and degree, plays at 'Aunt Sally', and does what no girl, in any tradesman's shop, pretending to only the elements of moral training, would have condescended to do. It was condemned a year ago as a blackguard act of the Duke of Beaufort. How must it be regarded in a lady?

Much worse trouble, however, was at hand than the blackguardly behaviour of a daughter-in-law. For a long time the health of Shaftes-

* President Andrew Johnson.

bury's second daughter, Mary, had been giving cause for anxiety; in the spring of 1860 she fell seriously ill. The trouble can be diagnosed as the condition known as *status asthmatica*, severe asthma complicated by an unresolved chest infection. In that age, when palliatives were few and ineffectual, inevitably she stood condemned to a terrible death.

Asthma is a disease frequently associated with psychological tension. Though Shaftesbury was a most loving parent, his love was of the kind which subjected his children to pressures too great to be borne by the weaker among them. Anthony had succumbed intellectually; now Mary was to collapse physically, probably suffering under the same strain. For the next eighteen months she and her mother spent most of their time in the mild climate of Torquay whilst Shaftesbury travelled up and down to London at greater expense than he could afford, or lived lonely and disconsolate in the big house in Grosvenor Square. Loving all his children with an almost painful tenderness, he was appalled by the sight of Mary's physical suffering and deeply disturbed by her mental agony. In August 1861 he wrote in his diary, 'Two things have been, and still are, in my heart – a prayer and a wish; a prayer for a comforting sign of her acceptance in Christ, a wish that she may go out in the bright day, and not in the darkness and solitude of the night.' Neither his prayer nor his wish was to be granted. Very early in the small hours of September 3rd Mary died in agony as a storm of wind beat against the windows and set the candles flickering in the draught.

The memory of that death-bed haunted Shaftesbury; it was to him 'a horror deep, dark, ineffaceable.' He came nearer now than at any other time in his life to doubting the goodness of God – 'I can understand the reason of ill-health and of death itself; but these long, severe, terrible, protracted sufferings in one so young disturb and baffle me.' His own health suffered under the strain; even when physical strength returned to him he felt his mental energy diminished. 'The electric spark in me is less vivid,' he noted sadly on November 29th. For Minny the strain had been almost more intense. Six weeks before Mary's death she had been seized with fainting fits and general collapse. So severe was the attack that for one moment both she and her husband believed it would prove fatal. She recovered, and at once resumed her place by Mary's bedside, but from now onwards she was to be more and more frequently subject to faintness, headaches, 'spasms,' and general debility.

Through no fault of their own Shaftesbury's surviving daughters were to be a source of intense anxiety to him. Vea and Conty (Hilda

was still in the schoolroom) did not possess those powers of attraction
with which both their mother and their grandmother had been so
conspicuously gifted. Their love affairs, or rather, lack of love affairs,
caused Shaftesbury many a pang. He himself suspected that 'there
is something in my personal character and career that has operated
perniciously on their prospects'; his lack of means may also have
scared away possible suitors. Though he could ill afford it, he had
scraped together the money necessary to launch Vea and Conty in
society; and, in spite of ill-health, their mother had assiduously
escorted them to the usual round of parties: 'Poor Minny must,
weak and tired as she is, go "into the world" that every opportunity
may be given. But what nausea, what pain, what humiliation, and
what loathing of the work, and what serious injury to health lie
under the smiles and small-talk a chaperone must put on!' Neither
Shaftesbury nor Minny was over-ambitious for their daughters; they
did not ask for sons-in-law of great wealth or station, only for 'true,
pious, worthy men.' But true, pious, worthy men, or, indeed, men
of any sort, were not forthcoming. The prospect for Vea and Conty
was bleak. An unmarried working-class girl could earn some sort
of a living as a seamstress, a factory worker, or a domestic-servant;
a girl of the professional classes could go out as a governess. None
of these alternatives was open to the unmarried daughters of an
impecunious earl; they could only look forward to 'a poor, solitary,
and dependent spinsterhood.' On top of all this grief and anxiety
came alarm for the youngest son, Cecil, who had to be removed
from school after a severe attack of meningitis and kept at home to
lead 'a listless, untroubled life,' and, his father greatly feared, an
idle, indisciplined one.

The diaries for this sad period record the deaths of many personal
friends and public characters. In particular Shaftesbury noted
the death of de Bunsen at the end of 1860, Cavour in the following
June, 'the learned, warm-hearted, highly gifted Southwood Smith' in
December, the same month that saw the unexpected death of the Prince
Consort from typhoid fever. When quoting Shaftesbury's comments on
the Prince's fatal illness Hodder tactfully omitted the final passage:

> I see and feel the shock to the Queen. She has never known sorrow
> and is unprepared for it. It will deprive her of reason. It will leave
> her melancholy, friendless, without a support, an adviser; no one
> to aid her in public affairs, no one in private. Her sons are growing
> up and requiring influence and restraint. She is wholly incapable of
> the duty. Mrs. Mashams, Duchesses of Marlborough, the follies,

the weaknesses of Queen Anne will be revived in the present peaceable, orderly, happy court of Queen Victoria.

In December 1861 Palmerston pressed Shaftesbury to accept the Order of the Garter, which he had declined when offered it by Aberdeen in May 1854. In his reply Shaftesbury urged various objections before coming to the real difficulty, 'the fees, which amount to a fearful sum.'[8] A few months later Palmerston repeated the offer, generously and tactfully taking the payment of fees upon himself. 'If a kindness can be enhanced by the way it is done, I am sure this is an instance of it,'[9] Minny wrote in her letter of thanks. This time Shaftesbury could not refuse.

In 1863 Palmerston followed up this kindness with another generous act. Shaftesbury's fifth son, Lionel, was to go into business as partner in a City firm, but for this he required a sum of money far larger than his father could provide. Palmerston came to the rescue by sending Minny five thousand pounds, accompanying his gift with a charming letter in which he begged to be allowed to pay his share of the cost of her son's start in life. Palmerston may or may not have been Minny's father, but after his marriage to her mother he invariably treated her as a daughter. As he himself had written to Minny long ago on December 18th 1856, 'when I married Emily I considered myself as adopting all her children as my own.'[10] In the diary entry recording Palmerston's gift Shaftesbury also refers to 'my equally kind and generous mother-in-law.' Some help too had come from his own mother. The dowager Lady Shaftesbury had been converted to Evangelicalism and now lived on amicable and even affectionate terms with her son, who frequently visited her at her home at Richmond. When she died, in August 1865, old, mindless, and stone-deaf, he rejoiced to think that 'her later years, I hope and believe, were very different from the earlier years.'

In spite of this generosity on the part of his relations, Shaftesbury's financial difficulties were such that in June 1863 he found himself unable to meet his household bills. Matters went from bad to worse until in December 1864 five friends, headed by Lord Kinnaird and the Noncomformist industrialist Samuel Morley, banded together to offer him an interest-free loan of £12,500. Shaftesbury, always so prickly where political preferment was concerned, accepted this offer of financial help in the same open and friendly spirit in which it was made. Among his papers is an envelope containing details of the transaction and docketed in his own hand, 'An heirloom, I hope; let it be preserved for my descendants.'[11]

Shaftesbury's financial difficulties had been much increased by the state of affairs at St. Giles. His many other commitments left him but little time to devote to the management of his Dorset estates, where he had left matters very much in the hands of his agent, Robert Short Waters. Though he knew this man to be neglectful and not very efficient, Shaftesbury believed him to be honest. Other people did not agree with this judgement. Gossip about mismanagement and peculation reached such a pitch that finally Palmerston decided to interfere. Not the least of the many services he rendered to Shaftesbury was the remarkably kind and tactful letter he wrote on November 29th 1861, urging that enquiry be made into Waters' doings. Shaftesbury, however, took no immediate steps, and it was not until 1863 that he discovered he had been cheated, or so he believed, of at least twelve thousand pounds. Being a just man, he took some of the blame to himself. 'I was too confident and not sufficiently attentive to my affairs,' he admitted; 'looking after other people's interests I forgot my own.' Some responsibility also rested with his accountants, who had audited the estate books carelessly, if at all. In these circumstances, rather than dismissing Waters, he generously allowed the agent to 'resign.'

This sorry business preyed much on Shaftesbury's nerves. Oversensitive and fearful of other people's opinions, he trembled lest he should be held up to scorn as lacking in method, in diligence, and in common sense – 'a sucked orange, an empty wine-cask, a clawless, toothless lion would be apt similitudes for me.'

In December 1864 Waters sued Shaftesbury for money which he declared to be owing to him, whilst one of his associates, a timber-merchant called Lewer, brought another suit over a tenancy agreement. 'Both for different objects have put me in Chancery, and a pretty waste there will be of time and spirits and money,' Shaftesbury wrote gloomily on December 12th; 'a successful suitor in the Court of Chancery is nearly always a ruined man.' On his part Shaftesbury now brought an action against Waters for malversation and embezzlement, but though he believed the man's guilt to be 'as clear as daylight' he found it exceedingly difficult to discover adequate proof. The various cases in which Shaftesbury, Waters and Lewer were involved copied the pattern of the famous case of *Jarndyce v. Jarndyce* in *Bleak House*; and, as so often where Shaftesbury was concerned, fact proved almost more Dickensian than Dickens' own fiction. Postponement followed postponement, appeal succeeded appeal, judgment contradicted judgment, the issue becoming all the time yet more complicated and obscure. 'What a thing is law,' Shaftesbury bitterly commented, 'and what things are accounts, and what a power is an astute and wicked man!' A century and more after the event it is impossible to judge of the extent of Waters' wickedness. All that can be said is that he was certainly negligent and possibly dishonest. He declared, for instance, that he had advanced Shaftesbury three thousand pounds, yet admitted to paying that sum out of the estate monies into his own account. After two years of litigation Shaftesbury found that he had already spent more than two thousand pounds on the expenses of suits which seemed likely to drag on indefinitely.

During Palmerston's second ministry Shaftesbury was concerned with no major pieces of social legislation. He did, however, make a great effort on behalf of the slum-dwellers displaced by the building of the railways and new streets which were being driven through some of the poorest areas in London. Evicted from their miserable homes, the inhabitants had no option but to cram themselves into already overcrowded dwellings in the same neighbourhood, since they could not afford to move farther away from their places of work. As long ago as 1853 Shaftesbury had brought this matter before the House of Lords. Now in 1861 and again in 1863 he pleaded the cause of these displaced persons and succeeded in securing a ruling that every Improvements Bill permitting the building of streets or railways must state the number of persons to be displaced, and must also go before a Select Committee whose special function would be to enquire into this aspect of the proposed scheme.

Although Shaftesbury was one of the small body of influential people who helped to organise Garibaldi's visit to England in April 1864 he makes no mention of this event in the diary. Meeting Garibaldi on arrival at Southampton, he accompanied him to the Isle of Wight to stay with Charles Seely,* the Member for Nottingham. Throughout Garibaldi's stay in London, Shaftesbury was constantly at his side, only refusing to accompany him to the opera. Though he was prepared occasionally to attend a theatre in order to give pleasure to Minny, Shaftesbury could not bring himself to tolerate opera, describing the newly-built Paris opera house as a temple to Venus, Bacchus, the sensual civilisation, to luxurious science, to licentious art.'

When Garibaldi agreed to receive Mazzini, the exiled Italian patriot suspected of revolutionary activities, Shaftesbury wrote to

---

* Later Sir Charles Seely, Bt., and father of the first Lord Mottistone, soldier, politician and author.

Palmerston to explain and excuse this meeting which might have
been regarded as politically unwise:

> Here is Garibaldi's explanation of Mazzini's visit. He does not
> believe Mazzini's guilt. His words were that, 'had he found
> Mazzini in prosperity he would have avoided all misunderstanding
> by not seeing him; but finding him in adversity, he could not
> throw him aside.' This is truly generous, if not politic.[12]

Everywhere he went the ordinary people greeted Garibaldi with
immense and enthusiastic applause; but with the politicians he was
not so popular. When it was thought advisable to curtail his stay in
England, Lord Granville told Queen Victoria, who had disapproved
strongly of his visit, 'The Duke of Sutherland has the real merit of
getting him away; the ladies of the family* and Lord Shaftesbury
are temporarily a little out of their minds.'[13] Palmerston, however,
wrote to the Queen in rather different strain:

> General Garibaldi has altered his arrangements. He has received
> invitations from an immense number of towns, and those invitations
> have been accepted. But those who have taken an interest about
> him, especially Lord Shaftesbury, thought that, politically and
> with regard to his health, it was very desirable that these visits
> should not be made.[14]

From now onwards a portrait of Garibaldi was to hang in the place
of honour in the library of the great house in Grosvenor Square. When
the hero left England he took with him a sheaf of notes on working-
class housing and a copy of the New Testament in Italian, all of them
gifts from Shaftesbury.

The keynote of this period had been Shaftesbury's relationship
with Palmerston, a relationship also involving his family. The hospitable house of Broadlands had been a well-loved second home to
them all, not least to the three girls, who found there the social
gaieties lacking in their own serious-minded and comparatively
poverty-stricken home. Evelyn held the pleasant and interesting
post of Palmerston's private secretary; Lionel owed his start in
business to Palmerston's generosity. To Minny, Palmerston had given
unstinted love and admiration; in a typical letter thanking her for
a present of Devonshire cream he describes the gift as 'like the giver,
excellent and perfect.'[15] The friendship between Palmerston and

* The Duchess of Sutherland was one of Garibaldi's chief supporters.

Shaftesbury himself is one of the curiosities of history. That Shaftesbury should so much prefer the godless, amoral, Whiggish Palmerston to the virtuous Tory Peel or the pious Tory Aberdeen is an anomaly that can only be explained by giving most of the credit for this happy relationship to Palmerston himself. Imperturbably good-humoured, generous, and full of sense, he was determined to be on the best possible terms with the members of his family, which, of course, included his wife's family also. Moreover, he knew a great man when he saw one; Palmerston valued Shaftesbury at his true worth, taking great pains to learn how to manage him, and refusing to be put off by prickly idiosyncrasies. In his turn, Shaftesbury responded to this kindly, sagacious treatment with a trust and an affection such as he gave to few other people.

The diary, at this period so brief and scanty, does, however, give a full account of Palmerston's death and of Shaftesbury's reaction to the event. In August 1865 Palmerston left Broadlands for a long visit to the Lamb family home of Brocket in Hertfordshire. Here he was in remarkably good form, vaulting over the park railings like a schoolboy. In October, however, he caught a bad chill, and though he rallied sufficiently to breakfast off mutton chops and port, his recovery was only temporary. Minny came down to Brocket to keep her mother company. Palmerston had loved her as a daughter; now he greeted her as she entered his room, 'Minny, come in, come in; you always seem to me like a sunbeam.' On October 17th Shaftesbury joined his wife at Brocket. Immediately on arrival he was summoned to Lady Palmerston's room, where he found her lying on the bed, prostrated by grief. Palmerston had suffered a sudden and serious relapse; the doctors had told her that no hope remained. She asked Shaftesbury to pray for her husband. 'Ah, have I not during many years prayed for you both, every morning and every night?' was the reply. 'Then pray with me now,' she begged of him.

Later in the evening the family gathered in Palmerston's bedroom. His doctor, Prothero Smith, a staunch Evangelical, asked the dying man whether he believed in regeneration through Christ. 'Oh, surely,' Palmerston replied with characteristic lack of zeal. William Cowper recited some prayers, then turned to Shaftesbury to ask him to continue – 'he knows your voice, and he will be touched to find that you are so near him.' Shaftesbury repeated prayer after prayer, and spoke of sin and forgiveness. He believed that Palmerston gave assent by 'a soft and peculiar sound, more like the breathing of the heart than an effort of the mouth.' At a quarter to eleven on the morning of October 18th Palmerston died very peaceably, leaving his son-in-law happily convinced that after a lifetime devoted to the things of this world, 'he acknowledged, accepted, and embraced our petitions, joined in the confession of sins, and trusted to the merits of the all-powerful Redeemer.' Shaftesbury of course may have been right in so believing, but he might not have felt quite so sure had he not chanced to be out of the room at the actual moment of death. Palmerston's dying thoughts had been of diplomatic affairs; his last words were, 'That's Article ninety-eight; now go on to the next.'[16]

On October 28th Palmerston was given a state funeral in Westminster Abbey. After commenting on the ceremony and the respectful behaviour of the immense crowds outside the Abbey, Shaftesbury wrote, 'The people mourned the loss of all this merit and service, but they did not perceive that, as the tomb closed over this Minister whom God had permitted for a while to be a bulwark against democracy, a bottomless pit was opened of religious, political, and social revolution.'

PART FOUR

When I feel old age creeping upon me and know that I must soon die – I hope it is not wrong to say it – I cannot bear to leave this world with all the misery in it.

Shaftesbury to Frances Powell Cobbe

Chapter 20

A TIME OF GRIEF

Palmerston had never seemed at home among the Victorians. Born in 1784, five years before the fall of the Bastille, by temperament and training he belonged to the age of Castlereagh and Canning. Shaftesbury had loved and admired this old Regency rake as he had never loved and admired any other politician. Palmerston was the last survivor of the leaders under whom he had served his political apprenticeship, the men with whom he felt himself to be in natural sympathy. Those who were now to come into power were of his own generation, but they were not of his way of thought. Though he was only three years older than Disraeli and eight years older than Gladstone he felt no affinity with either man; 'I am myself totally indifferent to both Gladstone and Disraeli,'[1] he wrote to William Cowper-Temple.* To many people there comes a time, usually at some point between their sixtieth and seventieth year, when the face of the world as they have always known it changes completely and they find themselves strangers in a strange land. This moment of truth came to Shaftesbury at Palmerston's death.

Politically, he found his own position completely altered. During Palmerston's tenure of office Shaftesbury's influence had not been confined merely to ecclesiastical patronage. As a near relative he could speak to the private ear of the Prime Minister, and although he had long ago abandoned his political ambitions he had none the less enjoyed this role of *éminence grise*. Palmerston's death reduced him to the status of an ordinary back-bencher. Because of his abandonment of party ties and his repeated refusals to take office he had nothing now that could give him any exceptional influence but his reputation as an upright man and a philanthropist; and such a reputation, as he very well knew, could cut both ways.

Though he no longer had any particularly close connection with political affairs, Shaftesbury remained regular in his attendance at the House of Lords, where he was honoured by all as the recognised

* As Palmerston's heir, William Cowper assumed the surname Cowper-Temple.

spokesman and champion of the poor. The great legislative battles on the social front had been won; all that remained to be done were mopping-up operations in the shape of amending acts to improve and extend existing laws, and measures to regulate conditions of employment in industries which had hitherto escaped control. Shaftesbury set about this work with all his old zeal and conscientiousness. As long ago as 1861 he had secured the appointment of another Royal Commission on Children's Employment. Its first report, published in 1863, was chiefly concerned with the employment of child chimney-sweeps, an abuse which Shaftesbury had not yet been able to put down, in spite of his many efforts in that direction. Other instances of children employed in shocking conditions were to be found in the brickmaking industry and in agriculture. For the present Shaftesbury left the brickfields alone, but as an agricultural landlord he felt particular concern for children working on the land. In the eastern counties especially it was customary for women and children to work in gangs, hired out to the farmers by a gang-master. Children of six and seven worked nine hours a day, before and after work trudging as much as five, six, or seven miles to and from their homes. Working in the fields in all weathers, beaten and ill-treated by the gang-masters, they suffered so much in health that the death-rate among children in the rural areas around Wisbech was almost as high as in Manchester. Many too were the complaints of the immorality resulting from the mixture of boys and girls in these rough and tough gangs. In 1865 Shaftesbury succeeded in setting on foot an enquiry by the Children's Employment Commission into this system of gang-labour. Two years later the publication of the Commission's report gave him the occasion to introduce a bill prohibiting field labour by any child under the age of eight and by girls under the age of eleven, and strictly regulating the gang-employment of women and girls. For lack of support he was obliged to drop the bill after its second reading. Later in the year, however, the Government brought in a similar bill which duly passed both Houses and became law.

This same year of 1867 the Government brought two bills before Parliament, the one extending the existing Factory Acts to cover all factories which employed more than a hundred workers, the other regulating conditions of employment in smaller workshops. In August both bills became law, giving Shaftesbury occasion to rejoice over the passing of 'the charter of justice and humanity' which brought to a victorious conclusion his thirty years' labour on behalf of the factory workers.

The year 1866 saw the beginning of one of Shaftesbury's most successful philanthropic schemes. The idea of a training ship was a happy inspiration, combining the practical with the picturesque. Both the Royal Navy and the Merchant Service were finding difficuty in manning ships at a time when hundreds of lads were running wild about the London streets, employed on nothing more profitable than holding horses, mud-larking, begging or pilfering. Meanwhile, disused but still serviceable vessels were cluttering up the Admiralty yards. Shaftesbury conceived the idea of fitting out one of these old ships, filling it with boys of the Ragged School type, and training them for a sea-going life.

On February 14th 1866 a hundred and fifty homeless boys were collected together at St. Giles' Refuge, in one of the poorest areas of London, and set down to a splendid meal of roast beef, plum pudding, and coffee. At the end of this feast Shaftesbury put the question, 'If a ship were fitted out and moored in the Thames how many of you would like to live aboard her and train as seamen?' The response was enthusiastic and almost unanimous. Thus encouraged, Shaftesbury approached the Admiralty and obtained the use of the fifty-gun frigate, *Chichester*. The notion of a training-ship caught the imagination of the public; funds were quickly forthcoming, and by the end of the year a hundred boys were already on board and started on a course of seamanship. Six years later, thanks to the generosity of Baroness Burdett-Coutts, one of the richest and most generous women in England, Shaftesbury was able to fit out a second ship, the *Arethusa*. Her successor, another *Arethusa*, is today moored in the Medway with two hundred boys aboard her to whom she is both school and home.

Another charitable work among boys in which Shaftesbury took a special interest was the Shoe-Blacks' Brigade, founded by a colourful character called John Macgregor, inventor of the Rob Roy canoe. As far back as 1851 Macgregor had thought to employ some of London's vagrant boys as shoe-blacks to clean the shoes of the many visitors to the Great Exhibition. When the Exhibition closed the Brigade continued to grow and flourish giving useful employment to many poor boys.

Some of the poorest and most neglected of the inhabitants of London were the costermongers, who, in Shaftesbury's day, herded together in their thousands in the slums of the City area. At night the donkey which drew the coster's barrow would sleep in the same room as the family, whilst the stock of fruit, fish or rotting vegetables was stored under the bed. Something about these wild and merry street-hawkers appealed especially strongly to Shaftesbury, who became President of the Golden Lane Mission to Costermongers, an institution founded by a post-office clerk called W. J. Orsman. Shaftesbury greatly liked and admired this man, whom he described in a period-piece phrase: 'Few things are more marvellous than to see what can be done by one man, however socially inferior, if he have but the love of Christ in his heart.' To prove his right to the title of 'coster' Shaftesbury bought a barrow, which he had decorated with his coat of arms, to be lent out to any brother coster who had not yet saved enough money to buy a barrow of his own. In return the costers presented him with a donkey which lived for many years at St. Giles, a source of great delight to visiting grandchildren.

These organised charities, Ragged Schools, training ships, missions, Shoe-blacks' Brigade, and the like by no means made up the sum total of Shaftesbury's philanthropic activities. Each day brought individual demands upon his time, his attention, and his very limited purse. When in London, each morning from eleven o'clock till one he held what might be described as a levee for people needing help and advice. Often, too, on returning home late at night from a meeting or a debate in the House of Lords, he would find poor people sitting patiently on his door-step, knowing that he would not turn them away until he had heard their troubles and done what he could to relieve them. On top of all this came casual encounters with individuals, as, for instance, the shepherd boy in Hyde Park who had never been allowed time off to go to church on Sunday, or the five-year-old girl who tumbled into the basement area of the Grosvenor Square house, or the other small girl literally thrust into his arms by her despairing father. To these, and to hundreds of similar cases, Shaftesbury gave unstinted care and personal attention; he would send little gifts to individuals, write letters in his own hand to orphan children, remind hard-pressed City missionaries of small promises of help too easily forgotten. Thieves, costermongers, boot-blacks, chimney-sweeps, every sort and kind of poor, down-and-out person, thought of him not as a distant benefactor but as a personal friend.

Where religious affairs were concerned Shaftesbury was now engaged in a battle on two fronts, on the one hand against neology, on the other against the Ritualists, so called because, unlike their predecessors the Tractarians, this new generation of High Churchmen set great store by ceremonial and ritual. In the fight against Ritualism Shaftesbury's fixed conviction that nobody was prepared to do him justice was strengthened by the behaviour of his fellow Evangelicals. Hodder tactfully makes no direct reference to this episode; it is therefore necessary to piece the story together from scattered and rather obscure entries in the diaries. It seems that by the late autumn of 1866 an anti-Ritualist movement had started up among the Evangelical laity. At a meeting held to elect a leader, at which the names of Shaftesbury and Lord Harrowby were put forward, Harrowby won on a show of hands, only one hand being raised in support of Shaftesbury. Harrowby, however, refused the position, whereupon the whole affair seems to have quietly petered out. Though on December 26th Shaftesbury had written 'I do not desire to be a leader where there is nothing to be led,' the entry for December 31st shows how great was the impression made upon him by this rejection by his own party:

It makes me reflect, and yet it almost makes me laugh, when I see how I have been deposed from the leadership of the Protestant party. The change is so sudden, and so complete, not by the tide flowing beyond me, but by it ebbing from me. I am precisely what I was; but my friends have become the reverse of what they were . . . Now I am candidly and fairly told that the Protestants want 'another sort of man,' that 'I am too well known,' 'my opinions are too extreme' . . . The announcement is a mortification to my self-love, but it saves me a world of trouble, speechmaking and responsibility.

On January 18th 1867 he again comments 'I am deposed from the throne of Protestant leader by general consent,' and goes on to describe his own position as he sees it:

I have been very long, too long, before the public; and I am satisfied that, were a successor at hand, I should be displaced tomorrow. But some beast is wanted to go to market, and 'the old Donkey' is as good as any other that can be had. Thus all externals fade away. I find myself alone, without advisers, without agents, without friends, without coadjutators, an ancient weather-beaten rock with the sea daily receding from it. There is wisdom and mercy in all this. It detaches one from life, and drives one more and more to pray for the Second Advent.

Two months later, in March 1867, Shaftesbury introduced a Vestments Bill, which sought to make it illegal for a clergyman to wear any ecclesiastical vestments except the surplice and hood prescribed by the 58th Canon of the Church of England. This measure aroused the anger of Samuel Wilberforce, who, declaring that the bishops were allowing themselves to be dragged at Shaftesbury's heels, denounced the bill as 'exactly the idea for his cramped, persecuting, puritanical mind.'[2] Though the bill failed to pass its second reading it nevertheless resulted in the appointment of a Commission on Ritualism. Shaftesbury refused to serve on this body, believing that it would lose all reputation for impartiality if it should include 'persons so prominent and so fixed as myself and the Bishop of Oxford.'[3] Samuel Wilberforce felt no such scruples about joining the Commission, with the inevitable result that Shaftesbury declared it to be 'as unfair, partial, and pre-judging as it can be ... the work, they say, of Samuel Oxon.'

Continuing his struggle against the Ritualists, in May 1868 Shaftesbury introduced the Uniformity of Public Worship Bill, which was thrown out by the Lords two months later, and in the spring of 1869 he introduced the first of a series of bills dealing with the Ecclesiastical Courts. Against his better judgement he had been persuaded by Haldane and an Evangelical lawyer called Stephens to take up this dry and difficult subject, which was nevertheless of some importance since the Anglo-Catholics, as the Ritualists were beginning to be called, were defying the authority of the existing courts. Since the question was one best dealt with by a lawyer or an ecclesiastic he would have done well to fall in with a proposal from Tait, who in December 1868 became Archbishop of Canterbury, that the bill should be withdrawn in favour of a similar measure brought in by Tait himself. Shaftesbury, however, felt that he stood pledged to the ultra-Protestant Church Association to bring in his own bill, which was promptly rejected by the House of Lords.

In the years following Palmerston's death the great political issue was electoral reform. In June 1866 the defeat of Russell's Reform Bill led to the fall of the Whig ministry. Derby took office, and, hoping to win Shaftesbury back to the Tory fold, asked him to join the Cabinet as Chancellor of the Duchy of Lancaster. The offer was refused almost as a matter of course. Hodder writes that Derby then offered Shaftesbury the Home Office, which was also refused. A passage in the diary suggests that had this second offer indeed been made it would have been considered very carefully. 'The Home Office alone would have given me a powerful status,' Shaftesbury wrote on June 30th, the day after he had refused the Duchy of Lancaster. The same entry expresses deep distrust of Derby's motives: 'I did not infer that he much wished me to aid him in the Cabinet, but only as a sort of picture to present to the country, the picture of a friend to the working classess.'

In the spring of 1867 the Tories brought in a Reform Bill of their own very similar to the measure they had voted against the previous year, giving the vote to all householders in the boroughs though not in the counties. Shaftesbury rightly held Disraeli responsible for this remarkable volte-face. In his opinion little blame attached to the Prime Minister, 'poor Derby, who, as Cerberus of old, is put to sleep by a soporific cube from Sybil Disraeli.' Shaftesbury himself was placed in an awkward dilemma. Much as he disliked the principle of household suffrage he believed that such a measure was bound to be granted, if not immediately then at most in two or three years' time. To oppose it was but lost labour. As a nominal Tory and a member of the House of Lords he saw the Reform Bill as a measure which he and his fellow peers could not approve but one which they did not wish to reject and saw little hope of amending. He knew well the pitfalls which awaited any speaker on this subject, yet where so important an issue was concerned he felt that he could not remain silent. On July 22nd 1867 he made a fine and temperate speech admitting the inevitability of Reform but arguing that it would have been wiser to proceed more gradually. 'I should have wished to hold up the suffrage as a great object of ambition to the working man,' he declared; 'I should have wished to hold it up as the reward of thrift, honesty, and industry.'

Shaftesbury's dislike of electoral reform was part of his belief in the aristocratic principle, which he held only less strongly than his belief in the Christian religion. He had set out to prove by his own actions and manner of life that aristocracy was an affair of service rather than of privilege and that an order of society based on the aristocratic principle was the one which conferred most benefit upon the nation as a whole and in particular upon the poorer classes. During this year of 1867 the collapse of this ideal seems to have been very much in his mind and he refers to it no less than three times in his diary. 'Long entertained a fond belief that, whilst making the welfare, physical, temporal, and spiritual, of the working-classes my primary object, a secondary one might be obtained in the contentment of the people, the repression of democracy, and the maintenance of our ancient institutions,' he wrote on March 2nd; 'it is now manifest that my aspirations will be fruitless.' On June 11th he wrote, 'It was my desire to do some good to the Constitution and show the benefit of hereditary property and large surfaces of land in single hands; I earnestly hoped that the devotion of a lifetime might prove the value of independence by succession and the non-necessity of labouring in a profession.' And on October 1st, 'My whole life has been spent in endeavours to build up the moral, social and political position of the "Aristocracy", but difficulties of many and various kinds and want of money have made oftentimes my practice contrary to my preaching.'

Want of money had indeed hampered Shaftesbury in his efforts to act the part of the ideal aristocratic landlord. Not without reason did he refer to his bank book as a 'fatal document.' From 1866 to 1868 his greatest anxiety concerned the progress, or rather lack of progress, in his law-suits. As time went on, bringing only 'fresh suits, fresh outlays, fresh anxiety,' a horrid doubt arose to trouble him: 'Is Waters an innocent man? Again and again has he called God to witness when uttering (as we all believed) the most cool and frightful falsehoods.' Yet Waters was not struck . dead like Ananias and Sapphira; instead, when his case was dismissed and costs given against him, he was bold enough to appeal to the House of Lords.

Both sides were employing some of the most distinguished lawyers of the day, of course at enormous cost. On March 1st 1866 Shaftesbury wrote a long summary of his financial troubles. The ill-considered schemes he had set on foot at St. Giles, brick kilns, land drainage, cottage building, he now saw as follies. His efforts on behalf of such causes as the Ten Hours Campaign had cost him far more than he could afford, whilst his philanthropic and religious interests had involved him in heavy expense. The Protestant College in Malta, for instance, a venture in which he had been deeply involved, had recently bankrupted, at the cost to him personally of nearly seven hundred pounds. Looking back, he summed up his errors with considerable insight: 'I acted upon feeling and trusted to the conclusions of my imagination, not realising the fact that there is no promise of miracles to supply what might be done by common-sense, and that mere warmth of heart is a very deceptive guide in the details of life.'

On May 6th 1868 Waters, who had meanwhile bankrupted, was due to stand his trial for embezzlement. Two days beforehand he fell ill of smallpox; 'it may be so,' Shaftesbury commented, 'but for him a' more opportune disease never occurred.' In any case, the bankruptcy made it difficult, if not impossible, for Shaftesbury to recover any money should judgment finally be given in his favour. The position appeared so hopelessly involved that a Dorset neighbour, Lord Portman, was moved to suggest that the matter be settled out of court and to offer his services to help bring about a reasonable solution. Both sides accepted his offer with considerable relief. It was eventually agreed that no further proceedings of any sort should be taken by either party and that all transactions between them should be regarded as terminated. On June 15th Shaftesbury wrote, 'This evening has, I believe, brought this painful and extensive litigation to a close.' He had not recovered his money, but at least he was free from the threat of further court action and from any increase to his already intolerable burden of legal expenses. The diary for February 13th 1869 gives a final, ironic postscript to the history of this unhappy affair: 'Waters is safe from all trouble in money matters, he has married a rich wife.'

Shaftesbury's financial burdens were not lessened by the discovery that Anthony was once more in debt, the result, or so his father believed, of Harriet's extravagance. Shaftesbury's disappointment over this daughter-in-law was a little solaced when, in 1866, Evelyn married Sybella Farquhar, a charming girl with a suitably Evangelical family background. A year later Lionel made an equally satisfactory marriage, his bride being Fanny Hanbury-Leigh. These two daughters-in-law became very dear to Shaftesbury, who described them as 'thorough darlings,' in marked contrast to poor Harriet, condemned as 'hard-hearted, insolent, mean, tyrannical and ungrateful.'

In the summer of 1867 Shaftesbury was seriously worried about Minny's health. Though she tried hard to convince him that her frequent ailments were of little importance his anxiety was not to be quieted – 'all is of consequence where she is affected.' But worse was to come. On July 27th Shaftesbury was summoned by telegram to Brighton, where Minny and the girls were staying. His favourite daughter, more congenial to him than any of his children except the long-dead Francis, 'dear darling Conty, that jewel of temper, simplicity and unselfishness,' had spat blood. For six years lung disease had been suspected; now it had declared itself.

The famous Dr. Gull was sent for immediately at the enormous cost of sixty pounds in fees. He could only recommend that the winter should be spent abroad in a warm climate, a prospect most unwelcome to Shaftesbury:

Must I then wander elsewhere and never see home at all? People already complain that we are seldom on our estate, and I am compelled, in grief, to add one more example among landowners of apparent neglect of duty.

The doctors however were insistent. By Christmas, Shaftesbury,

Minny and their daughters were settled in the Villa Liserb, at Cimiez
near Nice.

Here Shaftesbury filled his enforced leisure by reading, a pleasure
for which he could seldom find time at home. His choice of books
included the *Annals* of Tacitus, the autobiography of Benvenuto
Cellini, and Queen Victoria's recently published *Leaves from the
Journal of My Life in the Highlands.* He was fiercely critical of the
Queen's action in thus making public 'all that she thinks and does in
the innermost recesses of her heart and home.' A few years later he
himself was to give Hodder permission to publish unlimited extracts
from a much more revealing and personal journal. Various entries
clearly show that at this period Shaftesbury still had every intention
of destroying his diaries before he died. At the back of his mind,
however, there must have lurked some idea of publication; impossible
otherwise to explain why, in his harassed, overfull life, he should
have found time so frequently to write not a few hurried notes but
long, detailed, carefully-phrased and corrected accounts of his
thoughts, opinions, and actions.

The ostensible reason for the Riviera visit had been Shaftesbury's
own health (his digestive trouble was in fact both serious and persistent). He and Minny were in agonies lest the truth about Conty's
illness should leak out and ruin her chances of marriage – 'the girl
will be put down as a hopeless invalid, at least as one with a dangerous weakness, and though she may recover she will be "tabooed"
for ever.' In April 1868, however, business of many kinds compelled
him to return to England, leaving Minny behind with Conty, who
was no better but rather worse. On his return Shaftesbury found the
political scene greatly changed. At Christmas Russell had retired
from the leadership of the Liberal party, leaving that position to
Gladstone; in February, when ill-health forced Derby to resign,
Disraeli had become Prime Minister. The duel between the two
Victorian giants had begun.

The disestablishment of the Protestant Church of Ireland was the
question of the hour. When, in the summer of 1868, Gladstone
introduced a series of motions in favour of Disestablishment, Shaftesbury did not attempt to make more than a very short speech, and
that with difficulty – 'never before did a few words give me so much
trouble, anxiety, and vexation.' After an autumn General Election
resulted in the defeat of the Tories, Gladstone took office, declaring
'My mission is to pacify Ireland.' The first step towards that desirable goal was to be a bill disestablishing and disendowing the Irish
Church, which he introduced on March 1st 1869. When, at the end

of May, the bill passed the Commons and came up to the Lords, Shaftesbury was in a quandary. The Evangelicals were for once united in their opposition to Disestablishment. As the leading Evangelical he would be expected preferably to speak but certainly to vote against the bill. This he was reluctant to do, since he saw that if the Lords rejected it they would involve themselves in a hopeless struggle with the House of Commons, something he was always anxious to avoid. A year later, in July 1870, when the Lords threw out a bill abolishing religious tests at the Universities, he stated his point of view particularly clearly:

> It is a bad bill, no doubt, but it has been sent up three times by a House of Commons elected on universal suffrage, and it will be sent up again still worse, and we shall take it obediently and abjectly . . . If they [the Lords] resolve to maintain their position, and resist, year by year, even to the death, be it so. This, though neither safe nor cautious, may be sublime. But to exasperate by a little more delay, without the hope of escape or even change, is silly, wicked, and perilous. It may lead to an attack on the House of Lords itself which may deprive it of all capacity to be of use in the future.

Though Shaftesbury prepared himself to face the ordeal of speaking on the Disestablishment Bill he was secretly relieved when no opportunity to do so came his way. There remained the problem of voting:

> Shall I vote or shall I not vote? I have at once set aside all thought of voting for the bill. I would vote against it could I thereby save the Church or even justify its existence. But this is beyond all power. I should only add to the ruin of the Church and the degradation of the House of Lords . . . But it is a principle, say the most earnest declaimers. Very well, but is every principle to be maintained at every hazard?

In vain did he search the Scriptures and pray for guidance; he was driven to conclude that 'there are numerous political questions which the Bible does not solve.' Finally he decided not to vote.

The Disestablishment Bill brought Shaftesbury into conflict with Lord Salisbury, whom he was to recognise, though reluctantly, as a future leader of the Conservatives and to stigmatise as 'a blackguard without any heart.' Salisbury's speech on July 21st against

Disestablishment he described as 'shallower than ditchwater as to sentiment and substance.' In spite, however, of much determined opposition, the bill finally passed the House of Lords and became law.

In February 1869 Shaftesbury found himself in such financial difficulties that he was forced to sell some of the family jewels. Contemplating his position he wrote sadly, 'our blessed Lord endured all the sorrows of humanity but that of *debt*.' In similar circumstances he had often been helped either by his generous sister, Caroline Neeld, or by his equally generous mother-in-law. In June 1869 Caroline died, to her brother's great grief; in September, when he was taking the cure at Homburg, came news of Lady Palmerston's fatal illness. Seldom has a mother-in-law received such a tribute from a son-in-law as Shaftesbury paid to 'poor, dear, kind Mum':

> Until I lost her I hardly knew how much I loved her. To my dying hour I shall remember her perpetual sunshine of expression and affectionate grace, the outward sign of inward sincerity, of kindness, generosity, and love. Her pleasure was to see others pleased, and without art, or effort, or even intention, she fascinated everyone who came within her influence. Forty years have I been her son-in-law and during all that long time she has been to me a well-spring of tender friendship and affectionate service.

In the autumn of 1869 the gloom which Conty's illness had cast over the whole family was a little lightened by a happy event. Harriet, who could do nothing right, had so far produced four daughters. Great therefore was the rejoicing when in October she gave birth to a son. Shaftesbury was delighted by the welcome which the tenantry gave to this baby, the first heir to the earldom actually to be born at St. Giles. Satisfaction, however, was short-lived. At Christmas, Anthony and Harriet absented themselves from the family celebrations; worse still, they dismissed their 'pious, kind and affectionate governess,' planning to replace her with a foreigner, 'perhaps a covert Jesuit or an open infidel.' A further cause of distress was a Report by Edward Stanhope, one of the Commissioners sent down to Dorset by the Royal Commission on Employment in Agriculture. Though under no illusions about the state of the overcrowded, dilapidated cottages still existing on his estate, Shaftesbury had supposed that at least some mention would be made of his efforts towards improvement. The Report, however, proved to be most unfavourable. Shaftesbury believed that Stanhope had been deliberately misled by an old opponent of his own – 'the truth is, he saw little, he heard little; he took everything from Sidney Godolphin Osborne, who, to maintain his own calumnies, blinded the eyes of his wretched pupil.' This Report, combined with the discovery that, in spite of all the money he was spending on the place, St. Giles was receiving more Poor Law relief per head than any other parish in Dorset made Shaftesbury almost despair of achieving any real improvements to his estate. However, the appointment of a new agent in Waters' place at last brought about a change for the better, so that when he paid a visit of inspection in June 1870 Shaftesbury could rejoice to see all looking 'well and comfortable, becoming the property of a gentleman and a Christian.'

Abroad, the year 1870 was notable for the outbreak of the Franco-Prussian War; at home, for the passing of W. E. Forster's Education Act, which for the first time brought schooling within the reach of all children. This Act increased the Government grant to denominational schools and where no such schools existed set up elected school boards empowered to levy a local educational rate and establish non-denominational 'board schools.' Shaftesbury's attitude to education has been much misunderstood. He grieved that the passing of Forster's Act must mean the eventual disappearance of the Ragged Schools which could not come up to the standard necessary to qualify a school for the Government grant. He believed that the Ragged Schools best supplied the need of the type of child who attended them, and he feared that such children would benefit very little from the board school type of education. Nevertheless, in the main he supported Forster, whom he liked and respected personally, being convinced that this measure was the best that could be looked for in the existing circumstances. 'I laboured hard to aid Forster to carry it,' he wrote on Christmas Day 1870, 'because I believed, nay, almost knew, that this measure, if rejected, would have been followed by one, (and irresistibly followed) which would have involved a national apostasy by the public and statutory declaration that the word of God should not be admitted into any of the schools sustained by the Commonwealth.' Forster, on the contrary, had declared to him, 'Lord Shaftesbury, I would rather have my right hand cut off than be the means of excluding the Bible from our day schools';[4] and he trusted Forster to keep his word.

Shaftesbury had once been a believer in denominational teaching in schools; now he saw clearly enough that the most that could be hoped for was that the Board School curriculum should include Bible-teaching – 'What we ask for is simply this, that the Bible, and

the teaching of the Bible, to the children of this vast Empire should
be an essential and not an extra.'[5] This declaration begged the difficult question as to the exact form of such Bible-teaching. Forster's
Act, as finally passed, contained the Cowper-Temple clause, named
after Shaftesbury's brother-in-law, which laid down that the religious teaching given in board schools must exclude 'any catechism
or religious formulary distinctive of any particular denomination.'
Although this compromise was probably the only solution to the
problem, Shaftesbury was not far wrong when he described religious
teaching in board schools as 'such a meagre, washy, pointless thing
that though thinking people might complain of what was left out,
no living soul could make a grievance of what was left in.'

Shaftesbury did not disapprove of State education; he only disapproved of such education if it were 'godless.' He believed that the
success of the Ragged Schools had shown, as he himself had declared
long ago in 1850, 'that religion must be the alpha and omega of all
education given to the poorer classes.'[6] Odd though this statement
may appear in the light of modern educational theory and practice,
it is arguable that a convinced Christian like Shaftesbury must of
necessity see religion as the alpha and omega of everything, including,
of course, education. It should be remembered, too, that insistence
on the beginning and the end does not deny the importance of the
middle; to stress alpha and omega is not necessarily to overlook the
other letters of the educational alphabet.

On July 16th 1870 Shaftesbury notes that France had declared war
on Prussia, 'the Papal champion against the Protestant in continental
Europe.' There was no doubt as to where his own sympathies lay.
In the diary France is described as 'the stay of Anti-Christ, the power
by whose bayonets the Pope reigns in Rome,' whilst the King of
Prussia 'comes out in Teutonic and Christian glory.' Hating war
as he did, he had no sympathy with the French passion for *la gloire* –
'France seeks war as her element, her source of glory, her distinction in this world' – and he regretted that war correspondents should
refer to a battlefield by such euphuisms as 'the theatre of war'
rather than by the more horrifying and accurate term of 'the shambles.' After their defeat at Sedan on September 1st he believed that
the French should have made peace immediately; their determination to stand siege in Paris he regarded as both foolish and wicked.
He did all he could for the victims of the war, sitting on committees
to provide aid for the sick and wounded and for the relief of French
peasantry in the battle areas, and promoting schemes to help refugees
who had fled to England.

The troubles of his daughters continued to weigh heavily upon Shaftesbury's spirits. In October the engagement was announced between Queen Victoria's fourth daughter, Princess Louise, and Lord Lorne, heir to the Duke of Argyll. The Prince of Wales, who disliked the proposed marriage, wrote to the Queen, 'I suppose you know that Lorne was half engaged to one of Lord Shaftesbury's daughters, and that the family are naturally furious that he has thrown the girl over.'[7] Both Vea and Conty had been jilted by men whose names Shaftesbury was careful to leave unrecorded. The only reference in the diary to Lorne's engagement is a colourless entry dated October 14th:

> Lord Lorne is to be married to Princess Louise. This step will of course lead to the abrogation of the Royal Marriage Act and to the wiping out of many things 'that do hedge round the divinity of a King.'

A still more pressing anxiety was Conty's state of health. The continued fighting in France meant that when the doctors again ordered her south for the winter it was necessary to travel by the long, inconvenient route through Germany and across the Alps to the Italian Riviera. Here the weather was appalling – heavy snow fell on Christmas Day – and the hotels cold and uncomfortable. Conty fell alarmingly ill, and Minny collapsed, exhausted and in considerable pain. In February the party moved to the comparative comfort of Mentone, where Shaftesbury was reluctantly compelled to return alone to England – 'deep, deep sorrow to do so but there are other duties in the world than those solely domestic.'

At the end of March 1871 came the popular rising in Paris and the establishment of the Commune, news which aroused Shaftesbury's anxiety for his wife and daughters, who were still in France. He wrote to Henry Manning, now Roman Catholic Archbishop of Westminster, to express sympathy and horror at the murder of the Archbishop of Paris. A surprisingly friendly relationship already existed between Shaftesbury and Manning, who shared a common interest in the condition of the poor, and in particular the poor of London. Manning would send Shaftesbury copies of sermons and pastoral letters in which he had quoted Shaftesbury's own descriptions of slum conditions, and he would invite Shaftesbury to discuss social problems, even suggesting that they might join together 'to make a league among working men for Christianity and Christian education.' Shaftesbury, in his turn, wrote to Manning asking for information about Roman Catholic rules for auricular Confession; and later the two men were to find another common interest in their opposition to vivisection and the general use of animals in scientific experiments.

In July 1871 Shaftesbury moved a motion in the House of Lords calling attention to the employment of children in brickfields. This crying scandal is best described in his own words:

> I went down to a brickfield and made a considerable inspection. I first saw, at a distance, what appeared like eight or ten pillars of clay. . . . On walking up, I found to my astonishment that these pillars were human beings. They were so like the ground on which they stood, their features were so indistinguishable, their dress so besoiled and covered with clay that, until I approached and saw them move, I believed them to be the products of the earth. . . . I saw little children, three-parts naked, tottering under the weight of wet clay, some of it on their heads, and some on their shoulders, and little girls with large masses of wet, cold, and dripping clay pressing on their abdomens. Moreover, the unhappy children were exposed to the most sudden transitions of heat and cold, for, after carrying their burdens of wet clay, they had to endure the heat of the kiln, and to enter places where the heat was so intense that I was not myself able to remain more than two or three minutes. [8]

As a result of Shaftesbury's motion these ill-used children were brought under the protection of the Factory Acts.

All through the summer of 1871 Shaftesbury was in an agony of anxiety for his family. Conty had returned to England no better in health or spirits; in July, Cecil fell desperately ill of typhoid fever, and when, against all likelihood, he recovered, Minny collapsed, worn out by incessant nursing. The winter was to be spent once more on the Riviera, this year at Cannes. Here Shaftesbury found the mosquitoes fierce, the food inedible, and the wine 'pernicious.' Though a keen supporter of the Temperance movement, Shaftesbury much enjoyed a glass of good wine. He was no teetotaller but rather what was then known as a 'counter-attractionist,' a person who believed that slum-dwellers got drunk on beer and spirits either from lack of any other form of distraction or simply because they were thirsty and could find nothing else to drink. In his opinion the best preventive of drunkenness would be the provision of an easily accessible and ample supply of pure water.

At the end of January 1872 Shaftesbury was obliged to return to England, 'wrenched to the core' by the parting from his wife and daughters. He found some consolation in the company of Evelyn's small son, Wilfrid; but he lamented that Harriet would allow him no opportunity to see his eldest and favourite grandchild, Margaret, usually known as Poppy. He solaced his loneliness by writing frequent letters to Minny, whom he would address by terms such as 'Dearest of women.'[9] In one letter he described the service of thanksgiving at St. Paul's for the recovery of the Prince of Wales from his dangerous attack of typhoid fever. Shaftesbury commented on the presence of the Duchess of Manchester, whom he suspected of designs to ensnare the Prince, and he reproached the Queen for refusing to drive to St. Paul's in the state carriage with the famous cream-coloured horses – 'she is sure, if she can, to spoil everything.' For the Princess of Wales he had, as usual, nothing but praise. 'I pray that she may have every blessing in time and in eternity,' he wrote; 'may she be as good a wife and as good a mother as you are, and may her husband be as faithful to her as I, by God's mercy, have been to you.' Since both Shaftesbury and Minny were well aware of the Prince's many love affairs the wording of this prayer was perhaps not entirely happy. On February 29th a weak-minded youth called Arthur O'Connor pointed an unloaded pistol at Queen Victoria as she was alighting from her carriage. Shaftesbury sent Minny a cutting describing how the Queen had given her Highland servant John Brown a gold medal and an annuity 'as a mark of her appreciation of his devotion and presence of mind on the occasion of the attack on her Majesty.' 'This pretext for deifying John Brown will be seen through and the old story revived,' Shaftesbury wrote, referring to the rumours of a secret marriage between Brown and the Queen. He added the query, 'Is she wicked or mad?'

One particularly interesting letter to Minny touches on the subject of women in medicine. Though he was later to change his opinion, Shaftesbury was at this period against Women's Suffrage, but he strongly supported those pioneer women who were fighting for the right to train as doctors. Ever since 1866 he had regularly taken the chair at meetings of the Society for the Medical Education of Women. 'I only want to give these women a fair chance,' he wrote to Minny after one of these meetings, 'and as I said in my speech, if they are found adequate they will be a great addition to the practical science of society; and if the reverse, why then, they will return to their position as the great ornaments and comforters of mankind.' He added the affectionate rider, 'Of course, my dear, I was in the last part of that sentence thinking of you as the perfect type of the perfect part of the sexes.'

Among pioneer women doctors Shaftesbury particularly admired Elizabeth Garrett, afterwards Mrs. Garrett-Anderson. Though he refused to support her candidature for the Marylebone School Board, his letter makes perfectly clear his approval of her personally. It is dated October 25th 1870:

> If ladies are to sit on School Boards and undertake such wide and public duties, there is no one in England more fitted than yourself for posts where diligence and ability are required. But I confess to you that I am, for the present, behind the age in this respect; I do not dare to encourage a competition which eventually must make women the rivals of men in every occupation.
>
> If every lady were a Miss Garrett I should have no fear but a great deal of hope. Your own experience, modest as it may be, will tell you that it is not so.[10]

In the spring of 1872 a ballot bill, establishing a secret ballot at parliamentary elections, passed easily through the House of Commons. When this measure had been first introduced the previous year Shaftesbury had spoken out strongly against 'the fearful issues of secret voting.' Opposition to the secret ballot was one of Shaftesbury's most tenaciously held convictions. He had long recognised that Electoral Reform was inevitable, but he could not see that without the secret ballot such reform was almost valueless. Especially was this so in country districts. Shaftesbury's talk of the 'noble sentiment of public responsibility' was derisory nonsense to a labourer who stood to lose both his job and his cottage if he did not vote for the candidate approved by farmer or landlord. Although Shaftesbury prided himself on putting no pressure on his tenants but allowing them to vote as they pleased, in behaving thus he was in a tiny minority among country landlords.

Shaftesbury had often expressed a strong wish to make one great speech on the subject of the ballot; now his opportunity had come. Once again, however, he found himself unable to oppose a measure he heartily disapproved. He could not urge the Lords to vote against an important bill which the Commons had passed by a large majority; all he could do was point out the dangers inherent in the secret ballot and try to improve the bill when it went into Committee. Faced with such a difficult situation it was no wonder that on the day before he was to speak, which chanced to be a Sunday, he felt extremely unwell and found the utmost difficulty in keeping a check on his anxious thoughts. However, he succeeded in sticking firmly to his Sunday reading of the Bible and books of sermons, and the next day he made what was recognised as one of the most successful of all his speeches. 'Not unto us', he recorded humbly but joyfully; 'success, wonderful, overwhelming. It was indeed a marvel.'

This success, however, did little to lessen his depression. 'Where, except in America, have I any friends?' he asked himself on June 29th. The exception is an odd one, though Shaftesbury liked Americans better than he liked America itself. Perhaps the recent debates had revived memories of his long-ago acquaintanceship with Daniel Webster, the famous American statesman and diplomat, who had shared his dislike of the ballot and had urged him to oppose to the last the introduction of any such system. Perhaps he had in mind a more recent meeting with the poet Longfellow and with Senator Robert Winthrop, when he had found himself 'amazingly pleased with both of them.' Another American, Riverdy Johnson, had given him much pleasure by a speech to a great gathering of Ragged School children in which he described Shaftesbury as 'a nobleman by nature as well as by birth, one who has a grant of nobility from a higher source than Kings and Queens.' 'I cannot profess indifference to remarks of this kind,' Shaftesbury had noted gratefully on December 20th 1868, adding the comment, 'I esteem the man; I have a great fear, if not respect, for the country from whence he comes.'

On August 5th Shaftesbury had the pleasure of laying the foundation-stone of a 'workmen's city' at Lavender Hill, to be named Shaftesbury Park. This was a co-operative venture; and he especially rejoiced to see the working people making efforts to help themselves rather than depending on charity or on outside capital. The very next day there occurred 'a blessed event, a God-sent event'; Vea, now well over thirty, announced her engagement to Lord Templemore. Then the clouds shut down again, darker than ever before.

In August Shaftesbury returned from a brief holiday in Scotland to find Minny ill and in some pain. The doctor's report was, however, sufficiently favourable to allow him to leave London for St. Giles, where much urgent business awaited his attention. The next few weeks Shaftesbury spent in frequent journeys between Dorset and London. In the middle of September Conty fell so ill that for days and nights she lay in agonies, forbidden to make the slightest shift of position. She recovered slightly; and once more anxiety shifted from daughter to wife. On September 30th Sir William Gull, called in to see Minny, spoke ominously of 'a grave case.' On October 12th

Shaftesbury first saw, though he refused to recognise, the unmistakable signs of approaching death in Minny's face. On October 14th she was still well enough to go out for a short drive, but that evening she collapsed. Shaftesbury at last looked his fears straight in the face – 'my own dear, true, and precious wife; will God take away the desire of my eyes with a stroke?' At noon next day Minny lay dead.

Chapter 21

A VENERABLE FIGURE

Shaftesbury accepted this most bitter blow with simple and touching resignation. Sorrow for what had been taken away was mixed with thankfulness for what had once been given. 'To the memory of a wife as good, as true, and as deeply beloved, as God, in His undeserved mercy, ever gave to man' – so ran the inscription he composed for Minny's memorial tablet.

To his immediate shock and suffering the harshness of strict Evangelical practice added what was surely an unnecessary pang. 'Tonight will be a terrible event,' he wrote on the day of Minny's death; 'for the first time I must omit in my prayers the name of my precious Minny.' He suffered too from the pain which all bereaved people know remembering their faults and failings towards the dead – 'How many times have I, in my excitable spirit, said unjust and cruel things to her! What a placable spirit! What a power to forgive! and what a sublime power to forget!' He, whose nature was neither forgiving nor forgetting, had no thought now of Minny's little acts of rebellion, her fits of irritation over his unyielding routine of religious practice, the unjust and cruel things said long ago about the Jerusalem Bishopric. To Lady Gainsborough he wrote describing Minny as 'a sincere, sunny and gentle follower of our Lord.' Perhaps it was her sunniness that his shadowed spirit was to miss most of all in the years ahead.

Shaftesbury did not give way beneath the weight of his grief, but he knew very well that Minny's death was something from which he could never hope to recover. He who has lost an arm or a leg can learn to lead a useful, even a happy life, but never again can he be a whole man. 'Though the bereavement becomes less acute it never abates its heaviness,' Shaftesbury was to write eleven years after Minny's death. 'A man may continue the same to the world outwardly for work and for service, but inwardly he is really but the half of himself.' As Palmerston's death had changed and diminished the quality of Shaftesbury's political life, so, to a far greater extent, did

Minny's death change and impoverish his personal life, leaving it drained of gentleness and joy.

Shaftesbury's first thoughts had now to be for his invalid daughter Conty, whom he cared for with a pathetic tenderness, doing all in his power to make up to her for the loss of her mother – 'and such a mother!' Since the doctors were insistent that she must leave England immediately in November, he set out for yet another winter of exile on the Riviera. A week after their arrival at Mentone, Conty fell hopelessly ill. Though Shaftesbury grieved greatly that his child must die in a foreign land, in the very end came joy. Unlike poor Mary – tuberculosis is kinder to its victims than *status asthmatica* – Conty made what could be called a perfect death. Her last words were, 'I know I am going to die, I am so happy.' 'It is almost impossible even to weep for ourselves when we think of it,' her father wrote on the day of her death, December 16th, 'so truly blessed is her state, so wonderful her departure from this world.'

Within three months he had lost both his wife and his favourite daughter, yet he was not altogether unhappy. Describing himself as 'lost sometimes in floods of tears, but not of grief, almost of joy,' he found quiet comfort in counting over his dead, Francis, Maurice, Mary, Minny, Conty – 'What a band is now in Heaven!' The children still remaining to him rallied round to help and comfort, Hilda, from now onwards the home daughter, making him her particular care. D'Azeglio wrote a heart-broken letter, promising to come to St. Giles, painful though such a visit would be, because Minny would wish him to do so, 'and she must be obeyed.'[1] Best of all comforts was the return to work – 'There is still some misery to be mitigated, some souls to be saved.'

On his return to England after Conty's death Shaftesbury took up a new cause, and joined his fellow Evangelical, Samuel Plimsoll, in 'his glorious defence of the wretched, oppressed seamen of the Mercantile Marine.' Earnest, impetuous, and with little regard either for truth or accuracy, Plimsoll was a man who, left to himself, could be guaranteed to ruin the best of causes. In January 1873 he published *Our Seamen*, a book which awakened public interest in the scandal of overloaded, unseaworthy 'coffin-ships.' Unfortunately it also gave rise to a well-justified action for libel against Plimsoll. On March 24th Shaftesbury took the chair at a meeting in Exeter Hall called to urge that steps be taken to ensure that ships did not sail overloaded or in an unseaworthy state, and to demand improvements in the living conditions of seamen. A committee was set up and Shaftesbury chosen as President. His chief task was to restrain the ebullient Plimsoll, who badly needed to have at his side a counsellor who was both a skilled parliamentarian and a practised negotiator. Now, in spite of Shaftesbury's pleading, Plimsoll refused to give the apology which would have made it possible to drop the libel action. Surprisingly enough, he won his case, though he lost costs. Meanwhile public outcry had forced the Government to set up a Royal Commission to enquire into conditions on board merchant ships; and there, for the present, the matter rested.

A summer holiday in Scotland, usually spent with his friends the Burns of Castle Wemyss, was now to become part of the regular pattern of Shaftesbury's life. This year of 1873 it took the form of a cruise to the Western Isles, including Iona, Staffa, Rhum, Stornoway and Skye, where Shaftesbury refused to be impressed by romantic Dunvegan Castle, a home which might seem 'tolerable and even charming to a Macleod but maddening to anyone else.' This Scottish trip was followed by a visit to Vea in her married home in Ireland. Shaftesbury would not allow his abiding grief to spoil the genuine pleasure which he took in these holidays. It was at St. Giles especially that he felt the void, in the rooms, the walks, the flower-gardens, that still seemed touched by Minny's presence. Here in his own home his dead were 'never out of mind, hardly out of sight.' He, who loved the light of day so dearly, had always been moved to sadness at sunset; now in his loneliness he found the fading light and the dark, empty evenings excruciatingly melancholy. Worst of all was the silence, 'unbroken by that sweet silver voice that always had a tune to ravish my heart.'

He was troubled about the nature of that after-life in which he believed so firmly. Would he ever again see Minny as he had known and loved her? Could there be any real recognition, any meeting face to face, in that spirit world? Because he took the words of the Bible in so exact and literal a sense, the saying 'in heaven they neither married nor are given in marriage' particularly disturbed him – 'I may be to *her* and she to *me* no more than any other pardoned sinner accepted in the Lord.' As late as 1878 he was still puzzling over the problem and coming to no conclusion but a prayer, 'God in His consideration for our weakness and in His free mercy forgive us the errors and the grief.'

In religious affairs Shaftesbury's great concern was still the battle against Ritualism. The growth of the practice of auricular Confession* especially aroused his anger. On June 30th 1873 he took

* The practice of private confession to a priest, which Shaftesbury always described as 'the confessional,' a term properly applied only to the place where confessions are heard.

the chair at a huge Protestant protest meeting at Exeter Hall and delivered a speech exactly to the taste of his enthusiastic audience, who cheered him to the echo. He also helped to organise a monster petition against Confession to be presented to the Archbishop. 'The answer,' Shaftesbury noted mournfully, 'is "nuts".' In the middle of this Protestant uproar came news that Samuel Wilberforce, most able of High Churchmen, and the only bishop who had any sympathy with the Anglo-Catholics, had been instantly killed by a fall from his horse. Shaftesbury aptly quoted the famous epitaph, 'Between the stirrup and the ground mercy I sought, mercy I found,' and added, 'every kind feeling I ever had towards the Bishop is again alive.' To judge from the tone of the diary entries, the sum total of those kind feelings must have been extremely small.

The following year Shaftesbury was involved in more serious and wide-reaching action against Anglo-Catholics and Ritualism. A General Election held in January 1874 put the Tories into office with Disraeli as Prime Minister. One of the first measures to be introduced into the new Parliament was a Public Worship Regulation Bill, designed to put a stop to Ritualistic practices. Though this bill was concerned with a comparatively small issue affecting only the Church of England it aroused immense interest and excitement both inside and outside Parliament. Shaftesbury was deeply concerned with the Bill, which, in its final form, embodied much from his own rejected measures for the reform of the ecclesiastical courts.

Being a sensible man, Archbishop Tait had wished to avoid the necessity for legislating on this subject, but he was driven to do so by fear of Shaftesbury and the ultra-Protestant Church Association, who, if no official action were taken, planned to bring in a much more drastic measure of their own. Yielding to this pressure Tait drew up a memorandum outlining 'a simple, summary and inexpensive measure for securing obedience to the law.'[2] Complaints of ritualistic practices were to be heard by the bishop of the diocese, sitting with an advisory board of clergy and laity. If a clergyman refused to obey the bishop's ruling he was to be suspended. Tait was so anxious to placate Shaftesbury that he sent him a private copy of this memorandum with a request for suggestions and comments. In a highly unfavourable reply Shaftesbury objected to the scheme as leaving the Ecclesiastical Courts 'unpurged and even untouched' and as giving jurisdiction to a bishop instead of to a lay judge. He refused to co-operate with Tait in steering an Ecclesiastical Courts Bill through Parliament side by side with the Public Worship Bill; 'I could not consent to undertake it,' he wrote sourly; 'my experience of lawyers, laymen, bishops and chancellors is not agreeable as to the past nor encouraging as to the future.'[3]

When the Public Worship Regulation Bill came before the House of Lords Shaftesbury criticised it severely, objecting especially to the degree of authority conveyed upon the bishop – 'no man, whoever he may be, ought to be entrusted with absolute power.'[4] He planned to bring forward an amendment replacing the bishop by a lay judge to have jurisdiction of the whole country in 'ritual' cases, as proposed in his own rejected Ecclesiastical Courts Bills, and he was pleasurably surprised when Lord Cairns, the Lord Chancellor, approached him with a flattering promise of Government support – 'We shall make a good bill; and the amendments, as coming from you, will have great weight.'

Tait foresaw breakers ahead if he should give way to Shaftesbury on this issue. Following a series of controversial decisions by the Judicial Committee of the Privy Council, Anglo-Catholics were becoming increasingly defiant of the authority of a lay court in ecclesiastical cases. On the other hand, they professed to give special veneration and obedience to the bishops as the successors of the Apostles, and they would therefore put themselves completely in the wrong were they to defy the authority of a court presided over by a bishop. 'Hast thou appealed to Caesar? Unto Caesar shalt thou go.' However, Shaftesbury had behind him Cairns and the full force of the Government supporters. Tait realised that if he refused to accept this amendment he would be obliged to abandon the bill altogether. Faced with this alternative he gave way and accepted the substitution of a lay judge, thereby wrecking what little chance there was for the smooth working of the proposed jurisdiction. Having won his main point Shaftesbury could afford to be generous and agree to abandon various other subordinate amendments in order to help forward the swift passing of the bill, which became law on August 7th 1874.

Everything turned out exactly as Tait had feared and foreseen. The Act brought no credit to anyone except its victims, who qualified to rank as martyrs, though pigheaded ones. Anglo-Catholic clergy gloried in defying the authority of a secular judge and, to the dismay of the bishops, five of them actually went to jail for contempt of court. Shaftesbury had agreed to abandon an amendment depriving the diocesan bishop of his right to veto the hearing of any particular complaint. Using the loophole thus left open, in their anxiety to avoid further jail sentences the bishops vetoed nearly every hearing, thus making a laughing-stock of the Act. In his excess of anti-

Ritualist zeal Shaftesbury had been somewhat to blame for the introduction of this ill-advised measure; he was greatly to blame for its eventual failure.

What troubled him even more than the doings of the Ritualists were the findings of the new school of biblical criticism, a subject much in his mind at this period. As always, he showed himself to be less disturbed by the discoveries of scientists than by the discoveries of scholars. 'To science we can say in effect, "you are young, wait a little, all will be seen to be in harmony," ' he wrote on October 24th 1874. 'But what if these critics, full of learning, research, discriminating and puzzling power, declare that *you have not the word, the true text,* urge the number, variety, discrepancy of manuscripts, the errors, omissions, interpolations? This is puzzling, harassing, annoying. One prays that it can be answered though one is far from being able to do it. One has nothing ready for reply in public, and for reply to one's own mind.'

Where the Bible was concerned Shaftesbury was an undeviating Fundamentalist, horrified, for instance, by a speaker at a Bible Society meeting who suggested that the Gospels might be more highly inspired than the books of Chronicles. Shaftesbury cherished a particular attachment to the second book of Chronicles. 'The older I grow the more I love that book,' he had written as far back as 1854; 'it should be studied, weighed, and prayed over hour by hour by every man in public life.' Now, twenty years later, he expressed a wish that 'England would read our current history in the light of the second book of Chronicles,' presumably so that the English people might read, mark, learn and inwardly digest the fate of those rulers who did evil in the sight of the Lord. Shaftesbury could never solve the problems raised by the new school of biblical criticism because, looked at from a Fundamentalist stand-point, they were problems incapable of solution. Morally, his rigid religious views gave him an extraordinary strength; intellectually, they were a source of hidden, corroding weakness. A first at Oxford, he had a trained, scholarly mind which kept him uneasily aware that the findings of competent scholars could not be dismissed as untrue or conveniently ignored; yet this was exactly what he was trying to do. All would have been well if he could have brought himself to be more selective in his belief in the Bible, to admit, for instance, that the preface to St. John's Gospel was on an altogether higher level than the more bloodthirsty passages in the Old Testament. To this, however, he would never agree – 'It would be easier for me to give up revelation altogether, and reject the whole scriptures, than accept it on the terms, with the conditions, and the immediate and future limitations of it, imposed and exercised by "high criticism".' The Fundamentalist belief which made the Bible so dear to his heart could never be properly reconciled with the findings of his acute brain; as he himself had written, he could not discover a reply to his own mind.

Immediately after the deaths of Minny and Conty, Shaftesbury had risen to heights of virtual serenity; now he was back again in a pit of depression. Like so many elderly people, he believed himself to be either forgotten or deliberately passed over in favour of younger men. He complained, for instance, that he had not been asked to preside at the meeting of the Association for the Promotion of Social Science but that this honour had been given to Lord Rosebery, a man young enough to be his grandson and one 'whose public labours have been confined to a committee on racehorses.' Old and unwell, often in great pain from his chronic stomach trouble, he began to wonder whether he were in fact suffering from incipient cancer. His physical appearance too was changing. Reporting on one of his speeches, a Glasgow journalist gave a description of him very different from the picture of the young Ashley whose 'manly good looks' had been such an asset on a platform:

> Lord Shaftesbury is tall, gaunt, ungainly, with a nose almost as prominent as Mr. Disraeli's jaw, and a voice which seems to come from the other world. He has few of the physical advantages which commend an orator to his hearers.[5]

Bitter feelings within the family increased Shaftesbury's depression. We see Harriet only through her father-in-law's spectacles; it would have been interesting to have had her own version of the story. Though she is reputed to have been a difficult person she was surely not the monster that he made her out to be – 'she is morally what she would be politically were she Caligula, Commodus, or Caracalla.' Now she committed a supreme sin: 'my daughter-in-law, the wife of my eldest son, has joined herself to the Arch-Jesuit, Mr. Wilkinson* of Belgravia.' Harriet had turned Anglo-Catholic. Very soon, however, a still more remarkable conversion took place. On his return from his 1875 Scottish holiday, Shaftesbury was agreeably surprised to find Harriet very ready to be civil and friendly, whilst Anthony was, as always, loving and affectionate, showing himself most anxious to be on good terms with his father. No explanation of this change

* G. H. Wilkinson, of St. Peter's, Eaton Square, afterwards Bishop of Truro, later Bishop of St. Andrews, and Primus of the Scottish Episcopalian Church.

of front was ever forthcoming; but from now onwards all was to be peace and harmony. Several times Harriet is described as 'most amiable,' though still given to making excessive financial demands. Best of all, Shaftesbury could now see as much as he wished of Anthony's children. When he was at St. Giles they would come to him for Bible readings; and sometimes his favourite, Poppy, would join him on his early walk before breakfast.

In July 1875 trouble broke out again over Plimsoll. The Conservative Government had introduced a Merchant Shipping Bill embodying the reforms he had demanded. On July 22nd Disraeli announced that this bill would be abandoned for lack of parliamentary time. The scene which followed this announcement was long remembered in the House of Commons. Plimsoll lost his temper completely, shaking his fist at his fellow members and yelling, 'I am determined to unmask the villains who send sailors to their death.' He was allowed a week's grace in which to come to his senses and express regret for his behaviour. On the day after the uproar Shaftesbury wrote him a wise and tactful letter, commiserating with his feelings of disappointment but urging him nevertheless to apologise, advice which Plimsoll had the good sense to follow. 'Plimsoll modest, judicious, acceptable yesterday evening in his apology,' Shaftesbury wrote on July 30th, adding, however, the anxious query, 'Will he continue so? God give him counsel.'

The publicity given to Plimsoll's outrageous conduct coupled with the discreet apologies which Shaftesbury urged upon him served to arouse public feeling and force the Government to proceed with the Merchant Shipping Bill. As amended a year later, in 1876, this measure enforced the use of the load-line known as 'the Plimsoll Mark,' and gave to the Board of Trade stringent powers of inspection and regulation. The day of the coffin-ships was done.

When, in February 1876, Disraeli brought in the Royal Titles Bill allowing Queen Victoria to assume the title of Empress of India, Shaftesbury took it upon himself to head the opposition to the measure. As a non-party peer he felt he had a special duty to protest, thus making clear that the strong hostility felt towards the proposal was entirely non-political in origin. Nobody wanted the Queen to turn herself into an Empress, but nobody had the heart – or the nerve – to tell her so. The Queen herself, however, took special pains to discover Shaftesbury's opinion. He was summoned to Windsor, and sent, at her special bidding, to visit the Mausoleum at Frogmore with the Lord-in-waiting, Lord Torrington, who promptly seized the opportunity to ask for his views on the proposed title. 'They

are, that nothing could be worse,' came the uncompromising reply;
'there are many objections, and a main one is that it will make
Royalty ridiculous, which is more dangerous than to be hated.'
Torrington passed on this unpalatable statement to the Queen and
to Disraeli, getting himself rather unfairly scolded for his pains. On
April 3rd 1876 Shaftesbury moved an amendment to the Royal
Titles Bill proposing that an address be presented to the Queen
praying her Majesty not to take the title, Empress of India. He made
an extremely effective speech and succeeded in persuading the surprisingly large number of ninety-one peers to vote, though in a
minority, in favour of his amendment.

Like many old-fashioned aristocrats Shaftesbury was impervious to
the glamour of Royalty, and on occasion he could be positively off-
hand in his dealing with royal persons. In the summer of 1876, when
drinking the waters at Homburg, he was bidden to a dinner in honour
of the plump but popular Princess Mary Adelaide, Duchess of Teck,
mother of the future Queen Mary. Everyone had hoped to be able to
go home in good time; but after dinner was finished the Princess
made no move. Bored and exasperated, the guests sat on and on,
until at last Shaftesbury, who was in the place of honour next to the
Princess, rose to his feet, bade her a brief goodnight, and walked
out of the room, to the horror of the equerry but to the vast delight
of the rest of the company.

Gladstone, like Shaftesbury, had spoken and voted against the
Royal Titles Bill. The two men were not often to be found in agreement, but now they were to work together in a campaign of protest
against Turkish atrocities in Bulgaria. Gladstone, writes Magnus,
'took his stand squarely on the moral issue,'[6] a point of view very
congenial to Shaftesbury. 'The Opposition are going to work the
atrocities as a party question, and there is to be a great public
meeting with all the most red-hot politicians on the platform and of
course Lord Shaftesbury in the chair,' Disraeli wrote to Queen
Victoria on July 14th 1876, adding in his most waspish manner,
'Lord Shaftesbury is always ready to place philanthropy at the aid
of faction, as he did in the Royal Titles Bill.'[7]

When questions arose concerning the Turkish Empire, the thought
of the return of the Jews to Palestine was never far from Shaftesbury's
mind. 'When you are cutting down your next tree,' he wrote to
Gladstone, 'imagine you are cutting down that vast incubus to humanity, the dominion of the Turk, in whose absence from the Holy Land
lies the renewed presence of the Israelites in it.'[8] Doing his best to
interpret some of the more obscure biblical prophecies, he came to

the conclusion that 'the mystic Euphrates' would dry up on or about
January 1877 and that this event would coincide with the collapse
of the Turkish Empire. Meanwhile he joined whole-heartedly in
Gladstone's campaign, taking the chair at mass meetings both in
London and Glasgow, and writing to *The Times* to appeal for funds.

On April 28th 1877 Shaftesbury celebrated his seventy-sixth
birthday; but the amount of work he undertook would have taxed
a man in the prime of life. He still had strength and spirit to take
up new causes; the anti-vivisection campaign, the suppression of
child prostitution, the improvement of working conditions in the
cotton mills of India. Though he complained more and more frequently of loss of memory, increasing deafness, and general physical
and mental decay, he never took steps to lessen these troubles by
lightening his burden of work. Angered by what he took to be a lack
of public appreciation, he might resolve 'to bury myself in the dens
and back-slums of London, my first and fitting career, and appear
very little, if at all, in the House of Lords, platforms and public
assemblies'; his resolution was, of course, short-lived. Inevitably
the strain told on him; inevitably the bitter, self-righteous streak in
his character rose again to the surface, no longer softened and subdued by Minny's gentle good sense. As long ago he had declared
himself to be totally free from reproach in all his dealings with his
father, so now on May 2nd 1877, looking back over his long life,
he wrote, 'Against Thee only have I sinned – no, never once against
man.' A year later he repeated and enlarged on that amazing statement, at once so complacent and so spiritually arrogant:

> Love for Christ must necessarily include love for the human race,
> their temporal and, unquestionably, their eternal interests. Have
> I fallen short of this great command? . . . 'Against Thee only have
> I sinned,' and in my infirmity, do sin. Man, collectively, individu-
> ally, I bless Thee O Lord, has no account against me.

Overworked, over-strained, and therefore over-anxious, Shaftesbury was now faced with the ordeal of giving evidence before yet
another Select Committee on the Lunacy Laws. His work on behalf
of lunatics remains one of the least known, though one of the most
important, of his achievements. He himself wrote, 'Beyond the circle
of my own Commissioners and the lunatics that I visit, not a soul,
in great or small life, not even my associates in my works of philanthropy, has any notion of the years of toil and care that, under God,
I have bestowed on this melancholy and awful question.' For some

time he had been anxious to see this great work rounded off by an Act consolidating the lunacy laws. 'One work remains, great and wearisome, the consolidation of the lunacy laws,' he had written on July 3rd 1876. 'Lunacy was my first duty; let me make it my last.' Already he had spoken to the Conservative Home Secretary, R. A. Cross, urging the necessity for such a measure. The Select Committee of 1877 was not, however, concerned with consolidation. In spite of the findings of Walpole's Committee the public had remained convinced that it was possible if not easy to shut up a sane person as a lunatic. The question was taken up in the House of Commons by Thomas Dillwyn, who pressed for the abolition of private asylums and the appointment of a paid chairman of the Lunacy Commission in place of Shaftesbury, whom he regarded as old and incompetent. The result of this agitation was the appointment of a Select Committee to enquire into the working of lunacy law 'so far as regards the security afforded by it against violations of personal liberty,' with Dillwyn himself as chairman.

The thought of his examination before this Committee caused Shaftesbury great and natural perturbation. He saw himself standing up as the champion of the Lunacy Commissioners, their methods and achievements, and he feared that he would prove unequal to the task. An old man now, he was pitiably alarmed lest a failure of memory might cause him to look a fool. 'Shall fifty years of toil, anxiety and prayer, crowned by marvellous and unlooked-for success, bring me in the end only sorrow and disgrace?' he asked himself anxiously. Though the Committee was appointed in February, as the last witness he was not called until July. For months he fretted and agonised, 'never so weighed down and never so continuously unwell in all my life, oftentimes with sensations as though I should drop dead.'

When at last 'the hour of trial' arrived it ended not in disgrace but in triumph. The Select Committee treated him with all the respect and deference due to the greatest living authority on lunacy practice and reform. No hint of fading memory clouded his evidence; again and again he politely but firmly corrected his questioners on points of law or fact. Only once did he allow himself to be corrected, when, in a slightly comic passage of arms, a Scottish member of the Committee took him to task for remarking that the Scots were not a race remarkable for temperance.

Shaftesbury disliked the proposal to increase the number of Commissioners, believing that the existing small Commission had worked so well because 'we have fallen into each other's habits.'

The substance of his evidence was very much what it had been in 1859 before Stanhope's Committee, except on one important point. Then he had pressed for the abolition of private asylums; now he believed them to be so much improved that he would have them retained. He still thought it essential that lunatics should be admitted for treatment as soon as possible, and he was therefore irrevocably opposed to the suggestion that a magistrate's signature should be required for every certificate of lunacy, believing that this addition would cause unnecessary delay and unwelcome publicity. He claimed to be almost the only person still alive who could speak with personal knowledge of the conditions existing before the appointment of the Lunacy Commission, 'a state of things such as would pass all belief.' Whatever might have been true in those bad old days, he believed that under the beneficient control of the Commissioners it was all but impossible for a sane person to be wrongfully confined in an asylum. In their Report the members of the Select Committee followed Shaftesbury's evidence on all points. They refused to admit the necessity for a magistrate's signature, they approved the continuing existence of private asylums, and they declared that 'allegations of *mala fides* or serious abuses could not be substantiated.' Summing up the general position, they wrote, 'the comparatively trifling nature of the abuses alleged present a remarkable contrast to the horrible cruelty, apathy and indifference of half a century earlier.' Shaftesbury and his Lunacy Commissioners had won at least a temporary victory.

In December 1877 Shaftesbury found himself involved, or rather involved himself, in a quarrel with the highly respectable and respected Society for the Propagation of Christian Knowldege. In 1876 the S.P.C.K. had published *A Manual of Geology* described by Shaftesbury as a book 'of a most noxious character.' In vain had he sent a letter of protest to the Bishop of London – 'his Lordship's occupations did not permit him even to acknowledge its receipt.' Next year the S.P.C.K. added to their offence by publishing a more important book, *The Argument from Prophecy*, by Brownlow Maitland, attacking the already obsolescent method of proving the inspiration of the Bible by pointing to the literal fulfilment of biblical prophecies. This time Shaftesbury addressed his protest to the Archbishop of Canterbury, ending his six-page letter by removing his name from the list of S.P.C.K. members.[9] Though Tait asked him to withdraw his resignation he refused to do so and instead entered upon what Hodder describes as 'a long paper warfare' in which he continued to maintain extreme Fundamentalist views unacceptable even to his fellow-Evangelicals. In vain did Haldane beg him to retreat from this untenable position; his only reaction was to write Haldane down as 'waxed cold in his fervour and affection.' This difference of opinion was the beginning of a sad rift between the two old friends. 'Who is with me? Who? positively, I know not,' Shaftesbury asked himself on February 16th 1878. For once he was justified in supposing himself forsaken; in his unyielding Fundamentalism he now stood alone.

The outbreak of the second Afghan War was the cause of a more serious quarrel with Haldane. The British invasion of Afghanistan in the autumn of 1879 was denounced by Gladstone with what Shaftesbury described as 'a verbosity to exhaust a whole dictionary,' and stigmatised more succinctly by Shaftesbury himself as 'this calamity, and what is worse, this great sin.'[10] Haldane, who was of the opposite opinion, wrote in *The Record* strongly supporting the war. Shaftesbury was scandalised that an Evangelical paper should declare itself in favour of a policy of aggression, and he was also deeply hurt by what he believed to be Haldane's double-faced attitude:

> The only friend that I had remaining is not to be trusted. At the very time he was writing articles in defence of the war he was congratulating me on the 'noble opportunity' I had by the calling of Parliament to express my hatred of it. At the moment he was publicly censuring my letter for denouncing the war as a sin he was privately writing to me that he agreed with every word of it.

A week or so later he was writing of this old and trusted friend, 'cordially and freely do I forgive that feeble and double-faced man . . . but I can never trust him again or believe that he is sincere in anything.'

Haldane's defection, if defection it indeed was, left Shaftesbury with 'no one to speak to, no one to aid, no one to sympathise.' So much the more did he feel the loss of Minny, though he tried hard to transmute his grief into 'a staid deep sorrow, a calm and solemn reminiscence, desirable and healthy to the soul.' On December 18th, a day when he had written particularly bitterly about Haldane, he sought comfort in his loneliness by making a list of 'those noble, ardent, trustworthy, precious friends' on whom he could rely for help and sympathy in his philanthropic concerns. Shaftesbury had always been an isolated figure. Those who shared his personal memories and upbringing did not share his interests; those who shared his interests did not fit into the background of his private life. So now his list of friends – George Holland, Joseph Gent, T. B. Smithies and the like – included some men of money and standing but none from his own social class. A reader of the later diaries is struck by the absence of aristocratic names. After the death of his old friend the Duchess of Argyll he seems to have had no personal friends even among those Evangelical aristocrats, men such as Lord Kinnaird, with whom he sat on various committees and worked for such cases as Ragged Schools. The only exception seems to have been his brother-in-law, William Cowper-Temple, in 1880 created Lord Mount-Temple, and possibly the Burns of Castle Wemyss. In the social climate of that age it cannot have been good for Shaftesbury to associate almost entirely with people who could never forget that he was an earl.

In April 1880, following a General Election, Disraeli resigned and Gladstone once again became Prime Minister. 'Nothing will surpass the ignorance, the meanness, and the unpatriotic policy of the new holders of office,' Shaftesbury wrote on April 2nd, in the same entry also complaining of Disraeli's 'sinister influence over a bulrush Cabinet.' He was particularly perturbed when the well-known atheist, Charles Bradlaugh, elected as member for Northampton, refused to take the oath demanded of all members of Parliament because he would not pronounce the words 'so help me God.' So strongly did Shaftesbury feel about this matter that he declined Lord Granville's invitation to an official dinner – 'I durst not accept an official invitation from a Cabinet that contained Bright and Chamberlain and one of whose principal ministerial candidates was Bradlaugh.'

Shaftesbury had by now become a world-famous figure, treated on every hand with a respect which amounted almost to reverence, yet still he persisted in believing himself to be slighted and neglected. If anything could have persuaded him out of this fixed conviction it would have been the reception accorded him at a gathering held in the Guildhall on April 28th 1881 in celebration of his eightieth birthday. Among the many laudatory speeches was a particularly moving one by W. E. Forster, now Irish Secretary. Hodder glowingly describes the costermongers, flower-girls, and Ragged School children waiting outside to greet the arrival of their friend and benefactor, the immense crowd in the hall itself, the open expressions of affection, the tempests of applause when Shaftesbury rose to return thanks for an address and presentation made to him. His own account was less enthusiastic. He noted sourly that no literary or scientific men attended, no ecclesiastical dignitaries, no Conservatives of any importance – and he added that he had been hurt by the coldness of the excuses for non-attendance. The gathering had in fact been a representative one; and many of the celebrities who were unable to be present had sent him warm and touching birthday greetings. There was no truth at all in his bitter comment, 'I may be loved in Bethnal Green but I am despised in Belgravia.' By this time, however, his determination to see himself as the most disliked and unappreciated of men amounted almost to persecution mania.

Chapter 22

THE END

Hodder describes Shaftesbury's old age with rather pompous piety:

> As the outward man began to perish, the inward man was renewed
> day by day, and though the suppleness, strength and activity of the
> body began to fail, the well-exercised soul grew stronger. Beautiful
> it is, on a calm summer's evening, when the work of the day is
> nearly done, to watch the sun lingering in the heavens and trans-
> forming everything by its golden rays, and not less beautiful is
> it to gaze upon a saintly life when 'at evening-tide it is
> light'.[1]

There was in fact not much of the atmosphere of a calm summer
evening about Shaftesbury's old age; the years remaining to him
were not happy ones. Certainly his faith never failed; but he was
troubled about many things, and the older he grew, the more did
these troubles weigh upon his spirit. His bodily woes also increased,
until each day became a battle against deafness, weakness, discomfort and, all too often, acute pain. The thought of making a
speech or attending an official function was to him a nightmare.

Yet still Shaftesbury worked on. At the age of eighty he 'perambu-
lated' the London slums as he had done in his youth. On a blazingly
hot day in July 1881 he tramped in company with a sanitary inspector
through the worst parts of Whitechapel, visiting stinking alleys and
houses which he described as 'degraded pig-sties, dwellings not good
enough for dust-bins.' He had come to regard Housing as the most
important of all social questions. In a conversation with Cecil's
friend, Albert Grey, afterwards seventh Earl Grey and Governor-
General of Canada, he stressed the importance of the family as the
basic social unit and declared that 'the first thing we have to do is
to busy ourselves about the homes of the poor.'[2] He wrote two long
articles on the subject of Housing, and as late as 1884 spoke in the

House of Lords in support of Lord Salisbury's motion for a Royal Commission to enquire into the Housing problem, later giving evidence himself before that Commission.

Shaftesbury's interest in slum-dwellers, his concern with what he described as 'a lower depth to which we have to descend, not by fits and starts, but regularly and systematically,'[3] should have caused him to welcome the appearance of William Booth's Salvation Army, dedicated to the care and evangelisation of outcasts sunk beyond the reach of conventional churches and charities. Shaftesbury first refers to the Salvation Army on September 17th 1879, when he quotes Gamaliel's advice to the Sanhedrin, 'Refrain from these men and let them alone, for if this counsel or this work be of man it will come to naught, but if it be of God ye cannot overthrow it.' Three years later he was so convinced of the uncelestial origin of the Salvation Army that he described the movement as 'anti-Christian and most perilous.' He, who had once urged Christians to be 'abnormal, eccentric, wild, extravagant, but by every means we must preach Christ to the people,' now complained of 'doings . . . as extravagant and in expression as offensive, as any that ever disgraced the wildest fanaticism.' He pointed to the many missions 'which conduct their operations with abundant zeal and yet with modesty and sobriety.'[4] Maybe at the bottom of his heart there lurked a little jealousy towards the flamboyant Salvation Army which was stealing the publicity, and perhaps also the converts, away from those modest and sober missions to which so much of his own time and energy had been devoted.

In April 1881 Gladstone brought in his Irish Land Bill. Though Shaftesbury feared that this measure would endanger the sacrosanct rights of property not only in Ireland but in England also, he did not join whole-heartedly in the opposition to it but devoted himself to the secondary issue of preventing a serious clash between the two Houses of Parliament. He feared that the Bill would be uselessly opposed by the Conservative peers, 'who, as their habit is, do foolish things in a foolish way.' However, to quote his own words, 'God sent wisdom into the hearts of the Conservative leaders and they accepted the Commons' amendment.' When the Bill became law he praised Gladstone's moderation and dignity, and commented, as so often before, 'strange to say, was rejoiced in the safety of a pernicious measure.'

A year later, in February 1882, the Conservative peers acted as irresponsibly as Shaftesbury had feared by voting for an enquiry into the working of this Land Act. 'The issue last night was most serious,' Shaftesbury wrote to Gladstone on February 25th. 'The whole House of Lords must bear the responsibility; but I firmly believe that no one but Lord Salisbury desired such a result.'[5] Gladstone's Private Secretary, Edward Hamilton, noted with great satisfaction that 'even Lord Shaftesbury wrote to say he was horrified at Lord Salisbury's wilfulness.'[6] Nevertheless, the Land Act had not brought peace to Ireland. In May, Lord Frederick Cavendish, the newly appointed Irish Secretary, was murdered in Phoenix Park. Shaftesbury grieved especially for Lord Frederick's good and gallant wife, Lucy, and a month later he wrote bitterly, 'the condition of Ireland is murder made easy.'

Two other deaths this summer of 1882 much saddened Shaftesbury. In spite of their recent differences he mourned for Haldane, who died on July 19th, as for the dearest of his friends. In September came the death of Pusey – 'intensely and fearfully as I differed from him on many points of unspeakable importance,' Shaftesbury wrote, 'I could not but love the man.'

In 1881, 1882, and again in 1883, Shaftesbury as usual spent part of the summer in Scotland, but he was beginning to find such holidays too exhausting. He was happiest now at St. Giles, a place which could at last be described as a model estate, though not a very profitable one. When on a visit there a city missionary chanced to remark, 'I have a friend who prefers to be called a just rather than a good landlord because the term "just" implies a regard for the interest of both sides.' 'Your friend has the advantage,' Shaftesbury retorted; 'the scales are in his own hands and, depend upon it, they go down thump in his own interest.' True to the principle of putting his people's interests above his own, Shaftesbury had refused to follow the prevailing trend towards heavily stocked covers and strict preservation of game, and he had spent much more than he could afford in efforts to see his tenants properly housed. It was his delight to stroll through the village, to be greeted familiarly by the small children as 'Lord Shaffy,' and to note with pleasure the tidy cottages, each with its pump, its apricot tree, its pigsty and its quarter-acre allotment. Cottages with a parlour, kitchen and three bedrooms were let at the tiny rent of a shilling a week. Not surprisingly, the people appeared contented and well-behaved, and, to Shaftesbury's satisfaction, they were regular in their church going. 'The old place looks beautiful and happy,' he noted cheerfully on December 5th 1883. Yet, as he looked at his inheritance, he still feared for the future, not now because of his successor – he believed Anthony to be at last 'really doing good and rendering service in his generation' – but

because of the inevitable decay of the aristocratic order of society
in which he believed so profoundly. What he described as 'the mitigated feudal principle' was vanishing; 'the forthcoming land laws
will speedily demolish the great estates, and scatter the old families
to the winds, with all the tradition, feelings, habits and affections of
many generations.'

Après moi le déluge, but meanwhile life at St. Giles was pleasant to
Shaftesbury. The day started with a walk down to the lake. Behind
the library door he kept a bag full of bits of bread so that he might
always have a crust ready to feed to the ducks. Then, before breakfast,
came family prayers, attended by a long string of servants. Thirty
years afterwards one of Anthony's children still remembered with
pleasure her grandfather's beautiful reading of Bible passages. At the
end of prayers he invariably shut the book with a great bang, whereupon all the family dogs jumped up and barked loudly. Dogs were
everywhere, beside his desk as he sat writing, on either side of his
chair at dinner. In Minny's day pugs had been popular; now collies
were the favoured breed.

Shaftesbury's great pleasure was to fill the huge, ramshackle
mansion with his grandchildren. He loved to gather them round him
for a Bible lesson, or to watch as they rode the costers' donkey,
played at cricket or battledore and shuttlecock, and on wet days
scampered down the long corridors in exciting games of 'robbers' or
'prisoners.' To these children their grandfather was a magnificent,
rather melancholy figure possessed of an unexpected stock of funny
stories. Suddenly and unexpectedly, with a twinkle in his rather
remote blue eyes, he would produce some unsophisticated joke which
doubled them up in fits of laughter. They were well aware that this
grandparent was a famous man, known the world over for his work
on behalf of the poor and helpless. On one occasion they serenaded
him with some doggerel written for them by their Uncle Cecil and
sung to the tune of *God Bless the Prince of Wales:*

> God bless the Earl of Shaftesbury
>   For all the good he's done
> And bless the name we're proud to claim –
>   We're Ashleys, every one.

The splendid series of state-rooms hung with family portraits and
magnificent with gold silk wallpaper and upholstery were seldom
put to any use. Family life centred on the inner 'stone-hall' or on the
library, a long, book-lined room overlooking the lake. On Sunday

evenings the whole household and such villagers as cared to attend
gathered to sing hymns in the outer hall, where Minny had placed
the huge bust of Shaftesbury given her by the cotton operatives. Every
night, Sunday and weekdays alike, Shaftesbury never failed to have
a few minutes' conversation with Mrs. Toomer, once the children's
nurse and now housekeeper, before bidding her an affectionate
goodnight. His own 'den' was an unremarkable room at the back of
the house, its only attraction being a lovely view of the gardens
and lake. Here he had both a writing-desk and his narrow iron
bedstead covered with a patch-work quilt made for him by
Ragged School children. Of comfort there was very little; of luxury,
none.

One trouble marred the happiness of life at St. Giles, 'the financial
difficulties which crowd upon me like an armed host.' In 1882
Shaftesbury was driven to ask for a loan from his rich friend, George
Williams, who generously pressed the money upon him as a gift.
Nevertheless his commitments were so heavy that within a week he
was again complaining of debts encroaching upon him every hour.
Relief was to come only at the very end of his life, when, in April
1885, a group of friends sent him a cheque for £4500, accompanying
it with a letter which he described as 'a model of kindness, feeling,
and good taste.'

Attendance at the House of Lords was becoming more and more of
a trial to him; yet he still persisted, though forced to admit that he
often found it difficult to hear any word of the debate, so greatly
had his deafness increased. When, in February 1884, Gladstone
introduced his Reform Bill, Shaftesbury was, as so often before,
chiefly concerned to see that the Lords should not risk 'if not immediately their existence, certainly all their influence and power,' in a
battle they could not win. At the request of Rosebery, whom he
recognised as a coming man, he made a speech urging moderation
and compromise, which, though it displeased Salisbury and the
extreme Conservatives, earned him much praise elsewhere. Finally
it was proposed that a Re-distribution of Seats Bill should accompany the Reform Bill; and on these terms the Lords agreed to withdraw their opposition, much to Shaftesbury's relief.

Forced for once to give way to physical weakness, Shaftesbury
was unable to attend the closing stages of the debates on the Reform
Bill. With him mental depression and physical pain had now reached
an almost intolerable pitch of intensity. 'Yesterday a day of remarkable depression and pain,' 'a dreadful day of depression and pain',
'yesterday for pain and depression almost the worst day I ever had,'

'much lassitude and extreme pain' – so run the mournful, monotonous
entries. When the pain was acute he could only find relief by lying
flat on his back; every ten minutes or so he would break off his
occupation and rest until he was sufficiently recovered to be able to
continue. His reasons for declining a Sunday engagement, presumably one which did not conflict with his sabbatarian principles,
show how great was the pressure upon his time, his spirits, and his
powers of physical endurance:

> In the first place, Sunday is the only day I have to myself.
> Secondly, I am so deaf that I am a bore in society.
> Thirdly, I may be the whole while in great pain.[7]

Very seldom, however, did he thus excuse himself. Part of his
reluctance to refuse engagements arose from the strange conviction
that when he pleaded ill-health people believed him to be merely
malingering – 'sent my sorrowful and yet very true excuses, which of
course nobody believed.' Again and again this unhappy delusion
returned to trouble him. In April 1884, however, he was so unwell
that he was obliged to cease all work and take a short holiday at
Folkestone. The place seemed to suit him well, for he returned in
renewed health and spirits to face his last great battle over the
lunacy laws.

The findings of the 1877 Select Committee had not exorcised the
spectre of a sane person wrongfully incarcerated in an asylum. In
1884 the matter came to a head with the publicity attaching to
the case of the lady whom Shaftesbury referred to as 'that awful
woman, Mrs. Weldon.' Georgina Weldon was an eccentric who
believed that her pug dog had a soul and that the spirit of her dead
mother had entered her pet rabbit. Her husband tried to have her
shut up in an asylum, whereupon Mrs. Weldon rented Covent Garden
Opera House for a meeting to publicise her grievances, and started
a series of legal actions, including one against Shaftesbury and the
Lunacy Commissioners. Since the days of Waters and Lewer Shaftesbury had held law suits in peculiar abhorrence. This time he reported
that 'he got through it all very easily'; even so, the necessity to
appear in court added greatly to the strain upon his overtaxed
nerves and spirits.

On May 5th 1884 Shaftesbury spoke in the House of Lords against
a motion declaring the lunacy laws to be unsatisfactory and a danger
to the liberty of the subject. Though his speech was well received,
the motion passed both Houses, leaving the way clear for the intro-

duction by the Lord Chancellor, Selborne,* of a Lunacy Law Amendment Bill. All autumn Shaftesbury was too ailing to deal with any business or even to attend Church on a Sunday. By Christmas he was sufficiently recovered to travel down to St. Giles, where on January 16th he was thrown into great perturbation by a summons to London to discuss the terms of Selborne's Bill. Since he was not well enough to travel he was sent a draft of the proposed measure. Immediately he set about making corrections and annotations, and embarked on a correspondence with Selborne, which proved quite fruitless since neither side was prepared to give way.

On February 5th 1885, the day when Shaftesbury was at last able to return to London, the news of the fall of Khartoum and General Gordon's murder reached England. Old, ill, and occupied with his own troubles, Shaftesbury did not join in the storm of execration which now fell on Gladstone's head. He had considerable sympathy with Gladstone's unwarlike policy, and he only deplored the despatch of more British troops to the Sudan, an action forced on Gladstone by public outcry. A letter written on April 27th to Benson, who had succeeded Tait as Archbishop of Canterbury, shows Shaftesbury's undying hatred of war, and in particular of what would now be called an imperialistic war:

> The prayers must be for *peace, peace, peace.* There must be no mention of victory in conflict, or defeat of our enemies. The prayer must simply be that war be averted where it seems to be near, as with Russia; or that it should be quelled as in Africa, that peace be restored, and our armies speedily brought back in health and safety.[8]

On March 24th Shaftesbury recorded, 'went to the Lunacy Board for the last time.' He had resigned from the chairmanship of the Lunacy Commission, feeling himself in honour bound not to oppose a measure sponsored by the Lord Chancellor while continuing to hold office under that official, even though the office was an unpaid one. Selborne wrote immediately begging him to remain at least until the Lunacy Bill had been proposed and printed. Shaftesbury could not refuse such a request, although privately he took a wicked delight in quoting Disraeli's description of Selborne as 'the seraphic humbug.' When, however, the Bill came before Parliament, Shaftesbury found himself with no alternative but to resign because of his immovable objection to the clause which made it compulsory for a

* In 1872 Roundell Palmer had been created Earl of Selborne.

certificate of lunacy to be signed by a judge or a magistrate. On April 27th the Bill passed its second reading in the Lords, but it was not destined to become law. On June 9th the Liberal Government fell; the Bill quietly disappeared; and Shaftesbury resumed his old place as Chairman of the Lunacy Commission. After all, he was not to be thwarted of his wish to die in harness.

May 1885 was a month filled with meetings and speeches and with the business of the allotment of the fifty thousand pounds left to Shaftesbury by a Mrs. Douglas to divide as he thought best among deserving charities. Not till May 22nd was he free to go down to St. Giles, where, on Sunday May 24th, he enjoyed 'a *noble* day' reading the lessons at Morning Prayer and staying to receive Communion. Next Sunday, though suffering from 'lassitude so great that it was almost faintness,' he was well enough to repeat this programme and, a day or two later, to drive out to his old haunts at Brockington. On his wedding anniversary his thoughts naturally turned to 'my blessed, beloved, precious Minny.' Fourteen years had not served to blunt his sorrow; but he could now say, with thankfulness and resignation, 'she is in eternal safety and bliss; that is enough.'

On July 6th, under the title, *The Maiden Tribute of Modern Babylon,* the first of a series of articles by W. T. Stead appeared in *The Pall Mall Gazette* exposing some of the worst scandals of child prostitution. Shaftesbury was so shocked by these sensational revelations that, although too unwell even to write an entry in his diary, he dragged himself to the Home Office to discuss the matter with the Home Secretary, and the next night went down to the House of Lords for half-an-hour's talk on the same subject with Lord Salisbury. It was fitting that his very last effort in the service of oppressed humanity should have been made on behalf of these outraged and suffering children.

On July 25th Shaftesbury left London for Folkestone, hoping to benefit once again from the sea air. At first he rallied slightly; then it became clear, without shadow of doubt, that he was dying. Now, at the very end, his pain mercifully ceased, leaving him to undisturbed enjoyment of the visits of the many friends who came to bid him goodbye. To them he spoke very simply of the approach of death and of the comfort he found in his Christian faith. Sadly he resigned himself to the fact that he was too ill to be moved to his own home. There, however, he was determined that in the end he would be. Long ago he had written that, after death, 'my own desire would be to lie out on the naked hills.' Now, when one of the family, thinking that the proposed honour might give him pleasure, read him a letter

from the Dean of Westminster offering burial in the Abbey, his
answer came faint but firm: 'no – St. Giles, St. Giles.'

The old man lay waiting for death in a pleasant room looking out
over grass and trees and a distant view of the sea. His children
gathered round; Vea came from Ireland to take charge of the nursing
and to act as his secretary, since to the very end he insisted that all
letters must be punctually answered. W. E. Forster, who was himself
dying, was at pains to dictate a message saying how much he owed
to Shaftesbury's example in the conduct of public life. Almost
the last letter of all came from Edwin Chadwick. Every day Shaftesbury would name the passages from the Bible which he wished to
have read to him, always including the twenty-third psalm. The
autumn sun was streaming into the room when he died very quietly
in the early afternoon of October 1st. He had always dreaded death
in the dark.

Although in accordance with his own wish Shaftesbury was to be
buried at St. Giles, the nation was determined to honour him with a
funeral service in Westminster Abbey. From early morning on
October 8th, the day when this service was to take place, the pave-
ments along the route between Grosvenor Square and Westminster
were thronged with poor people, costermongers, flower-girls, boot-
blacks, crossing-sweepers, factory-hands and the like, waiting patiently for hours in order to catch a brief sight of the coffin as it passed
by. Each one of them, however ragged and poverty-stricken, was
wearing something black, even if only a ribbon or a scrap of old
material pinned on in token of mourning. These people mourned a
man who had fought all his life on their behalf, battling tirelessly
against indolence, ignorance and callousness in high places. This
they well knew, but they could not know that his hardest battle
had been with himself.

Shaftesbury was a personality flawed both by nature and by circumstance. He had the misfortune to be born with, as it were, a
mental skin too few; all his feelings were abnormally intense. Though
he had many saintly qualities he totally lacked the saint's serenity.
He could never achieve the detachment which marks the greatest
saints and also, some say, the most successful social workers. The
sight of a hungry, ill-treated child would reduce him to tears; he was
literally 'tortured,' to use his own word, by the thought of suffering.
Over-sensitive people often escape from the contemplation of pain
which is to them unendurable by turning their backs upon the un-

pleasant things in life, in some cases even opting out of responsibility for life altogether. Not so Shaftesbury; in the service of the poor he forced himself to encounter the most revolting forms of cruelty, disease, dirt and beastliness. In his determination to face up to facts which were to him almost intolerable lay his real heroism, maybe also his real saintliness.

Not only was Shaftesbury born hypersensitive; he was also born with an abnormal tendency towards depression. To write him down definitely as manic-depressive would be to stretch the existing evidence too far. Depression is one of the most common mental troubles; few indeed are the persons who have never experienced it. His diaries, however, show Shaftesbury's bouts of depression to have been unusually frequent and intense, seriously affecting his judgement and grossly distorting his view of his fellow men. Only those who have known similar depths of depression can fully realise the effort he must have made not to give way entirely beneath this appalling weight which so often fell upon him.

To these difficulties of natural temperament must be added others which had their origin in the circumstances of Shaftesbury's early years. It is usually believed that the roots of most psychological troubles are to be found either in an unhappy childhood or in an unsatisfactory sex-life. Shaftesbury was remarkably happy in his marriage, therefore presumably in his sex-life also. He had, however, endured a miserable childhood which had left him deficient in self-confidence and therefore over-assertive, greedy for the praise and affection which his parents had never given him, touchy, self-questioning, mistrustful, certain that everyone's hand was against him. A man of this type was ill-equipped for either parliamentary or philanthropic activities. Working against the grain of his own character, Shaftesbury trained himself in patience, politeness and tact, and in the very necessary art of concealing the passionate feelings which he allowed to overflow in the pages of his diary. Time and again, when men such as Oastler or Chadwick were wasting their energies in impotent rage, he remained outwardly cool and calm, and therefore master of the situation.

Shaftesbury himself would have described his achievement of self-mastery as a victory of grace over nature. With him religion was the first, and by far the most important thing in life; he found in it a power which enabled him to work on to the end in the face of difficulties, sorrow, and disappointment. Yet although religion may have been the cure, it was also a cause, and perhaps the most important cause, of his psychological troubles. Religion has three aspects, mystical, moral, and intellectual; those who ignore or over-stress any one of the three do so at their peril. Shaftesbury not merely neglected but flatly denied the value of intellect in religion – 'Satan rules in the intellect, God in the heart of man.' In a man of his intellectual ability the result was inevitably a sense of intolerable tension, an unresolved contradiction lying at the very heart of his personality.

A man so constituted might be forgiven if he made little or nothing of his life. Humanly speaking he could hardly be expected to achieve anything remarkable either for himself or for his fellow men. Though Shaftesbury had many and great gifts he also had faults which might have rendered those gifts useless. Both by temperament and by circumstance he seemed destined at best to a small success, at worst to complete failure. No man has in fact ever done more to lessen the extent of human misery or to add to the sum total of human happiness.

NOTES AND SOURCE REFERENCES

Abbreviations used

RA   Royal Archives, Windsor Castle
NRA   National Register of Archives
BM   British Museum
UCL   University College Library

Chapter 1

EARLY YEARS

1 Edwin Hodder, *The Life and Work of the Seventh Earl of Shaftesbury K.G.* (Cassell, 1887), Vol. I, pp. 41–42
2 Ibid., Vol. I, p. 39
3 NRA/SHA/MIS/62–5
4 Hodder, op. cit., Vol. I, p. 48
5 *Autobiography of Isaac Williams,* edited by G. Prevost (Longmans, 1893), p. 6
6 *Harrow School* Ed Laborde
7 For all following quotations from letters from Ashley, George Howard and Lady Morpeth see Castle Howard Papers
8 Barbara Blackburn, *Noble Earl* (Home and Van Thal, 1949), p. 24
9 *Journal of the Hon. Henry Fox,* edited by the Earl of Ilchester (Thornton Butterworth, 1923), p. 34
10 Ibid., p. 116

Chapter 2

THE YOUNG ARISTOCRAT

1 *Elizabeth, Lady Holland, to her Son, 1821–1845,* edited by the Earl of Ilchester (Murray, 1946), p. 18
2 For all letters to Lady Morpeth see Castle Howard Papers

3 J. L. and Barbara Hammond, *Lord Shaftesbury* (Constable, 1923), p. 124

4 *Elizabeth, Lady Holland, to her Son*, op. cit., p. 95

5 Castle Howard Papers

6 *Letters of Harriet, Countess Granville 1810–1845*, edited by the Hon. E. Leveson Gower (Longmans, 1894), Vol. I, p. 400

7 Castle Howard Papers

8 Ibid.

9 Leveson Gower, op. cit., Vol. I, p. 397

10 Hodder, op. cit., Vol. I, p. 65

Chapter 3

REFORM OF LUNACY LAWS AND PRACTICE

1 Kathleen Jones, *Lunacy, Law and Conscience* (Routledge & Kegan Paul, 1958), p. 135

2 Ibid., p. 80

3 Ibid., p. 82

4 Hodder, op. cit., Vol. I, p. 97

5 *Speeches of the Earl of Shaftesbury, K.G.* (Chapman & Hall, 1868), p. 144

6 Hodder, op. cit., Vol. I, p. 75

7 *The Correspondence of Charles Arbuthnot*, edited by A. Aspinall (Royal Historical Society, 1941), p. 119

8 Hodder, op. cit., Vol. I, p. 82

9 Ibid., Vol. III, p. 370

10 *Speeches of the Earl of Shaftesbury, K.G.*, op. cit., p. 369

11 *Elizabeth, Lady Holland, to her Son*, op. cit., p. 99

Chapter 4

LOVE AND MARRIAGE

1 BM/Peel Papers, 40400, f. 173

2 BM/Peel Papers, 40401, f. 20

3 David Cecil, *The Young Melbourne* (Constable, 1939), p. 37

4 Hampshire County Archives. Broadlands Papers 27/M/60

5 *Letters of Harriet, Countess Granville 1810–1845*, op. cit., Vol. II, pp. 42–43

6 Mabell, Countess of Airlie, *Lady Palmerston and her Times* (Hodder & Stoughton, 1922), Vol. I, p. 148

7 Leconfield and Gore, *Three Howard Sisters* (Murray 1955), p. 124

8 *Letters of Harriet, Countess Granville 1810–1845*, op. cit., Vol. II, p. 59

9 *The Lieven-Palmerston Correspondence, 1828–1856*, translated and edited by Lord Sudley (Murray, 1943), p. 17

10 John Prest, *Lord John Russell* (Macmillan, 1972), p. 71

11 Broadlands Papers, 27/M/60, Box M

12 Ibid.

13 Cecil, op. cit., p. 38

14 *Letters of Harriet, Countess Granville 1810–1845*, op. cit., Vol. II, p. 43

15 *Correspondence of Sarah Spencer, Lady Lyttelton, 1787–1870*, edited by her great-granddaughter, the Hon. Mrs. Hugh Wyndham (Murray, 1912), p. 283

Chapter 5

AFFAIRS POLITICAL AND FINANCIAL

1 Shaftesbury Papers

2 Hodder, op. cit., Vol. I, p. 129

3 Shaftesbury Papers

4 Ibid.

5 *Journal of Mary Frampton*, edited by H. G. Mundy, (Sampson Low, 1885), p. 378

6 Ibid., p. 380

7 Shaftesbury Papers

8 Ibid.

9 For Minny's letters to Ashley see Broadlands Papers, 27/M/60; for Ashley's replies see NRA/SHA/PC/128–160

10 *New Letters of Robert Southey*, edited by Kenneth Curry (Cambridge University Press, 1965), p. 385

11 Jack Simmonds, *Southey* (Collins, 1945), p. 153

12 *Memoirs of the Life and Writings of Michael Thomas Sadler, Esq., M.P., F.R.S.* Anon. (Seeley & Burneside, 1842), p. 403

13 Hodder, op. cit., Vol. I, p. 143

14 Ibid., p. 149

Chapter 6

CHAMPION OF THE FACTORY CHILDREN

1 Rhodes Boyson, *The Ashworth Cotton Enterprise* (Oxford University Press, 1970), p. 88
2 Ibid., p. 127
3 Mrs. Gaskell, *North and South* (Smith Elder, 1881 edition), p. 322
4 *Musings over the 'Christian Year' and 'Lyra Innocentium'*, by Charlotte Mary Yonge, together with *Gleanings of Recollections of the Rev. John Keble, gathered by Several Friends* (Parker, 1871), p. lix
5 J. T. Ward, *The Factory Movement, 1830–1855* (Macmillan, 1962), p. 422
6 Sir Reginald Coupland, *Wilberforce* (Collins, 1945), p. 77
7 Hodder, op. cit., Vol. I, p. 157
8 *Speeches of the Earl of Shaftesbury, K.G.,* op. cit., p. iv
9 J. C. Gill, *Ten Hours Parson* (S.P.C.K., 1959), p. 61
10 Hammond, op. cit., p. 35
11 Hodder, op. cit., Vol. I, p. 169

Chapter 7

RELIGIOUS VIEWS AND ACTIVITIES

1 Coupland, op. cit., p. 41
2 BM/Gladstone Papers. Add. MSS. 44773, ff. 13–33
3 BM/Gladstone Papers. Add. MSS. 44300, f. 43
4 Ralph Arnold, *History of England* (Mitchell Beazley) in preparation
5 BM/Peel Papers. Add. MSS. 40407, 21 December 1831
6 BM/Peel Papers. Add. MSS. 40407, f. 95
7 BM/Peel Papers. Add. MSS. 40401, f. 181
8 E. M. Forster, *Marianne Thornton, a Biography* (Edward Arnold, 1956), p. 15
9 T. R. Birks, *Memoirs of the Rev. Edward Bickersteth* (Seely, 1852), p. 102.
10 Owen Chadwick, *The Victorian Church* (A. & C. Black, 1966), Vol. I, p. 168
11 Henry Parry Liddon, *Life of Edward Bouverie Pusey* (Longmans Green, 1898, third edition), Vol. IV, p. 51
12 Christopher Dawson, *The Spirit of the Oxford Movement* (Sheed & Ward, 1933), p. xi

Chapter 8

QUEEN VICTORIA AND SIR ROBERT PEEL

1 Hodder, op. cit., Vol. I., pp. 214–216
2 *Manchester & Salford Advertiser*, 18 June 1836
3 Hammond, op. cit., p. 51
4 Hodder, op. cit., Vol. I, p. 228
5 *Correspondence of Sarah Spencer, Lady Lyttelton, 1787–1870*, op. cit. p. 283
6 RA/Queen Victoria's Journal. 13 September 1838
7 RA/Melbourne Papers. 20 June 1842
8 RA/P.P.Vic. 34/97
9 RA/Queen Victoria's Journal. 8 December 1837
10 RA/Queen Victoria's Journal. 15 May 1838
11 Mabell, Countess of Airlie, op. cit., Vol. II, p. 34
12 Ibid., p. 34
13 NRA/SHA/PC/145

Chapter 9

REFUSAL OF OFFICE

1 Hodder, op. cit., Vol. II, p. 65
2 *Wellington and his Friends; Letters of the First Duke,* selected and edited by the Seventh Duke of Wellington (Macmillan, 1965), p. 131
3 RA/Y/54/59
4 William Blake, *Songs of Innocence*
5 *The Victorian Church,* op. cit., Vol. I, p. 247
6 Ibid., Vol. I, p. 189
7 NRA/Palmerston Papers. GC/SH/4
8 Hodder, op. cit., Vol. I, p. 313
9 NRA/Palmerston Papers. GC/SH/14
10 Hodder, op. cit., Vol. I, p. 339
11 Ibid., Vol. I, p. 343
12 Norman Gash, *Sir Robert Peel* (Longman, 1972), p. 280

Chapter 10

CHILDREN IN COAL MINES

1   John Henry Newman, *Apologia Pro Vita Sua* (World's Classics edition, 1964), p. 148
2   Note in Prussian State Archives, 24 November 1841. Copy in possession of Miss Mary de Bunsen.
3   Newman, op. cit., p. 150
4   Liddon, op. cit., Vol. II, p. 265
5   Ibid., Vol. II, p. 262
6   Ibid., Vol. II, p. 264
7   Hodder, op. cit., Vol. I, p. 394
8   Ibid., Vol. I, p. 395
9   Ibid., Vol. I, p. 390
10 Liddon, op. cit., Vol. II, p. 265
11 Shaftesbury Papers
12 Ibid.
13 Hodder, op. cit., Vol. I, p. 398
14 Ibid., Vol. I, p. 403
15 Gash, op. cit., p. 331
16 Hodder, op. cit., Vol. I, p. 404
17 Robert Blake, *Disraeli* (Eyre & Spottiswoode, 1966), p. 171
18 Derek Hudson, *Munby, Man of Two Worlds* (Murray, 1972), p. 75
19 Hammond, op. cit., p. 83
20 John Morley, *Life of Richard Cobden* (Chapman & Hall, 1881), Appendix
21 Report of Children's Employment Commission, 1861.
22 *Speeches of the Earl of Shaftesbury, K.G.,* op. cit., p. 369

Chapter 11

POLITICAL AND PERSONAL TROUBLES

1   A. A. W. Ramsay, *Sir Robert Peel* (Constable, 1971 edition), p. 298
2   Hodder, op. cit., Vol. I, p. 449
3   Graham Papers. Microfilms in Bodleian Library, Oxford. 4 March 1843
4   *Sir Robert Peel, from his Private Correspondence,* edited by C. S. Parker. 1891. Vol. III, p. 114
5   G. M. Trevelyan, *John Bright* (Constable, 1925), p. 131
6   *Speeches of the Earl of Shaftesbury, K.G.,* op. cit., p. 87

Chapter 12

CORN LAW CRISIS

1 *Wellington and his Friends,* op. cit., p. 195
2 Hodder, op. cit., Vol. II, pp. 83–85
3 *Private Letters of Sir Robert Peel,* edited by George Peel (Murray, 1920), pp. 285–286
4 *Speeches of the Earl of Shaftesbury, K.G.,* op. cit., p. 131
5 Parker, op. cit., Vol. II, p. 168
6 Hodder, op. cit., Vol. II, p. 126

Chapter 13

PHILANTHROPIC WORK OUTSIDE PARLIAMENT

1 For this and all quotations on pp. 194–95 see *Ragged Schools,* article by Ashley, *Quarterly Review,* December 1846
2 Hodder, op. cit., Vol. I, p. 484 From *Household Words*
3 Hammond, op. cit., p. 260
4 Ibid., p. 258
5 *Speeches of the Earl of Shaftesbury, K.G.,* op. cit., p. 273
6 Ibid., p. 271

Chapter 14

DIFFICULTIES OVER THE TEN HOURS ACT

1 Hodder, op. cit., Vol. II, p. 245
2 David Cecil, *Lord M, The Later Life of Lord Melbourne* (Constable, 1954), p. 332
3 Hammond, op. cit., p. 132
4 J. T. Ward, op. cit., p. 363
5 Hammond, op. cit., p. 139
6 Ibid., p. 141
7 Hodder, op. cit., Vol. II, pp. 331–334

Chapter 15

THE BOARD OF HEALTH

1 UCL/Chadwick Papers. 6 November 1846
2 *Speeches of the Earl of Shaftesbury, K.G.*, op. cit., p. 279
3 Castle Howard Papers
4 R. A. Lewis, *Edwin Chadwick and the Public Health Movement, 1832–1854* (Longmans Green, 1952), p. 183
5 NRA/SHA/PC/13–18. 24 November 1849
6 *The Times* 16 May 1863
7 Lewis, op. cit., p. 183
8 UCL/Chadwick Papers. 12 September 1849
9 Castle Howard Papers
10 Castle Howard Papers. 28 February 1850
11 Castle Howard Papers
12 Castle Howard Papers. 18 January 1850
13 Lewis, op. cit., p. 244
14 *Hansard.* 22 July 1851
15 UCL/Chadwick Papers. 21 December 1849
16 UCL/Chadwick Papers
17 UCL/Chadwick Papers
18 Jasper Ridley, *Lord Palmerston* (Constable, 1970), p. 407
19 UCL/Chadwick Papers. 18 October 1853
20 NRA/Palmerston Papers. GC/SH/26
21 NRA/Palmerston Papers. GC/SH/27
22 *Speeches of the Earl of Shaftesbury, K.G.*, op. cit., p. 89
23 Castle Howard Papers. 9 September 1848

Chapter 16

EARL OF SHAFTESBURY

1 Hodder, op. cit., Vol. II, pp. 301–303
2 Ibid., Vol. II, p. 373
3 BM/Gladstone Papers. Add. MSS. 44300
4 Hodder, op. cit., Vol. II, p. 407
5 Shaftesbury Papers
6 Ibid.

Chapter 17

BISHOP-MAKER

1   Cecil Woodham-Smith, *Florence Nightingale* (Constable, 1950), p. 204
2   Shaftesbury Papers
3   Woodham-Smith, op. cit., p. 204
4   Ibid., p. 589
5   UCL/Chadwick Papers
6   Hodder, op. cit., Vol. II, p. 505
7   Shaftesbury's Diary. 2 November 1865
8   Hodder, op. cit., Vol. III, p. 193
9   *Letters of Queen Victoria*, Series One, edited Benson and Esher, Vol. III, p. 530
10   *The Victorian Church*, op. cit., Vol. I, p. 471
11   Hodder, op. cit., Vol. III, p. 9
12   Lambeth Palace Library. Tait Papers. 79/f. 48 et. seq.
13   B. E. Hardman, *The Evangelical Party in the Church of England* (Imprinted thesis, p. 68)
14   Hodder, op. cit., Vol. III, p. 33
15   Samuel Eliot Morison, *History of the American People* (O.U.P., 1965, New York), p. 592
16   RA/N/18/70
17   Lady Maud Warrender, *My First Sixty Years* (Cassell, 1933), p. 14

Chapter 18

RELIGIOUS CONTROVERSY

1   Hodder, op. cit., Vol. III, p. 197
2   NRA/Palmerston Papers. GC/SH/64
3   Liddon, op. cit., Vol. IV, p. 51
4   Hodder, op cit., Vol. III, p. 170
5   A. O. J. Cockshut, *Anglican Attitudes* (Collins, 1959), p. 64
6   NRA/SHA/PC/6
7   Quintin Hogg, *Shaftesbury, A New Assessment* (19th Shaftesbury Lecture, Shaftesbury Society; 1957), p. 12
8   *The Victorian Church*, op. cit., Vol. II, p. 20
9   NRA/SHA/PC/60

Chapter 19

PALMERSTON'S SECOND MINISTRY

1   RA/J/98/128
2   Hodder, op. cit., Vol. III, p. 85
3   Ibid., Vol. III, p. 82
4   Ibid., Vol. III, p. 92
5   Ibid., Vol. III, p. 90
6   NRV/Palmerston Papers. GC/SH/41
7   Shaftesbury Papers
8   Hodder, op. cit., Vol. III, p. 133
9   Broadlands Papers. 27/M/60
10 Broadlands Papers. 27/M/60
11 Broadlands Papers. 27/M/60
12 NRA/Palmerston Papers. GC/SH/2–70. 9 April 1864
13 *Letters of Queen Victoria*, edited Buckle (Murray, 1926), Second
    Series, Vol. I, p. 176
14 RA/A/32/48
15 Broadlands Papers. 27/M/60. 13 March 1862
16 Ridley, op. cit., p. 583

Chapter 20

A TIME OF GRIEF

1   Broadlands Papers. 27/M/60
2   A. R. Ashwell, *Life of the Right Reverend Samuel Wilberforce*
    (Murray, 1880), Vol. II, p. 206
3   Hodder, op. cit., Vol. III, p. 230
4   T. Wemyss Reid, *The Life of W. E. Forster* (Chapman & Hall,
    1880), Vol. II, p. 491
5   Hodder, op. cit., Vol. III, p. 264
6   Hammond, op. cit., p. 256
7   RA/Add. A/17/390
8   Hodder, op. cit., Vol. III, pp. 290–291
9   For all following quotations from letters to Minny see NRA/SHA/
    PC/149 et seq.
10 Shaftesbury Papers

Chapter 21

A VENERABLE FIGURE

1 Broadlands Papers. 27/M/60
2 Tait Papers. Vol. 203. 10 March 1874
3 Ibid. 27 March 1874
4 Hodder, op. cit., Vol. III, p. 346
5 Shaftesbury's Diary. 3 October 1874
6 Philip Magnus, *Gladstone* (Murray, 1954), p. 240
7 RA/H/S/137
8 BM/Gladstone Papers. Add. MSS. 44300, f. 82
9 Tait Papers. Vol. 231. 3 December 1877
10 Broadlands Papers. 27/M/60. 2 November 1878

Chapter 22

THE END

1 Hodder, op. cit., Vol. III, p. 481
2 University of Durham, Grey Papers. Memorandum of conversation, 22 July 1883
3 J. M. Weylland, *The Man with the Book*; Introduction by Shaftesbury (London City Mission, 1878)
4 Hodder, op. cit., Vol. III, pp. 438–440
5 BM/Gladstone Papers. Add. MSS. 44300, f. 106
6 *The Diary of Sir Edward Walter Hamilton,* edited by Dudley W. R. Bahlman, Vol. I, p. 229 (O.U.P., 1972)
7 Broadlands Papers. 27/M/60
8 Lambeth Palace Library. Benson Papers. Vol. 27, f. 96

SELECT BIBLIOGRAPHY

AIRLIE, MABELL, COUNTESS OF: *Lady Palmerston and her Times* (Hodder and Stoughton, 1922)

ARBUTHNOT, CHARLES: *The Correspondence of Charles Arbuthnot* (ed. A. Aspinall) (Royal Historical Society, 1941)

ASHWORTH, HENRY: *Letter to the Right Hon. Lord Ashley on the Cotton Factory Question and the Ten Hours Bill by a Lancashire Cotton Spinner.* (Manchester, 1833.)

ASHWELL, A. R.: *The Life of Samuel Wilberforce* (Murray, 1880)

BALLEINE, G. R.: *History of the Evangelical Party* (Longmans Green, 1908)

DE BERTIER DE SAUVIGNY, G.: *Metternich and his Times* (trans. Peter Hyde) (Darton Longman and Todd, 1962)

BEST, G. F. A.: *Shaftesbury* (Batsford, 1964)

BEST, GEOFFREY: *Mid-Victorian Britain* (Weidenfeld and Nicolson, 1971)

BIRKS, T. R.: *Memoirs of the Reverend Edward Bickersteth* (Seeley, 1852) 3rd edn.

BLACKBURN, BARBARA: *Noble Earl* (Home and Van Thal, 1949)

BLAKE, ROBERT: *Disraeli* (Eyre and Spottiswoode, 1966)

BOYSON, RHODES: *The Ashworth Cotton Enterprise* (O.U.P., 1970)

BREADY, J. W.: *Lord Shaftesbury and Social-Industrial Progress* (Allen and Unwin, 1964)

CARTLAND, BARBARA: *Metternich, the Passionate Diplomat* (Hutchinson, 1964)

CHADWICK, EDWIN: *Report on the Sanitary Condition of the Labouring Population of Great Britain* (ed. with an Introduction by M. W. Flinn) (Edinburgh University Press, 1965)

CHADWICK, OWEN: *The Victorian Church* (A. & C. Black, 1966)

CLARK, G. KITSON: *Peel and the Conservative Party* (Bell, 1929)

COBBE, FRANCES POWELL: *Life of Frances Powell Cobbe; by herself* (Bentley, 1894)

DRIVER, CECIL: *Tory Radical; the Life of Richard Oastler* (O.U.P., 1964)

FOX, HON. HENRY: *Journal of the Hon. Henry Fox* (ed. the Earl of Ilchester) (Thornton Butterworth, 1923)

Garibaldi's Visit to England in 1864 by Noel Blakiston. Extract from review in *Il Risorgimento* Anno IVI No. 3, Milan

GASH, NORMAN: *Mr. Secretary Peel* (Longmans, 1961)

GASH, NORMAN: *Politics in the Age of Peel* (Longmans, 1953)

GASH, NORMAN: *Sir Robert Peel* (Longmans, 1972)

GILL, J. C.: *The Ten Hours Parson* (S.P.C.K., 1959)

GRANVILLE, HARRIET, COUNTESS: *Letters of Harriet, Countess Granville* (ed. F. Leveson Gower) (Longmans Green, 1894)

GREVILLE, HENRY: *Leaves from the Diary of Henry Greville* (ed. the Viscountess Enfield) (Smith Elder, 1883)

HAMMOND, J. L. and B.: *Shaftesbury* (Constable, 1923)

HARDMAN, B. E.: *The Evangelical Party in the Church of England 1855–1865*. Ph.D. Thesis, 1963. Typescript, Anderson Room, Cambridge University Library.

HARRISON, J. F. C.: *The Early Victorians* (Weidenfeld and Nicolson, 1971)

HEASMAN, KATHLEEN: *Evangelicals in Action* (Bles, 1962)

HERZEN, A.: *Camicia Rossa* (Brussels, 1865)

HODDER, EDWIN: *The Life and Work of the Seventh Earl of Shaftesbury* (Cassell, 1887)

HOGG, QUINTIN: *Shaftesbury, A New Assessment* (19th Shaftesbury Lecture) Shaftesbury Society, 1957.

HOLLAND, LADY: *Elizabeth, Lady Holland to her Son 1821–1845* (ed. the Earl of Ilchester) (Murray, 1946)

HUTCHINS, B. L. and A. HARRISON: *A History of Factory Legislation* (King, new edition 1926)

INGLIS, BRIAN: *Poverty and the Industrial Revolution* (Hodder and Stoughton, 1971)

JONES, KATHLEEN: *Lunacy, Law and Conscience* (Routledge and Kegan Paul, 1955)

JONES, KATHLEEN: *Mental Health and Social Policy* (Routledge and Kegan Paul, 1965)

LABORDE, E. D.: *Harrow School, Yesterday and Today* (Winchester)

LECONFIELD, MAUD, LADY: and JOHN GORE: *Three Howard Sisters* (Murray, 1955)

LEWES, MRS. C. L.: *Doctor Southwood Smith; a retrospect; by his granddaughter* (Blackwood, 1898)

LEWIS, R. A.: *Edwin Chadwick and the Public Health Movement* (Longmans Green, 1952)

LIDDON, H. P.: *Life of Edward Bouverie Pusey* (Longmans, 1894)

LIEVEN, PRINCESS: *The Lieven Palmerston Correspondence 1828–1856* (trans. and ed. Lord Sudley) (Murray, 1943)

LIEVEN, PRINCESS: *The Private Letters of Princess Lieven to Prince Metternich* (ed. Peter Quennell) (Murray, 1937)

LONGFORD, ELIZABETH: *Victoria, R. I.* (Weidenfeld and Nicolson, 1964)

LONGFORD, ELIZABETH: *Wellington, Pillar of State* (Weidenfeld and Nicolson, 1972)

LYTTELTON, LADY: *Correspondence of Sarah Spencer, Lady Lyttelton* (ed. by her granddaughter, the Hon. Mrs. Hugh Wyndham) (Murray, 1912)

MAGNUS, PHILIP: *Gladstone* (Murray, 1954)

MARSH, P. T.: *The Victorian Church in Decline; Archbishop Tait and The Church of England* (Routledge and Kegan Paul, 1969)

MASTERS, DAVID: *The Plimsoll Mark* (Cassell, 1955)

MORLEY, JOHN: *Life of Richard Cobden* (Chapman & Hall, 1881)

NEUMANN, PHILIP VON: *Diary of Philip von Neumann* (ed. E. Beresford Chancellor) (Philip Allan, 1928)

ORCHARD, S. C.: *English Evangelical Eschatology.* Ph.D. Thesis, 1968. Typescript, Anderson Room, Cambridge University Library.

OWEN, DAVID: *English Philanthropy* (Harvard University Press, 1965)

PALMERSTON, LADY: *Letters of Lady Palmerston* (ed. Tresham Lever) (Murray, 1957)

PEEL, SIR ROBERT: *The Private Letters of Sir Robert Peel* (ed. George Peel) (Murray, 1920)

PETRIE, GLEN: *A Singular Iniquity; the Campaigns of Josephine Butler* (Macmillan, 1871)

PREST, JOHN: *Lord John Russell* (Macmillan, 1972)

RAMSAY, A. A. W.: *Sir Robert Peel* (Constable, new edition 1971)

REID, T. WEMYSS: *Life of W. E. Forster* (Chapman & Hall, 1888)

RIDLEY, JASPER: *Lord Palmerston* (Constable, 1970)

SADLER, MICHAEL THOMAS: *Memoirs of the life and writings of Michael Thomas Sadler;* anonymous (Seeley and Burneside, 1842)

SEELEY, JOHN: *Ecce Homo* (Macmillan, 1881, 5th edition)

SHAFTESBURY, EARL OF: *Speeches of the Earl of Shaftesbury* (Chapman & Hall, 1868)

SIMMONDS, JACK: *Southey* (Collins, 1945)

SIMON, SIR JOHN: *English Sanitary Institutions* (Cassell, 1890)

SMITH, FRANK: *The Life and Work of Sir James Kay-Shuttleworth* (Murray, 1923)

SOUTHEY, ROBERT: *New Letters of Robert Southey* (ed. Kenneth Curry) (Columbia University Press, 1965)

TREVELYAN, G. M.: *John Bright* (Constable, 1925)

WARD, J. T.: *The Factory Movement* (Macmillan, 1962)

PARLIAMENTARY PAPERS

Report of Select Committee on Pauper Lunatics in the County of Middlesex and on Lunatic Asylums. 1827

Report of Select Committee on Factory Children's Labour. 1831

Report of Commission on Employment of Children in Factories. 1833

Reports of Select Committee to enquire into the Operation of the Act for the Regulation of Mines and Factories. 1840 and 1841.

Commission on Children's Employment. First Report of the Commissioners. (Mines). 1842

Report of Select Committee on Lunatics. 1859

Report of Select Committee on Lunacy Law. 1877

INDEX

The seventh Earl of Shaftesbury, together with his brothers and sisters, used the full family surname, 'Ashley-Cooper'. For reasons which cannot now be ascertained his children and some, at least, of his grand-children, dropped 'Cooper', using only 'Ashley'. The present generation of the family has returned to the full name, 'Ashley-Cooper'. Shaftesbury's children and grand-children are therefore indexed under 'Ashley', his other relatives under 'Ashley-Cooper'.